£1·25

L.YAKIMENKO

Sholokhov

A CRITICAL APPRECIATION

PROGRESS PUBLISHERS
MOSCOW

Translated from the Russian by *Bryan Bean*
Designed by *Yuri Samsonov*

Лев Якименко
ТВОРЧЕСТВО МИХАИЛА ШОЛОХОВА
На английском языке

First printing 1973

Printed in the Union of Soviet Socialist Republics

CONTENTS

INTRODUCTION

*Low I bow, and as a son I kiss your
fresh earth, Cossack steppeland of the Don,
soaked with blood that will not rust.*

When I think of Sholokhov, two pictures spring to mind,
so different it is hard to believe that they are of one and
the same person. They are separated by many years,
years of dramatic historic events.

Sholokhov is standing in an unbuttoned sheepskin coat,
a fur hat casually tilted at an angle so that it partly
covers his high forehead, merry eyes smiling from a thin,
youthful face. The nineteen-year-old boy has just had
his first stories published. After receiving one of his first
author's fees from *Komsomoliya*, a youth magazine, he has
run gaily out into the yard with some friends and there
someone has snapped them for a souvenir of the occasion.
In spite of his youth he already has a wealth of experience
behind him: in those years young people became independent very early in life. He fought in the Civil War,
occupied the post of supplies commissar, pursued White
bands, and had been taken prisoner by them. Now he has
come to Moscow from his native Don region, intending
to study and vaguely dreaming of becoming a writer,
and it looks as though his dream is beginning to come
true.

"One day in April a stocky young fellow came into the
office, wearing an Astrakhan fur hat which was much
the worse for wear and a shabby coat thrown wide open,"
Ivan Molchanov, then secretary of the *Komsomoliya*
editorial office, recalls. "He took a manuscript from a side
pocket and placed it on the table. It was entitled *Melon
Field Keeper* and was signed by a completely unknown
writer 'M. Sholokhov'. Alexander Zharov and I read
the manuscript and immediately sent it to the print-
shop. Those were hungry days. I insisted that the authors

of the first number, which had not yet come out, should be paid something in advance. The next day I wrote out the first payment slip for Sholokhov."*

Then I see him many, many years later. Grey-haired, with wrinkles round his eyes, wearing a smart dress-coat, Sholokhov stands stiff and proud, a look of almost stern arrogance on his face, receiving the Nobel Prize from the King of Sweden.

More than forty years had passed since the first photograph was taken, forty years entirely devoted to literature.

Sholokhov wrote his first stories in 1923. Later, in 1926, they were collected in the book *Tales from the Don.* He began work on *And Quiet Flows the Don* in 1925 when he was twenty. The first book of *Virgin Soil Upturned* appeared in 1932. He was a war correspondent during the war, writing articles and stories. He began the novel *They Fought for Their Fatherland.* The end of 1956 saw the publication of his short story *The Fate of a Man.* In 1959 he finished the second book of *Virgin Soil Upturned.* The appearance of each of Sholokhov's books was in itself a great event. But, as is the case with all truly great works, it was an important event too for the reader when he discovered them for himself.

Sholokhov is one of those writers who prefer not to talk about the actual process of writing. Yet from what he has said here and there over the years, we can gain a pretty clear idea of the motive forces underlying his art.

The motive force at work in his writings is of course his love for his native region. He lives today in his beloved Don country where he spent his childhood, and where his youth passed in the turmoil of the Civil War. Veshenskaya village is as inseparably linked with Sholokhov as Yasnaya Polyana with Tolstoi.

Love for his native region means above all love for the people he has lived among: the farmers and soldiers, hunters and fishermen. "I wanted to write about the people I was born among and whom I knew,"** he was to say, looking back over his work on *And Quiet Flows the Don.*

* *Literatura i zhizn*, May 23, 1958.
** *Izvestia*, June 12, 1940.

The life of the people represents an inexhaustible source of material for Sholokhov. He cannot conceive his work without constant contact with the people who later stride across the pages of his novels.

Sholokhov maintains this contact when he is writing, when he rides to a field-camp and talks to the tractor-drivers round the campfire, or when merely chatting to an acquaintance he has bumped into in the street.

"During almost thirty years as a deputy to the Supreme Soviet of the U.S.S.R. I never once felt my duties to be a burden. On the contrary, I have got a tremendous amount out of the contacts my work involves," Sholokhov said at a meeting with voters in June 1966. Meeting new people and getting to know their lives, their joys and sorrows means live material for the artist. If the writer shuts himself up in an ivory tower, he can never hope to acquire that wealth of experience which daily contacts with other people can bring him.

The first book of *Virgin Soil Upturned* serves as a perfect illustration of this, for the whole book was the result of Sholokhov's direct participation in collectivisation, was in fact an answer to many of the difficult questions that arose during the revolutionary transformation of life in the countryside.

Sholokhov's speech in Stockholm after receiving the Nobel Prize in December 1965 seems to sum up the writer's views on art very neatly. Throughout his fifty years of activity as a writer, Sholokhov has never ceased to believe that art's noble purpose is to exert a salutary influence on mankind.

"To speak honestly to the reader, to tell people the truth, however bitter, to strengthen in the hearts of men their faith in the future and in their own power to create that future; to be an active fighter for peace throughout the world, and foster by one's writings other such fighters; to unite people in their natural and noble yearning for progress. The arts have a tremendous power over men's minds and hearts. I think a person has the right to call himself an artist if he directs this power to creating beauty in men's souls for the good of mankind."

Sholokhov draws his strength from reality—reality in its historical aspect, reality in its development, the reality of everyday life. His heroes move in the concrete, material world of things. They are reality itself, created with that precision of characterisation which gives each of them a unique, inimitable life of his own.

I am moved to stress this by the arguments which have flared up about realism. Sholokhov's works represent one of the most weighty and convincing answers to the question of the essence of realism in our age.

I approach the problems raised in these arguments as follows: has reality been exhausted as the only object of artistic apprehension, that is, reality explored for the purpose of obtaining the maximum objectivity, or does this objective approach to the picture of life and characters, this attempt to recreate the world of things in the world of art, no longer satisfy our perception of things, our aesthetic tastes and demands?

Are we to have reality as such, in all its hardness and complexity, or the reality of myth, reality distorted through the prism of purely individual, absolutely subjective perception, where the writer's ego serves as the model of the world?

Is it in fact essential that we make such a choice, or can various trends exist side by side in contemporary art? If so, we ought perhaps to examine and define the real potentialities inherent in these different trends.

Realism obviously presupposes a definite relationship between the artist and the world he lives in.

"I am one of those writers who see in unlimited opportunity to serve the working people with their pen the greatest honour and the greatest freedom.

"This is the source of everything, that is how I see the writer's, the Soviet writer's place in the world today." These are Sholokhov's words from his address in Stockholm.

Sholokhov the writer lives in a colourful world, the authenticity of which is confirmed by every line of his books. This world exists as given reality, which requires understanding and explaining. Sholokhov is involved in human society, and has a strongly developed sense of responsibility not simply towards life and man in the abstract, but towards those people whose vital beliefs and hopes he shares. This recognition of historical community, of man's capabilities and personal responsibility is the basic essence underlying Sholokhov's epos. The reality his works portray has its historical substantiation and social explanation.

Gorky apparently understood this. In 1932 he remarked in a conversation that "sensible people throughout Europe accept Sholokhov's works as reality itself".

Sholokhov's heroes—this applies equally to Grigory Melekhov, Semyon Davidov, Makar Nagulnov or Andrei Sokolov—not only exist in time but actually express the age they live in, living its hopes and quests, its joys and sorrows.

Sholokhov focusses his attention on apprehending the complex relationship between the individual and society, between personal urges and the character of the age. Through the arts man apprehends himself and the nature of the relationship between the individual and society, between man and Nature.

Art helps mankind put its great ideals into practice. Art which is imbued with the ideals of rejuvenating life is a source of inspiration, strengthening man's faith and hopes.

But art can only be so genuinely humanistic on condition that it has its roots in the people. In Stockholm Sholokhov spoke proudly, forcefully and ardently about what has always been and always will be the aim of his whole life.

"The historical path along which my people have advanced was no beaten track. They have gone forward as explorers, as pioneers of life. My aim as a writer has always been to pay tribute in all my works to this nation of toilers, builders and heroes, who have never attacked anyone, but have always known how to defend what they have created, to defend their freedom and honour, their right to build their future in the way they themselves have chosen.

"I would like my books to help make people better and purer in heart, to arouse love for man, and the desire to take an active part in the struggle for the ideals of humanism and the progress of mankind. If I have been at all successful then I consider myself a happy man."

Sholokhov's name already takes its place alongside such world-famous Russian writers as Gogol, Tolstoi, Dostoyevsky and Chekhov. "He is the most popular Russian writer in the West since Chekhov," wrote the well-known English writer and scholar C. P. Snow. "In England and America he is read far more than any of his younger contemporaries. You can now see paper-back editions of his works in any London book-store. I consider, as do many of my friends, that *And Quiet Flows the Don* is the finest book to have appeared anywhere in the last forty years."*

Ernest Hemingway said: "I am very fond of Russian literature. I owe a lot to its influence, to Pushkin, Lermontov, Dostoyevsky, Tolstoi, and of course Gogol's *Taras Bulba*. Of the modern writers Sholokhov is my favourite."**

One could cite numerous examples of remarks by famous writers, artists, scholars—and indeed readers from every walk of life—which witness growing interest all over the world in the works of Mikhail Sholokhov.

We find ourselves turning again and again to Sholokhov, to his experience, his knowledge and his works. It is over thirty years since he completed *And Quiet Flows the Don*, and more than thirty-five since the publication of *Virgin Soil Upturned*. Arrested in its flight by Sholokhov's mighty hand, the past lives in his books not only as a time that is over and done with, but (and this is the mark of truly great art) in relation to the present. It clarifies the present, and helps us draw up our future aims, moving us to think, argue and search.

* *Don* No. 5, 1965.
** *Izvestia*, March 19, 1960.

I

EARLY WORKS
The Azure Steppe
Tales from the Don

"The soft breath of the sun-warmed black earth could not stifle the finer perfume of the fading steppe violets. They grew on a stretch of abandoned fallow, popping up among the dry stalks of hart's-clover, spreading in a colourful pattern over the edges of an old field balk; and even on the flintily hard virgin soil their blue, childishly clear eyes looked out on the world from the withered grass of the previous year. The violets had lived their appointed time in this lonely and spacious steppe, and in their place, on the slope of the ravine, marvellously brilliant tulips were already rising, lifting their crimson, white, and yellow chalices to the sun, while the wind blended the varied perfumes of the flowers and carried them far over the steppe" (4, 641-642).*

Just such images of the faraway Don steppes must have sprung to the young Sholokhov's mind when he was working on his first stories in Moscow. The title he gave to his collected early short stories, *The Azure Steppe*, was most appropriate. On the Don they call the tulip the "azure flower". It was a simple image that conjured up his beloved, unforgettable native Don region.

"I wanted to write about the people I was born among and whom I knew," he was later to say.

These words do not only apply to *And Quiet Flows the Don*. All Sholokhov's works are deeply rooted in the soil of his native Don region.

Mikhail Alexandrovich Sholokhov was born on Kruzhilino farmstead, Veshenskaya village, on May 24, 1905.

"I was born and bred on the Don. It was there that I was formed as a man and a writer, and was educated

* All quotations are given according to: M. Sholokhov, *And Quiet Flows the Don*, Books 1-4, Moscow, 1967.

as a member of our great Communist Party. I am a patriot of my great, mighty country, and I am also proud to declare myself a patriot of my native Don region." Sholokhov spoke these words at a meeting with voters in 1937.*

Sholokhov's mother, Anastasia Danilovna Chernikova, came from a peasant family.

"I knew and loved the writer's mother well," A. Plotkin, who worked in Veshenskaya region at the time of the collectivisation, wrote in his memoirs. "She was a simple, modest old lady... always busy with something or other.... She was quiet and inconspicuous but very friendly. She always had a greeting and a kind word for everyone."

A. S. Serafimovich, a prominent Soviet writer, who stayed with Sholokhov at Veshenskaya, wrote: "His mother is a wonderful person, completely illiterate but with a strong, lively, penetrating mind. In order to be able to write to her son she set to and taught herself to read and write. There followed a happy correspondence between mother and son. Obviously he inherited from her the precious creative gift that made him a great writer."** She died during an air raid in 1942, when the nazis bombed the village of Veshenskaya.

His father, Alexander Mikhailovich Sholokhov, came from Ryazan gubernia. His son describes how he "sowed corn on bought Cossack land, served as a farm bailiff, as manager of a steam-mill and so on". He died in 1926.

Young Mikhail went to the parish school first. "Without finishing the school in Karginovo, I enrolled in a preparatory class at a Moscow lycee.... I studied for two or three years in Moscow, then continued at the Boguchary lycee. In 1918, I attended school here in Veshenskaya for a few months. In all I managed to complete four forms of high school."***

When the Civil War broke out Sholokhov exchanged his high-school studies for education in the hard school of life, in the fierce dramatic class struggle on the Don.

---

* *Artists and Men of Letters Who Are Deputies to the Supreme Soviet of the U.S.S.R.*, Russ. ed., Moscow, 1938, p. 40.
** A. Serafimovich, *Collected Works*, Russ. ed., Vol. 10, Moscow, 1948, p. 364.
*** F. Abramov, V. Gura, *M. A. Sholokhov*, Seminaries, Russ. ed., Leningrad, 1958, p. 132.

The fifteen-year-old boy joined a food supply detachment. At that time these detachments had to wage a stubborn struggle against the kulaks, who, relying on the support of armed bands, were hiding their crops in an effort to starve out the young Soviet Republic. "From 1920 I had a long period of service in a food detachment, travelling all over the Don region," Sholokhov wrote in his autobiography. "I chased White bands, who were in control of the region up to 1922, and they were chasing us. Naturally it involved getting into all sorts of scrapes...."

Sholokhov's early works—*Alien Blood*, *The Food Commissar*, and especially *Paths and Roads*, show just what sort of "scrapes" a young commissar could get into in those years. There was the constant danger of being struck down by a kulak bullet fired from round a corner, or of a sudden bandit attack. K. Potapov tells how Sholokhov was taken prisoner in a battle with members of Makhno's band near Konkovo farmstead. He was "interrogated by Makhno himself, and only escaped being shot because of his youth. Makhno promised him he would be hung should their paths ever cross again. The young Sholokhov took part in battles against Fomin's band, whom he was later to describe in *And Quiet Flows the Don*."[*]

Thus Sholokhov gained his early experience of the fierce, cruel class struggle on the Don, which provided so much of the subject-matter of his early stories and was to be expressed so powerfully in *And Quiet Flows the Don*.

The Civil War over, Sholokhov came to Moscow towards the end of 1922. What was it that prompted the seventeen-year-old youth to leave his home for the capital? Was he attracted by the recently opened workers' faculties? Or was it his dream of becoming a writer, the brave decision to launch out on that path that brought him hard-won happiness, world fame and the inevitable bitterness of many a hard blow?

In 1922 Sholokhov could hardly have imagined that his dream of becoming a writer might have any chance of coming true. When he arrived in Moscow the city was only just beginning to get over hunger and destruction, and

---

[*] K. Potapov's Afterword in: *And Quiet Flows the Don*, Russ. ed., Vol. 4, Moscow, 1953, p. 450.

the turmoil of the Revolution and the Civil War years. The NEP (New Economic Policy) period had just begun: privately owned restaurants and night clubs had opened, the "champions of free enterprise" walked around in expensive overcoats, their women in furs, and profiteers sold French perfumes and silk stockings, while long queues of unemployed formed outside the labour exchanges. There were violent contrasts at every turn.

Sholokhov's first impressions of this Moscow were reflected to some extent in his feuilleton "Three", published on October 30, 1923, in the newspaper *Yunosheskaya Pravda*.

The young man had a hard time in Moscow at first. He had to find a job to support himself, so he went to the labour exchange. I. Eksler describes how the young Sholokhov applied for work: "This young fellow in a tall grey sheepskin hat turned up at the labour exchange in Malaya Bronnaya Street. When asked his profession, he replied 'food commissar'."*

But the period of war communism was over and food commissars were no longer required. Sholokhov went to work as a loader, a navvy, a clerk and so on.

At the same time he began to write for a youth newspaper. His article "Ordeal" appeared in *Yunosheskaya Pravda* (then the official organ of the Komsomol Central Committee and Moscow Committee) on September 19, 1923, to be followed shortly after by "Three", and later "The Inspector", published at the beginning of 1924. Sholokhov's first attempts as a writer are of scarce literary importance in themselves and consequently do not appear in the writer's collected works. Yet even so, there were passages which testified to the young man's talent and fine powers of observation.

Sholokhov's career as a writer can be said to begin properly on December 14, 1924, with the publication of his story *The Birth-Mark* in *Molodoi Leninets*. The many stories later to be gathered together in the collections *Tales from the Don* and *The Azure Steppe* began to appear separately on the pages of various newspapers and magazines (including *Komsomoliya*, *Prozhektor*, *Smena*, and *Ogonyok*).

* *Izvestia*, June 12, 1940.

The collection *Tales from the Don*, published by the Novaya Moskva Publishing House in Moscow in 1926, carried a foreword by A. S. Serafimovich.

Serafimovich became Sholokhov's "literary godfather". Moreover, the two struck up a firm and lasting friendship. The older writer took a direct interest in the first book of *And Quiet Flows the Don*, and when it was published was the first to congratulate the young writer on his success in an article in *Pravda*, which extolled Sholokhov's talent and contained many penetrating observations about his work.

Sholokhov was all the more grateful for the support of such an experienced writer in that on the whole he received very little attention from his fellow writers at this stage.

In an article for Serafimovich's seventy-fifth birthday in 1938 Sholokhov wrote: "I am truly obliged to Serafimovich, for it was he who first supported me at the very beginning of my literary career, who first recognised and encouraged me.... I will never forget how in 1925, on reading my first collection of stories, Serafimovich wrote an enthusiastic foreword, and even wanted to meet me. Our first meeting took place at the First House of Soviets. Serafimovich assured me that I must continue to write and study. He told me to work very carefully on everything, and never to hurry. I have always endeavoured to follow this advice."*

2

Sholokhov began his career as a writer at a very significant moment in Soviet literature. A whole stream of young people were returning from the Civil War and entering the literary scene. They produced a flood of works that gave the new Soviet literature a fine reputation.

The representatives of the generation that had borne all the hardships of the Civil War on their shoulders were turning to literature still in their military greatcoats so to speak, and bringing to it "the whiff of grapeshot" they

* M. Sholokhov, *Collected Works* in eight volumes, Russ. ed., Vol. 8, Moscow, 1960, pp. 128-29.

had themselves experienced, the thunder of recent battles. Together they were creating a great epic of the October Revolution and the Civil War.

At the end of the twenties books by Soviet writers (*Chapayev*, *The Iron Flood*, *Cities and Years*, *The Rout*, *The Badgers*, the first books of *And Quiet Flows the Don*, and so on) began to appear in translation abroad, where they had a strange attraction even for the bourgeois reader.

This was of course not due to startlingly new literary devices, which were the basis of so many fashionable modernist trends. Nor was it due to the exceptional biographies of the writers, who were for the most part very young, although there was obviously a certain glamour in the idea of fame having come to a twenty-four-year-old youth who had taken part in the Civil War on the Don (Sholokhov), and a twenty-eight-year-old man who had fought as a partisan in the Far East (Fadeyev). But the main factor which accounted for their immense popularity was the books themselves, the life which they described.

They opened wide the door on the "mysterious" world of revolutionary Russia, with its battles that decided the fate of whole nations and states, the heroic deeds of the masses, the proud awareness of the importance of the victories gained, the unprecedented hardships, hunger and destruction, the bitter dramas and tragedies, inevitable in the great revolutionary upheaval which ushered in a new stage in the history of the world.

"When I was young and just setting out to become a writer—that is at the end of the twenties," wrote the Dutch writer Theun de Vries, "a German publishing house put out, apparently for the first time in Western Europe, a series which struck our imagination and our hearts. They were stories and novels by young Soviet writers who were themselves among the ranks of the revolutionary people and showed the world that race of new, strong fighters, who were sometimes rough but always healthy—the fighters and builders of socialism. There were the novels of Fedin, Gladkov, Fadeyev, Leonov, and Sholokhov. Ever since I have been very much under the influence of this new literature. It helped me form my own views on man and society. It forced me to recognise those social forces of which I had had only a very vague idea previously."*

Indeed, if we turn to the period in our literature Theun de Vries is referring to, we will find two words on the literary banners of the time: "Revolution and Man." The efforts of a whole generation of Soviet writers were turned towards understanding and interpreting the Revolution and the place in it and the attitude towards it of people of the most varied backgrounds.

"The war and the Revolution were our most important emotional experience. The single aim of our lives was to express this experience in art," Fedin wrote years later.**

The exceptional nature of the historical process underway, the simple fact that for the first time in history the masses were reorganising life in their own interests, was in itself enough to stimulate writers to conduct a ceaseless search for new methods. For if it were to remain faithful to life and "read the book of life" correctly, literature had to find new methods, new principles for creating works on a level with the age. The writers who nursed the new literature through its infancy had only recently been soldiers, and they were very bold in their thinking. For them literature was more than a vehicle for self-expression. They saw their high calling in terms of service to the people. It is clear from numerous statements made on the subject that they aimed to create a heroic literature, worthy of the people who had made the Revolution.

At a meeting in Paris in April 1949, Alexander Fadeyev said: "When the Civil War came to an end and we began to congregate from every corner of our vast country — young Party men, and even more non-Party men — we were amazed to find how similar the paths we had traversed were despite our very different circumstances. This went for Furmanov, the author of *Chapayev*, and for the young Mikhail Sholokhov, who was possibly the most gifted of us.... We came into literature wave upon wave, bringing our personal experience and our individuality. We were united by a sense of the new world being our own, and by our love for it."***

* *Inostrannaya Literatura* No. 11, 1956, pp. 182-83.
** K. Fedin, *Gorky Among Us*, Russ. ed., Moscow, 1943, p. 124.
*** A. Fadeyev, *Thirty Years*, Russ. ed., Moscow, 1957, pp. 459-60.

This sense of the world he lived in and wrote about being his own, and love for it, permeates all Sholokhov's early writings and indeed all his later works too.

Almost all the *Tales from the Don* are based on Sholokhov's personal experience in the establishment of Soviet power on the Don.

Tales from the Don were almost lost to the general public. The book was reprinted in 1931 in a very small edition (5,500 copies), and twenty-five years were to elapse before they were published again. Sholokhov himself was largely responsible for this. He considered them to be of scant literary value and was strongly opposed to their publication.

Now that the stories formerly gathered together under the titles *Tales from the Don* and *The Azure Steppe* have appeared in the first volume of the collected works of Sholokhov, the reader can see for himself how unjust the author was in judging them so severely. True, there are clumsy, rough passages, and some that jar somewhat. But the youthful freshness and the dramatic force of the conflicts and passions cannot fail to captivate the reader.

The young writer carefully examined the radical changes that the Revolution had wrought in the life of the Cossacks and tried to perceive the new features of life and people's characters.

At the same time Sholokhov's stories helped to dispel that false-romantic impression of revolutionary struggle, with "heroes" effortlessly overcoming their enemies, which was a feature of so many works written about the Civil War at that time. The writer showed the harsh reality of the fierce struggle that went on in the Cossack *stanitsas* both during the Civil War and in the first years of peace when Soviet power was being established on the Don. The Revolution affected the life of the people down to the very roots, dividing families and setting brother against brother, son against father. In *The Birth-Mark* the ataman of a White band kills his son who is in command of a Red Army cavalry troop. The Red Army man Shibalok kills the woman he loves when he learns that she has passed information to the Whites (*Shibalok's Seed*). Two brothers kill their father who had headed a drumhead court-martial which had sentenced Red Army prisoners to death (*Melon Field Keeper*). Kramskov, a White officer, has his father and brother, who are fighting in the Red Guards, shot (*Vortex*).

Tales from the Don literally reeks of powder and blood, so fierce is the struggle the writer depicts.

Many of the features of Sholokhov's talent which he was later to develop more fully are already present in these early stories. Sholokhov transmits the drama of the class struggle through poignant situations, where friends and even kinsfolk find themselves on opposite sides of the fence, thus showing the Revolution as a social upheaval of colossal magnitude affecting every aspect of human relationships.

One of the epic themes of world literature of the past was expressed with particular poignancy in *Tales from the Don*. Sholokhov penetrated life's small backwaters, and carefully examined the relationship between man and property, and how this affected people's character and psychology. And from the very start we observe that powerful motif which was to run through all Sholokhov's works: his rejection of a world based on blind egoism, inequality, the power of money, and the laws of the jungle.

The stories often centre on a struggle between two radically opposed forces: the conflict between people of the emergent world of socialism and those who cling tenaciously to the past—the kulaks and the whiteguards. Sholokhov sees the actual struggle he is depicting so dramatically as an expression of the conflict between irreconcilable principles: humanism, and care for the welfare and happiness of the recently disinherited, on the one hand, and the savage tenacity of people who will stop at nothing to retain their privileges, wealth and possessions, on the other.

The characters of the people building Soviet power on the Don were formed in the crucible of ceaseless struggle with the class enemy, now latent, now exploding in a new fierce burst. The young author gave all his love and sympathy to these people. There is Yefim, a Red Army man and former shepherd, responsive to other people's griefs, mortal enemy of the kulaks "whose day is done" (*Mortal Enemy*); Grigory, a young orphan, a herdsman, then a Komsomol member, who longs to study so as to be able to govern "our republic" (*The Herdsman*); Petka Kremnev, secretary of a Komsomol cell, who bravely takes upon himself all the most difficult and dangerous tasks (*Paths and Roads*); and the amiable Foma Korshunov (*The Bastard*).

For all their differences in age, character and experience, these people all have one thing in common: the Revolution has inspired them all to take part in building a new life.

In *Tales from the Don* Sholokhov gave a genuine, authentic account of the fierce class struggle which continued on the Don after the Civil War was over, an account that is imbued with confidence in the inevitable triumph of the new.

There are strong connecting links between *Tales from the Don* and Sholokhov's novels. Some of the stories are closer to *And Quiet Flows the Don*, others to *Virgin Soil Upturned*, but for all the difference in their literary worth they represent a good running start to a life of great creative achievement.

II

And Quiet
Flows the Don

Chapter One

THE NOVEL IN THE MAKING.
ITS PLACE IN SOVIET PROSE
OF THE TWENTIES AND THIRTIES

1

In 1925 Sholokhov left Moscow and returned to his native Don region. From that time forth his whole life was to be dedicated to writing.

In 1925 the twenty-year-old budding writer Mikhail Sholokhov took the firm decision to return home, there to write a big book about the Don.

The young writer looked upon his first book as a modest unsuccessful attempt to write about his native region. When he left Moscow for the Don Sholokhov was still unsure as to how he would cope with his plans.

Sholokhov was planning to write a novel about Cossack life. "I began to write the novel in 1925," he was later to relate. "But originally I had no intention of such a large-scale work. The idea of showing the role of the Cossacks in the Revolution appealed to me especially. I began with the part they played in Kornilov's march on Petrograd. There were Don Cossacks in the 3rd Cavalry Corps, which took part in the march." Such, in the author's own words, was his original plan for a novel about the life of the Don Cossacks.

Sholokhov wrote about four signatures of the novel, which was entitled *The Don Epic*. But he was not satisfied with what he had written. He felt that the reader was left in the dark as to why the great majority of the Cossacks took part in the struggle against the Revolution.

"Who are these Cossacks? What is this Don Cossack region? Is it not something of a *terra incognita* for the reader? Such considerations led me to drop the work I had begun. I began to think of a much more encompassing novel," Sholokhov wrote in 1937. *

* *Izvestia*, December 31, 1937.

From what Sholokhov says we see that he originally intended writing a novel about the role of the Don Cossacks in Kornilov's attempted coup, but that while working on it he realised that the events leading up to the October Revolution could not really be understood properly unless he turned to the past, especially pre-war life, and the First World War. Sholokhov strove to shed light on the historical role of the Don Cossacks, and this in turn made it necessary for him to widen his sights to take in the grandiose conflicts of the whole revolutionary epoch.

The next year Sholokhov began work on the first volume of the novel as we know it, which describes the life of the Cossacks in the pre-war and war years.

At that time Sholokhov evidently suffered moments of doubt which are so familiar to writers, even the greatest: a feeling of hopelessness, when awareness of the vastness and singularity of the task that lay before him coupled with a deep sense of responsibility and tremendous perfectionism seemed to crush him and paralyse him with the thought that his efforts were useless.

Yet Sholokhov was only twenty when he set out to write *And Quiet Flows the Don.* He had but two years of writing behind him and the thin book, with a foreword by Serafimovich, in which his first stories were collected had not yet come out. And here he was alone, in an out-of-the-way Don village, far from the main literary centres, where he could have relied on the friendly support and approval of more experienced writers.

In 1932, when he was already world famous as the author of the first volumes of *And Quiet Flows the Don*, Sholokhov described this period in his "Autobiography" written for the magazine *Prozhektor*: "In the autumn of 1925 I set about writing *And Quiet Flows the Don*, but dropped it after three or four signatures. I felt it was beyond me." He went on: "I originally began with 1917, with General Kornilov's march on Petrograd. A year later I came back to it, and than changed my mind and decided to show the life of the Cossacks before the war."

The events described in volume one led up to the February Revolution, to the events in Petrograd and Kornilov's offensive. Naturally, in volume two Sholokhov used many passages from his first version.

"I began with an account of Kornilov's offensive, what now forms the second volume of *And Quiet Flows the Don*," Sholokhov told I. Lezhnev. "I had written some pretty good passages when it occurred to me that I had started off in the wrong place. I put the manuscript aside and started again, this time with the old days, with the life of the Cossacks before the war, which formed the first three parts, that is volume one, of *And Quiet Flows the Don*. When I had finished volume one and came to describe the events in Petrograd and Kornilov's offensive, I returned to my first manuscript and used it for volume two." *

The story of how Sholokhov first tackled *And Quiet Flows the Don*, the direction in which his thoughts were turning, is in itself significant. It helps one understand that universal law of art, whereby the success of the artist is explained first and foremost by his ability to discover and reveal "new worlds in life".

Of course it would be ridiculous to put this down merely to the fact that Sholokhov was the first in our literature to write of the Don region and the Don Cossacks on such a scale and with such understanding and sympathy. After all, a writer is not an ethnographer. We have seen how when the twenty-year-old writer set out so keenly to write his novel in 1925, he was still a long way from writing the book that was to earn him such fame.

From the first chapters of what now forms volume two of *And Quiet Flows the Don* it is easy to pick out the heroes of his first version and imagine the roles they were to play. I get the impression that in the original arrangement the writer was keeping very much to the literary traditions of the day, to those tenets which had come to have the force of unwritten laws. There was Bunchuk, the Communist who carried on propaganda among soldiers at the front, and the monarchist officer Listnitsky. There were powerful descriptions of the fighting and suffering which led up to the February Revolution. Ivan Alexeyevich Kotlyarov was also apparently there in embryo form.

A careful reading of the present fourth part leads one to the conclusion that Grigory Melekhov was most

* I. Lezhnev, *Mikhail Sholokhov*, Russ. ed., Moscow, 1948, p. 228.

probably not among the heroes of the first version. He makes casual short appearances, and he is completely absent from the passages about the Kornilov campaign. Grigory's successive promotions and his part in the fighting at this stage (for which Sholokhov himself admits using passages from his original version) are described in brief, fleeting episodes rather like movie sequences, totally uncharacteristic of Sholokhov.

And Quiet Flows the Don really got going when Sholokhov abandoned what he had so far written and turned to the life of the Cossacks before the war, that is, when he found what was to become the nucleus of the book: the Melekhov family and in particular Grigory. Thus Sholokhov came round to the epic simplicity of the opening as we know it: "The Melekhov farm was at the edge of the village...."

However, Sholokhov did not confine himself to the Melekhov household, but went on to widen the focus to the revolutionary storms which were gathering over Russia and the Don....

Little by little as he worked painstakingly over volumes one and two he was to develop and widen the subject-matter of the novel. His original plan of a portrayal of the role of the Cossacks in the Kornilov campaign was gradually enlarged into a grandiose four-volume epic of the Great October Socialist Revolution and the Civil War and the role of the Don Cossacks in these great events.

Sholokhov worked on the first two volumes of *And Quiet Flows the Don* from 1925 to 1928.

The literature of the 1920's produced a powerful, dramatic panorama of the revolutionary transformation of the country. Literature raised a wide range of questions, such as Country and Revolution, man and history, freedom and necessity, humanism and duty, class and universal values, will-power and weakness, the biological and the social, the conscious and the instinctive, and so on. The explosive material of politics invaded the arts. In this electric atmosphere "eternal" problems were charged with the excitement of new discoveries and became matters of life and death. By the answers he gave to this or that question a writer defined his position vis-à-vis the people and the Revolution, the events which had shaken the world.

Almost all the literary groups of the twenties went in for innovation, in most cases understood in the purely formal sense, as a rejection of tradition and the experience of the past. Yet if we look back over the complex history of Soviet literature it is not hard to see that all that was best and avantgarde in the true sense of the word in the literature of the twenties, was a result of fruitful study of the great works of the past, and assimilation of the artistic achievements of Maxim Gorky.

Stefan Zweig, himself one of the finest writers of our age, spoke in 1928 of what struck him so about Gorky.

"I would include Gorky's alert mind among the few real wonders of our age. I can think of nothing in art today that comes anywhere near the clarity and accuracy of his vision. Not a hint of mystical haziness darkens his vision, not a smear of falsehood marks the crystal-clear lens, which neither magnifies nor minifies, never twists or distorts the image, or gives a false picture, never exaggerates light or darkness. Gorky always sees clearly, and he always sees the truth, and the truth he sees is peerless and the clarity inapproachable. Everything on which his honest, incorruptible gaze alights—and his eye is the most truthful and accurate instrument in art today—remains completely intact, for it misses nothing, distorts nothing, changes nothing but reflects only the purest, most exact reality."*

Zweig's words do not strike one merely as an expression of boundless admiration for great talent. It is notable that he insistently drives home in different ways one and the same idea—"the peerless truth" and "inapproachable clarity" of Gorky's works. Is there in fact anything special and unusual in what Zweig called "Gorky's alert mind"? Was he not perhaps exaggerating when he included it "among the few real wonders of our age"? Obviously he was not referring to the greatness of Gorky's talent, for Tolstoi and Dostoyevsky, to whom we shall be returning on several occasions, do not yield to Gorky in this respect. Why, then, did Zweig single out Gorky with such insistence from among the great realist writers?

From a careful reading we get the impression that

* Stefan Zweig, *Begegnungen mit Menschen, Büchern, Städten*, Berlin-Frankfurt am Main, 1955, pp. 101-02.

Zweig is endeavouring to understand that qualitatively new outlook on the world, that new approach to solving life's problems, which distinguished Gorky and which took the form of a new *artistic method*, being reflected in his art.

Zweig considered it was Gorky's philosophy of life which gave him such confidence and force in his art and his capacity "to miss nothing, distort nothing and change nothing". He saw Gorky's strength to lie above all in his "indissoluble kinship with the people".

"Gorky never once doubted the invincibility of the people," Zweig wrote. "He believed in his people, and his people believed in him. Those great prophets Dostoyevsky and Tolstoi still feared revolution like a serious illness. Gorky was convinced that the sound health of the Russian nation would overcome this 'illness'. It was because he knew the masses and understood the Russian people, as a son knows his mother, that he never felt that mystical horror of the future which tortured these two great prophets of Russian literature. He knew that his people, any people, was strong enough to withstand all upheavals and overcome all dangers."*

This kinship with the people, and the consequent possibility of capturing life in all its real essence and recreating the flow of existence is the great achievement of the art of our age. It is particularly interesting to note how this principle was grasped by Stefan Zweig, a writer who was himself far from what was later to be called socialist realism.

Right from the outset Soviet literature asserted the indestructible bond between art and the life of the people. The best works of the twenties truthfully portrayed the heroic reality of the Revolution and the Civil War, the people in arms, freeing themselves from the fetters of the past. They showed the mighty change which had occurred in the position, perception and psychology of millions of working people.

The leitmotif of Soviet literature of the twenties, the People and the Revolution, was caught up by Sholokhov in *And Quiet Flows the Don*. He was fascinated by the life of the people at the great turning-point in their history

* Ibid., pp. 103-04.

and attempted to reveal the guiding principles which lay behind the Revolution, and show how they affected every aspect of life.

In writing his novel Sholokhov drew on the rich traditions of Russian literature which always endeavoured to discover the real needs and aspirations of the masses and comprehend their historical role. In creating his epic of the fortunes of the people in the Revolution and deciding on the artistic method to adopt, Sholokhov naturally turned for guidance to those masters of the epic genre, Tolstoi and Gogol.

From the time the first volumes of *And Quiet Flows the Don* appeared the work has often been compared to Tolstoi's *War and Peace*, and indeed the two works have a great deal in common, in the vast sweep of reality they portray, their epic structure, dramatic narrative and deep psychological penetration. The reader could not fail to note how the traditions of the Russian nineteenth-century classics were being continued in the new Soviet literature still in its infancy.

In many ways Sholokhov was also continuing the Gorky tradition. This similarity was not so much a matter of style or method but of fundamental ideological and aesthetic principles.

Sholokhov was a great admirer of Gorky both as a man and a writer. What attracted Sholokhov most in Gorky's works was his pride in man, his love for man the fighter, and his belief that the world would be transformed by the efforts of the working people. Sholokhov considered this revolutionary, humanistic element at the root of Gorky's art to be the writer's greatest gift to posterity.

"Gorky dearly loved those who struggled for a bright future for mankind and with all his heart and soul hated the exploiters and shop-keepers, and the petty bourgeois dozing in the quiet slough of provincial Russia."* It is unlikely that this brief newspaper report gives Sholokhov's speech word for word, but it expresses what was on the writer's mind, when along with all his fellow countrymen he was mourning the passing of "the stormy petrel of the Revolution", the great friend and teacher of all Soviet writers.

* *Molot*, June 23, 1936.

Sholokhov presented to Gorky a copy of the first book of *Virgin Soil Upturned* with a very warm and friendly inscription.

Sholokhov was working on *And Quiet Flows the Don* at the same time Gorky was writing his epic chronicle *The Life of Klim Samgin*. These outstanding works of Soviet literature both show the power of socialist realism. As the past recedes never to return, the new life emerges victorious before our very eyes on Sholokhov's vast canvas of the Revolution and the Civil War. Even the lives of those characters in the novel that seem to be least involved in social developments are radically affected by the events of the Revolution, by the course of history. The purport of the revolutionary changes is revealed in the flow of life itself, in the complex of human destinies and the amazing human variety of the characters.

2

Sholokhov spent fifteen years writing *And Quiet Flows the Don*. At first the writer lived and worked in circumstances that were far from ideal. He met with doubts and reservations even from those who were closest to him. "When he began work on *And Quiet Flows the Don* Sholokhov shut himself up in his father-in-law's study," wrote an *Izvestia* correspondent. "His relations joked that he was writing 'a real novel', and over the title: 'What a title! He tells you it's a novel and it turns out to be a river!' But Sholokhov did not lose faith. He was determined he was going to write 'a real novel'." *

Sholokhov finished the first two volumes in 1927 and the novel began to appear in the earlier numbers of the magazine *Oktyabr* in 1928.

On April 19, 1928, *Pravda* carried an article by A. S. Serafimovich on it, which was full of sincere praise for the young writer: "Sholokhov has never once said 'class' or 'class struggle'. Yet, as is the case with very great writers, the class stratification is imperceptibly woven into the narrative, the descriptions of people, and the

---

* *A Collection of Literary Criticism on Mikhail Sholokhov*, Russ. ed., Rostov-on-Don, 1940, p. 139.

chain of events and gradually grows and makes itself felt more and more as the grandiose age is unfolded before us. From the egg of some small, reasonably good, 'promising' stories a very special writer has hatched, unlike any other, with his own promising artistic personality."*

In the summer of 1931 Sholokhov sent book three of the novel to *Oktyabr*. He had worked hard on it and made many changes in the chapters previously published.

Sholokhov gradually brings Mikhail Koshevoi forward to occupy one of the most important places in the book, as a sort of antipode to Grigory Melekhov.

There is a much stronger patriotic note. The narrative had developed freely with a truly epic sweep. Sholokhov's portrayal of individual Red Army men, such as the fearless commander Likhachov; his description of sailors going into the attack singing the *Internationale*, of commanders and commissars marching into battle ahead of their men; his account of the fighting in the war-ravaged lands of the Don, of the terrible fate that befell the captured Veshenskaya Communists, and of the heroism of the people in arms are all tremendously powerful and pervaded with absolute faith in the triumph of Communist ideas. Sholokhov gives a masterly philosophical and artistic interpretation of these historical events, showing the people in arms as the only bearers of all that is beautiful and truly heroic.

Through such leading figures in the White Army as Denikin, Krasnov and others, he shows the Whites' venality and the way they were serving the Germans and the Allies. Both the monarchists and the Don autonomists are revealed in their true colours, as unpatriotic and enemies of the Russian people. Drawing on a wealth of documentary material Sholokhov shows that the various counter-revolutionary governments which succeeded one another on the Don were anti-popular and antinational.

The publication of book three of *And Quiet Flows the Don* was attended by considerable difficulties. Part six of the novel which dealt with the Upper Don uprising of 1919 in particular raised a storm of protest.

* A. Serafimovich, *Collected Works*, Vol. 10, p. 362.

Book three had begun to appear in Nos. 1-3 of the magazine *Oktyabr* in 1929 and publication was thereafter interrupted until 1932 (*Oktyabr* Nos. 1-8 and 10).

The history of book three is more than just a part of Sholokhov's biography, it is of great importance in understanding several essential aspects of socialist realism. For surely when a writer refuses to hide or draw the veil of silence over often contradictory and ambiguous historical facts but insists on delving into them and establishing their true place in history, this is not merely a question of fearlessness and great strength of mind but a purposeful method of reading the book of life, which permits him to perceive and demonstrate the historical process with the maximum of objectivity.

History was not something hostile to the writer or influencing him from without. By putting himself in the position of those who consciously and deliberately created the reality of the Revolution he transcended time and found that depth of understanding without which creative freedom is unthinkable. In this way he was able to shed light on the tragedies and mistakes and reveal all that was false and which obstructed development and progress.

The Upper Don uprising was one of the most tragic episodes of the Civil War. It broke out in February 1919 at the rear of the Red Army under the kulak Socialist-Revolutionary slogan "For Soviet Power Without the Communists". One of the documents of the time mentions how the Red Army men were not a little astonished to see the insurgents' red banners with the slogan "Long Live the Soviets! Down with the Communists!"*

Considerable forces had to be diverted to deal with the insurgents and this undoubtedly accounted to a large extent for the success of Denikin's thrust towards Moscow.

After a painstaking study of a mass of data Sholokhov ventured to explain the causes of the revolt.

Part six of the novel, which told of the Veshenskaya rising, was finally completed after a great deal of effort had been spent on it. Its publication was largely held

---

* *The Civil War in Russia 1918-1919. Strategic Account of Attacking Operations on the Southern Front, January-May 1919*, Russ. ed., Moscow, 1919, p. 46.

up due to opposition from leading members of the RAPP.*

This was a difficult period for Sholokhov. The enemies of Soviet literature were doing their utmost to slander the writer, maintaining that he had plagiarised the first two books of the novel.

But Sholokhov was not one to give way before any attacks, prejudices or narrow-mindedness. He fought for his book, upholding historical truth as the *sine qua non* of true artistic worth. The young writer not only demonstrated true civic courage, but showed unshakeable faith in the strength and ability of socialist art to tell the truth, however unsavoury it might be.

In a letter to Gorky of June 6, 1931, he made fun of those fellow writers who understood the tendentiousness of Soviet literature in grossly oversimplified terms.

"Some of my fellow writers who read part six and did not know that what I described was the historical truth, were strongly prejudiced against it," Sholokhov wrote. "They protest against 'artistic fancy' carried over into life. Moreover, this prejudice is reflected in the notes that have been written in the margin of the manuscript, which are often quite ludicrous. In the chapter where I describe the Red Army entering Tatarsky village, there is the following sentence:

"'The riders (Red Army men) were bouncing up and down in the saddle in a most ungainly fashion.' A mark has been placed against this sentence with the following exclamation: 'Who?!... Red Army men bouncing up and down in a most ungainly fashion? Can one say such things about Red Army men?!... That's counter-revolution!'

"The person who made this indignant comment is doubtless unaware of the fact that the Red Army men were not cavalrymen, and that when they fought in the cavalry they rode appallingly badly: it was quite a common thing for a horse's back to get chafed. Anyway, it is impossible to ride in a dragoons' saddle without bouncing up and down. It's quite a different matter from riding in a Cossack saddle which has a high pommel and a cushion. Besides, anybody, even if he knows how to sit properly

* The Russian initials of Russian Association of Proletarian Writers (*Rossiiskaya assotsiatsia proletarskikh pisatelei*), 1925-1932.

in a dragoons' saddle, sits badly compared to a Cossack. I just don't understand why the comrade who made the comment was so infuriated and expressed his revolutionary zeal with such a roll of the 'r'. The important thing is not that they rode badly, but that so doing they beat people who rode excellently. These are all unimportant minor details. The indispensable condition they are imposing on me if I want to have part six published is the removal of a number of passages which are dearest of all to me (lyrical passages and some others). The interesting part about it is that ten men propose discarding ten different parts and to please them all I'd have to get rid of three-quarters of the whole...."

In the same letter Sholokhov describes the true circumstances which led to the Veshenskaya uprising, on the basis of numerous documentary and eyewitness reports. He writes as follows:

"Now for a few remarks about the uprising:

"1. It arose as a result of exaggerated encroachments on the interests of the middle-peasant Cossacks.

"2. Denikin's emissaries took advantage of this situation. Working in the Upper Don region, their job was to direct the sporadic outbreaks of discontent into a single massive movement. A typical feature of the revolt was the fact that the vast majority of the 'outsiders' (not Cossacks) who had hitherto been the mainstay of Soviet power on the Don, fought on the side of the insurgents, forming detachments which fought more desperately and consequently better than the Cossack insurgents.

"Some 'orthodox' 'leaders' of the RAPP who read part six accused me of justifying the uprising as I pointed to the fact that the Upper Don Cossacks were annoyed because their interests had been seriously encroached upon. Is that really so? I merely drew a picture of the harsh reality which preceded the uprising without any exaggeration either way....

"But, Alexei Maximovich, I had to show the negative aspects of the policy which deprived the Cossacks of their special status and encroached on the interests of the middle-peasant Cossacks, for otherwise I could not reveal the causes of the uprising. For not only do people not rise up but even a flea doesn't bite just like that, without any reason.

"In part six I introduced a lot of characters who only pay lip-service to Soviet power.... Setting them off against Koshevoi, Stockman, Ivan Alexeyevich and others, I wanted to show that not all were such overzealous activists, and that these overzealous people distorted the idea of Soviet power....

"I feel, Alexei Maximovich, that we have by no means done with the problem of the middle peasant, and neither have the Communists in those countries which will follow the road of our Revolution."*

It is clear from this letter that the "orthodox" "leaders" of the RAPP rejected book six of *And Quiet Flows the Don* above all because they had a speculative approach to the historical process, taking it to be an absolutely positive *fait accompli*. The trouble was that they used it as an *a priori* postulate to "sanctify" all past events and situations. But "impeccability" as an initial postulate is least of all applicable to the historical process, which involves millions of people, different classes, social groups and so on.

Both in his novel and in his letter to Gorky, Sholokhov pointed out the causes of the Veshenskaya uprising. But a writer who merely limited himself to indicating the causes, without following up all the real and possible consequences, would be behaving like the proverbial ostrich.

The inability to feel and comprehend events in their historical perspective inevitably leads to the distortion of the essence of those events.

Those who apply the evaluation of the historical process as a necessary and desirable development to all events and facts are adopting the position of Candide whom Voltaire made such fun of for his insistence that "all is for the best in the best of possible worlds".

The truth can only be found through a concrete historical analysis of all the causes and results of a given event.

Sholokhov showed that there were people on the Don in 1919 who, like his Malkin, distorted the very "idea of Soviet power". In fact Serafimovich had written about this in 1919 in his article "The Don", published in *Izvestia*.

* First published in: I. Lezhnev, *Sholokhov's Path*, Russ. ed., Moscow, 1958.

"At times it was necessary to shoot Communist hangers-on and even Communists, who had disgraced themselves by abuse of their power and coercion, and to advertise the measures taken far and wide..."; "the reform of the existing social structure was carried out without due regard for the special features of the economy, life and psychology of the Cossacks, without due regard for the conditions actually existing.... "*

The fact that Sholokhov was farsighted enough to understand the causes did not mean that he justified the events. With great dramatic force he showed that the revolt, supposedly raised "for Soviet power" and which involved thousands of working Cossacks and "outsiders", was anti-popular and anti-national both in essence and in its consequences.

Perhaps Sholokhov's amazing powers of penetration, his deep insight, are most of all apparent in the vicissitudes of Grigory Melekhov, whom the struggle against the people brings to spiritual bankruptcy, loss of faith and the will to live even.

Sholokhov widened his sights further and further. The insurgents join up with whiteguard troops. One would have naturally expected the insurgents, surrounded as they were on all sides by superior Red Army forces, to welcome the link-up. Sholokhov shows that this was by no means the case. The mask of illusion was thrown off to reveal the bitter truth, the tragedy of these deluded, deceived people who were roused to wage a criminal war against the working people's Revolution.

Sholokhov's honest description of events as they actually happened helps the reader understand what the people went through in the years of the Revolution and the Civil War. The attempt to find a third alternative led to war against the Revolution, and only served the interests of the exploiter classes. History itself made Communist ideas the only possible answer to the requirements of the people.

Sholokhov's "poetic affirmation of the course of history" was the result of his understanding of the fundamental principles of historical development, and his ability to express them through the style of the narrative, charac-

* A. Serafimovich, *Collected Works*, Vol. 8, pp. 100-01.

ter grouping, the individual fortunes of his heroes
through various means at a writer's disposal.

Thanks to the support and intervention of Gorky book
three of *And Quiet Flows the Don* was finally published,
and Sholokhov set to work on book four.

3

Sholokhov was to spend a long time writing book four.

"Everything had existed long since in rough," he later
said, "but I was constantly reworking it."*

The size of the novel apparently took its final shape
in 1934-1935. "*And Quiet Flows the Don* will be a novel
in four books," the writer declared.

He also spoke of the abundance of real-life material
which had to be incorporated in book four, and the difficulties and the responsibility involved in his work on the
concluding parts of the novel.

"To include such an abundance of material in one book,
as you will understand yourself, is no easy task. This
accounts for the slow rate at which the book is getting
written. I have been working at it for a long time now.
I did consider adding another book to the novel, but
rejected the idea. I must finish it."

It was about this time, it would seem, that the plan
of book four finally took definite shape. The writer was
already quite clear in his mind about the events Grigory
Melekhov was to go through.

"At the end of book three Melekhov is in command of
an insurgent division near Veshenskaya. He strikes out
northwards from here, towards Balashov, and then is
forced to retreat with the White armies to Novorossiisk.
After the Whites have been crushed in the South and the
Cossack armed struggle is over Melekhov joins the Red
Army, and fights on the Polish front with the First
Mounted Army.... He later joins an outlaw band."**

With reference to the socio-historical significance of
Grigory Melekhov's vicissitudes, Sholokhov insistently
warned:

* *A Collection of Literary Criticism on Mikhail Sholokhov*,
p. 134.
** *Izvestia*, March 10, 1935.

"Melekhov's destiny is a purely individual phenomenon and I have no intention of suggesting that it is typical of the middle-peasant Cossacks. I take him away from the Whites, of course, but I will not make a Bolshevik of him. He is no Bolshevik."*

Sholokhov deliberately spoke of the "individuality" of Grigory Melekhov's destiny, for there was a general tendency to generalise in literature at the time, to use the typical individual as representative of the mass, and Sholokhov was constantly warning us to be on our guard against a crude, oversimplified likening of Melekhov's destiny to that of the middle peasants. It was apparently this which led several critics later, in 1940-1941, to make the mistake of dividing Melekhov's life into two stages: the typical and the individual, untypical.

The necessity of making Melekhov's role in the Revolution clear led to a certain amount of reshuffling of the other characters. Sholokhov refrained from introducing any new figures. The Communist Mikhail Koshevoi was to come to the fore just before the end of the novel.

"Koshevoi stands out among the Bolsheviks in book four. I shall bring him into the foreground and focus more attention on him. It is extremely difficult to introduce any new characters into the novel, Bolsheviks or otherwise."**

The way the two former friends' paths diverged in the Revolution was intended to make clear the social justice of what was happening by force of contrast.

In writing book four Sholokhov strove for psychological authenticity and at the same time for a deep social and philosophical comprehension of the life of Grigory Melekhov. To this end he counterposed his mercurial, vacillating hero with a man who was resolutely going out to meet the truth of the age.

Big changes were made to Aksinya's role in the final version. The writer's original intention was that she should stay "alive to the last chapter". "She won't have children, but neither will she know heartbreak,"*** Sholokhov said.

* Ibid.
** Ibid.
*** Ibid.

But Sholokhov abandoned his original plans for Aksinya whereby she was to come out of stormy events and violent upheavals unscathed, to live in joyless peace with the world and herself.

Aksinya was caught up in the vortex of the revolutionary upheavals of the age. She grew in stature to become a woman truly great in love and unafraid of risking all in her quest for happiness. She goes to her grave triumphant and unbroken. Struck down by a bullet, she falls in a flight of happiness, like a bird on the wing, just when it seems that her dreams are about to come true: her Grigory was beside her—her husband, her beloved, father of Mishatka and Polyushka whom she had brought up as her own, tasting all the joys of motherhood. It seemed nothing could separate them now: ahead lay the Kuban, the land of her hopes, of the happiness she had dreamed of for years. In a ravine far out in the steppe Grigory buries a happy Aksinya....

I feel that Aksinya's end was dictated not so much by the inner logic of the character as by the desire to strengthen the tragic note of Grigory Melekhov's culpability. For, after all, he was responsible for the death of this proud, passionate woman.

It is now possible to see exactly when it was that Sholokhov began to perfect part eight, chapter by chapter. Part seven was published in *Novy Mir* at the end of 1937 and the beginning of 1938 (1937, Nos. 11-12; 1938, Nos. 1-3). The writer dated the rough copy of part eight *December 17, 1938*. This is apparently when Sholokhov began the final stage of his work on the novel.

In 1939 Sholokhov mentioned in the course of an interview: "I shall definitely finish it in February."* And indeed the eighth and last part of the novel was published in Nos. 2 and 3 of *Novy Mir* for 1940.

Soviet literature in the thirties was largely concerned with showing the new Soviet man in the making, which it did through the representation of life in its most varied aspects. Some books showed this process of universal historical significance through the reality of the day, others by revealing the way the typical features and qualities of socialist man developed.

* *Molot*, March 20, 1939.

The great variety of themes and genres in the literature of the thirties was indicative of the great spiritual wealth of Soviet man, who was not only striving to comprehend the present and his place in it and the recent past of the Revolution and the Civil War, but was also carefully studying the whole history of his people and its outstanding figures.

Books of the most varied styles and genres were equally important in this—books like Ostrovsky's *How the Steel Was Tempered*, Alexei Tolstoi's *Peter the Great*, Sholokhov's *Virgin Soil Upturned*, Gorky's *Life of Klim Samgin*, Fedin's *The Rape of Europe* and Fadeyev's *The Last of the Udeghes*—and all of them represented different facets of one and the same method, socialist realism.

In the last parts of *And Quiet Flows the Don* Sholokhov was attempting the difficult task of translating the laws of historical development into convincing, concrete artistic terms.

The vast canvas of events of his epic was remarkable for its force and a wealth of colour, the unexpected changes in people's fortunes, the amazing wealth of individual personalities. For all its dramatic force, the narrative was nonetheless imbued with lyricism. The writer was able to conjure up the whole gamut of human emotions, from buoyant humour to tragic hopelessness.

"Art is never arbitrary if it is honest, unconstrained art. No, it is a holy scripture about life and man—its wretched and great, funny and tragic creator,"* Gorky wrote to Fedin.

This lofty conception of honest, unconstrained art certainly applies to Sholokhov's novel, which is imbued with love and respect for the working man.

And so the eighth and last part of *And Quiet Flows the Don* was published in *Novy Mir* (Nos. 2 and 3) in 1940. Thus Sholokhov's work on his novel—the weightiest in Soviet literature which had taken years of colossal effort to complete—was finally over. Right from the start, from the publication of the first two books, interest in the novel had been tremendous. The novel had conquered an exceptionally wide section of the reading public. It was argued about, and the appearance of each new

*K. Fedin, *Gorky Among Us*, Russ. ed., Moscow, 1944, p. 151.

part was awaited with great excitement. It would be no exaggeration to say that the novel became an event in the life of the people. The concluding part was received with enthusiasm. "You remain stunned by its power for a long time after you've finished reading it.... The book is remarkable among other things for the way it makes you think. And one of the things you think is: what a great writer there is living in our day."*

There was lively discussion on the novel in the press following the publication of the last part. Not one of those who wrote about it denied its tremendous artistic power, and indeed how could they? The dozens of newspaper and magazine articles, both those that were enthusiastic over the work and those that were more reserved in their praise and contained critical comments, were all visibly stunned by the great truth and artistic power of *And Quiet Flows the Don*.

---

* Y. Lukin, "The Concluding Part of *And Quiet Flows the Don*" *Literaturnaya Gazeta*, March 1, 1940,

Chapter Two
THE TRAGEDY OF GRIGORY MELEKHOV

1

Mikhail Sholokhov was the first writer to give such a broad picture of the life of the Don Cossacks, and the first to create an epic of the Cossacks' role in the Revolution.

The Don Cossacks who never knew serfdom were a caste apart from the ordinary peasants. The difference was not only in their education—Cossacks were brought up to be bold and resourceful and prepared for military service from childhood. The tsarist government had always encouraged them to consider themselves a special caste, and to look on the "muzhiks" and town workers with contempt. They were brought up as loyal servants of "tsar and country".

Grigory Melekhov had had it impressed on him since childhood that "Cossack" was the most honourable of titles. Indeed, the biggest insult among the Cossacks was to call someone a muzhik.

When Stockman, the underground Bolshevik organiser, intervened in the murderous brawl that had broken out between Cossacks and Ukrainians and said, "Long ago serf peasants ran away from the landowners and settled along the Don. They came to be known as Cossacks," he is met by the angry cry: "The swine wants to make muzhiks out of us!" (1, 189). This caste alienation, so carefully cultivated by the tsarist authorities and the Cossack landowners, officers and kulaks was to manifest itself with particular acuteness during the Civil War, in the separatist movement whereby the Don Cossacks strove to secede from revolutionary Russia and set up their own "Cossack system".

The Cossacks were won over by a big allotment of land. As one of the heroes of Serafimovich's story *On the Brink* put it, speaking of the Cossacks who had helped put down the 1905 Revolution, "they stuffed themselves on land".

The way the Melekhovs—who were middle Cossacks— lived is clear from the words of the head of the family Pantelei Prokofyevich: "Even without this year's harvest we've got grain enough for a couple of years. Praise be, we've got our bins full to the lids and some more elsewhere...."

The Cossacks exploited the peasant "outsiders", and the landless settlers. But the poor and middle Cossacks worked the land themselves with the help of their families. "Me and the old man slaved away day and night," says Ilyinichna, and in the novel we see the life of toil of many Cossack families.

In *And Quiet Flows the Don* Sholokhov lays bare the social heterogeneity of the Cossacks at the time of the Revolution.

Cossack generals and officers like Listnitsky owned vast estates—thousands of acres of land. The kulak Miron Korshunov had accumulated great wealth and power on his Tatarsky village. He employed permanent labourers, bought up land, and went in for thoroughbred livestock breeding. The merchant Mokhov and his partner Atepin squeezed the poorer Cossacks, making loans for interest.

Cossacks like Mikhail Koshevoi, unable to cultivate their own land, worked as hired labourers. Others, like Ivan Alexeyevich Kotlyarov, abandoned the land and went to work at Mokhov's mill, becoming semi-peasant, semi-worker. Among these poorer villagers arose a deep discontent with the existing state of things. A worker at Mokhov's mill, nicknamed Knave, remembered 1905 and nursed a seething hatred towards the wealthy and a longing for revenge. He was confident that there would be another revolution and that the time would come to get even with the oppressors.

Before the war and Revolution came and stirred up the whole country Grigory Melekhov never even thought of social problems. The Melekhov family, although not rich, were reasonably well-off and respected. Grigory loved his farm and the work on it. We see him haymaking, harvesting, ploughing in autumn. He felt an inner need for work. Without it life lost its meaning and when he was away at war, his mind returned again and again to his near and dear ones, his native village, and work in the fields, and he was gripped by a deep nostalgic yearning. "It would be good to have his hands on the plough-handles and walk along the damp furrow behind the plough, his nostrils greedily drinking in the raw, fresh scent of crumbling earth, the bitter smell of grass cut by the plough-share."

Grigory Melekhov grew up in a society which greatly respected military valour. The Cossacks went to church and attended village assemblies dressed in military uniform with shoulder straps, and decked out with all their medals. Awards like the St. George Cross evoked great respect and admiration for the bearer. This attitude to tsarist awards which had been instilled in Grigory from childhood, was to do him much harm in the future, leading him astray from the right path on which the Bolshevik Garanzha had set him when he was in hospital.

"Serve as you should. Service for the Tsar will not be in vain," Grigory's father writes to him when he is doing his army service before the outbreak of war, signing the letter: "Your father, Senior Sergeant Pantelei Melekhov" (1, 313). His father was more than his parent; he was a Senior Sergeant. For Pantelei Prokofyevich this military title meant that added respect was due.

Cossack families were patriarchal. The father was the senior member of the family and absolute master of the household. He could have the village give a disobedient son a public birching. Fear of his father and absolute obedience to him was instilled in the Cossack from childhood, and such obedience and respect for their elders was taught not only in the home but in the army too during military service. Thus the senior Cossacks had the right to punish their juniors.

Pantelei Prokofyevich kept a firm hand over his family. When in a rage he was capable of beating Grigory over the back with his crutch, and giving his wife what for if she took the part of a member of the family who had been disobedient. This did not prevent the Melekhovs from being a loving, close-knit family. When Grigory rushed on Stepan Astakhov, who was beating his wife Aksinya almost to death because of her affair with Grigory, Pyotr did not hesitate to join his younger brother.

The two brothers' love for one another is apparent throughout the novel. Pyotr's death at the hand of the Communist Koshevoi during the Civil War is one of the blows that drives Grigory onto the path of struggle [against the people.

In spite of his mettlesome, touchy nature, Grigory got along pretty well with his family. When his father decided to marry Grigory, who had "disgraced him" by carrying on with Aksinya, he tamely led Natalya to the altar. Of course this was largely due, too, to youthful thoughtlessness and his underestimating the strength of his feelings for Aksinya.

Grigory loves his home and family and is attached to his native village. He had never felt discontent with the way of life he had grown up with. Even when he broke with his family and went into service he was not divorced from village life. True, he did dream of going away to the Kuban, far, far away to where "beyond the rolling hills, beyond the long grey road lay a welcoming land of blue skies, a fairy-tale land with Aksinya's love, in all its rebellious late-flowering strength, to make it the more attractive" (1, 223). But the fairy-tale tone which Sholokhov adopts in this passage conveys how unrealistic and impracticable this dream was. Grigory is due to be called up for military service and this keeps him from going right away from the village. Even so, he would have been unlikely to leave his native parts. When Aksinya proposed that they throw up everything and go to the mines "far away", Grigory answered her with surprising cool-headedness and sensible clear-sightedness: "You're a fool, Aksinya, a fool! You talk away, but you say nothing worth listening to. How can I leave the farm? I've got to do my military service next year.... I'll never stir anywhere away from the land.... I'll never leave the village" (1, 80).

Indeed Grigory misses the farm and the village when he and Aksinya are working on Listnitsky's estate at Yagodnoye. "I miss the village, Pyotr," he complains to his brother (1, 284), and eagerly asks him for news of home in a tone which leaves no doubt as to how important it is to him.

Although Nagulnov in *Virgin Soil Upturned* is somewhat similar to Grigory in character, there is this big difference: whereas the former breaks forever with his rich family because of his early born dislike for "property", Grigory never really burns his bridges and always leaves a chance for a reconciliation with his family and the village. When his father and brother suggest he return it is because they sense this. When Grigory, who is serving in the army, is informed that Natalya is living with his family and that she is waiting for him, he gives an evasive, non-committal reply, merely saying that Aksinya has a child by him, and that he cannot abandon it.

This strong attachment to his farm, to his land typical of the peasants generally, was particularly strong in the case of the relatively well-off middle peasant. Throughout the Civil War Grigory never forgot for a moment that he had his own land, his own farm.

2

Grigory Melekhov's great humaneness reveals itself in everything. In a violent family drama, in the trials of war, and in the minutiae of everyday life—everywhere he demonstrates the strong sense of justice, self-respect and passionate love for life.

When he accidentally cuts a little wild duckling in two while mowing he stares with deep compassion at the little ball growing cold in his palm. The pain he felt was a manifestation of Grigory's characteristic love for all live creatures, for people and for nature.

It was only natural therefore that Grigory should have been so distressed when he first came face to face with the horrors of war. For a long time he could not get over his first battle and the Austrian he had cut down. "I cut down a man, and I'm sick at heart because of him, the swine!" he confides to his brother (1, 404). He begins to have doubts about the point of the First World War and is haunted by an uneasy feeling of its being as futile as it is disastrous.

As a farmer, Grigory has a strong sense of kinship with the world around him. This organic relation to nature and the capacity to appreciate its beauty has long appeared in Russian literature as a measure of man and his spirit. Man's attitude to nature was a favourite method of characterisation with Lev Tolstoi, whose negative characters have as a rule a limited awareness and appreciation of life in all its facets. Sholokhov adopts this method widely in *And Quiet Flows the Don*. The paucity of spirit of Colonel Listnitsky is revealed in his inability to appreciate the beauty of the Don steppe, while the rich natures of the Communists Likhachov and Podtyolkov are expressed in their full-blooded response to the beauties of nature. Sholokhov's favourite characters— Grigory, Aksinya and Pantelei Prokofyevich—live and move in the world of nature with its wealth of colour and sound.

We see Grigory early in the morning on the day his brother is due to leave for the summer training camp, leading his horse down to the Don to water it. "Slanting across the Don lay the wavy never-ridden track of the moonlight. Over the river hung a mist, and above it, the stars, like sprinkled grain. The horse set its hoofs down cautiously. The slope to the water was hard going. From the farther side of the river came the quacking of ducks. A sheat-fish jumped with a splash in the muddy shallows by the bank, hunting at random for smaller fry.

"Grigory stood a long time by the river. The bank exuded a dank and musty rottenness. A tiny drop of water fell from the horse's lips. There was a light, pleasant void in Grigory's heart, he felt good and free from thought" (1, 30).

The scene is described as if through Grigory's eyes. There is nothing unusual about it for him, it is part of his everyday life. Yet he sees the stars as being "like sprinkled grain". He notices in passing the quacking of ducks, and his attention is drawn to the splash a fish makes jumping, which for him, keen fisher that he is, evokes an almost tangible image of the sheat-fish hunting at dawn. Sholokhov shows amazing skill here in the way he reveals Grigory's response to nature. He rejects a conventional phrase to describe the beam of moonlight on the river and uses instead the typical Don word for track, and the expressive term "never-ridden". This is more than a precise description. It gives the narrative a touch of local colour so that we see Grigory standing by the river looking at the track of moonlight and sensing, rather than being consciously aware of it, the transparent path, untrodden by man.

The reader cannot help feeling that the "never-ridden track of the moonlight" is part of Grigory's own personal experience, and that he is part of this joyous world of light and colour.

The landscape in which we see Grigory is far more than a setting for the action in progress. Sholokhov always tries to make us feel that Grigory is a part of the world he moves in. For Grigory, Aksinya's hair "smells like henbane" (1, 45) and "the faint scent of the winter wind, or perhaps of fresh steppe hay, came from her fresh cold mouth" (1, 225). By means of these and similar poetic comparisons the author tries to transmit Grigory's sensitivity, his appreciation of a woman's beauty. In fact Sholokhov endows Grigory with a sharp appreciation of all that is beautiful.

A character's real nature and aesthetic significance is frequently revealed through his environment and his relationships with other characters. Grigory's appreciation of beauty is revealed in the story of his relationship with Aksinya and Natalya, for example. His love for the proud Aksinya, whose wild, fatal beauty does not fade with the years, and his life with Natalya—also beautiful but in quite a different way, a faithful, loving wife and mother—throw much light on his character.

Grigory is a man of strong passions and resolve. His love for Aksinya with all its violent ups and downs is remarkably strong and deep. When he comes home on leave to convalesce after his discharge from hospital and learns that Aksinya has been "carrying on" with young lieutenant Listnitsky, he gives him a fearful beating, drops Aksinya and returns home. But neither Aksinya's faithlessness, nor life with Natalya, nor even the children could douse his passion, and he spent many a night at the front yearning for Aksinya.

Grigory's highly developed sense of personal dignity and his consciousness of being any man's equal was bound to lead to many a sharp conflict in a class society with its laws of subordination and oppression—as indeed it did.

While the new recruits were passing muster Grigory felt a strong dislike for the white-handed officers. His "rough swarthy fingers" happened to lightly brush "the sugar-white hand" of one of the officers. The officer snatched his hand away, rubbed it on the edge of his greatcoat, frowning fastidiously, and drew on his glove. Grigory noticed his action and straightened up with a bitter smile. Their eyes met, and the officer flushed. and raised his voice: "What's all this, what's all this, Cossack?" (1, 308). On a later occasion, when a sergeant-major swoops on him with raised fist by a well in Radzivillovo, he addresses him with fearful hatred in his voice: "Look here ... if you strike me—I'll kill you. Understand?" (1, 333). And the sergeant-major who, encouraged by the officers, was used to settling things with his fists, turned on his heel and walked away.

In the grey routine of army life Grigory often felt a wall of silence between himself and the smart, idle officers. It was only natural that he, a working man used to earning his living by the sweat of his brow, although not fully aware of the class division of society, should nonetheless understand perfectly well that landowners and officers belonged to a different world, and that he should despise these parasites and idlers who were his "superiors". This feeling was to grow in him, and during the Civil War his deep, searing hatred for the oppressors and parasites would erupt on many an occasion.

Grigory was always ready to take up arms when human dignity was insulted. He was ready to use his fists on the Cossacks who raped Franya the housemaid, and would have, had they not tied him up and threatened to kill him; and when on the parade ground the troop commander asked him why a button was missing from his greatcoat, Grigory, overwhelmed by the memory of what had happened, felt like crying for the first time in years at his powerlessness.

This was Grigory Melekhov at the outbreak of the First World War.

3

The art of moulding an impressive, powerful literary character is a difficult and complex one. We may feel that we have learned a lot about Grigory Melekhov from the everyday life of himself and his family, from his complicated and confused relationships with Natalya and Aksinya. The swarthy Cossack with his sombre, somewhat savage expression, hot-tempered to the point of recklessness, proud and always ready to uphold his self-respect, resolute, abrupt, tender and rough, stands before the reader as real as if he were of flesh and blood. There is remarkable strength in his slightly hunched body, his darting glance, the way he works and the dashing figure he cuts in the saddle. Yet we cannot really know the young Grigory completely until we have examined the socio-historic environment he lived and grew up in.

And Quiet Flows the Don is a freely flowing narrative, with many characters and events but indirectly linked to the main heroes. Yet, at the same time, every scene, every chapter, throws light on the complicated and ill-starred life of Grigory Melekhov, often from the most unexpected angle.

The picture we are given of the life and fortunes of the Don Cossacks, while being of interest in itself, at the same time serves as an indirect means of characterisation, throwing additional light on Grigory Melekhov.

We know next to nothing, for example, of Grigory's attitude to the war when it first broke out; we do not know what he thought it was all about when he found himself flung into the bloody conflict. Sholokhov is a clever writer who leaves nothing to chance. He switches the scene of action to Tatarsky village and to Stockman, slowly but surely sowing the seeds of unrest and discontent with the existing order among the poorer Cossacks, thereby furthering their awakening to class-consciousness. Stockman tries to explain the causes of war, the struggle among capitalist states for markets and colonies. Those he talked to apparently understood him, but they were a small group, numbering ten at the outside.

The village elders spoke of the war in very different terms. Talking with the old men in the market place, Pantelei Prokofyevich told them how Grigory had written that there would soon be war. The old men recalled past wars and exchanged prognoses:

"'But there won't be any war.... Look at the harvest.'

"'The harvest has nothing to do with it. It's the students giving trouble, I expect.'

"'In any case we shall be the last to hear of it. But who will the war be with?'

"'With the Turks, about the sea. They can't come to an agreement on how to divide the sea.'

"'Is it so difficult? Let them divide it into two strips, like we do the meadowland.'

"The talk turned to jest, and the old men went about their business" (1, 319).

Such primitive notions about war and its causes were only possible in an isolated community, and in a place far removed and isolated from the main proletarian centres.

The account of the first battles in which Grigory took part is preceded by the lively, picturesque scene of the general mobilisation of the Cossacks. Sholokhov describes the animated, motley crowd in the square, interspersing the narrative with dialogue in a masterly fashion. The excited chatter of the crowd in the square seems to buzz in the reader's ears as if he were there himself. The women, attired in their holiday clothes, lined the fences along the streets. The commission inspected the horses. Many of the Cossacks were drunk.

"'But suppose there's a war?'

"'Pah, my friend! What country could stand up to us?'

"In a neighbouring group a handsome, elderly Cossack was arguing heatedly.

"'It's nothing to do with us. Let them do their own fighting, we haven't got our corn in yet.'

"'It's a shame! Here we are standing here, and on a day like this we could harvest enough for a whole year.'

"'The cattle will get among the stooks!'

"'And we'd just begun to reap the barley!'"

This sober, circumstantial talk (clearly elderly Cossack farmers are speaking) is interrupted by joking and complaining at the tavern being closed leaving them nowhere to drink. Then a "blood-stained and completely drunk" Cossack is led into the village administration. Tearing open his shirt he shouts: "I'll show the muzhiks! I'll have their blood! They'll know the Don Cossack!" which causes a ripple of laughter and comments of approval.

"'That's right, give it to them!'

"'What have they grabbed him for?'"

"'He went for some muzhik!'

"'Well, they deserve it.'

"'We'll give them some more!'

"'I took a hand when they put them down in 1905. That was a sight worth seeing!'

"'There's going to be war. They'll be sending us again to put them down.'

"'Enough of that. Let them hire people for that, or let the police do it. It's a shame for us to'" (1, 343-344).

These masterfully penned scenes, quite apart from the validity they have in themselves, are also important both for the picture they give of the environment in which Grigory was brought up and the help they give in understanding the ideas with which the young Cossack was equipped when he entered the war. Grigory had a minimal grasp of politics, limited to his naive ideas about the tsar, the country, and his military duty as a Cossack. He displayed great courage in battle, and was the first in the village to be awarded a Cross of St. George, but he did not think very hard about what he was fighting for. As time went on and battle followed battle he grew more and more weary and disillusioned and became increasingly perplexed and tormented by doubts.

While in hospital Grigory met up with the clever and sharp-tongued Bolshevik soldier Garanzha, whose words, as powerful as they were true, turned the whole system on which his life had hitherto been based into a smoking ruin. "It had already grown rotten, eaten up with the canker of the monstrous absurdity of the war, and it needed only a jolt. That jolt was given, and Grigory's artless straightforward mind awoke" (1, 512). With horror he realised that what Garanzha said about the senselessness of the war was true. He was unable to sleep and awoke Garanzha in the night. Blazing with anger he asked him: "You say we are being driven to death for the benefit of the rich. But what about the people? Don't they understand?" He struggled with the question of how to stop the war. "So you think everything has to be turned upside down?... And what will you do with the war when you've got the new government?... How are you going to root out war, when men have fought for ages?" (1, 513, 514). Garanzha had an answer for everything, and on saying goodbye to him, Grigory thanked him with feeling: "Well, khokhol, thank you for opening my eyes. I can see now, and I'm not good to know" (1, 516).

It is impossible to overestimate the importance of Grigory's first political schooling. It was to bear good fruit in the first months of the October Revolution, when spurred to action by it he was to side with the Bolsheviks and lead the Cossacks into the struggle against the Whites. And despite the fact that he was soon to wander from the true path, it nonetheless gave a mighty jolt to his ideas and feelings.

Grigory returns home on leave, and his discontent with the war and rage against those who drove people to the slaughter, combined with his own wounded self-esteem explode in the scene where he beats Listnitsky mercilessly. His family and the entire village soothed his tortured soul, flattering him with unconcealed adulation. After all, here was the first Cossack from the village to have received a Cross of St. George home on leave. The old men talked to him as an equal. He caught sidelong, respectful glances following him wherever he went. People took off their hats to him as he walked by and the women and young girls did not conceal their admiration. His family were almost ingratiatingly attentive to his needs. Pantelei Prokofyevich strode proudly along beside him on their way to church or to the market place. It was only natural that it should have gone to his head. After all, there were few who could hope to command such respect. The truth Garanzha had revealed to him, and his bitter invective faded into the darkest recesses of his mind. The time-honoured order seemed unshakeable, the deep-rooted Cossack concepts of honour, and military valour which had been instilled in him throughout his life once again assumed their former exciting attraction. "Grigory returned to Tatarsky one man, and went back to the front another.... Mentally still unreconciled to the senselessness of the war, nonetheless he faithfully defended his Cossack honour" (2, 55, 56); he seized "every opportunity of displaying reckless prowess, risking his life in madcap adventures, changing his clothes and going into the enemy's rear, capturing outposts, and feeling that the pain for other men which had oppressed him during the first days of the war had gone for ever" (2, 59-60).

With the advent of such an important historical event as the imperialist war, bringing in its wake so many serious and unexpected consequences, and with a revolutionary situation rapidly developing in the country it was important that the spotlight be trained for a while on Grigory's socio-political awareness. Sholokhov brings him into contact with various people professing very definite social views of a radically different nature. The Cossack Uryupin and the soldier Garanzha are the litmus-paper on which we can observe the various changes Grigory's views undergo.

Grigory meets up with Uryupin at the front during the war. Uryupin preaches a loathsome philosophy of contempt and hatred for man, and indeed epitomises the ideal of the Cossack warrior, loyal to tsar and country, so dear to the hearts of the governing classes of tsarist Russia. He is a true product of the bourgeois-landowner class society with all its inhumanity and callousness.

Uryupin's cynical advice to Grigory who is still tormented by the memory of the Austrian he had killed, is: "Cut a man down boldly!... Don't think about the why and wherefore. You're a Cossack, and it's your business to cut down without asking questions.... You mustn't kill an animal unless it's necessary, but destroy man! He's a heathen, unclean; he poisons the earth, he lives like a toadstool!" (1, 433). Grigory takes an active dislike to him from the outset. He fires a shot at Uryupin when he learns that he has cut down a Hungarian prisoner in cold blood. When Uryupin refers to the incident some time later Grigory informs him: "If I'd killed you I'd have had one sin the less on my conscience" (1, 490).

Grigory's instinctive humanity, sucked in with his mother's milk, finally triumphed in Grigory over the philosophy of annihilation professed by Uryupin. The obvious senselessness of the war aroused uneasy thoughts, anguish and discontent in him. At this juncture the author brings Grigory into contact with Garanzha, and face to face with a great human truth. For a while democracy and humanism gain the upper hand in Grigory over his class and property prejudices.

Grigory begins his tireless search for a great truth, a solution valid for the whole people. Later he was to renounce his search as a naive childish dream, and turn to finding a solution which only took Cossack interests into account. He returns home from hospital, convinced that he has the right answer and knows on which side the truth lies.

His break with Aksinya and the reconciliation with his family and the village is accompanied by a return to the ideas of military duty and Cossack honour fostered in him from childhood.

Here begins the tragic story of a strong, volatile man's harsh ordeals and painful vicissitudes in the vortex of the Civil War. Grigory's soul becomes a battle ground where the great human truth being put into practice by the people in revolt is locked in a mortal combat with the dark, evil forces of the deep-rooted habits of the old world with its property interests and class feelings. The "self-willed and merry lad" traverses a terrible, thorny path, strewn with irreparable losses. The struggle against the people, against the great truth of life leads him on to an ignominious end. A tragic figure will stand before us amid the ruins of the old world, a broken man for whom there is no place in the life that is beginning.

4

Grigory was to lose many fine human qualities from choosing the wrong path in the Revolution and finding himself at odds with the people. On his return to the war after resting at home and being thoroughly immersed in his Cossack world again, Grigory pals up with Uryupin. There are no longer the quarrels and incidents between them that there had been, and Uryupin's influence is more clearly discernible in Grigory's changed character and psychology. "The pain for other men ... had gone." Grigory's heart "had grown hard and coarse", and suddenly we are struck by the painful realisation of the awful connection between the time-honoured Cossack way of life and traditions, and Uryupin's degenerate, inhuman philosophy. The reader suddenly finds himself associating the Melekhov family and their way of life with Uryupin and his heinous ideas.

Sholokhov's remarkably skilful oblique characterisation is one of the chief attributes of his talent. While giving the reader much food for thought, he never hands out ready-made conclusions or presses his own opinions on him.

We are told very little about Grigory's life at the front after his return from leave. What we do know we learn from a few brief general accounts by the author or from Grigory's reminiscences. The focus is on the changes that had taken place in Grigory's character and outlook. "With cold contempt he played with his own and others' lives.... But he knew that he no longer laughed as in former days; he knew his eyes were sunken and his cheekbones stood out sharply; he knew that if he kissed a child he could not look straight into those clear, innocent eyes. He knew what price he had paid for his crosses and medals" (2, 60). This was the Grigory that met the Revolution.

But Garanzha had sown a live seed in his soul. Grigory did not forget the words of his intelligent, bitter room-mate in the hospital. Once he tried to explain the main essence of Garanzha's teaching to Uryupin. As was to be expected, Uryupin expressed complete disagreement: "There's no sense ever comes from these revolutions, only mischief. You remember this, that what we Cossacks need is our own government, and not any other! We need a strong tsar.... We've got nothing in common with the muzhiks...." (2, 62). He tried to persuade Grigory that the Cossacks had their own special interests to defend. But Grigory disagreed and complained that he "always thinks along one track" (2, 63).

Grigory tries to avoid adopting a parochial Cossack view of the future and take the wider interests of the people at large into account as Garanzha had taught him. Thus the way is paved for his going over to the Bolsheviks in the first months of the Revolution. He opposes Uryupin, this tsarist and inveterate defender of Cossack class privileges, though he does so weakly and vaguely, as if himself doubting the truth of what he is saying. This is the complex character Sholokhov creates for us: a man for numerous reasons prone to grave political doubts and hesitation, who has great difficulty in feeling his way amid the apparent chaos of the revolutionary upheavals.

The Great October Revolution and the Civil War that
followed faced Grigory Melekhov with a serious dilemma:
what direction should he take and with whom should
he go along?

The Bolsheviks brought peace to the war-weary country. Most of the front-line Cossacks were tired of the war
and sided with them.

At the outbreak of the Revolution Grigory's sympathies
for the Bolsheviks were still weak and little developed.
He had never had any firm political convictions, nor was
he to find any throughout the Civil War. His lack of firm
social beliefs is revealed in the story of his relationships with two people—Lieutenant Izvarin and the
revolutionary Cossack Podtyolkov.

Izvarin served in the same regiment as Grigory. Unlike
Uryupin he was well-educated, widely read and an elo-
quent speaker, and he poisoned Grigory's mind with
the dangerous ideas of Cossack autonomy and separatism.
Son of a well-to-do Cossack, he campaigned for the seces-
sion of the Don Province from revolutionary Russia.
Grigory had heated arguments with him. How could
the Don live without Russia, he wanted to know, when
they had nothing except wheat. But Izvarin easily
triumphed over the semi-literate Grigory in these verbal
duels.

It is notable that in their arguments both Izvarin
and Melekhov treated the Cossacks as a single, united
people apart and that neither of them saw them as being
divided by class differences. This social blindness was
indeed Grigory's Achilles' heel.

Brought up in a traditional property society, Grigory
is unable to grasp the completely new, unprecedented
order on which the new society is to be built. He is
unable to break out of that vicious circle of concepts
of the life based on property relations which divides
people into hostile classes.

"If the Bolsheviks get the upper hand it will be good
for the workers and bad for the rest. If the monarchy
returns, it will be good for the landowners and suchlike
and bad for the rest," Izvarin impressed on Grigory
(2, 252-253). "In real life it never works out that everybody

gets an equal share," Izvarin had said, and Grigory was to repeat these words himself.

Grigory came into contact with Fyodor Podtyolkov, then a sergeant-major in a Guards battery, but later to become the first chairman of the Don Revolutionary Committee. Grigory tries to give a paraphrase of Izvarin's "autonomist" arguments, but Podtyolkov confounds him with the incontestable truth of his answers:

"The atamans will go on just the same as before, oppressing the people who have to work. You will go before some 'Excellency', and he'll give you one on the snout. A fine life indeed! Better hang a mill-stone round your neck and jump into the river.... Once you've overthrown the tsar and the counter-revolution you must see the government passes into the hands of the people. That story about the old times is all fairy-tales. In the old days the tsars oppressed us, and now if the tsars don't, somebody else will" (2, 257).

There is confusion and unrest in the region. Kornilov's Volunteer Army is being formed on the Don. In Novocherkasskataman Kaledin gathers units that have remained loyal to the old regime. At Kamenskaya, front-line Cossacks elect a Revolutionary Committee.

Grigory Melekhov joins the struggle on the side of the Revolution. He commands a Red Guard detachment in the battle at Glubokaya against the forces of Chernetsov, composed mainly of officers, and has an important clash with Podtyolkov there. On Podtyolkov's orders the Cossacks massacre Chernetsov and the officers taken prisoner. With his usual impetuosity Grigory challenges Podtyolkov.

There is more than humaneness behind this instinctive movement: all his latent discontent is bursting to the surface.

"He wanted to turn his back upon the whole hate-riddled and incomprehensible world. Behind him everything was entangled, contradictory. The right path was difficult to trace; the ground quaked under his feet as in a bog, the path branched in many directions and he felt no confidence that he had chosen the right one. He had been drawn towards the Bolsheviks, had led others after him, then had hesitated, and his heart had cooled. 'Is Izvarin right after all? Who are we to trust?'" (2, 341).

It is in this tortured state of mind that Grigory returns home to recuperate after being wounded by a whiteguard bullet. The right path was indeed difficult to trace. He was to spend the whole Civil War trying to do so.

Grigory's ignorance of the laws of historical development strengthens his aversion to the war and his longing to return to his home and his old life. His desire to retire from the struggle only arises when he finds himself at the cross roads and does not know which way to take. The vital question for us, therefore, in our examination of the ill-starred life of Grigory Melekhov, is what was it that made his search for the truth so difficult, that harrowed him and caused him to waver so?

6

Grigory Melekhov belonged to the "petty bourgeois or semi-petty bourgeois working masses" for whom vacillation between the bourgeoisie and the proletariat was inevitable. The outcome of the revolutionary struggle was finally decided, as Lenin pointed out, by these millions finally coming down on the side of the workers and poor peasants.

"...And if anything decided the issue of the struggle against Kolchak and Denikin in our favour, despite the fact that they were supported by the Great Powers, it was that both the peasants and working Cossacks, who for a long time remained in the other camp, have in the end come over to the workers and peasants—and it was only this that finally decided the war and brought about our victory."[*] These words are from a speech Lenin addressed to working Cossacks in 1920.

By making the hero of his epic a man from a middle-peasant background Sholokhov was able to reveal one of the cardinal problems of the Revolution, and its great socio-political experience. His bold, fearless portrayal of the tragedy of a man from the people who was richly endowed by nature and should have allied himself with the revolutionary forces but failed to do so, was a revelation in our literature, for he was bringing layers of life to the surface which had been hardly touched upon before.

[*] V. I. Lenin, *Collected Works*, Vol. 30, p. 396.

Lenin gave a very accurate definition of the contradictory nature of the peasant toiler: "The peasants are half labourers and half property-owners."*

In Grigory Melekhov Sholokhov gives a penetrating psychological analysis of the struggle between deep-rooted property habits and the affinities of the toiler.

Throughout the Civil War Grigory remains firmly opposed to the idea of sharing out the Cossack land. As soon as the land is mentioned the property instinct comes out in him, the instinct to defend his property, if necessary with his life.

Immediately after his return home from serving in the Red Guards Grigory tries to convince his father and Pyotr that land should be given to those "outsiders", from other provinces who have been living on the Don for a long time. "I want a Soviet government," he replies to his father's question as to what side he is on (2, 352). Pantelei Prokofyevich, that firm limb of the Cossack law, explodes with anger, while Pyotr energetically tries to talk him round. The comfortable life at home (Sholokhov chooses his moment well to give an account of a fine spread in the Melekhov house) with its regular settled routine, the artless delight of the family when, yielding to Natalya's entreaties, he wears his officer's tunic and his crosses ("'You look like a colonel!' Pyotr exclaimed in delight") is irresistibly pleasant to Grigory, and awakens all his class and property feelings.

These new feelings first burst forth shortly before the execution of Podtyolkov. The Cossack hierarchy are leading the Cossacks against Soviet power, against the Red Guard detachments retreating from the Ukraine. The White officers mobilise the Cossacks in many districts of the Don Province. Mikhail Koshevoi, Knave, Christonya and Grigory gather at Ivan Kotlyarov's house. Mikhail and Knave propose that they go and join the Reds. Ivan Kotlyarov hesitates, for he has his family to think of. Grigory angrily opposes the idea, and when Knave went on to insist that they ought to leave, angrily cut him short: "Not so fast! Your position is different, there's nothing to keep you, you can go where you like! But we've got to think it over carefully. I've got a wife and

* Ibid., p. 510.

two little children.... You can wag your tongue, you whipper-snapper! You're just what you've always been. You've got nothing but your jacket to your name...." (2, 421-422). These are the haughty, angry vituperations of the Cossack with his own farm for whom the homeless, unfortunate Knave does not merit even the most basic human respect. It is significant here that the main pre-text Grigory gives for not leaving is that he has his homestead and family to think of.

Grigory had not wished to leave and join the Reds. Instead he fought for anti-revolutionary forces of the Don Army. Deceived by slogans calling for autonomy for the Don region the Cossacks rose against Soviet power.

Grigory's views undergo a sharp change at this point. He believes that he is fighting to defend the Cossack lands from the encroachments of the Tambov, Ryazan and Saratov muzhiks led by the Bolsheviks. Angered against the Bolsheviks he considers the counter-revolutionary struggle perfectly justified. But he sees that the majority of the Cossacks are little disposed to fight and are prepared to adopt a conciliatory attitude.

The Red Army struck the Cossacks some hard blows and by the autumn of 1918 the front defended by ataman Krasnov's whiteguard army was beginning to collapse. Whole groups of Cossacks deserted their detachments and returned home to wait uneasily on their farms for the arrival of the Red Army. Grigory also deserted and stayed on in the village to await further developments. It was not long before the Red Army was passing through Tatarsky, pursuing the fleeing White forces, and Soviet power was once more established on the Don.

Everything that was fermenting inside Grigory, seething beneath the surface, was to burst forth in his conversation with Ivan Alexeyevich Kotlyarov, now Chairman of the village Revolutionary Committee. This frank confession was the result of long, painful meditations. The conversation revealed all Grigory's inner contradictions, his inability to overcome his property and class interests. It represents a most important point on his tortuous path, throwing much light on his future, explaining a great deal.

One winter's evening Grigory dropped in at the head-quarters of the District Revolutionary Committee, and there ensued one of those scenes which Sholokhov handles so masterfully, where he brings characters together in a dramatic situation in which they naturally reveal to the reader many important features of their nature. In this case Sholokhov has brought together three old friends. Not so long before Grigory and Ivan Alexeyevich had refused to go off and join the Reds, giving the excuse that they had their families to think of. But even at the time Ivan Alexeyevich had had an uneasy sensation that he was not acting according to the dictates of his conscience. He guessed that with Grigory it was something else.... At the assembly that was held after the Reds came to the village, Grigory met Ivan Alexeyevich and his old friend Mikhail Koshevoi. Mikhail had worked as a drover and then been drafted into a disciplinary company, where he had been kept under close surveillance to prevent him from joining the Bolsheviks. The day before the Whites had abandoned the village Ivan Alexeyevich had gone out to meet the Reds and had come into the village with them. Grigory had deserted his regiment, staying on at home. "How is it you stayed behind, Grigory?" Ivan Alexeyevich had asked, his friendly tone betraying sincere concern for Grigory. "And how about you?" was Grigory's answer. "Thinking of my commission? I risked it and stayed on here. I nearly got killed yesterday.... I was sorry I hadn't cleared out. But now I'm not sorry...."

"We should have cleared off to the Reds when we had the chance. We wouldn't be looking so silly now if we had," Ivan Alexeyevich added (3, 189). He had understood his mistake and was trying to make amends for it. But it has not even crossed Grigory's mind that he had chosen a dangerous, slippery path right back at the time of Podtyolkov's execution.

Now, in January 1919, Grigory meets Ivan Alexeyevich and Mikhail Koshevoi with his ideas already matured. He speaks directly, with an almost desperate frankness, for Kotlyarov and Koshevoi are as yet people in whom he can confide, and he may even be secretly hoping that they might be in sympathy with his views. Grigory asks Ivan Alexeyevich what the Bolsheviks are giving the Cossacks. "Are they giving us the land? Or liberty? Are they making everyone equal? We've got enough land to choke ourselves with already. And we don't want any more liberty or we'll be knifing each other in the streets. We used to elect our own atamans, but now they're set over us. This government will bring the Cossacks nothing but ruin. It's a peasants' government, and we don't need it. And we don't need the generals either. The Communists and the generals are all alike: they're all yokes on our necks" (3, 210-211).

Grigory had become a firm supporter of Cossack separatism. He tries to substantiate the idea of the special position of the Cossacks as a class apart, united in their outlook and aspirations.

Ivan Alexeyevich is a simple, semi-literate Cossack, groping his way towards the great social truth of life, following what his heart tells him to be right. He answers Grigory with firm conviction:

"'The rich Cossacks don't need it, but how about the others? You fool! There are three rich Cossacks in the village, and how many poor? And what will you do with the labourers? No, we can't take your view of it. Let the rich Cossacks give up a bit of their own wealth and pass it on to the poor. And if they won't, we'll take it, with their flesh as well! We've had enough of their lording it over us! They stole the land.'

"'Not stole it, but conquered it. Our forefathers poured out their blood for it, and maybe that's why the earth is so fruitful....'"

It is significant that Grigory should try to find an explanation and justification for the special class position of the Cossacks by referring to those far-off days. For the autonomists glossed over the present social class structure of Cossack life with legends of the past. Ivan Alexeyevich makes short work of Grigory's arguments: "That doesn't make any difference; they must share it with those who need it. But you—you're like the weathercock on a roof. You turn with the wind. Such men as you cause trouble" (3, 211).

Ivan Alexeyevich, who had opposed the imperialist war at the front and raised a Cossack squadron against Kornilov, and was thus not without political experience, faces Grigory with the simple fact that the Cossacks do not constitute a single class. "There are all sorts of Cossacks," he points out.

Grigory is unwilling rather than unable to see this. For him the Cossacks are a united whole, with their own special interests. This is what enables him to believe in the possibility of the Cossacks having their own special path in the Revolution. Ivan Alexeyevich does not pull his punches, but points out to Grigory the way his special, "third" way inevitably leads.

"It's a long time since I saw you last and I won't deny that you've changed. You are an enemy of the Soviet Government," he says tersely. But he cannot bring himself to raise his eyes and look Grigory in the face, in view of his lingering attachment to him.

"I don't think you used to hold those views," Mikhail Koshevoi had remarked at the beginning of the conversation with the deliberate intention of wounding Grigory with the memory of the time when he had fought for the Reds. From then on he listened in silence but with mounting anger against his former friend.

These three Cossacks are three very different individuals. Despite the apparent similarity of their social position, and the fact that they felt the same about most things not so long before, a clear distinction in their class sympathies has now become apparent and, more important, they are divided over the most fundamental thing, what they understand by the truth and the meaning of life. In their heart of hearts Ivan Alexeyevich and Mikhail Koshevoi were toilers, and their feelings as such put them on the side of the revolutionary people of Russia, whereas Grigory had property class prejudices.

Ivan Alexeyevich chose the right path in the complex situation at the beginning of the Civil War and refuses to be turned away from it by anybody. He found the true way only after hard experience and much thought, and once he has found it he is ready to stick to it to the death if necessary. This simple, semi-educated man was head and shoulders above Grigory. He had risen to the noble humanistic awareness of the need to share other people's burdens and difficulties. He is constantly concerned for the workers, the poor and hungry, for all oppressed mankind. The way ahead is also clear to Koshevoi. He is filled with hatred for Grigory, who is attacking what is dearest to him, the Soviet, working people's government which he serves with all his heart and soul.

After the conversation Grigory continued to be tortured by the same doubts: "There's not one truth in this life. The one who wins eats the one who doesn't. And I've been looking for a truth that doesn't exist, wearing my heart out over it, going from one to the other. In the old days, they say, the Tatars tried to grab the Don lands and make us slaves. And now it's Russia. There can be no peace with them! They are foreign to me and to all the Cossacks" (3, 216).

7

By the time the Veshenskaya counter-revolutionary uprising broke out in the rear of the Red Army in February 1919, Grigory had weighed and decided everything. We see an embittered man furiously defending the world of private property which he realises is being threatened. All his former hesitations and doubts evaporate and he cannot even understand what there had been to think about.

"What had there been to think about? Why had his spirit tossed like a hunted wolf in search of a way of escape, of solving contradictions? Life seemed absurdly, wisely simple. Now he believed that there never had been any truth under whose wing all might shelter; now he thought that each had his own truth, his own furrow. For a piece of bread, for a strip of earth, for the right to live, men always had fought and always would fight so long as the sun shone on them, so long as the blood flowed warm in their veins....

"The path of the Cossacks had crossed the path of the landless peasantry of Russia, the path of the factory people. Fight them to the death! Wrest from them the rich Don earth, washed with Cossack blood. Drive them as once the Tatars had been driven beyond the borders of the province. Strike Moscow, fasten a shameful peace on them!" (3, 259, 260).

In this reasoning of an enraged property owner whose interests are being threatened we hear centuries of falsehood, the voice of that passing world where it is every man for himself and man preys on man. The seeds Izvarin had sown in Grigory's heart had taken well and were bearing fruit. He accepted Izvarin's false credo as the truth, attracted by the fact that it seemed to offer the possibility of a third path in the Revolution.

The Veshenskaya uprising, in which a large number of the Upper Don Cossacks for a variety of reasons took part, seemed to confirm Grigory's attitude. The Cossacks appeared to be opposed to both the Whites and the Communists, with their kulak Socialist-Revolutionary battle slogan "For Soviet Power Without the Communists!" The fighting took place in the rear of the Red Army and had no connection with White Army forces. The insurgents continued to use "Comrade" as the common form of address, a sort of "Cossack Republic" was set up, and Grigory felt that his path in the Revolution was henceforth clear. This mistaken conviction was all the stronger in him in the early days of the uprising because he felt he had merged with the Cossack masses. *He had never sought for a personal truth, but for a truth under whose wing all the Cossacks might shelter.* It is because he sees himself as defending Cossack interests that he throws himself with such desperate fervour into the thick of the conflict.

As commander of an insurgent division Grigory would seem to have definitely chosen his path. His grief and bitterness when he learns his brother Pyotr has been shot by Mikhail Koshevoi is such that it is as if nothing could ever reconcile him with his brother's killers. In this scene Sholokhov makes the reader feel all the power of those complex circumstances which bind Grigory to the past. Grigory's behaviour was not only influenced by class feelings but also by considerations of family loyalty: combined, they led him to defend that order which was crumbling under the blows of historical necessity.

The hard school of experience, however, soon revealed the true nature of the events taking place, whom and what interests Grigory was really serving when he led the Cossacks into battle. It is not long before he is seized by fresh doubts as to whether he has after all chosen the right road, and he has "a rebellious feeling of the injustice of his cause".

This feeling arises after Grigory has been questioning a captured Cossack who had fought for the Reds. He had originally ordered him to be executed, but taking pity on him had had him released.

Anxiety and caustic bitterness stir within him blotting out the self-satisfied joy he feels as he watches the dense lines of horsemen, his men, streaming past him. He is suddenly struck by the thought: "And above all... who am I leading them against? Against the people.... But who is right?"

"The intoxicating strength of power faded from his eyes, and the anxiety and bitterness remained, bowing his shoulders with their unbearable heaviness" (3, 302).

So it is that, as a result of his experiences, Grigory is once more assailed by indecision and painful doubts. At the insurgents' headquarters he meets a Cossack who has come from Alexeyevskaya *stanitsa* to apply for help in raising the Cossacks there against Soviet power. "If we had sent you troops, would you have risen? All of you?" Grigory asks. His question betrays the doubt that was torturing him, which gave him no rest. His insistence on the word "all" immediately gives the reader a clear insight into the direction his thoughts were taking. The Cossack's answer only confirms Grigory's doubts: "Well, I don't know about that.... The good farmers would, of course." "What about the poor?" Grigory insists, and the way he continues to question the man after Kudinov, the insurgents' commander, had rudely told him to go back whence he came, reveals how deeply concerned he was. As to whether the poor would rise or not the man answers: "The loafers, you mean, why the devil should they rise? This government's just the thing for them, a real holiday!" (3, 317). Grigory frowns thoughtfully.

Kudinov introduces Grigory to "Comrade" Georgidze who also works at the insurgents' headquarters. "He's a lieutenant-colonel and he's been through a staff training college." Grigory feels a vague inward anxiety and causeless anger. Suddenly he guesses the truth. "What if the Cadets purposely left these educated officers with us in order to stir up revolt in the rear of the Reds and to guide us along their own way?..." (3, 325). It is not long before Grigory's suspicions are confirmed.

Sholokhov reveals all these transitions and inward struggles indirectly through *the events described*. The important role the latter play in bringing out the inner workings of a character's mind is typical of Sholokhov, who skilfully chooses the most historically relevant and representative events with this in view. The chain of inner feelings and ideas is closely interwoven with the action. Thus Grigory's talk with the Cossack at staff headquarters serves to reveal thoughts which are going on so deep down in Grigory's consciousness that he himself is not all the time fully aware of them. They are disclosed not by direct description of the hero's inner life, but in a more complex, roundabout way, through such outward signs as the tone and sequence of his questions, the causeless anxiety and anger he feels when he shakes hands with the whiteguard lieutenant-colonel, and so on.

Sholokhov does not only show how various thoughts and feelings arise: he also reveals the social causes that give rise to them. Grigory feels great hostility towards the gentleman colonel whose presence at the headquarters worries and angers him, for he has no wish to serve the Cadets. He plies the Cossack with questions—he would like to believe that the Cossacks have their own Cossack truth, that he is serving it and it alone. But he is tormented by doubts, and in a drunken conversation with a friend, all that is simmering inside him suddenly bursts forth: "We'll kill the colonel. He stayed behind on purpose.... Kharlampy! Let's give in to the Soviet Government. We're in the wrong" (3, 355).

It is these feelings that lead Grigory to understand that the cause he is fighting for is anti-popular and provoke his admission to Kudinov: "I think we went wrong when we began the rising" (3, 325).

8

The struggle against the people in the camp of the counter-revolutionaries brings Grigory to moral bankruptcy and he seeks escape from reality and his painful, tormenting doubts in drink.

"After four days of incessant carousing he began to show signs of its effects: he went baggy and blue under the eyes, and his glance was senselessly stern" (3, 351).

Even Ilyinichna's patient, long-suffering maternal heart is moved to speak. As he goes back to the front when his leave is over, she makes the sign of the cross, and kissing him says reproachfully: "Grigory, think what you're doing! Look what fine children you've got, and perhaps those you killed had children too. When you were a lad you were so gentle, but now you're always frowning and your heart must be like a wolf's. Listen to what your mother says, Grigory" (3, 428). .

Out of boundless maternal love the old woman had addressed these sharp words of criticism to her youngest son. How many sleepless nights and suffering had driven her to utter these words to which Grigory responded with a cheerless smile!

The struggle against the people has atrophied many of Grigory's finer feelings. When reproaching him with having been unfaithful Natalya says, "Aren't you ashamed?", Grigory smiles as if she is being childishly naive and exclaims: "Huh! Ashamed!... I've forgotten how to be ashamed. How can you feel shame when all your life's messed up? There you are killing people. You don't know what all the mess is about...." (3, 392).

This man who loved life so was gripped by such a feeling of futility that his own very existence seemed completely pointless.

"...Grigory thought with sober indifference: 'I've lived and experienced everything in my day. I've loved women and girls, I've ridden the steppe, I've rejoiced in fatherhood, I've killed men and faced death myself, and delighted in the blue sky. What new thing can life show me? Nothing! And I can die! It won't be so terrible. I can play at war without risk, like a rich man gambling. My loss won't be so great'" (3, 359).

There is a mortal weariness, a terrible indifference in these thoughts. He returns again and again to thoughts of death which sap all his vital energy. He looks on death without bitterness or regret, as a relief from his errors and delusions.

More and more frequently Grigory's near and dear ones compare him to a wolf. For both Sholokhov himself and

his heroes, the words "wolf", "wolf-like" have the force
of a sharp moral condemnation. Grigory himself had
said to Pyotr during the imperialist war: "They've set
us fighting one another, worse than a pack of wolves.
Hatred everywhere" (1, 404). And now he is being likened
to a wolf.

In a cri-du-cœur his mother says his heart "must be
like a wolf's", and his sister Dunya feels the same. By
likening Grigory to a wolf Sholokhov forcefully accen-
tuates the whole tragedy of the soul-destroying changes
that take place in him. He resorts to this motif at the
time of the Veshenskaya uprising, when Grigory is struggling most actively against Soviet power, abandons
it when his feelings as a toiler get the upper hand again,
to return to it in the last part of the novel, where it rings
more strongly than ever while Grigory is fighting in
Fomin's band. Sholokhov uses this wolf motif to typify
the evil class feelings which so mar the nature of this
tragically misguided man from the people.

In a terrible frenzy, in the heat of battle, Grigory
cut down four sailors. For the first time in his life he
collapses in a fit.

"...In a moment of horrible clarity of mind, he tried
to get up. But it was no use and, turning his tear-stained,
distorted face to the Cossacks standing around him, he
shouted in a broken, savage voice:

"'Who have I killed?'

"For the first time in his life he writhed in a fit,
shouting and spitting foam from his lips:

"'Brothers, there's no forgiveness for me.... Kill me....
Cut me down, for the love of God! Death ... put me to
death....'" (3, 367).

In this moment of lucidity Grigory condemns himself
and the struggle he is waging against the people.

Like retribution, out of the blue, a terrible, sharp
pain grips his heart, everything goes dark before his
eyes and the ground seems to slip away beneath his feet.
Grigory can find no rest, no escape from his tormenting
thoughts. He no longer believes in the justice of what
he is doing, and is gripped by a vague remorse, an intui-
tive sense of guilt.

"...You never think what it is that's gnawing at my
heart, sucking my blood.... Life's taken a false turn,

and maybe I'm at fault in that too.... We ought to make peace with the Reds and attack the Cadets. But how? Who will bring us into touch with the Soviets?" (3, 392).

Grigory is wrestling desperately with contradictions which are insoluble for him. There is a deeply tragic note in his words to Natalya: "I hardly care for the children and I haven't a thought for myself. The war's dried it all out of me. I've grown hard.... Look into my soul and you'll find it's black as an empty well...." (3, 393).

The words "empty" and "black" intrude again and again in Grigory's thoughts and speech. When he thinks or speaks about himself he can find no more fitting words than these to express his bitter, painful thoughts. Grigory Melekhov's soul had indeed become black and empty.

9

Losses, changes and painful inward struggles all leave their mark on a man. Sholokhov reveals the hidden mechanism of his hero's progress towards spiritual bankruptcy, the external signs of which are so obvious, with merciless truth. The constant interaction of what is going on deep down inside a character and his outward behaviour, gives Sholokhov's novel its characteristic dynamic unity. He has a rare talent for showing man in constant motion. By capturing a character's essence at every given moment with such remarkable truthfulness, he is at the same time conveying his changeability. We see before us man as a traveller on the road of this bitter-sweet life with all its ups and downs.

Not so long ago we saw Grigory as a youth "with his youthfully thin, round neck and the unconcerned fold of his continually smiling lips". With the passing years, in the trials of battle and everyday life, we see him change before our very eyes and become "the manful giant of a Cossack who had lived through and experienced so much, with eyes puckered wearily, with rusty tips to his black moustache, a premature greyness at the temples, and deep furrows on the forehead...." (4, 12).

Sholokhov is a past master of the art of portraiture which has long been an important feature of Russian prose. A. S. Serafimovich was the first to point out this side of his talent. In 1928 he wrote: "He doesn't 'write in' characters like so many carefully drawn sketches. People spill out into the pages of his book like a lively, colourful crowd, where every individual has his own nose, his own wrinkles, his own eyes with their crow's feet, his own accent, and walks and turns his head in his own particular way."*

In realist art portraiture in the widest sense of the word—which is far more than a mere description of outward features—is used as an important means of individualising characters. We cannot imagine the Russian novel with its penetrating psychological studies without portraiture.

In the literature of the 19th century the description of the hero on his very first appearance often gave the reader an insight into his personality. The Russian novelists strove to capture the essence of the hero's personality through outward features.

Today a novelist would hardly begin with a detailed description of a character's appearance, how he is dressed, his age, etc.

"One cannot make a ten-page portrait of a hero, give his appearance and size, and say what sort of a person he is, and then let him start to act. This is the wrong method to employ," declares Alexei Tolstoi. "It is quite static, whereas a hero's portrait should come from the action, from struggles and conflicts, from the way he behaves. The portrait gradually takes shape from the lines and between the lines, between the words, emerging gradually, and the reader can imagine it for himself without any description."**

Thus the portrait does not anticipate events, but takes shape out of them. We are more interested in what a man looked like in given circumstances, when our interest has already been caught.

The portrait is built up like a mosaic in the course of the development of the action. The undoubted importance which drama plays in the modern novel can be clearly seen here.

Obviously one cannot talk of a law in all this, but such is apparently the general trend.

* A. S. Serafimovich, *Collected Works*, Vol. 10, p. 360.
** Alexei Tolstoi, *Collected Works*, Russ. ed., Vol. 13, Moscow, 1950, p. 322.

There has been a fundamental change in the opening of the narrative, representing a swing in the direction of greater dynamism. Accordingly, *And Quiet Flows the Don* opens with the account of Prokofy Melekhov's return from war with a Turkish wife, and only after this dramatic introduction are we treated to a condensed description of the Melekhov family. "And that was how the hook-nosed, savagely handsome Cossack family of Melekhovs, nicknamed 'Turks', came into the village."

In the first description of the Melekhov family the author makes no attempt to paint a detailed family portrait like on a canvas, where all members of the family would be given equal importance.

"Under the weight of the passing years Pantelei Prokofyevich grew gnarled and craggy; he broadened and acquired a stoop, but still looked a well-built old man. He was dry of bone, and lame (in his youth he had broken his leg while hurdling at an Imperial Review of troops), he wore a silver half-moon ear-ring in his left ear, and his beard and hair retained their vivid raven hue until old age. When angry, he completely lost control of himself and undoubtedly this had prematurely aged his buxom wife, whose face, once beautiful, was now a perfect spiderweb of furrows.

"Pyotr, his elder, married son, took after his mother: stocky and snub-nosed, a luxuriant shock of corn-coloured hair, hazel eyes. But the younger, Grigory, was like his father: half a head taller than Pyotr, some six years younger, the same pendulous hawk nose as his father's, the whites of his burning eyes bluish in their slightly oblique slits; brown, ruddy skin drawn tight over angular cheek-bones. Grigory stooped slightly, just like his father; even in his smile there was a similar, rather savage quality" (1, 15-16).

In the family portrait of the Melekhovs, Ilyinichna, Pyotr, Dunya, and especially Darya (Pyotr's wife), are all pale and sketchy beside the powerful figures of Pantelei Prokofyevich and Grigory, largely because it is not a self-contained episode, but evolves out of the course of events, being dictated by the story of Prokofy Melekhov's marriage with the Turkish woman and the extraordinary circumstances of their son's birth, which requires a sequel. Describing the Melekhovs as they have become many years later, the author puts the spotlight on Pantelei Prokofyevich and Grigory, who are the most truly representative members of the family.

The very term "portraiture" implies the presence of features which force us to speak in terms of the writer's talent for "painting", in terms of colour and tone, vividness, etc. And indeed the writer depicting a character's outward appearance has essentially the same artistic aims as the artist painting a picture. Both try to create an illusion of life, to capture their characters' constantly changing inner world and outward appearance. The writer is almost bound to resort to the idiom of painting, to such means as colour, chiaroscuro and so on.

A perfect example of a modern Soviet writer who consciously aims at this is Konstantin Fedin, whose characters are depicted as vividly as if they had been painted on an artist's canvas. This is amply illustrated by the following portrait from *Early Joys*, where Tsvetukhin and Pastukhov spring to life as if at the strokes of an artist's brush: "The first to alight wore a black cape fastened with a gilt chain with lion-head clasps and a soft black felt hat that gleamed like a raven's wing. He himself was dark-complexioned, with a clipped moustache as black as tar. The second was dressed casually in a pea-green summer coat with a light nap and a sand-coloured felt hat with a lilac ribbon. His face, slightly flabby and complacent but still young and well cared for, looked as though it had been tinted with pastels and gave the same impression of lightness and showiness as his clothes."*

Fedin describes his heroes' outward appearance largely in terms of light and colour, dwelling on the colour of their clothes with loving attention. With the trained eye of an artist, he picks out the pattern of light and shade that plays on an object or a person and, fully aware of its expressiveness, uses it with consummate skill for purely literary, narrative purposes.

Fedin's mastery of colour and light effects is so delightfully entrancing in that it testifies to the truly unlimited power of words.

* K. Fedin, *Early Joys*, Moscow, 1967, pp. 31-32.

Another great modern novelist, Alexei Tolstoi, saw man in constant motion. His portraits are never isolated still-lifes, "*in camera* miniatures" so to speak, but take shape organically out of the action. He "inscribes" his characters in a particular milieu, space, etc., with amazing skill.

A perfect illustration of this is provided by the description in his novel *Peter the Great* of the arrival of Sanka Volkova —a woman whom fortune has raised from a tumble-down village hovel to boyars' halls—at the Buinosov mansion. Note the manner the author has chosen to describe her entrance, dress, and the impression she produces on the ancient, arrogant and not very clever family.

"The valet opened the door (an old-fashioned one, low and narrow), and a pink-gold dress rustled. A pair of bare shoulders were thrust forward, and then head back, a look of indifference on her beautiful face, eyelids lowered, boyarinya Volkova entered. She stood in the middle of the hall. Her rings flashed as she grasped her abundant skirts, lace-trimmed and sewn with roses, and advancing one foot—a satin slipper with a three-inch heel—she made a French curtsey keeping her forward leg straight. Her powdered coiffure with the ostrich feathers swayed from side to side. When she had done, she raised her blue eyes, smiled revealing her teeth and said: 'Bonjour Princesse'".

It would be difficult to imagine a more thorough description of her appearance, clothes, behaviour, etc. Sanka stands before us, completely alive from her powdered coiffure with the high ostrich feathers to the tip of her satin slippers with their high French heels.

But this is all revealed through the kaleidoscope of a swift succession of actions. It is a far cry from those portraits where the artist paints a model who is "sitting" for him, so to speak.

The reader is not an outside spectator viewing a canvas portrait of Sanka. The succession of the poses, and the spacial depth achieved give the reader a physical sensation of movement taking place before his very eyes. In describing Sanka's entry to the Buinosov house, the author seizes on various portrait details. They are determined by space, the surroundings, the historical features of the place and so on.

Fedin's and Tolstoi's character-studies are calculated above all to produce a visual effect, and this is what makes it possible to speak of them being essentially linked to painting. But while Fedin gives a precise, detailed description of a character in a particular position (mainly in terms of colour, and chiaroscuro), Alexei Tolstoi sees his characters in a rapid succession of positions, each of which reveals a certain pictorial detail and which taken together give a very dynamic portrait.

Sholokhov's art is also visual. He tries to give a striking picture of man in motion. But he not only "paints", he describes a character too. Even where his art is most pictorial, it is almost always a penetrating psychological study at the same time. He is not only interested in giving an expressive portrayal of a character's outward appearance, but in revealing the way he behaves, his general temperament, his mood at a particular moment. Sholokhov's portraits are of a man in a certain situation, mood and so on.

In that first family portrait of the Melekhovs which we have already referred to, the author is not only striving to produce a strong visual impression, giving the reader a vision of each member; he is at the same time revealing their nature.

When Pantelei Prokofyevich, for example, is presented to us, we are not merely told what he looks like ("He was dry of bone, and lame ... he wore a silver half-moon ear-ring in his left ear" and so on), but are given the key to his very nature, to the way he behaves in all sorts of different situations. "When angry, he completely lost control of himself and undoubtedly this had prematurely aged his buxom wife, whose face, once beautiful, was now a perfect spiderweb of furrows." This is more than a reference to strained family relations or an explanation of the premature wrinkles on Ilyinichna's face: it is a purely psychological detail which is an essential part of the portrait of Pantelei Prokofyevich.

In his *Diary of Youth*, the young Lev Tolstoi wrote: "Strictly speaking it is impossible to describe a man, but it is possible to describe the impression he has made on me."

Tolstoi was apparently trying to draw a line for himself between the methods the portrait painter has at his disposal and those open to the writer. Yet when reading Lev Tolstoi, Sholokhov, Alexei Tolstoi, Konstantin Fedin, one feels they are painting with words, and are as much masters of colour as the painter.

Obviously Lev Tolstoi's formula does not cover the portraits he drew of his characters, any more than it does in the case of many other great writers, Dostoyevsky for example. But it does express what Tolstoi and many others were striving to achieve in their portraits.

Sholokhov's approach to character-description is rather similar to Lev Tolstoi's. It is not only the outward appearance of a man that interests him but what Tolstoi loosely called "the impression he has made on me".

Sholokhov's portraits of his heroes are almost always imbued with a particular mood, a definite feeling, and possess to a large extent what we might well call a psychological descriptive element.

This is well illustrated by the scene where Aksinya sees a wagon draw up in the Melekhovs' yard with Grigory lying in it, and does not know whether he is dead or alive. "There was not a drop of blood in Aksinya's white face. She was standing leaning against the wattle fence, her hands hanging lifelessly. No tears glittered in her misted black eyes, but there were so much suffering and dumb entreaty in them that Dunya halted for a second and said reluctantly... 'He's alive, alive!'" (4, 328-329).

The shock Aksinya receives is not only expressed outwardly (in her paling, her hands dangling lifelessly, etc.). The purely pictorial touch "no tears glittered in her misted black eyes" is but a preamble to a powerful direct description of Aksinya's feelings as reflected in her eyes: "there were so much suffering and dumb entreaty...."

Alexei Tolstoi, to take an example, usually avoids such psychological details in his portraits. He apparently holds that characters' inner drama can and ought to be revealed in their movements, what they say, etc. Take the scene where Peter I is paying his last respects to the dead Lefort. "He stood there for a long time, one hand resting on the edge of the coffin. He bent and kissed his beloved friend's brow and hands. His shoulders began to tremble beneath the green caftan, the nape of his neck stiffened.... He left the dais weeping like a child, and stopped before Sanka. She nodded sadly. 'There'll never be another friend like him,' he said. He buried his face in his hands, and shook his curly hair tousled from the journey. 'We shared everything, joys and sorrows. We thought with the same mind....'"

Sholokhov, on the contrary, describes both a character's feelings and their outward expression. Sholokhov's predilection for psychological details in his portraits links him to the Tolstoian tradition.

The outward appearance of a character will only be impressed on the reader's memory if the writer manages to seize on those features which are most typical and permanent. It is not merely a question of purely outward features, though they have their place in the portrait. Aksinya's plump figure and the fine, fluffy curls on her neck, Grigory's swarthy face and hawk nose, Pyotr's corn-coloured hair, and Khristonya's enormous size and deep, rumbling bass voice are all details which help to make the characters stick in the reader's mind. The younger Sholokhov was often not averse to introducing bizarre details, although, for example, Pantelei Prokofyevich's half-moon ear-ring does not glitter on the pages of the book for long. With his remarkable ability to penetrate deep into the minds and feelings of his characters, Sholokhov would think nothing of abandoning a striking detail once it had ceased to have any essential importance. What was the point of the ear-ring? It really serves to stress the oriental streak in Pantelei Prokofyevich, and has no psychological significance. The oriental in Pantelei Prokofyevich is much more in evidence in his quick temper, the way he completely lost control of himself when angry—characteristics inherited by Grigory and Dunya and even little Mishatka.

Obviously such typical outward features as Aksinya's plumpness, Grigory's swarthy face and Pantelei Prokofyevich's limp have nothing to do with the characters' psychology. A lot would be lost if a writer tried to gear all the features of his heroes' outward appearance to their character.

The dynamics of Sholokhov's portraits lies in the subtle interplay of outward and inner features. He specially and consistently singles out those essential outward features which best correspond to a character's inner nature.

The most striking feature of Aksinya's appearance are her black eyes. But they are never described purely in terms of colour. Now they smoulder with the consuming fire of passion and love for Grigory, now they are "sprinkled with the ash of fear", and so on. The expression in Aksinya's eyes reveals one of the most important essential features of her nature—her passion, her fiery temper.

Like Fedin, Sholokhov is fond of using colour when he comes to describe eyes. But in doing so, he almost invariably adds some psychological detail which gives us a deep insight into the character's nature.

The art of character-drawing is particularly difficult in a complex epic narrative. The heroes are often absent from the scene for a long time, yet somehow the reader must not be allowed to forget them. There is no need for the author to describe them each time they reappear however, as long as he reminds the reader of their most typical features. Often just one particular detail is sufficient for the character to spring immediately to mind again.

One of the chief methods used in *And Quiet Flows the Don* in the case of the Melekhovs, is the insistence on common family traits. Again and again we are reminded of Grigory's "burning eyes bluish in their slightly oblique slits", his pendulous hawk nose, his stoop, his angular face, his rather savage smile. The repetition of these details in all sorts of situations impresses them on the reader's memory, making the character extraordinarily familiar, almost physically tangible.

Dunya too is described on several occasions as having the Melekhov family features. "Dunya was like her father, dark and sturdy. She was fifteen now, her figure still girlish and angular ... her black eyes in their long, rather slanting sockets, still sparkled bashfully and mischievously" (1, 315-316).

We are also frequently reminded of the family likeness in the descriptions of little Mishatka, Grigory's son. "The little boy, with morose eyes and knitted brows, was cast in the Melekhov mould: the same long slits of black, rather sombre eyes, blue prominent whites, the spreading line of brows, and swarthy skin" (2, 346) and later: "Sullen, with the Melekhovs' ungracious look" (4, 234).

The constant repetition of the Melekhov family features in Grigory, Dunya and Mishatka, just as the insistence on such characteristic details as Pantelei Prokofyevich's limp, Aksinya's plump figure and black eyes, Darya's fine eyebrows, Listnitsky's soft plump chest and so on, is only one element of the character-drawing in the novel, though of course a very important one. But perhaps even more important is the way the author concentrates on the changes that take place in a character as a result of his experiences.

After recovering from a serious illness, Grigory looks on the world around him as if discovering it anew. "With eyes expressing a slight astonishment he gazed at the new world which had been revealed to him; a simple, childlike smile hovered on his face, in strange contrast to his harsh features, to the expression of his animal-like eyes, and softening the harsh folds at the corners of his lips" (4, 330).

The only characteristic feature remaining is "his animal-like eyes". The rest are new traits resulting from what he has been through ("the harsh features", "the harsh folds at the corners of his lips"), or details which reflect his actual mood ("eyes expressing a slight astonishment", "simple, childlike smile", etc.).

Sholokhov's descriptions of Grigory usually combine typical, permanent features with outward signs of deep changes, the description of these outward signs serving to supplement and clarify the psychological details and give the reader a deep insight into the workings of the character's mind. In fact Sholokhov describes the hero's outward appearance most often when he wants to draw our attention to a particularly important state of mind.

After his first battle in the imperialist war Grigory was tormented by a dreary inward pain. Try as he may, he could not forget the Austrian he had killed. "'Pyotr, I'm played out,' he tells his brother. 'I'm like a man who only needs one more blow to kill him....' His voice was cracked and complaining, and a dark furrow (only now, and with a feeling of anxiety, did Pyotr notice it) slanting diagonally across his forehead, made a startling impression of change and alienation" (1, 403).

The furrow that Pyotr noticed with such anxiety was

the visible expression of Grigory's spiritual crisis in the first months of the war.

A character's appearance may be described in various ways: direct narration by the author; through his own eyes (as in Gorky's *Life of Klim Samgin*, where the hero frequently looks at himself in the mirror); as seen by other characters. The latter approach makes for a highly emotion-charged description.

What makes the furrow across Grigory's forehead the powerful descriptive detail is the way it goes to his brother Pyotr's heart and the fact that it appears in an emotion-charged psychological context (Grigory's cracked, complaining voice, Pyotr's feeling of anxiety and so on) which reveals the hero's state of mind.

As events unfold dramatic tension builds up in the descriptions of Grigory Melekhov. In depicting Grigory at the beginning of the Civil War, Grigory taking part in the Veshenskaya uprising, or fighting in Fomin's band against the young Soviet state, Sholokhov sadly recounts the vacillations, and grave changes for the worse of his hero.

More and more frequently the words "harsh", "malicious", and "cruel" occur in descriptions of Grigory's face, particularly his eyes. With time they become characteristic features of the greatly changed Grigory who has so often shed the blood of working people and Red Army men, the fighters for Soviet power.

"There was a harsh expression on his sunburnt face, with its cheekbones covered with an unhealthy fullness of flesh. Stretching his dark muscular neck, he thoughtfully twisted the end of his sun-bleached moustache and stared fixedly at the wall with *eyes grown cold and bitter during these past few years*" (3, 123-124. Author's italics).

The changes years of bitter fighting have wrought in Grigory's appearance are referred to again and again: "the bags under his eyes", "the spark of senseless cruelty in his eyes", "his deathly pale face with its unwinking, staring gaze" which the Cossack woman watches "with loathing and pity", "his tired, drooping eyes", "the prematurely grey hair round his temples".

More and more attention is focussed on the inner changes as reflected in Grigory's outward appearance, while the purely descriptive details of his outward appearance gradually fade into the background.

One of the last descriptions we have of Grigory is after he has run away from Fomin's band. His joining the band was a most fatal mistake which brought him so low that it would be practically impossible ever to rise again. Looking at him while he slept, Aksinya sees not the man whom she had known so well, and who was so close, so dear to her, but a total stranger, harsh and frightening.

"His black lashes, their tips bleached by the sun, quivered very gently; his upper lip stirred, revealing his firm clenched white teeth. She looked at him more closely and only then noticed how much he had changed during the past few months of their separation. There was a harsh, almost cruel expression in the deep vertical furrows between his brows, in the folds of his mouth, in the prominent cheekbones. And for the first time it occurred to her that he must be terrible in battle, on a horse, with bared sabre. Lowering her eyes, she glanced at his big knotty hands and sighed for some reason" (4, 676-677).

Sholokhov gives a ruthlessly realistic portrait of this Grigory, with his firm clenched white teeth bared and his big knotty hands, which not so long before had grasped the plough, but were now those of a bandit; but for Aksinya's feelings as she looks mournfully at him, it would indeed be a cruel portrait....

Very little remains of Grigory's many fine, outstanding qualities. They seem to have vanished to be replaced by the terrible marks left by time and the changes tragic experience has wrought.

Grigory's descent along the sloping path towards moral bankruptcy, which Sholokhov reveals with such power in his hero's outward appearance, makes him age disastrously quickly. We are shown this through the eyes of his near and dear ones, his sister Dunya and Aksinya, who think and speak of it with pain and sorrow.

"'Oh, but you've grown old, Brother!' Dunya said commiseratingly. 'You've gone as grey as a wolf'" (4, 91).

In her thoughts Aksinya tried to ignore his new, "wolf-like" appearance. She somehow saw him not as he was, but as he had been as a young man.

"My dear, Grisha darling, the grey hairs you've got!" (4, 676). Her words sound like a lament for the irretrievable past.

The last glimpse we have of Grigory is through the eyes of his little son Mishatka.

"Mishatka glanced at him in terror and dropped his eyes. He guessed that this bearded and terrible-looking man was his father...." (4, 690).

This is a spot-on definition of what Grigory Melekhov has become. "Bearded and terrible-looking" is all that remains to be said of this once handsome and strong man.

Thus Sholokhov depicts through portraiture the end Grigory Melekhov's break with the people brought him to.

10

Sholokhov needed to be a good psycho-analyst to portray a character with such a complex, contradictory nature as Grigory Melekhov. We have mentioned a few of the methods Sholokhov uses in the character-drawing in *And Quiet Flows the Don*, how he creates the social and historical environment in which Grigory was born and bred and its influence on the hero, how he shows Grigory's relationship to his family, nature, work and women, and the characteristics and qualities he reveals in the process. These are all different aspects of one and the same thing, depending on the writer's ability to penetrate man's inner world and correctly reveal the motives of his actions.

The writer has a complicated and very precise instrument at his disposal if only he knows how to handle it, and that is psychological analysis. Every writer has his own highly individual way of using it, depending on his own particular talents, the aim he is pursuing and also his choice of subject-matter. But be that as it may, the fact remains that this instrument is absolutely essential to the writer who is trying to create a character of depth and which rings true.

No character is complete unless the influence social and human relations have on him is revealed, unless we can see the deep links between his feelings and actions, which tell us whether he is a fully integrated personality or spiritually alienated (such characters as Pechorin and Rudin come to mind), without an analysis of his passions, a gift for grasping the most distinctive traits of his personality. Sholokhov, being a fine representative of socialist realism, draws from the arsenal of Russian and world literature this incomparable weapon of psychological analysis.

Sholokhov was writing about the life of the people at a turning point in history, and the picture he gave could not be a true one unless it was complete, unless, that is, he made a complete analysis of the characters involved, drawing on all the artistic means at his disposal.

A special feature of Sholokhov's rare talent is the way he gives his powerful picture of two social worlds at war not only on the level of large-scale historical events but through a penetrating analysis of the equally dramatic inner struggle between old and new with man's soul as the battlefield.

By his deep analysis of Grigory Melekhov's inner life, through the prism of a highly personal struggle between contradictory social feelings, Sholokhov reveals those concrete historical conditions which determine the movements of man's soul. He is interested above all in the causes giving rise to a clash of thoughts and feelings, and the conditions for their socio-historical actualisation. This side of Sholokhov's analysis arose as a result of the application of the historical method to aesthetic theory, which was developed by Gorky and was embodied in the theory of socialist realism.

Both the course and the result of the struggle between contradictory social feelings have a wider social importance. The struggle arose under the impact of revolutionary storm, with the development of the conflict between two worlds. It is not a question of abstract spiritual conflicts, the victory of certain moral principles; Grigory Melekhov is searching for the social truth, and his search is made dramatic by the Civil War, when he is forced to act quickly and make snap decisions at every step. One mistake brings another in its wake and even the most seemingly insignificant step is often fatal and irreversible so that in the final analysis an action is justified not by personal moral criteria, but in the light of a higher truth asserted by the people in their revolutionary struggle. It is as if on the vast canvas of *And Quiet Flows the Don* history passes judgment on Grigory Melekhov, on his doubts and vacillations.

Thus Sholokhov's psychological analysis has the aim of judging man. While Tolstoi judges man on the basis of ethical criteria, through the approval or condemnation discernible in the writer's own tone, with Sholokhov poetic affirmation of the objective laws of historical development comes to the fore. The humanistic aim of the Revolution is the invisible judge whose sentences have the higher authority of objective justice.

Sholokhov gives a penetrating all-round analysis and judgment of the life of Grigory Melekhov and all its vicissitudes. He gives a sufficiently complete picture of the history of the Don Cossacks during the Revolution and the struggles of the revolutionary people to enable one to distinguish where Grigory is to blame for his errors and where they are justified by history. The final ruthless sentence history metes out on Grigory is the terrible end he comes to.

Yet the struggle between conflicting social feelings in Grigory, however important, is only one aspect of Sholokhov's psychological analysis. There are numerous others in the novel. Aksinya and Natalya are revealed largely in terms of their all-consuming, passionate love; Ilyinichna, through her powerful maternal feelings, and so on. Grigory would be as a pale shadow compared to the strong, clear character we know, if we were shown only his social feelings.

But the Grigory Melekhov we know is a real human being living a real life. He reveals the whole gamut of human emotions in all kinds of situations. The picture is complete. We see the struggle that rages in his soul between conflicting social sympathies and the joy and satisfaction he gets from work on the land, which makes him feel at peace with the world; we see his feelings for his "beloved, unforgettable" Aksinya, which neither time nor separation can alter, and his coldness towards Natalya and later his love for her, the mother of his children, this woman who gave up her whole life irrevocably, right to the end, to her one and only Grigory; we see his terrible grief at Natalya's death, his fatherly devotion to the children, to those dear, tiny creatures he had given life to. As these scenes unfold we learn more and more about Grigory's nature, and a clear-cut, dynamic character takes shape before our eyes which is remarkably true and authentic. The great range of Sholokhov's psychological analysis is one of the most attractive features of his talent.

Sholokhov is a writer of passion. His vivid characters have an unquenchable thirst for life. Sholokhov clothes such eternal strong emotions as love, misery, joy and suffering in flesh-and-blood characters, in a highly distinctive, unique manner.

The story of Grigory and Aksinya's tragic love runs through the whole novel. Sholokhov describes the strength of their feelings for one another, and the development of their love with all its ups and downs, in a manner that is at once amazingly accurate psychologically and by no means detached.

Aksinya is ready to make any sacrifice for the sake of her all-consuming passion. A married woman, she fearlessly flouts the moral code and customs of the village. But Grigory, still a carefree youth, is not prepared to overcome the obstacles, and breaks with her. Grigory doesn't forget Aksinya however, and continues to feel an irresistible attraction towards her, and his love which at first had been a mixture of brute desire and tenderness, gradually becomes more and more spiritualised. When he is away fighting during the First World War and the Civil War he often looks back on their life together at Yagodnoye as the happiest period of his life. Whenever he thought of Aksinya, he would remember his childhood and vice versa, and this subtle observation of Sholokhov's speaks of the feelings which bind Grigory and Aksinya far better than a lot of words could. Aksinya is a part of him for ever, just as much as his childhood is.

Grigory's recollections are an important element in the character-drawing. They always appear in sharp contrast to the vicissitudes of his life, and are like a ray of bright sunlight piercing the gloom of his errors. He always remembers his childhood and Aksinya in specially hard moments, in direct proportion to his sufferings. After his conversation with Ivan Alexeyevich Kotlyarov, Grigory was seized by a feeling of "deep, never silenced exasperation" as it became clear to him that "he stood at the parting of the ways, struggling between two elements and rejecting them both" (3, 213). He was thinking of this while carrying a sledge-load of munitions bound for the front. As the bullocks plodded along the road, he lay huddled against the ammunition cases and, burying his face in the hay, which "smelled of dry clover and the sweet haze of July days", dropped off to sleep. In his sleep he dreamed that he and Aksinya were walking together "through high-standing corn". Aksinya was as she had been five years before, and he saw her "more vividly than ever before". A sudden jolt awoke him. They had met a line of sledges carrying corpses of people that had died of typhus. Grigory turned away from bitter reality and returned to his dreams of the half-forgotten past. Again, during the uprising, when Grigory, tortured by the thought that he had chosen the wrong path, sought oblivion in drunken carousals and chance amorous adventures, he would suddenly remember Aksinya as the love he would never forget and "childhood floated through his memory like a sunny day".

Five long years had passed, and Aksinya was once more living with her husband who had returned from POW camp, when she and Grigory met again. It seemed that time and people had separated them forever. They had both aged and events had left their mark. Grigory, now commander of an insurgent division, was coming to the painful conclusion that he had made a serious and possibly fatal mistake in taking part in the struggle against the Soviet government. The day he was due to return to the front he led his horse down to the Don to drink. Aksinya was drawing water and deliberately dallied when she saw him. Sholokhov describes their swiftly alternating feelings with remarkable subtlety, showing real understanding of the "dialectics of the soul".

As Grigory approached Aksinya, who was deliberately filling her pails slowly, "sad memories passed before him in silvery flight". Aksinya turned as she heard his footsteps, and an assumed expression of surprise appeared on her face, "but her joy at the meeting and her old pain gave her away". "A miserable, distracted smile" appeared on her face, a recognition of her inability to master her agitation and hide her true feelings. "Grigory's heart was shaken with pity and love."

He said "Good morning" and, after a slight pause, "Aksinya dear". After the common everyday greeting the "Aksinya dear" sounds as a burst of irrepressible feeling, expressing love that has survived the years and

suffering at their long, painful separation. This one
phrase gives the psychological key to the whole of the
bitter conversation that follows.

"'Good morning, Aksinya dear.'

"'Good morning.'

"Aksinya's voice was a strange mixture of surprise,
affection and bitterness.

"'It's a long time since we last spoke to each
other.'

"'Yes, it's a long time.'

"'I'd even forgotten the sound of your voice....'

"'You forget quickly.'

"'Was it so quickly?'"

A painful silence followed which seemed to separate
them again for a short while. The author expresses this
in the "hint of vexation and bitterness" Grigory's voice
betrays when he asks: "Well, haven't we anything to
talk about? Why are you silent?" Aksinya, who has
regained her self-command, replies coldly: "It seems
we've said all we had to say...." (3, 420, 421).

Only an artist with a deep understanding of human
psychology can capture the way the heart beats with
such precision, and depict the kaleidoscope of the feelings.

The two of them face one another, Grigory worn out by
his trials and worries, the proud Aksinya, older now but
still beautiful, and he suddenly begins to tell her of his
love, with almost naive frankness: "But I just can't
tear you out of my heart, Aksinya. Here I've got children
growing up, and I'm myself half grey, and how many
years lie like an abyss between us! But I still think of
you. In my sleep I see you and I love you still. And
sometimes as I'm thinking of you I begin to recall how
we lived at Listnitsky's. How we loved each other...!
Sometimes as I look back on my life it seems like an
empty pocket turned inside out...." (3, 421).

Grigory's words have a note of sad resignation about
them, he seems to have no hope of regaining Aksinya's
love and makes no effort to do so. Life has sapped his
strength, he is no longer his former active self, able to
give himself heart and soul to something that excites
his feelings.

"I too," the words sprang to Aksinya's lips, involun-
tarily expressing her love for him alone that had been

pent up inside her for so long. Recollecting herself immediately, she tried to give the impression that she had
spoken quite casually. "But I must go ... we're standing
talking...." (3, 421). But Aksinya was incapable of guile,
and with a sudden surge of passion, which lit her face
with a youthful blush, she reminded him that it was
there, by that very spot, that their love had begun, and
a cheerful note crept into her voice.

But even when Aksinya was his again, and what he
had longed for had come to pass, Grigory did not regain
that peace and happiness and faith in life that had once
been his. "Well, life has taken a new turn, but my heart
is still cold and empty.... Even Aksinya can't fill that
emptiness now...." (3, 429). Such are his painful thoughts
as he leaves home to return to his regiment and once
more "squander away his and others' lives" in battles
against the Red Army. But he no longer dared ask even
himself why, and for whom he was fighting. He was
afraid to face up to the terrible truth.

11

Character is never a separate element in Sholokhov's
books. It is revealed as an integral part of a composite
picture of life in all its complexity which, by showing
social class sympathies and antipathies, family relationships, loves, hatreds, friendships and so on, brings out
all the character's traits and qualities.

However far Grigory goes along the road of moral
degradation, we always sense that he is somehow not
quite a true representative of the whiteguard counter-
revolutionary movement. Sholokhov makes this felt and
indeed helps us understand why it is so in Grigory's
relationships with Uryupin and Mitka Korshunov.
Grigory knew Uryupin from having served at the front
with him. His acquaintance with Mitka Korshunov went
back much further: they had been born the same year,
gone to school and chased women together, and Grigory
had married Mitka's sister. Yet they never felt close,
there was always a coldness in their relationship.

However much the war may have degraded Grigory, he
never sunk as low as to accept that degenerate denial

of the value of human life, that indifference to man, which Uryupin preached, and indeed demonstrated to him on several occasions.

Uryupin's inhuman "philosophy" stripped of rhetoric and fine phrases expressed the true nature of the guiding principles behind the punitive war fought by all the White armies, which tried to pacify the people's "mutiny" by shootings and hangings.

Chernetsov, the organiser of counter-revolutionary officer detachments on the Don, and Listnitsky, a loyal Kornilovite, have a lot in common with Uryupin.

The notebook Grigory took from the pocket of a dead Cossack, a student, contained the following reference to Chernetsov: "Before my eyes our Squadron Commander Chernetsov cut down a German hussar.... On the way back I saw Chernetsov's face, intent and controlledly cheerful—he might have been sitting at the card table, instead of in the saddle, having just murdered a man. Squadron Commander Chernetsov will go far. A capable fellow!" (1, 428). Chernetsov fully demonstrated how "capable" he was in the Civil War, executing miners and ruthlessly massacring workers and revolutionary Cossacks.

Many of those who took part in the White counter-revolutionary movement demonstrated this same propensity for senseless murder. Sholokhov shows that a delight in butchery often went hand in hand with fierce hatred for the working people.

Uryupin was a fierce opponent of the Revolution. As a whiteguard, Listnitsky spoke with bitter anger of the "mutinous scum", the "damned people". Mitka Korshunov was also morally degenerate. In the Civil War he quickly worked his way up to the rank of officer of a punitive detachment.

The author puts us on our guard against Korshunov from the very first moment the future butcher appears in the novel. His actions, the way he "playfully" lashes the sleeping Grigory with his whip, his seduction of Liza Mokhova and the "despair, anger and fear" with which he asks her father for her hand, his cruel, heartless taunting of Natalya, all dispose us badly towards him, as does that first description we have of his eyes: "His round, yellow eyes glistened impudently in their narrow slits. Mitka's pupils were long, like a cat's, making his glance swift and elusive."

Throughout the novel the author makes a point of showing us that cruelty innate in Mitka's nature from childhood, but which was to assume such monstrous proportions when he was serving in a punitive detachment.

"Say what you like, gentlemen, there's no one to beat Korshunov. He's not a man, he's a dragon!" his commander would exclaim admiringly.

Korshunov is driven in his punitive "exploits" by a bitter hatred for the Soviet government, which has deprived him of his wealth, the biggest farm in Tatarsky village.

Sholokhov shows the Chernetsovs, Uryupins and Korshunovs to be true outcasts, who, with their contempt for the people and denial of the most elementary human values, have really renounced the right to be considered human beings.

On learning that Mitka Korshunov has brutally murdered the family of the Communist Koshevoi, Pantelei Prokofyevich refuses to let him into his yard. "I don't want you to soil my house!" the old man says resolutely. "We Melekhovs have no kinship with executioners, know that!"

Mitka replies furiously: "I know you! I see you through and through, I see the sort of spirit you breathe out! You didn't retreat across the Donets, did you? You went over to the Reds, didn't you? That's just it! You all ought to be treated like the Koshevois, you sons of bitches!" (4, 149, 150).

Of course only Mitka, blinded with rage and hatred, could seriously accuse Pantelei Prokofyevich of sympathy towards the Reds. The old man had his own firm ideas about Cossack honour, and Ilyinichna expresses them with wise simplicity to Natalya, approving her husband's behaviour. "Mitka has turned out a real scoundrel. He's found himself a fine job! Look at him! Not serving like other Cossacks in the real forces! Joining the punitives! And is that the Cossacks' task to be executioners, to hang old women, and to cut down innocent children with their sabres?" (4, 150-151). Grigory Melekhov had been brought up on such ideas of Cossack honour, and he was never to be false to them.

Even fighting together on the side of the whiteguards was never to bring Grigory close to Mitka Korshunov and his likes, and indeed could not, for they were fundamentally different not only in their behaviour, but in their mental and emotional make-up.

In the Revolution Grigory had the opportunity of choosing a different path from the one he actually embarked on.

12

Grigory harboured an undying hatred for the tsarist autocracy, for generals and officers, gentleman parasites and idlers. These were the feelings of a man of the people, which had been awakened by the Great October Revolution.

Grigory's characteristic sense of dignity and self-respect developed during the years of the Revolution. This is revealed with particular force in the scene with General Fitshalaurov. The general's bass voice thundered louder and louder as he tried to give a good dressing-down to Grigory, whom he saw as an upstart lieutenant from the ranks, and who had dared moreover not to carry out his orders. As the whiteguard general stood shouting at him pounding the table with his fist, Grigory could contain himself no longer and, rising, said in a thick voice: "I must ask you not to bawl at me!" Then, lowering his voice almost to a whisper, warned: "If you, Your Excellency, attempt to lay even your little finger on me, I shall sabre you on the spot!" (4, 130). The general looked at him in silence for a long time, then dropped heavily into his chair.

Even if Grigory had ever had any respect for generals and officers, the war and the Revolution would have destroyed it for good. He soon came to have a very low opinion of the whiteguard generals and gentleman officers, who dreamed of regaining their lost estates, wealth and privileges.

Grigory, a hard-working peasant, speaks with fury in his voice to a fellow peasant about the alien, hostile world of the parasite officers: "Look at their hands.... And look at mine, hard as a horse's hoof! They can bow and scrape, but when I come into a room, I knock into everything. They smell of toilet soap and all sorts of womanish creams and paints, but I smell of horse-piss and sweat. They're all educated, but I hardly got through a church school. I'm foreign to them from my head to my heels...." (4, 120).

Grigory was sharply aware of the bottomless abyss which lay between him and the gentleman parasites. He was always feeling the haughty contempt of the foppish whiteguard officers for him, a poorly educated Cossack, and he could never forgive them for it. "They think we're made of different dough, that an uneducated man, one of the ordinary folk, is some sort of cattle" (4, 121).

The meteoric rise to fame in the Red Army of simple people who not so long before had been despised and slighted did not go unnoticed by Grigory. He spoke with frank admiration and with a touch of envy of Budyonny, a sergeant in pre-war days and now a famous Red Commander who had given "the generals of the staff a good hiding", and of "some Moscow locksmith", a Red regimental commander, who had smashed and put to flight the troops led by one of the most famous Cossack generals. All this brings Grigory to understand the main thing in the war. This is "the cause you're fighting for". He himself no longer believed in the cause he was fighting for.

The Revolution had left an indelible impression on Grigory's mind. *Although it so happened that he often fought for the old order, he rejected it with all his mind and soul and was convinced there could be no return to it.*

Whenever he comes into contact with representatives of the whiteguard counter-revolutionary movement, they always arouse protest in him, and awaken in his soul that deep feeling for democracy which attracts him to the Bolshevik cause.

Thanks to this positive side of his nature, he himself is quite aware that he would be more at home fighting for the Reds. "I may be a blockhead to you, but you wait a bit! Give me time, and I'll go over to the Reds, and with them I shall be heavier than lead. And then you well-mannered and educated parasites had better not fall into my hands! I shall wring out your guts, and your souls with them!" (4, 127).

This was no playful threat spoken in jest. Grigory was to carry it out by fighting with the Red Army against Wrangel and the White Poles.

In his psychological analysis of Grigory, Sholokhov uses what is known as *self-analysis*, that is letting the hero reveal himself by judging his feelings and actions in his own thoughts and words. All Grigory's observations quoted above can be considered essentially as self-analysis.

Gorky makes extensive use of this method in his *Life of Klim Samgin*. The hero's double-dealing and skilful dissimulation are revealed at those rare moments when he has the courage to be honest with himself. All that is false and trivial which has been carefully hidden comes to the surface, and we realise just how much has been kept from us. He admits his absolute lack of talent, his secret sympathies for the Black Hundreds, and his willingness to become an agent provocateur. To demask Samgin Gorky uses the method of self-analysis, and does so with consummate artistry.

In *And Quiet Flows the Don* we have quite a different use of self-analysis. Grigory is a straightforward, extrovert person and does not reveal himself through shy, secret self-confessions but by speaking forth his feelings and sympathies loud and clear for all to hear. When he resorts to self-analysis it is for the purpose of examining not individual, personal things but his social feelings.

Sholokhov employs the method of self-analysis in order to disclose his hero's thoughts and feelings more and more frequently as events unfold, and these self-confessions assume an ever greater importance. Grigory does his utmost to know himself and judge his actions. This is always true of him, but especially so after the Upper Don insurgents have joined forces with the White armies. He begins to ask himself who he is after all, for whom is he shedding his blood, what is he risking his life for, and on which side his true sympathies lie. Quite openly and with obvious pleasure he decides that his sympathies are not with the generals and officers he so despises, and his farmer sentiments begin to come to the fore when he frankly declares what he thinks of himself. He is automatically making a stand for things directly opposed to the aims of his actions, to what he is fighting for.

When the insurgents join up with Denikin's whiteguard forces Grigory feels as if something has snapped inside him. This man of boundless courage, who not long before had spared neither his own life nor the lives of those entrusted to his command in battle, is no longer prepared to take risks, does not want to fight even. Grigory no longer has the conviction, however false and illusory, that he is defending Cossack interests in battle.

Another important element in the character-drawing in the novel is the method of disclosing the hero's inner world through *inner monologues*. This, along with self-analysis, plays a large part in revealing the thoughts and feelings of Grigory Melekhov.

Lev Tolstoi was one of the greatest masters of this method in Russian literature. Indeed he was largely responsible for creating this useful way of giving the reader free access to the innermost workings of a character's mind. The inner monologue opens wide the doors for psychological analysis, making it possible for the writer to disclose the deepest, often contradictory movements of the human soul. Tolstoi's innovations have had an important influence on the subsequent development of literature. Sholokhov, as many other Soviet writers, owes a great debt of gratitude to their masters in the art of psychological analysis, writers like Lev Tolstoi, Chekhov and Gorky.

However individual Sholokhov's great talent may be, *And Quiet Flows the Don* nonetheless does owe something to Tolstoi, both as regards sentence structure and the nature of the hero's inner monologues. Although such passages may be few and far between, they are nonetheless important evidence of Sholokhov's literary roots.

There is a typical Tolstoian note, for example, in Ivan Alexeyevich Kotlyarov's inner monologue as a prisoner of the White Cossacks. "He realised that he would get no further than Tatarsky, that here he would die; and he did not want his family to see his death" (3, 459).

Sholokhov's inner monologues vary from reflections of the hero expressing the movements of his soul through a short talk with himself, to lengthy considerations of important aspects of historical development. When Grigory sets free a captured Red Army Cossack, we have an inner monologue which discloses the contradictory feelings he is beset by. "He ... stretched out his arms ... at a loss to know why he had gone out and given this order for the prisoner to be released.... He was a little irritated with himself for his sudden feeling of pity—what else but unthinking pity had forced its way into his mind and prompted him to release an enemy? Yet he was glad...." (3, 299). Grigory was tortured by "a rebellious feeling of the injustice of his cause".

Sholokhov usually spotlights the culminating moments in Grigory's spiritual development through an inner monologue. On his way home after serving in a Red Guard detachment, Grigory is thinking of his place in the Civil War on the Don. This is a turning-point introducing the first stage in his political vacillations, and it is expressed through an inner monologue: "He wanted to turn his back on the whole hate-riddled and incomprehensible world...." (2, 341). The same method is used again when, at the outbreak of the Veshenskaya uprising, Grigory's angry feelings as a property owner come to the fore and his actions are henceforth dictated by the ideas of Cossack separatism. He thinks with a blind hatred of the Soviet government; and his searchings for social justice, for a truth under whose wing all might shelter, seem to him empty and aimless. "What had there been to think about? Why had his spirit tossed like a hunted wolf in search of a way of escape, of solving contradictions?" (3, 259).

Sholokhov usually employs represented direct speech in these monologues, that is, the hero's actual thoughts are given in the third person. As a rule, this is explained by the fact that these are thoughts going on in the innermost recesses of the character's mind, of which he himself is not always quite aware. Hence the author's frequent recourse to such expressions as "he was thinking disconnectedly and aimlessly", "he vaguely considered", introducing such passages. This use of the third person in the inner monologues makes the construction more simple and unconstrained syntactically and at the same time is a means for the author to subtly introduce his own succinct judgments on the character's innermost personal thoughts.

At the outbreak of the Upper Don uprising Grigory is convinced that he has at last reached a final, irrevocable decision to fight Soviet power to the death for the rich Don earth, for the right to own it. With the subtle touch of a true master of style, Sholokhov makes use of impersonal direct speech here to convey the temporary nature of Grigory's private-ownership instincts. The author's suspicion that Grigory will once more be assailed by doubts and inner struggles is expressed in one of the first sentences in the passage, in the words "as if": "It was as if those days of search for the truth ... had never been." The author's opinion is voiced more strongly further on. There is a note of bitter irony in the repetition within such a short space of "now he believed" and "now he thought". Grigory has changed—for the worse. But the insistence on "now" and the use of "thought", "believed", clearly indicate that these feelings were likely to be temporary.

One of the original versions of this inner monologue ended with Grigory considering himself and the other Cossacks "the tsar's landowners".*

In the version published in the magazine *Oktyabr* (No. 2, 1932) Sholokhov dispensed with this remark as being incompatible with Grigory's character. With his hatred of generals and officers, Grigory could hardly be expected to compare himself with the landowner parasites. In fact, most interesting changes were introduced throughout the monologue, whereby, using the more flexible device of impersonal direct speech, the author is better able to express his doubts that Grigory has reached a final, irrevocable decision, in a manner which does not jar as being incompatible with the future development of the character. In the original version Grigory's doubts as to the existence of an all-embracing truth are given in an unreservedly positive form: "There had never been any such truth."**

---

* "We are all the tsar's landowners. Each Cossack had the right to twelve desyatins of land. Defend the land" (M. Sholokhov, *1919*. Unpublished extract from *And Quiet Flows the Don*, Russ. ed., Moscow, 1930, p. 22).
** Ibid., p. 21.

The corrected version adds an all-important subtle shade of doubt as to the finality of Grigory's decision: "Now he believed that there never had been any such truth."

There is also an emotional justification of Grigory's thoughts in the final version which the original lacked. Before the uprising Grigory had hidden to save himself from arrest, and he knew that his father had been arrested. The original version read: "Each had his own truth, his own furrow—he thought."* In the later version this is expanded to: "Furious and embittered, he was thinking that each had his own truth, his own furrow."

The improvements Sholokhov introduced for the appearance of this section of the novel in *Oktyabr* are extremely significant and bear witness to his maturing talent. They not only represent a deeper and more flexible approach to Grigory's state of mind, but show that Sholokhov was already taking into account the subsequent fortunes of his hero concentrating on Grigory's contradictoriness and duality at this stage where he had apparently overcome his doubts once and for all.

Grigory's instinctive sympathies as a working man soon come to the fore in the ensuing conflict, and finally gain the upper hand. But his action against the Soviet government is most blameworthy, and it is difficult for him to erase his guilt and correct his mistakes. He is once more assailed by conflicting doubts and Sholokhov again resorts to an inner monologue at this vital moment in his hero's spiritual development.

"He vaguely considered that it was not his job to reconcile the Cossacks with the Bolsheviks; for that matter, he could not himself be reconciled with them. But he felt that he could not and would no longer defend all these people who were alien in spirit, who were hostile to him—all these Fitshalaurovs, who had a profound contempt for him, and whom he despised no less profoundly" (4, 141).

It was his hatred for the generals and officers that drove Grigory to leave the White Army.

* Ibid.

13

Volume four is the book of reckonings. Every episode, every scene, every detail even, is significant. They are chosen and put together with a sense of artistic measure and consistency which admits no excess, nothing superfluous. The reader is kept in a state of constant suspense as Grigory's ill-starred life draws to its conclusion.

Part eight sees Grigory returning home after being demobbed from the Red Army. As he crosses the brown, faded autumnal steppe he recalls his childhood, and dreams of a life of peace and happiness with Aksinya.

Our last meeting with Grigory was a long time ago. We lost sight of him in Novorossiisk when a Red mounted patrol rode round the corner and swept towards him and his companions who had also taken part in the Upper Don uprising. From the account of Prokhor Zykov we learned that Grigory had served in the Red Army, fighting against Wrangel and the White Poles. Much has happened at the village during his absence. His mother has not lived to see her youngest boy's return; Dunya has married Koshevoi who is chairman of the village Soviet; Aksinya has returned to her home, after recovering from typhus.

But what of Grigory? What is he like now? We see him as a new person, as one does after a long absence, when changes stand out particularly sharply, through the eyes of a chance acquaintance. Sholokhov's idea of letting us see Grigory through the eyes of a chance companion, the widow who drives him home, is a master stroke. He could have chosen to show us the new Grigory through a meeting with his near and dear ones—Aksinya, Dunya or Prokhor Zykov—or by himself, giving an objective description. But, realising that these methods would not do—description by the author here would be too detached, while Aksinya or Dunya with their excitement and joy at the meeting would have given a distorted impression—he chooses to show us Grigory through the inquisitive, penetrating, experienced eyes of the widow.

As the bullocks plod steadily along, dragging the creaking cart, the woman began to find life boring, and surreptitiously examined Grigory, his concentrated face, his half-closed eyes. "He's not so very old, though he is grey. And he's a queer fellow somehow. Screwing up his eyes all the time. What's he keep doing it for? You'd think he was tired out, you'd think somebody had been using him as a cart-horse.... He looks as though he'd seen some trouble in his time. But he isn't bad-looking really. Only a lot of grey hair, and his moustache is nearly grey too. But otherwise he's not bad. What's he thinking so much for?" (4, 498).

It is almost as if the simple woman is speaking aloud to herself, one can even hear her tone of voice. The way Grigory keeps "screwing up his eyes" and looks tired out as if "somebody had been using him as a cart-horse" reminds us of the years of fighting he has behind him, "seven years in the saddle". But more than that, this description of Grigory arouses pity and a vague feeling of anxiety for his future. Somehow we cannot believe that he is at last coming home to port, to a peaceful family life. And indeed life still did have many a sorrow in store for him....

The great emotional power of this portrait of Grigory lies in the masterly way Sholokhov combines weariness of the war and all his past delusions with premonitions of the tragic finale.

Rich, expressive imagery is characteristic of Sholokhov's prose; every line, every phrase vibrates, is alive. Every comparison is absolutely authentic, clear and dynamic and is imbued with that strong feeling which plucks at all the reader's heart-strings.

The concluding chapters of the novel are permeated with a noble grief. In Fomin's band, in the forest, Grigory's ill-starred life works to a close, to a living death, while the reader, passionately involved in the hero's fortunes, looks on with horror, and asks himself again and again: what is the ultimate cause of Grigory Melekhov's tragedy, why did this strong, passionate, talented man come to this ignominious end?

14

When he returns to Tatarsky, after being wounded fighting the Whites, Grigory realises perfectly well that he ought to have stayed with the Red Army until the end of the Civil War. As he himself explains, he did not return to the front because he was angered by the way the Commissar and the Communists in the squadron did not trust him: "Towards the end I couldn't stand their distrust any longer." There were obviously important reasons for their distrust of him, and in fact Grigory himself unconsciously expresses them. It was not just a question of his past service with the Whites. The fact is Grigory was not entirely reconciled to the Soviet government. After much painful trial and error he finally came to be neither for Reds nor Whites, but for what was in fact bandit anarchism. There was a strict consistency in his actions, which Sholokhov reveals with remarkable penetration into a life full of complications and contradictions in his description of Grigory's inevitably tragic end.

By continuing to struggle against Soviet power as a member of Fomin's band, Grigory is sealing his doom. As well as breaking with the revolutionary people he is cutting himself off from the Cossack masses. It is Prokhor Zykov's character that helps us understand the personal element responsible for Grigory's downfall.

He appears with Grigory about half way through the first volume, on the eve of the First World War, and pops up again and again throughout the novel thereafter, playing an especially large role in the last few parts.

From the time of the uprising Prokhor faithfully follows Grigory wherever he goes. He is in fact a tragi-comic counterpart to the hero, with almost identical fortunes. The simple Cossack expresses in a joking manner many of the problems which assail Grigory, and shows the tragi-comic aspect of the hero's drama, without depriving it of its poignancy.

When the insurgents join forces with the White Army, Grigory feels that something has snapped inside him and he no longer has any wish to fight. Prokhor feels very much the same way about it, but his sense of humour does not desert him. Speaking to the master of the house in which they were quartered, he declares: "The better the beast under you, the faster you can get away from the enemy. I'm not out to catch them; but if we find ourselves in a tight corner, then I'm the first to show my heels. That's me. I've had my face to the bullets for so many years now I'm fed up with it!" (4, 83). When the time comes to sew on his epaulets, Grigory sighs and says: "I wouldn't mind if I never saw them again!" (4, 101) and his words express all his bitter hostility to the officer clique and the feeling that he is fighting for a cause that is alien to him as a Cossack farmer. Prokhor also has his say as to what he thinks of epaulets: "They've been waiting for us, damn them! Now we may wear them, but we'll never wear them out. They'll last out our time. I said to my wife: 'Don't sew them on so they'll never come off, you fool! Just tack them on so that the wind can't blow them away, and that'll be all right.' You know the state of our affairs. If we get taken prisoner they'll see at once that even though I'm not an officer, I'm a senior non-com" (4, 102).

The combination of grim irony and humour in Prokhor's speech lends it a special colour. This comic note in Prokhor's worries, just like the tragi-comic touches in Pantelei Prokofyevich in the later parts of the book serve a definite purpose. The outcome of the Civil War was quite obvious, and attachment to the past, while still retaining the gravity of tragic trials and errors in the case of Grigory Melekhov, had nonetheless no further purpose in life. The sufferings of Prokhor Zykov and Pantelei Prokofyevich assume a tragi-comic character. They are laughing at themselves through their tears and sorrows. These defenders of the old order already appear absurd and amusing even to themselves, and this is Sholokhov's masterly way of bringing the reader's attention to the fact that the old was passing away forever.

For Prokhor the war against the Soviet government has long ceased to have any justification whatsoever, and he cannot wait to see it over.

"What do you think, Panteleyevich? Haven't we poured out enough blood on the earth?" he asks Grigory after the insurgents have joined forces with the Whites.

"'About enough.'

"'But what do you think, will it be finished soon?'

"'It'll finish when they've smashed us.'

"'Well, it's a gay life we've run into, the devil be praised! Mebbe the sooner they smash us the better" (4, 107-108).

There is a certain guarded caution in Grigory's "about enough". He recognises his fault and secretly fears the reckoning, and is perfectly aware of the futility of continuing the struggle. Prokhor, on the other hand, takes a devil-may-care attitude and is not afraid to speak his mind. He uses every possible means to shirk the actual fighting, awaiting defeat as the only just outcome of the inglorious struggle with the revolutionary people. He continues to trail around with the Cossack counter-revolutionary armies out of sheer inertia. Actually, he has long since withdrawn from the conflict. In fact Prokhor, who tagged along with Grigory all the way to the sea, came to the conclusion that it was high time to finish this fratricidal strife long before his commander did. The beginnings of Grigory's divorce from the Cossack masses, that was subsequently to bring him terrible solitude, can be traced back to the time they were approaching Novorossiisk. Prokhor Zykov and thousands of other Cossacks came through the hard school of experience to be finally reconciled to the Soviet government. Grigory, however, persisted in his error, and came to adopt a position of hopeless anarchistic denial of everything: "I don't want to serve anybody any more. I've fought more than enough for my age, and I'm absolutely worn out. I'm fed up with everything, with the Revolution and with the counter-revolution" (4, 519).

Grigory speaks of himself with bitterness and cruel scorn: "...Ever since 1917 I've been going round and round in a circle, reeling like a drunken man. I broke away from the Whites, but I didn't join up with the Reds, and I float like dung in a hole in the ice...." (4, 532).

Grigory's lack of firm social convictions, his anarchistic nihilism, meant that a strong jolt could send him off in any direction. He joined Fomin's band, but he joined it alone, Prokhor remaining in the village. When Prokhor asked him if he would be called to account for his service with the Whites, Koshevoi answered him rudely and abruptly: "You're only a sheep," and drawing a sharp distinction between Prokhor and Grigory, continued: "There'll be no questioning of orderlies, but Grigory will have to face the music when he turns up" (4, 467).

Grigory's class prejudices as a property owner were stronger, his vacillations more marked, and his guilt greater before the people and the Soviet government. His unquestionable talent, his abilities as a commander, his courage and military skill, as well as the faith the Cossacks had in him, had all combined to give him a position of authority in life. He drew others after him, and the more hundreds, even thousands that repeated his mistakes, the greater and more unredeemable his personal guilt was.

"You started the rising.... The old debts have got to be paid off in full," Mikhail Koshevoi says threateningly (4, 517, 520).

Grigory avoided the reckoning only at the price of cutting himself off from the people once and for all. It was a terrible price to pay as he soon realised.

On a road out in the steppe Grigory chances to meet a fellow villager from Tatarsky. "Will you be making your peace with the Soviet government soon?" the old man asks, and, in reply to Grigory's evasive answer, continues: "It isn't well, Grigory Panteleyevich; on my word it isn't well!... As my old mind sees it, it's time to end it!" (4, 602). An old woman he asks for a scythe also has no sympathy for him: "As he passed the old woman he distinctly heard her mutter: 'There's no destroying you, damn you!'" (4, 664).

These words are said of a man who not so long ago was being told: "You are our pride. How would we live but for you!" A great change had certainly taken place in the mood of the Cossacks. As he roams the steppe with Fomin's band, Grigory is alienated from the Cossack masses. Sholokhov puts those words of censure into the mouths of old people, with the wisdom and experience of a life-time's work. Coming from them it is particularly convincing, for they represent the wisdom of that part of the people who passed through all the trials of the Civil War, and only after many mistakes, often gradually and not without apprehensions, came to accept the new truth, and to recognise Soviet power as the only lawful government.

Grigory's moral bankruptcy stands out particularly clearly against the background of the picturesque Don countryside.

Spring came and the snow melted on the fields, and the mighty Don overflowed its banks. Grigory would gaze at the watery expanse, and at night would stand listening to cries of the innumerable flocks of northward-flying geese. One day he saw a large flock of swans. "The morning glow was flickering brilliantly beyond the barrier of the forest. Reflecting its light, the water seemed rosy, and the great, majestic birds, with their heads turned to the sunrise, seemed rose-coloured also. Hearing a rustle on the bank, they flew up with a sonorous trumpet-call, and when they rose above the forest, Grigory was dazzled by the astonishing gleam of their snowy plumage" (4, 619).

Here we have an example of that realistic symbolism typical of Sholokhov's poetics. The beautiful, majestic birds, the dazzling gleam of their snowy plumage, suggest the purity of childhood, something fine and good that has been lost for ever. For Grigory is now an outlaw, racked by suffering and yearning. With him we see "the sun-hazed steppe, the guardian mounds showing azure along a distant ridge", the "marvellously brilliant tulips" rising in the place of the fading steppe violets. Scene after scene passes before us, one more beautiful than another.

This description of sunny spring bursting forth in a riot of colour is a powerful, tragic contrast to the gloomy, empty Grigory, who is but a spectator looking on at the great feast of life. It is in these moving terms that Sholokhov shows how Grigory has cut himself off from nature, no longer understands or feels a part of the surrounding world, has become an outsider.

As he gazed around him, he would be seized by a lacerating pain in his breast. Then he would lie down on the ground, which was warmed by the spring sun, and the pain would slowly pass.

Grigory realised that he was an outcast, a mere brigand. "Nobody needs us; we're hindering everybody from living and working in peace. A stop must be put to this, and about time too!" In a last burst of energy, a last attempt to put himself on the right track, he runs away from the band and, collecting Aksinya from the village, sets off for the Kuban. But Aksinya meets her death on the way.

Grigory buried his Aksinya in a deep ravine at dawn. The scene is described in a masterly fashion. The short, jerky sentences with the frequent pauses convey a sense of repressed emotion, as if a man is finding breathing difficult and has to stop and make an effort to control himself every so often. Grigory is quite crushed with grief. He had suffered and cast about desperately after Natalya's death, but his sorrow then had been that of a man in pain, wounded but living. Aksinya's death was a mortal blow to him, his heart and spirit were broken.

The picture of a man broken by sorrow is given in very simple, short, sharp strokes, as a concise enumeration of outward details. Grigory tried to rise and, as if struck by some unknown force, "he fell flat; but he at once jumped to his feet in terror. He fell yet again, striking his bare head painfully on a stone." Unable to rise, he knelt and automatically began to dig a grave with his sabre. He was seized by a choking feeling, and "to breathe more easily he tore open shirt at his neck". When he had buried Aksinya, he took his farewell of her, "firmly believing that they would not be parted for long". He remained on his knees beside the grave for a long time, "his head bowed, his body swaying a little. Now he had nothing to hurry for. Everything was finished" (4, 684-685).

But the scene does not end on this note. Sholokhov adds a final moment of great pathos to reveal the great depth of Grigory's suffering. The author himself introduces it with the words: "The sun rose above the ravine through the smoky haze of a burning wind from the east." Deeply moved already, the reader is stirred still more by the gloomy severity of this image. Grigory raised his head and saw above him "the black sky and the blindingly glittering, black disk of the sun". This is a man who has nothing left in life. Nothing could make up for his irreparable loss. One of his last links with the joyous, triumphant world of life has been broken. How better could Grigory's boundless suffering over the loss of his Aksinya be conveyed than by this image of "the black sky" above him, and "the blindingly glittering, black disk of the sun"? Yet Sholokhov goes on to give the fullest possible picture of the broken Grigory. The powerful description of the spring fires in the steppe symbolises the epic grandeur of all that Grigory has been through. War had indeed ravaged his life like an all-consuming fire.

"In the early spring, when the snow vanishes and the grass which has been buried under it during the winter begins to dry, fires break out in the steppe. Flames driven by the wind fly along in streams, greedily consuming the dry foxtail grass, leaping over the lofty stalks of the thistle-grass, slipping across the brown heads of the mugwort, spreading out in the hollows. And afterwards the acrid, burning smell of charred and cracked earth hangs over the steppe. All around, the young grass grows a merry green, innumerable skylarks flutter in the azure heaven above, migrant geese feed on the nourishing herbage, and the bustards settle for the summer and build their nests. But wherever the steppe fires have passed, the dead, charred earth blackens ominously. No birds nest on it, no animals come, and only the wind, winged and swift, carried the dove-grey ash and the dark, pungent dust far over the steppe.

"Like the steppe scorched with fires, Grigory's life also turned black. He had been deprived of everything which was dear to his heart. Pitiless death had taken everything from him, had destroyed everything. Only the children were left. But he himself still clung convulsively to the earth, as though his broken life was indeed of some value to himself and others" (4, 685-686).

A broken, morally bankrupt and utterly unhappy man is the tragic image of Grigory we carry away from the last few pages of the novel.

Sholokhov's novel shows with a tremendously convincing force that there is no third way in the Revolution, that fighting against his people leads a man to moral bankruptcy and dehumanisation.

In a way, Grigory represents the last in a long line of characters from Russian literature who were crippled by bourgeois property relations.

Hatred for the world of private property, for class society and its crippling effect on man, and the affirmation of the new, truly human world of socialist society, runs through all Sholokhov's writings like a leitmotif. It is present throughout *And Quiet Flows the Don* and is reaffirmed in *Virgin Soil Upturned*. Thus militant humanism is the most important single feature of Sholokhov's art, and he is thereby following in the footsteps of the father of socialist realism, Maxim Gorky.

15

Grigory Melekhov's tragic fate was not only the inevitable logical outcome of the socio-historical conflict, but was dictated by the authenticity of the character Sholokhov has created.

A faithful representation of the historical process in a work of literature boils down to *authenticity*. The quality of authenticity in a work of literature is an aesthetic category, for it means the correspondence between what the writer has created with the aid of his imagination and objective reality.

Obviously there can be no question of absolute correspondence, for the flow of life is not directly reproducible, but applied to a literary work with the aim of establishing the correspondence between the product of the artist's imagination and the world of reality, authenticity is a most important criterion for judging realistic art and for gauging a writer's understanding of the laws of history and what is of essential importance.

At the same time authenticity is a hall-mark of true art, one of the most important conditions for the characters and action to ring true.

Sholokhov endows Grigory Melekhov with many typical features, but in so doing makes him not an ordinary, run-of-the-mill character, but a vivid, strong individual. Grigory does not nurse his doubts and torments in the depths of his soul, waiting behind the scenes until the troubled times have past. He is a strong, active individual, who takes to horse, brandishing his sabre, throwing himself into the thick of the battle. His doubts and torments are nearly always revealed through his direct participation in events. First he fights against the whiteguard officer detachments of Chernetsov for the establishment of Soviet power on the Don, then he incites the Cossacks to anti-popular revolt, leading them against the armies of the Revolution. Next we see him "atoning for his sins" by fighting with the Red Army against Wrangel and the White Poles, and after his return home he once more takes up arms against the Soviet order, joining Fomin's outlaw band. Grigory's flights from one side to the other, his tormenting doubts as to whether he has chosen the right path, clearly reveal the struggle going on in his soul between his property instinct and the working man's psychology. They were typical of the middle peasants as a whole but various factors contributed to aggravate them in his case and make it much more difficult for him to see his way.

The path of the middle Cossacks in the Revolution was different from that of the middle peasants in general. The laws of revolutionary development naturally applied to them too, but the Cossacks had been a privileged military caste for centuries, and so they only came to accept Soviet rule after a long and fierce struggle.

Yet Grigory was not exactly typical of the majority of middle farmer Cossacks, for, as we have said, a number of factors combined to make him something of an exception. His commanding role in the Upper Don uprising, for example, aggravated his guilt before the Soviet government and made his reconciliation with the people more difficult.

Socially conditioned vacillation, typical of millions of non-proletarian toilers, when carried to extremes and not finally ending in joining the revolutionary people, inevitably led to an ignominious end. This was a general law of historical development, disclosed and made more understandable by all that was unique and individual in the fortunes of Grigory Melekhov. For Sholokhov the typical is that which correctly reflects the regular features of social development. This treatment of the phenomena of life reveals the progressive outlook of Sholokhov the writer and Communist.

One of the most impressive features of Sholokhov's talent is his remarkable ability for presenting the life of an age in all its complexity and diversity through a highly individual character, creating *a literary figure as a phenomenon of the age.*

In Grigory Melekhov's life, vacillations and searching for the social truth, Sholokhov embodies the chief conflicts of the time. In the armed struggle between the two camps in the Revolution and the Civil War the petty bourgeois was torn by conflicting feelings, his property instincts and the psychology of the toiler. In the period when the old world of private property and exploitation and the new world of socialism were locked in mortal combat, Grigory Melekhov stood at the crossroads. From his personal experience in the Revolution and the Civil War he felt that the past was doomed, that it was hostile to him, but he could not understand the great justice of the new world that was being born out of the bloody conflict because he was confused by his property instincts and class prejudices. He nursed the delusion that there was a special, third way in the Revolution, a just Cossack order that would reconcile the property owner and the toiler, but it turned out that in battle he was serving those very generals and officers he so detested. He lost heart, decided to make peace with Soviet power and gladly joined the Red Army. But again he felt he was not at home. "Nothing is clear to me even now," he declares sorrowfully when he returns to his native village after being demobbed from the Red Army.

With the ardour of a truly great humanist writer Sholokhov convincingly demonstrates through the life of his hero that man's only road, however many sufferings and labours he may encounter on the way, is that which leads to the new truth of the age.

16

Sholokhov's works show that the most dramatic conflicts and the most tragic characters (such as Grigory Melekhov, Makar Nagulnov and Andrei Sokolov) are historically authentic and have the power to move us only if the writer's standpoint is based on an understanding of what is desirable and inevitable for the people.

The concept of the tragic, as an aesthetic category, is revealed not only in the writer's attitude to reality but also in the depth of his understanding of what is taking place.

A writer who judges events and his heroes' lives from the standpoint of Communist ideals is able to penetrate the essence of the tragic. Sholokhov's sympathy with his hero, Grigory Melekhov, does not mean that he justifies him. He was able to identify the historically inevitable with the desirable. One of the great merits of socialist realism was the fact that it refrained from idealising the innocent victims of history, all those suffering heroes of the novels of the twenties who were unable to understand where true justice and truth lay. *And Quiet Flows the Don*, with its penetrating analysis of the causes and results of Grigory Melekhov's tragedy, the tragedy of a man of the people who stood between two principles and rejected them both, and its author's clearly expressed condemnation (in which his own judgment has the support of history), represents an important step forward in the development of socialist realism.

Art and literature, while being the most subjective of human activities, by their very nature aspire to an objective apprehension of the world, representing man's attempt to know himself and his fellow human beings as they really are.

Nineteenth-century realism had as its conscious aim the important aesthetic task of truthfully reflecting reality.

"Art is the reproduction of reality, the world repeated, as if created anew," wrote Vissarion Belinsky in his article *A Look at Russian Literature of 1847*.

A definition of this kind could only be born where the soil of realism had already been well tilled. It is full of pride in the magic ability of realist literature to recreate in a novel way before our very eyes the colourful flow of life in all its complexity.

Naturally, a fundamental aesthetic criterion of this art was truth to life.

It was inevitable that a question should arise which was to torture many generations of writers: How can the writer's appreciation of reality be made most faithful and convincing?

This question is of especially vital importance in our day, when decadent bourgeois tendencies are belittling and renouncing realism, when modernist groups are claiming their highly subjective and arbitrary concepts of reality to be truly innovatory.

For many bourgeois writers the historical process appears as something terrifyingly unpredictable and unintelligible, and most of them try to escape reality by burrowing into the most intimate feelings of their heroes. This inability to grasp where justice lies often results—even in cases where the writer's subjective approach is honest—in fortuitous and shaky ethical values, an absence of criteria of what is truly beautiful and so on.

These writers are somehow alienated from the historical process, and are not free to make judgments about it because of their limited ability to understand it.

Without faith in the future there can be no art. It is as essential to a writer as the air he breathes. Lev Tolstoi once declared, striking a strong polemical note: "One mustn't write only about what is in the world. If there is to be any truth in what you are describing, you must write not about what is, but about what ought to be...."

These words of the great writer and apostle of truth of course by no means represent an appeal to retire from the contradictions and conflicts of real life. In insisting on the necessity for understanding "what ought to be" he was maintaining that true art is inseparable from a bright ideal. In other words, he is saying that the writer must believe in the future if he is to be able to understand the present.

But in our dramatic age, humanistic faith, optimism alone, is not enough. The true strength of the writer's ideals is not only revealed in the creative process but is put to the test in life itself. It is no longer sufficient for the artist to penetrate and understand the conflicts of the age, he must also apprehend the general laws of historical development, for only such apprehension, as the example of Gorky shows in particular, can enrich faith with the power of scientific foresight.

Apprehension of the general laws of historical necessity is the "scientific rock-bed" that assures true creative freedom in our modern times, as is borne out by the development of socialist realism in Soviet and world literature. The writer can attain this knowledge as a "poet", that is, as a man who knows the bitter, unsettled state of contemporary capitalist reality from personal observations, from direct apprehension of numerous facts and facets of life, or he can attain it as a thinker, from his grasp of the progressive theories of Marxism-Leninism. More often than not we find a complex amalgamation of the two.

Alexei Tolstoi was for a while a White emigré, and then returned to revolutionary Russia. His long, hard road to understanding can be seen in the lives of the heroes of his trilogy *Ordeal*. He explains what enabled him to achieve the great range of his art in an article entitled *Marxism Has Enriched Art*.

"Only now that I am mastering the Marxist interpretation of history, now that the great teaching which was put to the test in the October Revolution gives me clearness of purpose and a method in reading the book of life, do I know real creative freedom, breadth of subject-matter, a wealth of themes such as no one life can encompass."

In order to enter the realm of true creative freedom, a writer has to free himself from narrow egoistic views and sympathies, but more than that, he has also to understand the purpose and meaning of the great historical facts that confront him.

In modern conditions he must find the strength to freely and fearlessly come out on the side of those who are building the road to the future for all mankind.

The very concept of necessity or regularity is impossible unless the writer himself understands through his own experience his indissoluble link with the popular masses, with the lives of the simple people who as a result of heroic efforts have become the masters, directors and creators of life. Only then will the writer's own sympathies and antipathies be ultimately determined by an understanding of what is good and what is bad for the people, and the deeper this understanding and the more it is imbued with the writer's feeling, his own personal "concern", the more authentic and convincing the picture he creates will be.

This is why the question of the writer's link with life is of paramount importance in the aesthetics of socialist realism. Every aspect of the life of the working people and their titanic efforts to transform the world is a constant source of creative energy and an emotional stimulus to the socialist realist writer.

Thus socialist realism means above all art that is truly "popular" in the original sense, art that is directly and consciously defending the people's interests, art inspired by an understanding of the ultimate end of the development of the present stage of world history.

For the socialist realist writer a knowledge of the modern scene, a keen interest in people, their personal and social relationships, their standing in society and every detail of present-day reality, however small, means a direct involvement in life. He not only stands up openly on the side of the forces of progress, but tries to aid their important historical advance by the very content of his art.

Alexander Fadeyev endowed Levinson, the hero of his novel *The Rout*, with that "simple science it is so hard to acquire ... of seeing everything as it is, in order to change what is and approach what is being born and is to be".

These words are an accurate definition of the militant approach of the socialist realist writer to exploring life. This is the basis of that drive towards the future which is the great quality of Soviet literature.

The writer who adopts this approach understands the historical process not merely as a natural result of the struggle between certain conflicting interests, but as something in which he is directly involved, and as his personal concern coincides with the aspirations of the masses, with the real content of the historical process, it is bound to lead to true objectivity. The principles of socialist realism give the writer more scope for artistic expression than any other creative method.

It is hard to imagine a more difficult task than that which was Sholokhov's declared aim in writing *And Quiet Flows the Don*. "I am describing *the Whites' struggle with the Reds* and not the other way round. This is the big difficulty," Sholokhov declared at a meeting with workers at Rostov-on-Don in 1930 (author's italics).

While previous works about the Civil War had told mainly of those who grew up and matured together with the Revolution and found themselves as individuals in the struggle for the people's happiness, *And Quiet Flows the Don* tells of those who lost their way and suffered irreparable losses in the process.

A considerable part of the Don Cossacks took part in the counter-revolutionary struggle, and many of the Cossack men and women in Sholokhov's novel either took part in it or were sympathisers.

Considering the events and characters Sholokhov chose to portray, and the great understanding and sympathy he evinced in doing so, it would have been easy for him to adopt the standpoint of his heroes as if sharing their historically justified illusions. It is easy to imagine, for example, how the life of Grigory Melekhov could have been presented in a work by a gifted writer who professed realism but who did not have Sholokhov's outlook, of a writer, that is, who judged his hero's life "in itself", purely as his "inner life" and not in relation to those fundamental changes which were taking place in the position and awareness of the people.

The result might well have been a "luckless" Grigory, broken by the inevitable course of historical events, "a sacrifice on the altar of history". Remember how Aksinya described to Grigory what she had said to Mishatka when he came to her crying because the village boys wouldn't play with him. "He burst into tears, and such bitter tears too! 'The other boys won't play with me, they say my daddy's a bandit. Mummy, is it true he's a bandit? What are bandits?' I told him: 'Your daddy isn't a bandit at all. He's just—unlucky'" (4, 680). And remember the last conversation between Grigory and Mikhail Koshevoi. The "reckoning" was indeed hard.

"'I've already told you, Grigory, and there's no point in getting upset about it: you're no better than they are; in fact, you're worse, you're more dangerous.'

"'How am I? What are you getting at?'

"'They're rank-and-file Cossacks, but you started the rising.'

"'I didn't start it, I was only commander of a division.'

"'Isn't that enough?'

"'Enough or not, that's not the point.... If the Red Army men hadn't planned to kill me that evening, I might not have taken any part in the rising.'

"'If you hadn't been an officer no one would have touched you.'

"'If I hadn't been taken for the army I wouldn't have been an officer.... That's making a long story of it.'

"'Both a long and rotten story.'

"'In any case it can't be gone over again, now it's past and done'" (4, 517).

Grigory was wont to explain a lot of the things he had done as depending on circumstances beyond his control, each complicating the issue, and creating a vicious circle from which there was no escape.

A writer who interpreted what took place merely from the point of view of Aksinya or Grigory, would be revealing but a part of the truth of the life he was attempting to portray.

Sholokhov adopted a broad approach, convinced that the whole truth could only be revealed against the background of history, and that history in our day means above all the development of the people's revolutionary struggle. It was this approach alone that could enable him to treat the personal and social aspects of Grigory's tragedy so objectively, and stress its historical implications.

Many attempts have been made by critics both at home and abroad to define Sholokhov's creative method. In the late twenties and early thirties critics of the RAPP group came out with some very primitive judgments, criticising Sholokhov on the grounds that in *And Quiet Flows the Don* he himself is basically adopting the position of the wavering middle farmer Cossacks and is hence unable to see on which side the truth lies, and attached to him the label of "objectivism". Although such judgments smacked unmistakably of vulgar sociology, the word "objectivism" became firmly linked with Sholokhov, some criticising him for it, others praising him.

In 1949 the German writer Willi Bredel wrote of Sholokhov: "He presents in a truly objective manner, in gentle, exciting and bright colours, people on both sides, their searchings, their mistakes, indecision and vacillation, their human grandeur and their human imperfection. He reveals the social and psychological origins of their views. He neither judges nor condemns but merely shows: such is life."*

This interpretation of Sholokhov's method combines different concepts. The attempt to understand true objectivity as an equally-balanced, impartial approach to the representatives of both camps can only mean that the artist is placing himself above the classes, on a height out of earshot of the shouts and din of battle. The writer is left to judge both sides, presenting them both in their "human grandeur" and "human imperfection". This is all very well, but what is the measure of this grandeur and imperfection? What guarantee have we that the judgments made are impartial and just, that they do indeed reveal the essence of characters' natures?

* *Heute und Morgen*, 1949, Heft 3, p. 147.

These questions are extremely important, not only in connection with the arguments that are raging around socialist realism. Their solution is of essential significance in any aesthetic system.

Lenin's remarks on the nature of a truly objective approach to the world provide an important clarification of this subject. Although Lenin was actually concerned with producing a definition of historical materialism, there is nonetheless much in common with literature in this point of departure, for literature is one of the forms of cognition of the world and man's place in socialist reality.

Lenin insisted that the materialist's aim is to represent the historical process correctly and precisely. He explains how this can be achieved in *The Economic Content of Narodism*, where his remarkable analysis of the two approaches, that of the "materialist" and that of the "objectivist", defines the essence of the truly objective approach to reality:

"The objectivist speaks of the necessity of a given historical process; the materialist gives an exact picture of the given social-economic formation and of the antagonistic relations to which it gives rise. When demonstrating the necessity for a given series of facts, the objectivist always runs the risk of becoming an apologist for these facts; the materialist discloses the class contradictions and in so doing defines his standpoint. The objectivist speaks of 'insurmountable historical tendencies'; the materialist speaks of the class which 'directs' the given economic system, giving rise to such and such forms of counteraction by other classes. Thus, on the one hand, the materialist is more consistent than the objectivist, and gives profounder and fuller effect to his objectivism. He does not limit himself to speaking of the necessity of a process, but ascertains exactly what social-economic formation gives the process its content, *exactly what class* determines this necessity.... On the other hand, materialism includes partisanship, so to speak, and enjoins the direct and open adoption of the standpoint of a definite social group in any assessment of events."*

* V. I. Lenin, *Collected Works*, Vol. 1, pp. 400-01,

These ideas of Lenin have a direct bearing on socialist realism. In art life, historical reality, does indeed appear in a variety of different individual fortunes and experiences. The realist writer contemplates the reality of his age and, if he wishes to be truly objective, to create characters which are authentic models of his contemporaries, he must seek the explanation for the actions of the masses, for people's behaviour and feelings, not in the mystical will of providence, but in the conditions of the life of a particular society.

Only art based on the materialist approach to the world can rise from accepting "a given series of facts" as inevitable to explaining them.

The writer can only judge the historical process freely and develop his own standpoint when he is able to understand and explain the class contradictions inherent in the process.

Lenin's words define that ideological basis which is the essential prerequisite for the application of the historical method in artistic thought.

Gorky repeatedly insisted that one of the important advantages of the socialist realist viewpoint is that it enables the writer to explain the past, understand the present and glance into the future. Indeed, the writer can only understand the present if he sees it as a link in the chain of historical development. The past reveals the true nature of the conflicts of the present, while only the artist who glances into the future can see the way to their settlement.

Surely this is the explanation for the historical optimism of such works of Soviet literature as *The Rout*, *And Quiet Flows the Don* and so on, that treat essentially tragic subjects. Facts, characters and events are so grouped that the historical tendency is perfectly clear.

However, a writer is not a dispassionate recorder of the inexorable course of history. Every line he writes reveals his understanding of events, his emotion, anger and love. The partisanship of the socialist realist writer is expressed not merely in his correct understanding of historical necessity, but in his open defence of the interests of the people and progressive Communist ideals.

One of the chief features of Sholokhov's method is the way he brings his heroes before the judgment of history, so to speak. At the same time his heroes are not passive spectators or powerless "victims of history" such as have sometimes been sympathetically portrayed in Soviet literature. Characters like Grigory Melekhov and Mikhail Koshevoi throw themselves into the thick of the fray, partly in order to find the truth, but also because they know their strength and feel capable of having some influence on the course of history.

"Over there people are settling their own and others' fates, and here I am minding a lot of mares," Mikhail Koshevoi thought bitterly, when he was living out in the virgin steppe with only the wind and the horses for company (3, 41).

During the Veshenskaya uprising Grigory Melekhov's hard experiences and bitter reflections lead him to understand the anti-popular nature of the struggle against Soviet power. "Life's taken a false turn, and maybe I'm at fault in that too," he says to Natalya (3, 392).

The up-and-do nature of Sholokhov's heroes is in itself an innovatory feature born of the Revolution. To the simple man, whose thoughts not so long before had revolved exclusively round his strip of land and the joys and sorrows of family life, the Revolution brought the awareness that he was settling "his own and others' fates".

Yet Grigory Melekhov and Mikhail Koshevoi often found themselves in a different camp, and their actions could not be judged on the basis of their own personal justifications. If the writer was to be truly objective, it was not enough for him to describe the flow of events in which, as Engels put it, men seek the motives of their actions; he must be fully aware of the forces which determined the outcome of the conflict, the direction of future historical development.

Sholokhov shows us the very heart of life, its conflicts and contradictions, and its truth is revealed not through the author's assessments but in the advance of history itself. The progressive trend of development, seen and correctly understood by Sholokhov, is the criterion by which all his heroes' actions are judged.

Sholokhov, whom the critics accused of objectivism, was possibly one of the most biased writers in the history of literature. Throughout Sholokhov's writings the reader is continually aware of the author's attitude to the characters and events he is describing. Sholokhov makes no attempt to hide his ardent concern but the reader is never handed out ready-made judgments. These are to be sought in the images themselves, in their aesthetic content and in the culmination they attain.

The progressive outlook of this great Communist writer enables him to shed light on the deepest substrata of human life, to show all the complexity and inherent contradictions in the transition from one social order to another. By revealing life as it is, by showing countless people in conflict, Sholokhov teaches us to love some and despise others.

Chapter Three
THE MASSES

1

The true realist writer sets out to give an accurate and authentic picture of man in relation to his fellow human beings and the surrounding world. Thus it is essential in the long run that he understand and explain the historical process.

Soviet writers refused to recognise the influence of any powerful outside factors in the historical process, as was only to be expected from people who themselves fought in and won the Revolution and the Civil War. It was only natural that they should see the explanation for all that had taken place in the revolutionary struggle of the people, that is in reality itself. Indeed, one of the great innovatory features of socialist realism was this enthusiastic epic sweep which determined not only the subject-matter but also the composition and style of the works of Soviet literature.

One of the main aims of Soviet literature was to discover the best means of depicting the historical activity of the people through the lives of individuals or groups of people, and to show the reader the grandeur of the collective achievement of the masses. The people become a leading character in the great epic.

And Quiet Flows the Don presents the people at a turning point in history. The ten years the novel covers are full of events of momentous historical importance — the carnage of the imperialist war and the resulting 1917 Revolution in Russia which marked the beginning of a new era.

Sholokhov's heroes are workers and peasants, and work is an essential part of their life.

Lev Tolstoi had condemned the idle, immoral life of the ruling classes and extolled the life of the toiling masses, seeing the highest good in work for the benefit of humanity. Like the hero of his novel *Resurrection*, he understood that this was a new, beautiful world.

"'Yes, a different, entirely new world,' Nekhlyudov thought, as he looked at those dry, muscular limbs, the coarse home-spun clothes and the sunburnt faces with their expression of tenderness and suffering. He felt he was surrounded by entirely new people with their serious interests, their present joys and sorrows, their human life of toil.... And he felt the joy of the traveller who has discovered a beautiful, new, unknown world."

The literature of socialist realism was to be the true explorer of this beautiful, new world. For Gorky's aesthetics, work and the capacity for revolutionary activity are inseparable categories.

"For me work is a sphere which fires my imagination with unlimited inspiration," Gorky wrote. "I believe that all the mysteries and tragedies of our life will only be solved through work, and that it is the only thing that can make the alluring dreams of equality and justice come true."*

Sholokhov possesses a rare gift for penetrating the very essence of the simple working man's character, revealing his thoughts, feelings and aspirations with warmth and understanding. Grigory Melekhov, Aksinya, Pantelei Prokofyevich, Ilyinichna and Natalya are among the immortal characters of Russian and world literature.

Sholokhov's heroes are peasant Cossacks whose whole life is based on hard work, and we see them in their daily round.

Ilyinichna is "bent with toil", and Pantelei Prokofyevich is always on the go so that it is difficult to imagine him not occupied with some task or another. We see him repairing a shoe or harness by the light of the oil lamp on a winter's evening, or going out to see to the cows. In the spring and summer he is always out in the steppe, mowing or sowing, reaping or threshing.

"Hard-working" figures as one of the most positive epithets in the novel. "He's a hard-working lad", people say approvingly of Grigory, while "hard-working Natalya" soon won the hearts of her parents-in-law.

---

* Maxim Gorky, *Collected Works*, Vol. 15, pp. 227-28.

The proud and beautiful Aksinya is rarely to be seen unoccupied. She fetches water from the Don, whitewashes the house, milks the cow, and gathers the hay in the wake of the mowers. During the hard years when there is hardly a man left in the village she repairs the roof and goes mowing and sowing with Dunya.

The heroes of the novel are often described as having "skilful hands, itching for work", "toiler's hands", "fingers roughened by work".

Sholokhov's descriptions of work are almost always concrete and visual. He shows us his heroes actually at work, the way they work. We see Pantelei Prokofyevich at the mowing, for which the whole village turned out as though for an annual holiday: "His hook-nose shone as though freshly varnished, the sweat clung to the hollows of his swarthy cheeks. He smiled, baring a close-set row of white, gleaming teeth in his raven beard, and, with his wrinkled neck bent to the right, swept the scythe through the grass. A seven-foot semicircle of mown grass lay at his feet" (1, 64). Grigory is described during the reaping: "He could hardly open his parched lips. He gripped his pitchfork closer to the prongs in order to get a better leverage on the heavy swathes, and breathed spasmodically. His dripping chest itched from sweat. From under his hat it poured down his face and stung his eyes like soap" (1, 110).

The perspiration dripping off Grigory is a very concrete image which immediately conveys the intensity of his strenuous effort.

Throughout the novel—in the descriptions of working people, in the succession of farming scenes, in the recollections of the Cossacks torn away by the war from the land and pining for work—we find an insistence on a life of toil as the only real life for a man.

Sholokhov sees work as belonging to the aesthetic category of the beautiful, and this is what gives that exciting poetic quality and moving lyric power to the workaday scenes in the novel. The poetry of work is a leitmotif of *And Quiet Flows the Don*.

Weary with the long war, Grigory longs "to walk along the soft furrow left by the plough-share, whistling to the bullocks; to hear the trumped call of the cranes; to brush the flying silver gossamer from his cheeks, and to drink in the autumnal scent of earth raised by the plough" (3, 120-121).

Note how the language here is not that of common, everyday speech. *"The trumped call of the cranes"*, *"the flying silver gossamer"*, *"to drink in the autumnal scent"*, are all poetic expressions, and in fact not a single detail in these lines is on the level of common speech. The passage is intended to convey the beauty inherent in the simplest everyday tasks. And indeed this scene of autumn plowing, scrupulously accurate down to the last detail, arouses a sense of beauty and gives true aesthetic pleasure.

We find what has so often been expressed in literature in prosaic terms as gloomy and monotonous being treated as something aesthetic. Sholokhov was after all describing the hard life of the peasants in pre-revolutionary Russia, yet he managed to single out and reveal the poetry of labour. Even the most humdrum features of workaday life are full of significance and bring him pleasure.

When Grigory was travelling home to recuperate after his wound, his heart warmed within him as he remembered his former life.

"...When he thought that soon it would be time to get the harrows ready for spring, the willow mangers would have to be woven, and that when the earth was unclothed and dry he would be driving out into the steppe, his labour-yearning hands gripping the plough handles, feeling it pulse and jerk like a live thing; when he remembered that soon he would be breathing in the sweet scent of the young grass and the damp-smelling earth turned over by the plough-share, his heart warmed within him. He longed to clean the cattle-yard, to toss the hay, to smell the withered scent of the clover, the quitch, the pungent smell of dung" (2, 341-342).

Sholokhov poeticises labour as a mighty constructive force giving his heroes physical vigour and moral health. Prolonged inactivity is an intolerable burden for them.

2

While poeticising labour and the real life of toil of the Cossack farmers in contrast with the idle, hence futile life on the Listnitsky estate, Sholokhov never donned rose-coloured spectacles. He did not hesitate to reveal the evil power of property instincts that had such a grip in Cossack life, showing how it disfigured human beings and dehumanised them.

One-armed Alexei Shamil had been quarrelling with his neighbour Kashulin over a strip of land for six years. "Alexei beat up the old man every spring, although the strip that Kashulin had grabbed was not big enough to swing a cat in anyway" (1, 196).

The private property instinct made itself felt in the sphere of family relations too, in the idea which still persisted in village life that the paterfamilias was the indisputable lord and master. When Stepan exercised his rights and beat Aksinya with calculated brutality, the villagers merely displayed an unhealthy curiosity. As for Ilyinichna, she had borne countless beatings from her husband when both of them were young.

It took a woman truly remarkable strength and courage to live and raise her children in these conditions where she was deprived of her true dignity as a human being and a mother.

It was not done to freely demonstrate one's tenderer feelings in public. The description of Grigory's wedding with Natalya whom he does not love is truly horrifying. "Scowling, Grigory kissed his wife's insipid lips and sent a hunted glance round the room. A crimson fever of faces. Coarse, drunkenly muddy glances and smiles" (1, 139).

Sholokhov purposely gives a naturalistic description of the wedding, thereby adding a satirical note to the scene. He is openly sympathetic towards Grigory, the mettlesome young Cossack forced by village conventions to give up his Aksinya and marry Natalya.

Sholokhov shows us another unpleasant side of Cossack life—the way pillage in wartime was considered quite natural and lawful, merely as a sign of Cossack bravado.

There is a scene in book one where a Cossack who has stolen a watch belonging to an inhabitant of a village near the frontier meets with the open approval of his fellow Cossacks:

"'The likes of us can't help stealing.'

"'Everything sticks to a Cossack's hand.'

"'Let them be more careful about their things!'

"'A nimble fellow, that!'" (1, 353).

During the Civil War the defenders of "the quiet Don" became an army of looters, pillaging the families of Red Guards and those suspected of Bolshevik sympathies and stripping prisoners naked. Pantelei Prokofyevich, always with an eye to the farm and the family interest, becomes a regular looter during the Civil War. He comes to the front to see Grigory, and carries off everything he can lay his hands on in the house of a Cossack who is away fighting for the Reds. Deaf to tears and entreaties of the Cossack's wife, he loads everything onto his wagon, from horse-collars and clothes to the bath-house boiler.

The predatory nature of the world of property can best be seen in the lives of the wealthy merchant, Mokhov, and the richest farmer in the village, Korshunov.

Alarmed by the February Revolution, and feeling that a fatal blow had been struck to the world he lived in, Mokhov recalled an incident that had occurred long before at the mill, when he had ordered his scales-man not to give flour to a Cossack who had made a fuss about being given short weight. Now he was to admit to himself, "I got my money by shady means.... I've squeezed others...."

The Korshunovs' house with its iron roof standing in a spacious garden surrounded by a strong high fence, was every bit as good as that of Mokhov the merchant. The tight-fisted old Miron Korshunov owned fourteen pairs of bullocks, fifteen cows, a herd of horses and brood-mares, and a flock of several hundred sheep. His whole life had been spent accumulating wealth and he was a hard taskmaster who drove his seasonal and permanent labourers until they almost dropped. Both "outsiders" and poorer Cossacks went to him hat in hand. There was a strong human drama behind the inconspicuous-looking Mikhei, a regular farm-hand employed by Korshunov. Ruined by fire, he had left his family to become a labourer, had taken to drink, and was soon a wreck of what he had been.

Sholokhov's description of life in Tatarsky village reveals the *social heterogeneity of the Cossacks*, exploding the myth of the Cossacks being a solid caste.

Korshunov can easily afford to send Mitka off to do his military service on a fine thoroughbred charger perfectly equipped, but the Melekhovs have to sell some cattle to get a steed for their son. Fedot Bodovskov complains to the Bolshevik organiser Stockman whom he is driving from the railway station to the village: "I sold my bullocks and bought a horse and they rejected him.... It's enough to ruin you!" (1, 218). In Fedot Bodovskov's guileless chatter Stockman sees the seeds of discontent with the existing order. Discontent was mounting among the poorer Cossacks—people like the mill-hand Timofei, nicknamed "Knave", his assistant David, the engineman Ivan Alexeyevich Kotlyarov, and the young Cossack Mikhail Koshevoi.

The October Revolution and the Civil War toppled the old world of exploitation and injustice, the whole order based on private property relations. One of the victims of this struggle between the old and the new was that gifted man of the people Grigory Melekhov.

Sholokhov presents history as *the history of the revolutionary development of the masses.* He shows the Revolution and the Civil War not as a sudden explosion of elemental forces, but as an event dictated by the laws of historical development, prepared by the existing social and economic conditions. This is why he goes to the trouble of showing the reader the life of the Cossacks before the war, revealing the class stratification and the mounting discontent and protest.

In his account of the dramatic events of the First World War, the Revolution and the Civil War, Sholokhov attempts to depict the steady growth of the working people's awareness, their unprecedented upsurge of creative revolutionary energy. Both in mass scenes and in the private lives of individuals Sholokhov showed that the development of the masses towards political awareness and understanding of their true interests came as a result of their participation in the revolutionary struggle and through the work of the Communists.

We see from the activities of Stockman as early as book one how far the Party had penetrated the popular masses.

At first sight the very fact of a Bolshevik worker turning up in an out-of-the-way Cossack village may seem a bit far-fetched, but as it happens Sholokhov was showing things as they really were. Strong Party underground organisations were not confined to such proletarian centres of the Don Province as Rostov, Novocherkassk, Shakhty and so on, but existed in the smaller centres too, as revealed in S. Kudinov's recently published memoirs about the heroic underground activities carried on by the Social-Democrat organisation at Kamenskaya *stanitsa*.

Stockman turns up in the small Cossack village of Tatarsky on the eve of the First World War. Despite the fact that Stockman is a pale character beside the other heroes of the novel, lacking as he does their rich inner life, we feel *the strength of the Party* behind his reserved manner, seriousness of purpose and tenacity.

Stockman sees the social heterogeneity behind the comfortable façade of Cossack life, and is able to pick out those of the villagers who are likely to be receptive to revolutionary ideas.

Stockman first comes up against the savage aspects of the village life one day at the mill, when a brawl erupts between Cossacks and "outsiders" over some quite trivial matter. He arrives on the scene as the Cossacks are about to spring to horse and pursue the "outsiders" who have made off in their wagons. It is not purely humanitarian motives that move him to intervene. He bravely takes advantage of this tense, dangerous moment to put over a bit of useful propaganda, explaining to the Cossacks that they are descended from the Russians, and are peasants just like the "muzhiks", Ukrainian or Russian, are. The local authorities realise that the important thing is not the fact that Stockman intervened, but what he said. This is clear from the way the inspector who arrives shortly after to examine Stockman in connection with the disturbances at the mill asks: "What did you talk to the Cossacks about on the day of the fight at the mill?"

When he had gradually, carefully gathered a small group of poorer villagers Stockman began his work by exploding the myth that the Cossacks were a caste apart. He suggested they read a book entitled *A Short History of the Don Cossacks*, in which the unknown author, starting with "the free life of the past", went on to scoff at "the tsar's government and the Cossacks themselves who had hired themselves out to the monarchs as their henchmen".

Stockman cleverly guided the heated arguments that broke out. It was no easy task to destroy the ideas the Cossacks had been "fed with their mothers' milk", but he "ate into the simple understandings and conceptions like a worm into wood, instilling repugnance and hatred towards the existing system". And the young Mikhail Koshevoi is moved to say bitterly, somewhat perplexed: "It's not our fault such shame was brought upon the Cossacks."

Thus the seeds of the great truth were sown in an out-of-the-way Cossack village. They were to bear rich fruit in the years of the war and Revolution.

Mikhail Koshevoi did not forget what he had learned from Stockman and when he was at the front he came out again and again against the senseless war. As Uryupin remarked he was always crowing about it "like a cock on the wall". Once when the Cossacks were retreating in disorder under heavy enemy machine-gun fire, Mikhail Koshevoi cried out: "The people are swine, swine! When they've poured out all their blood, then they'll learn what they're being shot down for!" (2, 71).

Sholokhov presents the First World War in all its grim reality, showing the bloody battles, the incompetence of the tsarist commanders which lead to enormous casualties, life in the trenches with the filth and the lice, and the mortal weariness of the Cossacks and the ordinary soldiers, among whom discontent was mounting as they began to wonder what on earth they were fighting for.

"I haven't been out of the trenches since 1914. Never had a home or family of my own, but I've got to fight for someone," Knave complains bitterly to Ivan Kotlyarov whom he has met by chance in a village near the front. They speak of Stockman with a burst of feeling that comes somewhat unexpectedly from these rather stern men.

"'D'you remember Stockman?'" Ivan Alexeyevich asks. "'He was a good fellow, our Osip Davidovich! He'd tell us what it was all about. He was a man, if ever there was one....'

"'Do I remember him!' Knave cried, shaking his tiny fist and crinkling his little bristly face into a smile. 'I remember him better than my own father'" (2, 34).

We see how the Bolsheviks prepared for the Revolution in the trenches, telling the people what it was all about, why they were being sent like lambs to the slaughter.

The "bitter Ukrainian", Bolshevik Garanzha, opens Grigory Melekhov's eyes to the futility and pointlessness of the imperialist war. Garanzha makes but a brief appearance in the novel and then disappears for good. Yet like so many of Sholokhov's characters he remains implanted in our memory. One senses an experienced Bolshevik agitator in this man from the people. A simple soldier, formerly a village blacksmith in the Ukraine, Garanzha is able to present the most complicated things in simple terms so that they are readily understandable. The following passage is typical of Garanzha's terse speech, garnished with proverbs and invectives. "The tsar's a grabber, and the tsaritsa's a whore, and they're both a weight on our backs.... The factory-owner drinks vodka, while the soldier kills the lice. The factory-owner takes the profit, the worker goes bare. That's the system we've got. Serve on, Cossack, serve on!" (1, 512).

Garanzha speaks in the simple front-line jargon in which the soldiers' developing class-consciousness was expressed. It is easy to see how convincing his caustic remarks would be to the discontented front-line soldiers fed up with fighting. Why, he was speaking to them in their own language!

The clever Bolshevik gradually destroyed all Grigory's former ideas about the tsar, the country, and his own military duty as a Cossack, leading him to conclude that revolution was inevitable.

Garanzha finishes a night-time conversation that Grigory was long to remember with words expressing passionate faith in the victory of the Revolution: "Away with frontiers, away with anger! One beautiful life all over the world" (1, 514).

But Garanzha was only one of a whole host of Bolshevik soldiers, who bravely spoke out against the war and paved the way for the victory of the Revolution.

Ilya Bunchuk was another Bolshevik working among the Cossacks in the trenches. Sholokhov emphasises the man's fierce tenacity. "There was nothing remarkable about the man. Only the firmly pressed jaws and the direct challenging glance distinguished him from the rank-and-file Cossacks around him" (1, 562).

Bunchuk had joined up as a volunteer in order to master the art of war and prepare himself for the coming class struggle.

"Those who sow the wind shall reap the whirlwind," he says solemnly to round off a conversation with *sotnik* Listnitsky in which he has made no attempt to hide his views.

The work of the Communists at the front helped the soldiers and Cossacks understand the senselessness and disastrous nature of the war, teaching the masses that the war could not be ended without a radical change in the existing system, that is by revolution. Their work bore fruit; even the Cossack units were "demoralised", as the monarchist officer Listnitsky put it.

Sholokhov follows the development of the Cossacks' mood right through the war, showing how they gradually came to press for peace *en masse*.

When the Cossacks are being mobilised for the war, a confident voice pipes up: "Pah, my friend! What country could stand up to us?" But another Cossack remembers how he had helped to put down the strikers in 1905, and suggests they'll be sent again to do the same. He is interrupted by yet another who says: "Let them hire people for that, or let the police do it. It's a shame for us to."

But both those who hoped they were being sent to put down disturbances and those who considered it shameful sang the song of *The Quiet Don*, marching on "in obedience to the monarch's call".

After a few years of war the Cossacks sang another song, with the mournful words: "He'll ne'er come back again."

The February Revolution showed that the Cossacks did not want to fight. They came out openly against the continuation of the war, there were cases of refusal to obey orders, and frequent spontaneous meetings were held. The following sort of talk was heard:

"'...If there's been a revolution and all the people have been given their freedom, they ought to stop the war, because the people and us Cossacks don't want war! Am I right?'

"'You're right!...'

"'We're sick of it!...'

"'Down with the war! Let's go back home.'"

Much Cossack blood had been spilt, Cossacks had looked death in the face many many times, and others besides Koshevoi and Bunchuk had tried to get them to see the truth before the Cossacks became fully aware that "the people and us Cossacks don't want war" and that the Revolution meant freedom for all, thus attaining an understanding of the inevitability and desirability of revolutionary changes.

3

With the Civil War and the division of the country into two armed camps, the regions with a predominantly Cossack population (such as the Don, the Kuban and the Terek) became strongholds of the counter-revolution.

A considerable part of the Cossacks, stirred up by the counter-revolutionary officers and kulaks, rose against the Soviet government in 1918, and fought an anti-popular war against Soviet Russia.

In April 1918 "there was a great cleavage in the Don Province. The front-line Cossacks of the northern districts—those watered by the rivers Khoper, Ust-Medveditsa, and the Upper Don—withdrew with the retreating detachments of Red Guards, while the Cossacks of the lower districts drove and pressed them towards the frontiers of the province" (3, 7).

Sholokhov shows that the causes for this great cleavage were socio-historical rather than strictly territorial. "The poorer Cossacks of the north" had long been "the main stronghold of all rebels", while the richer Cossacks of the south had remained faithful to the establishment, defending the tsar and their privileges.

What we see in Tatarsky was the general pattern throughout the region: the Revolution split every village into hostile camps battling to the death. On the one hand there were such inveterate enemies of Soviet power as the Korshunovs, on the other the revolutionary Cossacks—Koshevoi, Kotlyarov and so on.

Those Cossack toilers who were led into the struggle against Soviet Russia were to follow a tortuous path. Some of them finally came round and recognised the Soviet government, while the others ended their days eking out a miserable existence in the slums of Istanbul, Paris and Belgrade.

Sholokhov's dramatic account of the complicated fortunes of the Cossacks in the revolutionary struggle gives a most authentic picture of the struggle between the two worlds.

While having his attention chiefly focussed on the lives of the main characters—Grigory Melekhov and his family, Aksinya, Natalya, Koshevoi—the reader frequently has to widen his sights for mass scenes and the appearance of numerous incidental characters, so that he has an impressive canvas of the Civil War, a whole world that is bursting at the seams with life.

The author gives a broad panorama of the revolutionary camp. He describes battles in the Don steppe, then brings Grigory into contact with Red Army prisoners of war in scenes which show the great strength and courage of the defenders of the Revolution, of the Red Army men and their commanders, and again shows the bitter fighting in which the destiny of the people is being decided. In this kaleidoscope of events and characters we are confronted by the giant *image of the people*, the hero of the greatest Revolution ever carried out.

The insurgent Cossacks look on the Reds they are about to engage with "vague anxiety, akin to fear". Grigory and his squadron watch the Red lines approaching.

"...He and the rest of the Cossacks were astonished to see a horseman, evidently the commander, riding on a high-standing white horse in front of the first line. There were two more in front of the second line. The third line was also led by a commander; beside him fluttered a banner, like a tiny crimson patch of blood against the dirty yellow background of the field.

"'Their commissars go in front! That's heroic of them!' Mitka Korshunov laughed with admiration.

"Meanwhile the wind brought the indistinct strains of singing to the hill-side. The lines of Red Guards wound along unevenly, and their voices came faintly, lost in the sultry, spacious steppe. Grigory felt his heart beating violently and spasmodically. He had heard that soul-gripping refrain before! He had heard the sailors singing it when he had been with Podtyolkov at Glubokaya, devoutly removing their caps, their eyes gleaming passionately" (3, 99-100).

The banner, looking like "a tiny crimson patch of blood" as it flutters against the dirty yellow field in the distance, and the indistinct strains of singing reminding Grigory of the sailors at Glubokaya, "devoutly removing their caps, their eyes gleaming passionately", singing the *Internationale*—these inspired details bring the scene to life so that the reader is gripped by that thrilling sensation which heroism arouses.

Such emotion-packed scenes of heroism abound in the novel. Here is a good example when Grigory leads his Cossacks to the attack against the survivors of the Red forces which had crossed the Don and now found themselves pressed to the river.

"Not more than a hundred paces separated them from the Red Army men when, after three volleys, a tall, swarthy-faced, black-whiskered commander rose to his full height from behind the hillock. A woman dressed in a leather jacket was supporting him. The commander was wounded. Dragging his shattered leg, he stepped down from the mound, took a firm grip of his rifle with its fixed bayonet, and hoarsely commanded:

"'Comrades! Forward! Smash the Whites!'

"Singing the *Internationale*, the little handful of brave men advanced into the counter-attack, advanced to death.

"The hundred and sixteen who were the last to fall on the bank of the Don were all Communist members of the International Company" (4, 35).

In this epic of the people locked in mortal combat with the old world for a new, happy life, we naturally meet *a whole host of incidental characters*, every one of which must be impressed on the reader's memory, however brief his appearance in the novel. This can be achieved only if these minor characters are there for a purpose, that is if their words, thoughts and actions represent some important feature of the period, help characterise a particular social group, and thereby add something to the general picture of the age the author is trying to draw.

Likhachov, commander of a Red Army punitive detachment, is just such a character, and although he makes a very brief appearance the reader does not easily forget him.

Likhachov is wounded and taken prisoner by the Cossacks who rose against Soviet power. Though in great pain, he stoically bears it and refuses to answer any questions. When the commander of the insurgent forces asks him to write to his detachment calling on them to surrender, he spits in his face. Full of hatred for his enemies, and firm in his belief that the cause he is fighting for is just and that the Revolution will ultimately be victorious, he is prepared to face anything. His character is most fully revealed in the tragic scene of his death.

Every word in this small scene has been weighed up and chosen with loving care so that it carries a tremendous impact. Likhachov is being driven to Kazanskaya. "He walked in front of his mounted guard, lightly stepping over the snow, his eyebrows knitted." These brief external details lead us straight to the character's inner world. The tall, heavily built Likhachov "steps lightly" because he is not afraid of death and is full of contempt for his captors. At the same time, his knitted eyebrows betray his thoughtful mood, his premonition of death. In the forest he passes a birch tree which catches his attention. Sholokhov does not go into long details about his character's state of mind, but expresses it through a single striking image. Likhachov sees not simply a white birch but a "*deathly* white birch", and the reader, who hitherto has only been able to guess vaguely at what might happen, is suddenly gripped by a strong premonition as he sees this image through the eyes of a man whose end is near.

Sholokhov expresses in an extremely vivid manner the fortitude and unbroken faith in the triumph of life with which Likhachov meets his death. "As he passed a deathly white birch, he smiled quickly, stopped, stretched out his sound arm, and tore off a twig. On it little buds were already swelling with the sweet March juices...."

This almost involuntary burst of joy at the sight of the swelling birch buds is a glimpse into the soul of a man who is in love with life, and who firmly believes in its ultimate triumph over death. There is a childlike purity and beauty in this big, stern man who "thrust the buds into his mouth and chewed them, gazing with misty eyes at the trees fresh with the young spring, and smiling at the corners of his lips.

"He died with the black petals of the buds on his lips. Seven versts from Veshenskaya, in the grim sandy dunes, the guards cut him down with bestial fury" (3, 271-272).

Men like Likhachov may be killed but never vanquished. He and the birch tree coming to life again after the winter merge for us into a single moving symbol of the eternal triumph of life over death.

This poetic scene testifies to the inexhaustible store of possibilities the truly gifted artist has at his disposal for capturing the most various aspects of reality. There are many writers, past and present, who recount acts of heroism in high-flown rhetorical language which makes the general effect seem terribly forced and unnatural. Sholokhov's description is simple, authentic and poetic, and this is why Likhachov's heroic death transcends the strictly personal, and acquires the force of an affirmation of the great cause he was fighting for in the Don steppes.

Sholokhov proceeds from that socialist realist concept of man the fighter which Gorky spoke of thus: "For me man is always victorious, even when he is wounded and dying."*

Sholokhov presents the Civil War in terms of contrast, a method frequently employed by Lev Tolstoi.

In *War and Peace* Tolstoi contrasts the criminal acts of the invaders with the popular war which reveals the best features of the Russian people. He uses the same method of contrast to show the emptiness of high society and the moral grandeur and courage of the true patriots. Thus, the description of the soirée at Julie Drubetskaya, where the ladies are preparing lint that will never reach the wounded, and exacting a fine for the use of French, is situated between two extremely significant chapters. The first contains the impassioned and profound conversation about Russia's woes between Prince Andrei and Kutuzov, and the second describes the preparations for the Battle of Borodino. After a scene in Hélène's salon, with a description of her latest affairs with two important personages, we meet Pierre, thoroughly shaken by

---

* A. M. Gorky, *Articles on Literary Criticism*, Russ. ed., Moscow, 1937, p. 215.

all he has seen and experienced on the day of the battle. The hungry and miserable Pierre is fed and made comfortable beside the camp fire by some soldiers. On the one hand we have the grandiose events of the life of the people, and on the other the affectation and pitiful emptiness of the life of high society.

In *And Quiet Flows the Don* Sholokhov is constantly contrasting the world of the revolutionary people with the ugly world of the whiteguards and interventionists which is doomed to perish.

The contrast is all the more dramatic and powerful in that it is often contained in a single chapter, or even in a particular episode, as in the scene with the captured Red musicians, where Sholokhov makes a perfectly ordinary situation—there were in fact cases of groups of musicians being captured—into a powerful episode reflecting the clash between two hostile worlds.

The episode is narrated simply and straightforwardly, which makes it all the more convincing. A fat, smug Cossack officer wanted to show off his power over the prisoners and make fun of them, and ordered them to play his beloved *God Save the Tsar*. But it turned out that none of them knew it. When the captain threatened to have them shot immediately, "one of the bandsmen, an elderly man with a wall-eye, began pushing himself to the front of the group. Clearing his throat, he asked:

"'Will you allow me? I can play it.' And without waiting for permission, placed his sun-bleached flute to his trembling lips.

"The wailing mournful sounds that rose solitarily over the spacious merchant's yard brought a wrathful frown to the captain's brow. Waving his arm he shouted:

"'Silence! Stop that beggar's whining!... Is that what you call music?'"

It is ironic enough that the call for the tsarist anthem was answered by *"an elderly man with a wall-eye"*, a masterly stroke which heightens the satirical note. There is even more satirical irony in the *"wailing mournful sounds"* that then rose. The tsarist anthem is shown as having outlived its day, and the reader cannot help feeling that this applies to the whole White camp who dream of the day when its strains will sound once more throughout "great, indivisible" Russia.

The author's aesthetic conceptions force the reader to draw moral and political conclusions. Such is the nature of true art.

It is quite another matter when the oafish officer calls on the musicians to play the *Internationale*.

"And in the hush that had fallen on the yard, in the sweltering heat of noonday, the protesting trumpet blasts of the *Internationale* suddenly rang like a call to battle in majestic unison.

"The captain stood with his feet apart, lowering like a bull at a fence. He stood and listened. His muscular neck and the bluish whites of his half-closed eyes became infused with blood.

"It was too much for him.

"'Stop!' he roared frantically.

"The band broke off as one man. Only a French horn was a moment late and its passionate strangled blast hung in the torrid air.

"The musicians licked their parched lips and wiped them with their sleeves and dirty palms. Their faces were tired and listless. Only one dusty cheek bore the trace of a tear" (4, 72).

This small dramatic episode packs far-reaching implications: two anthems, two worlds, two social orders.

While the "wailing mournful sounds" of the tsarist anthem rise "*solitarily* over the *spacious* merchant's yard", and every detail in the description evokes a feeling of protest and suggests the weakness, loneliness and impending doom of the supporters of the old order, the *Internationale* rings majestically and triumphantly, and the whole description is in quite a different style, heroic and enthusiastic. The strains of the *Internationale* are "like a call to battle" ringing out "in the hush that had fallen on the yard, in the sweltering heat of noonday". The "majestic unison" of the "*protesting trumpet blasts*" is like the triumphant march of the armies of the Revolution amid the smoke of battle, like an affirmation of the power of the people, which finally overcomes all its enemies.

The description harmoniously combines epic grandeur with warm humanity. Sholokhov does not overlook "the lesser actors" on the stage of history. Although we are not told directly what the musicians felt as they played the *Internationale* surrounded by enemies—"their faces were tired and listless" is all we are told—the "trace of a tear" on "one dusty cheek" and the "passionate strangled blast" of the French horn are enough to communicate the dramatic tension and indicate their true feelings.

The situation may be a tragic one but the feeling that predominates in the passage is one of joy and the belief that in spite of temporary set-backs and defeats the revolutionary cause will triumph in the end, that victory belongs to it by right from the outset.

Sholokhov's aesthetic tenet that the people are the sole bearers of beauty and heroism, runs through every scene of "And Quiet Flows the Don", uniting the most disparate elements into a compound whole.

Sholokhov's passionate interest in life in all its facets is apparent throughout the novel. He looks into the ferment and picks out everything that comes to view: the disciplined revolutionary cohorts, strong in their awareness of their aim; some tragic figures who are tortured by doubt and indecision; the staunch defenders of the old order, blinded with hatred for the new; and here and there people who have apparently left no mark at all on the course of events....

This *humanity*, this desire to see and understand everything, is the hall-mark of truly great art.

Incidental characters streak across the vast canvas of the epic like falling stars, gleaming for an instant and then disappearing without trace—or so it seems, for a human life always leaves something behind. Sholokhov is a truly great humanist writer in that he never disregards even what may seem insignificant at first sight.

One such character is Maxim Gryaznov, the Veshenskaya horse-thief whose life is described in passing. Caught up in the whirlwind of the Revolution, he found himself in a Red Army unit. He procured a horse for himself—an amazingly swift horse, admired and envied by all. And then the horse was killed, and so was Gryaznov himself, now one of Bunchuk's machine-gun crew.

The author inserts the following brief epitaph: "Maxim Gryaznov, Tatarsky Cossack, former horse-stealer and of late a drunkard, had departed this life."

There is no mistaking the fact that Sholokhov's sober words make one stop and ponder over this seemingly futile life that has been so suddenly cut off. After all this was a *human* life.

Sholokhov's wise, humane gaze penetrates all the complexities of life. We feel his warm sympathy throughout the novel.

Critics have often dwelt at some length on the young widow in the last part of the novel, and we have already mentioned how she serves to show us the new war-weary Grigory returning to his native village. But Sholokhov does not go in for purely "auxiliary" characters, that is, they are never there merely because they serve a purpose, and here too the writer's loving, wise heart reveals a hidden drama, of which the character herself is not aware, a life broken by the war.

At the very beginning of the description the author stresses the dissonance between the woman's youth and beauty and the marks the unclean life she leads have left on her appearance.

"She was certainly a very good-looking woman, and well built. Her massive breasts, out of proportion to her height, rather spoilt her figure, while a *slanting scar* on her round chin gave her face *a hard-boiled look and seemed to age* her ruddily brown face, which around the bridge of her nose was sprinkled with golden freckles as fine as millet seed" (4, 493-494; author's italics).

Returning home in a quiet, sad mood, fed up with the war and longing to get down to work, to live with his children and Aksinya, and paying more attention than usual to the world around him, Grigory helps us penetrate the young broken life behind this outward appearance.

Her husband had been killed. "We only spent a month together, and then he was taken off into the army. I manage somehow without him. It's easier now young Cossacks have come back to the village, but before that it was hard.... So now you know, soldier! That's my life!" (4, 496).

Her calculated coquetry, her coarseness and cynicism, her wasted youth and unshed tears, everything about her luckless life which is all there before us in this brief scene is too much part of the tempestuous times she is living through for us to judge her harshly.

"Poor kid!... Life has done a lot to you in twenty years," Grigory says commiseratingly, and we feel that this is Sholokhov speaking (4, 501).

Sholokhov's breadth of vision and his ability to penetrate life's hidden dramas and passions is one of the most significant features of his talent.

Behind all the great momentous events lie so many bitter, everyday dramas, like the seemingly quite unremarkable story of the young widow.

It would be a long job to count up exactly how many characters there are in *And Quiet Flows the Don*, and I don't intend to try, but there are somewhere in the region of eight hundred. That every one of them, however brief its appearance, is a definite individual speaks of the author's remarkable ability to observe the essential in a character and capture it in a few short strokes.

The incidental characters that crop up all the time, either in the orbit of the heroes' entourage or independently, give the novel that authenticity and completeness as a picture of life which is an essential feature of realism.

The colourful world that swarms with life on the pages of Sholokhov's novels is as real as life itself, and the writer's talent is as inexhaustible as his material.

A "cheery Cossack" makes a brief appearance, just a couple of pages, at the beginning of book four. He awakes Aksinya, who has fallen asleep in tears under a full-flowering bush of hawthorn, and tries to persuade her "to have a spot of sin". There is an abrupt transition from the preceding scene with its lyrical mood and tragic undertones (Aksinya contemplating a lily of the valley and recalling her "long life so meagre in happiness", as if she has a premonition that her end is near) to this prosaic episode, this cynical display of raw passion. But life is full of such transitions, and the strength of true art lies in the fact that it recognises them and reproduces them. As the involuntary object of the Cossack's pressing attention Aksinya reveals the purity and strength of her love for Grigory. Shortly before she had come to visit Stepan, her unloved husband, at the front and had suffered bitter humiliation. Yet although she had "come back" to her husband, she all the time thought of Grigory, her one and only true love.

Despite all the compromises Aksinya was forced to make, she was rarely immoral in her behaviour, as was, for example, the dissolute Darya. Aksinya's compromises were forced upon her, that was her drama. There was no leading her into a casual "spot of sin", as the rather coarse scene with the Cossack in the forest shows. This episode tells us a lot about Aksinya, and at the same time purges her, so to speak, of her humiliating meeting with Stepan.

When she says: "I'm the wife of Grigory Melekhov!" it is not purely a matter of self-defence. Her words are a cri-du-cœur expressing the faith and hope of her hard, mixed-up life.

This apparently incidental episode serves to show the reader the pure, poetic side of Aksinya's soul. It is also a particularly good example of Sholokhov's concise character-drawing.

The Cossack makes an extremely brief appearance. "Beside her stood a young white-moustached and white-toothed Cossack, holding his saddled, white-nosed horse by the rein. He was smiling broadly, shrugging his shoulders and tapping his foot, and in a rather hoarse but pleasant tenor voice singing the words of a merry song" (4, 19).

There is a playfulness that only a writer sure of his talent permits himself in "*white*-nosed horse" and "*white*-moustached and *white*-toothed Cossack". This insistence on "white" fits the picture of the merry, roguish young Cossack perfectly and at the same time links him and his horse in our minds. An inexperienced writer would hardly have been able to refrain from telling us more about the appearance of the Cossack and his horse. Yet if one tries elaborating on the description, referring to the horse's coat or going on to describe the Cossack further, one will realise immediately that this merely encumbers the narrative and spoils the whole picture by dividing the reader's attention. The Cossack and his horse would naturally appear to the awaking Aksinya as a single striking vision.

On the other hand to write that he stood "holding his saddled ... horse by the rein" would be insufficient, for a truly artistic description must contain some detail, however slight, to set the reader's imagination going. The horse's white nose is just such a detail, creating as it does the illusion of a complete impression. Besides, Aksinya naturally saw the Cossack and the horse's head beside him first of all and the horse's white nose was naturally immediately associated in her mind with the "cheery Cossack's" broad smile, white moustache and white teeth.

Thus the reader assimilates the new character without any effort, and his knowledge of human nature and the times is the richer for this glimpse of a man with his particular expression and mood.

And Quiet Flows the Don is a battlefield where a mighty battle of ideas is being waged. Some of these ideas are rooted in the old society which is being destroyed, others are the young shoots of the new world which is being born, but behind them all stand the classes, social groups, people.

As a man sincerely concerned for the future, Sholokhov tries to show the power of ideas to which he is inimical and which could lead certain sections of society astray and wreck the life of individuals. It would have been a pure distortion of reality to try and simplify what really happened, drawing the veil of silence over unpleasant or undesirable things that actually occurred.

The dramatic tension of the novel lies in the fact that it tells of the fortunes of the people, of human life. It is sufficient to remember the merciless truth with which Grigory Melekhov's life is presented.

By bringing Grigory into contact with representatives of the different camps, Sholokhov is able to show the universal significance, the humanistic strength and beauty of Communist ideas, and the poverty and narrowness of those egoistic private-ownership views which blinded Grigory.

Podtyolkov, a simple, uneducated Cossack like Grigory Melekhov, but raised by the Revolution to the post of chairman of the Don Council of People's Commissars, is awaiting execution after being taken prisoner by the White Cossacks. Barefooted and half-naked as he is, he speaks to them before his death. His speech is a model of revolutionary humanism. It is full of heroic faith and love for mankind, even for those who have lost their way. His comrades are killed before his eyes, but in the last few minutes he has left on earth he turns to the deluded White Cossacks. He is unbroken, and clings to his convictions even in the face of death. "...They heard Podtyolkov's voice raised passionately. Surrounded by old men and front-line men, he was shouting:

"'You're blind ... ignorant! The officers have tricked you, they've forced you to kill your blood brothers. Do you think it will end with our death? No! Today you are on top, but tomorrow it will be your turn to be shot. The rule of the Soviets will be established all over Russia. Remember my words! You are shedding the blood of others in vain! You're a lot of fools.

"'...On behalf of the toiling people, in their interests we have struggled against the rats of generals, not sparing our lives. And now we are perishing at your hands! But we do not curse you! You have been bitterly deceived. The revolutionary government will come, and you will realise on whose side was the truth. You have laid the finest sons of the quiet Don in that pit....'" (2, 494-496).

Podtyolkov's prophecy was to come true. After two years of bitter fighting, "the revolutionary government came" and the Cossacks did indeed realise "on whose side was the truth".

In *And Quiet Flows the Don* Sholokhov shows *the triumph of Communist ideas, their acceptance by the people*. It would be difficult to find anything that sums up the main idea that runs through the novel better than Gorky's words: "The truth essential to life has always triumphed."*

* Maxim Gorky, *Collected Works*, Vol. 24, p. 297.

Chapter Four
DECLINE AND FALL OF THE MELEKHOV FAMILY. ETHIC AND AESTHETIC ASPECTS

1

The lives of the heroes of *And Quiet Flows the Don* are determined by the dramatic events of the age of the Revolution and Civil War.

Mikhail Koshevoi, Ivan Alexeyevich Kotlyarov and many others took an active part in the struggle for a new life where poverty would be abolished and there would be fair shares for all. Kotlyarov bravely faced death at the hands of the deluded Cossacks in his own village, while Koshevoi returned to Tatarsky some years later to take part in building the new life.

The Korshunovs and the Listnitskys took up arms in defence of their privileges. Miron Korshunov was shot for inciting the people against the Soviet government, while Yevgeny Listnitsky, already a broken man after the war against the toiling people, could not take the news of his wife's infidelity and shot himself.

Grigory Melekhov wavered between the two camps, and his part in the struggle against the people led him to an ignominious end. Natalya and Aksinya who had linked their fates with that of this "unfortunate man" both perished, and the whole strong Melekhov family was gradually destroyed before our very eyes.

The life of the people changed course sharply and headed off along the new untrodden path. Of the whole Melekhov family only Dunya was to set out on this road with little Mishatka, Grigory's son, and Mikhail Koshevoi.

The idea of historical necessity underlies the whole structure and composition of *And Quiet Flows the Don*. The onward march of history and the inevitable triumph of the Revolution finds artistic expression in the heroes' lives. The revolutionary struggle determines both the events and the characters' lives. Sholokhov presents the relationship between the individual and the people, and man and his age in all its complexity.

The story of the Melekhov family is one of the most important of the several plots in the novel, which opens with an account of the family and closes with the scene of Grigory's return to the empty Melekhov house.

The inevitable doom of the old order—one of the main ideas behind the novel—is expressed with remarkable dramatic power through the disintegration and destruction of this family of peasant toilers who clung assiduously to the past.

An aura of prosperity hung over the Melekhov household. The firm hand of the thrifty Pantelei Prokofyevich made itself felt in everything.

The hot-tempered head of the family would stand for no nonsense and was quick to take stern measures in cases of disobedience or argument even. He brings his crutch down on Grigory's back, uses his fists on his long-suffering wife and whips Darya with leather reins when she tries to "replace" her husband in his absence. His will was law in the family. Such was the age-old custom, encouraged by the church teaching of obedience to one's elders. The Cossack paterfamilias was absolute ruler in his household.

Grigory married Natalya purely on his father's orders, and thus began the protracted family drama, from which Grigory, Natalya, Aksinya and Stepan were to suffer greatly, and which was to give Pantelei Prokofyevich many a grey hair and Ilyinichna many a premature wrinkle.

The discontent with the existing order among the poorer Cossacks in the village, and their revolutionary conversations in Stockman's lodgings; Grigory's departure from his home to go into service on the Listnitsky estate; Aksinya's courageous revolt against the slavish position of women; all this bears witness to the deep contradictions inherent in the old way of life, and to the approach of the revolutionary storm.

For Pantelei Prokofyevich the existing order was consecrated by time and custom. He did all he could to get Grigory to return to his lawful wife, trying to appeal to Aksinya's conscience and threatening his son with all kinds of punishment. The village considered that Grigory had smeared the family name, and for Pantelei Prokofyevich what the village thought was law. He bore this misfortune heavily, and when Grigory returned to the fold crossed himself and wept for joy.

The old man speaks with tremendous respect of the tsar and the generals. Everything the counter-revolutionary general Kaledin said at the village meeting was for him the incontrovertible truth. He is terribly proud of his two sons for having been promoted officers for their service at the front, and cannot refrain from ridiculous boasting of their merits. When Grigory returns home on leave he drives him right through the village before making for their street. "I saw my sons off to the war as rank-and-file Cossacks, and they fought their way to officers' rank. Don't you think I'm proud to drive my son through the village? Let them look and be jealous! It's balm for my heart, lad," Pantelei Prokofyevich declares artlessly (2, 343).

Pyotr took after his father in this respect. Cunning and rather dull, he was not averse to flattery and toadying to his superiors, and soon climbed the ranks during the war. With his officers' epaulets he felt he had attained the highest possible happiness. They seemed to open the way for him to a free and untrammelled life. He made it into the world of the oppressors and lords of life, but with the outbreak of the Revolution all his dreams went up in smoke in the mighty class conflict.

Unlike his brother, Pyotr was firmly for the old order. "I shan't stumble like you, Grigory.... You couldn't drag me to the Reds with a rope round my neck ... there's no sense in it, it's not in my line," he says to Grigory (3, 29).

Although the two brothers grew up in the same social conditions, their mentalities are very different. Sholokhov makes a profound analysis of both the social and personal motives of his heroes' actions.

Grigory is a searcher after the truth, with a strong sense of justice and awareness of his peasant class origins. He feels cramped in the stuffy atmosphere of the old world and suffocates under the added burden of the senseless, murderous war. He attaches little importance to ranks and medals. Many of the views instilled in him from childhood onwards undergo a radical change during the war and in the Revolution. As he says to the Socialist-Revolutionary Kaparin: "Ever since 1915, when I got my first sight of war, I've been thinking that God doesn't exist. Not at all! ...We front-line men have got rid of God, he's only for the women and old men now. Let them find comfort in him. There isn't any finger of God, and there can't be any monarchy" (4, 629). Again and again, in the most varied circumstances, Grigory's healthy toiler's feelings overcame his property views and prejudices.

Pyotr on the other hand was the man of property from head to foot. The Revolution shattered his dreams of leading a free officer's life. He felt it encroached on the Cossacks' privileges, on their land, and did not hesitate to take up arms against the Soviet government and the "muzhiks". During the Civil War he sends cartloads of booty home. "Pyotr's got a fine eye for the farm," Pantelei Prokofyevich says with unconcealed admiration in his voice. "He gave me clothing, a horse, sugar...." (3, 117). Unlike Grigory, who not only did not pillage himself, but forbade his subordinates to do so, Pyotr was quite unscrupulous in this matter.

Grigory never conceals his views; far from it, he voices them openly and forcefully. Pyotr on the other hand adapts himself to circumstances, biding his time. He has the same abiding hatred for the Soviet order as the kulak Ostrovnov in *Virgin Soil Upturned*. When the Cossacks of his regiment leave the front and rise against Krasnov, Pyotr goes with them. He worms himself into people's confidence, making them forget he had been an officer. But at the meeting in Veshenskaya when Red Army men take the floor, Pyotr cannot contain himself and, glaring at the Cossacks, mutters to himself in impotent rage: "Scum! Blasted peasants! Bastards!" (3, 143).

Pyotr's death at the hands of Koshevoi was the first hard blow that the Civil War brought the Melekhov family. From then on death was a frequent visitor at the Melekhovs' house.

We see the influence of the revolutionary events on the nature and mentality not only of such characters as Grigory Melekhov, Mikhail Koshevoi, Kotlyarov and so on, but of people set in their way of life like Pantelei Prokofyevich.

The lively, quick-tempered old man of the opening chapters ages before our very eyes. The war and his anxiety for his sons' lives, the false alarm about Grigory's death, all this left its mark on him. He began to go grey and "tears came too easily". The alternation of bitter woes and unexpected joys was too much for the old man and we see it telling on him.

At first a stern, dignified figure, Pantelei Prokofyevich becomes a fussy old chatterbox. Though no lover of braggarts himself, he really begins to crow when Grigory is awarded the Cross of St. George. Why, the whole village is talking of his son's exploits, and even Mokhov gives him a present for Grigory. "These are gifts to our hero. Sergei Platonovich read about his deeds in the papers and has sent him some sweets and tobacco.... Do you know, the tears came to his eyes," the old man boasted (1, 473-474).

Pantelei Prokofyevich's boastfulness is revealed time and again with an unfailing sense of humour in all sorts of situations. With deep psychological penetration Sholokhov shows that this new trait in the old man's character appeared when his life sharply changed for the worse. It was as if he took to bragging about his son so as to make up for the sorrows he had suffered, and which he knew might again descend on him at any moment. This is but one of the tragi-comic motifs which Sholokhov introduces in his portrayal of Pantelei Prokofyevich.

Pantelei Prokofyevich is very hostile to the Revolution. Like Pyotr, he condemns Grigory for "fraternising" with the Bolsheviks and joining with the "muzhiks". As a delegate to the Army Council, he votes for the election of General Krasnov, firmly believing that he is the man to defend the Don from the Bolsheviks. He takes advantage of the Civil War on the Don to enrich himself. "Why shouldn't you take from those who've gone over to the Reds? It's a sin not to take from them," he tells the angry Grigory (3, 117-118).

All his life Pantelei Prokofyevich had worked to get rich. To that end he spared neither himself nor his family. He seized whatever he could, wherever he could, for the home. But the Civil War swept through the village. First one side then the other was on top, and the government changed hands accordingly. More than once Pantelei

Prokofyevich had to hurriedly leave his home and hearth and "retreat", and each time he returned it was to see further destruction and damage.

Pantelei Prokofyevich took a grip of himself and set to repairing and restoring things, but he was fighting a losing battle. The tight-fisted old man who had formerly taught his family to go careful on the matches, and make do without a lamp in the evening ("kerosene is expensive"), ceased to worry about such things, as a form of self-defence to ward off suffering for his losses. He tried to depreciate, at least in his own eyes, all the property he had accumulated at the cost of so much toil. More and more frequently we find him making attempts to console himself which would be amusing if they were not so pathetic: "You know that pig was nothing but trouble..." (4, 289); "It wasn't much of a barn...." (4, 314). "Anything the old man had had to abandon was always no good at all, so he said. It was the way he had of consoling himself" (4, 301).

But material losses were only half Pantelei Prokofyevich's woes. His strong, united family disintegrated before his very eyes, and try as he may he could not preserve the strict old order in his household.

In his description of the changes in the Melekhov family Sholokhov shows how far-reaching the impact of the events of the Revolution was. The great storm affected the whole of the old order directly or indirectly. The bitter Civil War struggle disrupted the unity of the Melekhov family and brought about its destruction.

The first to break away was Dunya, who combined the Melekhov stubbornness and hot temper with great feminine charm and impetuosity. Yet when the situation required it, her Melekhov tenacity and obstinacy would come to the fore. She went against the whole family in her pure love for Mikhail Koshevoi. We can easily appreciate her great courage and the strength of her feelings if we remember that the rumour was circulating in the village, that Mikhail had killed her brother Pyotr, as indeed was the case. Dunya stands up for her right to love whosoever she chooses, and she is spared Aksinya's grief and suffering, for times had changed. The old order was collapsing and Dunya went forward to meet the new, her head held high, undismayed by Grigory's fearful threats or her father's angry cries. "You can't command the heart," she said quietly but resolutely (4, 92). Knowing that she is in the right, and aware of her own strength, Dunya does not argue but shuts herself up in her own shell, loses all interest in household affairs and breaks away from the family.

Natalya is estranged from her in-laws in her deep suffering when she learns of Grigory's new liaison with Aksinya; and after Pyotr's death Darya seeks every opportunity to leave the house and do as she pleases.

Pantelei Prokofyevich could not fail no notice what was going on, but there was nothing he could do. The old order was crumbling and his authority as master of the household and head of the family had been blown to the four winds.

Pantelei Prokofyevich is a changed man. He still chides and scolds, but he is quite aware that his authority has gone. Darya is always answering him back, Dunya is sullenly disobedient, and Ilyinichna contradicts him more and more frequently. His temper, which once terrorised the whole household, is no longer to be taken seriously and often provokes laughter.

A rich vein of sparkling humour runs through the whole novel and brightens the darkness of the tragic concluding chapters. There are harmless and spicy jokes, funny stories, songs, and tales of yore that warm the listeners' hearts with joy and laughter, and malicious jibes. Sholokhov captures the healthy humour and talent of the people, their ability to spot what is funny in life and derive amusement from it. Indeed laughter and tears, or joys and sorrows, are not far removed from one another in life, and laughter and joking often help people overcome their hardships and woes. During one of the hardest periods in his life Grigory thinks: "It's a good thing we Cossacks like our fun. Jokes come to stay with us more often than sorrow. By God, if life were all serious I'd have hanged myself long ago" (4, 598).

Sholokhov does not introduce jokes and humorous characters and situations merely to relieve the tension. The humour stands in its own right no less than the drama. Sholokhov is trying to present a complete picture of an age, and humour is as much a part of life as tragedy.

Pantelei Prokofyevich is a truly tragi-comic figure,

due to the discrepancy between what he was and still wants to appear and what he has become. Formerly thrifty to the point of stinginess, he got into the habit of depreciating things to console himself for their loss. Whereas he had formally tyrannised the family with his violent temper, his outbursts are later impotent squawks of rage that no longer intimidate anybody, and are often even laughable.

One such instance is a scene where all the family are gathered at the dinner table. Pantelei Prokofyevich has returned to the village after the Reds have retreated and Grigory is home on leave. Grigory angrily tells Dunya that from that day on she is to forget even to think about Mikhail Koshevoi and she quietly but resolutely replies that "you can't command the heart". At this Pantelei Prokofyevich flies into a rage with his disobedient daughter and roars: "Hold you tongue, you daughter of a bitch! Or I'll give you such a hiding that you won't have a hair left on your head! You hussy! I'll go this minute and get some reins...."

The ensuing row, which promised to be like one of the violent family scenes which were such a common occurrence in life before the Revolution, turns out to be highly comical due to the way Darya turns the argument. With an arch, apparently meek way of making the most biting replies to her father-in-law's threats, Darya shows that it is no longer so easy as it used to be to bring a disobedient daughter to heel.

"'But, Father, we haven't got one pair of reins left. They've all been taken,' Darya interrupted him, a meek look on her face.

"Pantelei shot a furious glance at her and, not lowering his voice, continued to unburden his soul:

"'I'll get a saddle-girth, and I'll drive all the devils out of you....'

"'The Reds have taken the saddle-girths too,' Darya intervened, this time in a louder voice, but still gazing at her father-in-law with innocent eyes.

"But that was too much for Pantelei. He stared at his daughter-in-law for a second, turning livid with dumb fury, his mouth silently gaping (at that moment he looked like a pike hauled out of the water), then hoarsely shouted:

"'Shut up, damn you; may a hundred devils take you! They won't let me say a word. What do you call this?'" (4, 92-93).

Darya is not afraid of the old man's wrath; what is more, she engages him in a battle of words and makes fun of him, only maintaining an outward semblance of respect. There is a touch of irony in the word "meek", for this "meek look" hides feelings which are far from submissive. They come more into their own in her next reply which she makes "in a louder voice", challengingly, gazing at her father-in-law "with innocent eyes", which are in fact as innocent as her look is meek. Darya wins this round over her father-in-law. The old man's confusion and powerlessness are evident in his hoarse cry, "shut up, damn you" and his plaintive "what do you call this?"

Sholokhov builds up the humour to an outburst of laughter in a masterly fashion.

Pantelei Prokofyevich flies off the handle and again unleashes his fury on Dunya. "...Killing will be too good for you. A fine wooer she's found! A gallows-bird has captured her soul! Is that what you call a man? Do you think I'd have such a Judas as my son-in-law? If he ever falls into my hands, I'll put him to death myself. Only give me one more back-answer, and I'll get a willow switch and I'll give you...." At this point Ilyinichna staggers her husband by saying—either in all innocence or to stop the shouting:

"'Why, you could look all over our yard with a light in broad daylight and you'd never find a willow switch.... You can scrape out every corner of the yard and you won't find so much as a twig to light a fire with. That's what we've come to!'

"Even in this artless remark Pantelei detected an evil intent. He looked fixedly at the old woman, then jumped up like a madman and ran out into the yard.

"Grigory threw down his spoon, covered his face with his hand-towel, and shook with soundless laughter.... They all laughed except Dunya. Now a more cheery note reigned at the table" (4, 93).

Only recently it would have been an unheard-of occurrence for the head of the family to be made look so ridiculous in his own house. The humour here hinges on the fact that Pantelei Prokofyevich's behaviour is anachronistic, and in laughing at him we are laughing at the old, patriarchal life which not so long ago had caused so much pain and suffering (it should suffice to remember how Pantelei Prokofyevich forced Grigory to marry Natalya, and how he had tyrannised Ilyinichna in her younger days) and the apparently unshakeable structure of which had altered radically under the impact of the Revolution.

At the same time the author uses this comic scene to show the damage and losses the Melekhov family have suffered. Indeed, they no longer had reins or saddle-girths, or even willow switches in their yard.

With consummate skill Sholokhov uses local colour to build up a comic situation with far-reaching implications.

In the scene in question the humour arises from the fact that the apparent reason why Pantelei Prokofyevich is powerless to carry out his threats is that his usual means of inflicting punishment have been destroyed or carried off. The hot-tempered old man is not used to being thwarted and his fury mounts in the face of these material obstacles. When Darya answers him back the first time he shoots a furious glance at her and continues, but when she answers him back again he is beside himself. "He stared at his daughter-in-law for a second, turning livid with dumb fury, his mouth silently gaping...." Sholokhov compares him to a pike that has just been hauled out of the water and it would surely be impossible to find a better image to describe the old man's expression at that moment as he sits stunned and powerless, quivering with fury. This portrait detail greatly heightens the humour of the situation. Ilyinichna's seemingly casual remark about it being impossible to find a willow switch "with a light in broad daylight" is the last straw for Pantelei Prokofyevich and he runs berserk. He "looks fixedly at the old woman" and jumps up "like a madman". Sholokhov deliberately exaggerates in describing Pantelei Prokofyevich in this scene in order to make his anger humourous.

This whole comic scene, where Pantelei Prokofyevich's rage is out of all proportion to the immediate cause, is the author's way of showing the true reason for the old man's powerlessness, which is the fact that he can no longer expect to be the absolute master in his own house he had been in the past.

Pantelei Prokofyevich is at the same time a comic and a tragic figure and leaves one with very mixed feelings.

Old as he was, he was called up to fight when the Whites ordered general mobilisation. Although he had often upbraided the Cossacks for not wanting to fight, and to judge from his talk he was the bravest of the brave, he showed no inclination to back up his words with action and sought every opportunity to pop home from the front. "I'm no youngster to go marching forty versts a day, to dig trenches, to attack at the double, and to crawl along the ground, ducking the bullets. The devil himself couldn't do it!" he complains to Ilyinichna when he returns home lice-ridden and ravenous. When it comes to actually fighting Pantelei Prokofyevich disassociates himself from those he himself has always said to be defending the Cossack rights against the Red Army. He deserts and hides up at home and is only saved from a shameful flogging at the hands of a Kalmyk punitive detachment bacause his son is an officer. "Well, I'll hide myself a lot better this time!" he thinks as he makes his way home (4, 305).

Pantelei Prokofyevich was a firm supporter of the Cossack rights and the old order until it came to doing something. He is comical because his deeds are so far from corresponding to his words.

"Don't you worry about the war: our men will get the better of those peasants," Pantelei Prokofyevich says blithely with a bellicose air. Without batting an eyelid he declares: "If it wasn't for this trouble with my leg I'd show them how to fight the enemy!" (4, 319). And this is the same Pantelei Prokofyevich who ran away from the advancing Red Army so fast that he left a new coat behind in his haste, and later made sure he didn't have to go back by getting a false medical certificate! He boasts about Grigory, not forgetting to put a good word or two in for yours truly in doing so. "And how could he help being a hero when you know whose son he is? When I was young I, too—I say it without boasting—I was no worse than him! My leg prevents me or I wouldn't let him better me even now!" (4, 317).

The old man has become a pitiful figure with his petty vanity. It is as though forced cheerfulness and empty boasting are part of an attempt to ward off the hard blows of fate.

Fate certainly did not spare the Melekhovs. In a very short time the formerly happy, bustling household was reduced to half its number. Natalya was the next to go after Pyotr. After Grigory's continued infidelity she could not bear to have his child, and died after ridding herself of it. Pantelei Prokofyevich bitterly mourned her death, for he had loved her as his own daughter. When he heard there was no hope, he went off by himself and wept aloud. Less than a month later the scent of incense and cornflowers filled the Melekhov house once more. The gay, dissolute Darya drowned herself in the Don.

Pantelei Prokofyevich shuddered at the thought of the dangers Grigory was exposed to at the front. The thought of further sorrows after all he has had to bear, was too much for him. The old man became permanently sunk in gloomy thoughts and was haunted by the fear of further misfortunes. Sholokhov gives a subtle, penetrating analysis of the old man's state of mind. On hearing the news that Christonya and Anikushka have been brought home dead, he heads straight for the protective silence of the autumnal forest. "In one year death had struck down so many dear ones and friends that at the very thought he was oppressed, and all the world faded and seemed to be enveloped in a film of black" (4, 323).

Pantelei Prokofyevich's perplexity at all that was going on, at the great events which were disrupting the whole old order of life that he was accustomed to, and his weariness from the hardships and losses he had suffered, left their tragic mark on him. His thoughts turn towards death. Everything reminded him of it: "...The falling leaves, and the geese flying and crying through the azure sky, and the drooping withered grass...." (4, 325). When they were burying Darya he picked a spot in the cemetery for himself. But the old man was fated to die far away from his native parts. When the Red Army drove the Whites and the interventionists out of the Don steppes Pantelei Prokofyevich retreated with them. He died of typhus in the Kuban country and was buried there, far from home, by his son and Prokhor Zykov.

Only Ilyinichna, Dunya and Grigory's children remained in the Melekhov house.

Ilyinichna is moved forward to become one of the most important figures in the last part of the novel. This sad figure of a peasant mother is among the truly immortal characters of Russian and indeed world literature.

In the early part of the book Ilyinichna appears as little more than a foil for Grigory and Pantelei Prokofyevich. The young Sholokhov seems to have been more interested in clear-cut, striking characters, and frequently seized upon unusual, arresting details in his character-drawing. Thus, for example, throughout book one Sholokhov stresses the fact that the hawk-nosed, oriental-looking Pantelei Prokofyevich wore an ear-ring in his ear. When the family receive the news that Grigory has been killed in action it is the old man's grief, not Ilyinichna's, that is described, as if the author feels that deep sorrow can be represented more dramatically through the sufferings of a broken man. Ilyinichna's sufferings are alluded to in passing and she then fades into the background.

Ilyinichna is the indefatigable, bustling housewife, always inconspicuously occupied with the household chores, and taking little part in events. Pantelei Prokofyevich directs all the family affairs. He might feel it necessary to discuss important matters with his wife, but he nonetheless usually acted as he himself thought fit. When Pantelei Prokofyevich drove Grigory from the house, Ilyinichna could do nothing to influence him.

Yet later in the book this fine, courageous woman comes into her own. We learn most of what we know of her past from part seven, where the author penetrates the depths of her mother's heart, and reveals the rich, heart-warming inner world that is concealed there and which so rarely shows on the surface.

The great humanity of Sholokhov's art is especially apparent in the scenes where Ilyinichna mourns the death of her son Pyotr, or is full of sadness and longing for Grigory and in the descriptions of Pantelei Prokofyevich's sufferings. One of the finest features of this peasant couple's nature is their love for their kinfolk. In portraying the better side of the toilers' nature Sholokhov continues Gorky's theme of exalting labour. He shows how all that was finest in such characters as Pantelei Prokofyevich, Ilyinichna, Natalya, Grigory and Aksinya sprang from working peasant life.

Sholokhov referred to Ilyinichna as a hard-working woman and indeed she had worked all her life with no respite. She was the first in the family to get up and the last to go to bed. Not only did she have all household chores and the children to see to, but she had to work hard in the kitchen garden and in the fields as well. No wonder her hands were coarse and callous.

Ilyinichna's great moral strength and fortitude are stressed again and again. Just how hard her life had been we can see from the following passage, where she is trying to console Natalya. Laying her "work-worn hand" on her daughter-in-law's head, she says: "You're terribly touchy, you youngsters, God's truth! The least thing and you go into a frenzy. If you'd lived as I had to live when I was young, then what would you have done? All his life Grisha hasn't raised a finger against you, and still you're not satisfied, but you must go and carry on like that. You want to throw him over, and you go off into a fit, and I don't know what you didn't do. You even brought God into your dirty business.... Well, tell me, you poor thing, is that good? But when I was young my game-legged devil used to thrash me almost to death, and that all for nothing, all over nothing. I hadn't done the least thing to deserve it. He himself behaved abominably, but he worked his temper off on me. He used to come home at dawn, and I would scream and cry and fling reproaches at him, and he would give his fist its sweet will.... For a month I'd go about as blue as iron all over, and yet I lived through it and brought up the children, and not once did I try to clear out" (4, 219).

This account gives us a clear picture of the cheerless life that was a woman's lot in a Cossack village before the Revolution. Ilyinichna was not complaining when she described her life to Natalya, she was merely trying to protect her family and Grigory's children by appealing to her daughter-in-law to face things with courage and fortitude.

Sholokhov refers to Ilyinichna as a "wise and brave old woman" and again later as "the proud and brave-hearted Ilyinichna", thereby expressing the great inner beauty and grandeur the old woman revealed throughout her hard life, her fortitude in the face of so many troubles and woes.

Although Ilyinichna did not understand the events that were taking place before her very eyes during the Revolution and the Civil War, thanks to her experience and maternal instincts she often showed more perspicacity, wisdom and humanity than Grigory or her husband.

When Ilyinichna hears how Grigory has cut down a number of sailors in battle, she makes no bones about upbraiding her son, and scolds him for his ruthlessness. She backs up Pantelei Prokofyevich when he drives Mitka Korshunov from the yard, having learned how Mitka had brutally put the Koshevoi family to death because Mikhail was a Communist. "Why, at that rate the Reds might have sabred me and you, and Mishatka and Polyushka, for Grisha's doings. But they didn't; they had mercy," she declares indignantly to Natalya (4, 151). Dunya tells how when Darya shot the captured Communist Kotlyarov, Ilyinichna "was afraid to stay the night in the same house with her, so she went to sleep with the neighbours". All these episodes testify to Ilyinichna's profound humanity.

The war did not spare the old woman. Death snatched away her husband, her son, and many of her kinfolk and dear ones. "...She lived on, broken by suffering, grown old and pitiful. Much sorrow had she known in her life, perhaps too much" (4, 453). Sholokhov is unable to repress his sympathy and love for Ilyinichna, as is evident from his sudden intrusion with "perhaps too much". The motif of suffering becomes more and more powerful in the description of the last days of Ilyinichna's life.

Ilyinichna awaits the return of her youngest with great anxiety. In a near-frenzy of grief she says to Aksinya: "It can't be that I've been robbed of my last son. God has no cause to punish me.... I've only got a little time left to live now—only a very little time left to live, and my heart's had enough sorrow without that! Grisha's alive! My heart has had no sign, and so my darling's alive!" (4, 422).

These words convey many subtle shades of feeling. Ilyinichna's maternal heart refuses to believe that Grigory is dead. "But I don't believe it!" she exclaims. "It can't be.... God has no cause to punish me." This angry exclamation, emphasised by the repeated negations, gives way to deep sorrow, a premonition of her own approaching death. "I've only got a little time left to live now—only a very little time left to live...."

The great emotion behind Ilyinichna's words is conveyed with particular force by the rhythmic repetition which is a feature of the oral folk poetry tradition. "Grisha's alive!" is like an invocation, and her last words—"my darling's alive!"—are a cry of love and faith straight from the depths of her mother's heart.

The means Sholokhov employs to obtain this tremendously strong impact are really very simple. He uses few words and well-worn ones at that, but he chooses and organises them in such a way that the reader is deeply moved. The exclamation and repetition create language rich in intonation which perfectly expresses the sequence of emotions, from angry denial and sad meditation to the surge of feeling which she gives vent to in her defiant outburst.

Grigory was constantly on the old woman's mind, to the exclusion of all else, during her last days. "I've grown old.... And my heart is aching after Grisha," she tells Dunya. "It's aching so much that nothing pleases me, and it hurts my eyes to look out on the world" (4, 438).

There can be but few examples in world literature of subtle shades of maternal feelings being expressed with such moving power, warmth and understanding.

When Ilyinichna learned that Grigory was alive and well, she began to await his return with the utmost impatience. She imagined he might come home at any moment, and every day she cooked extra food, and after dinner always set a pot of cabbage soup on the stove, so that there would be a hot meal ready for him. Whenever Mishatka was disobedient she told him just to wait until his father came home and he'd be for it. She had Prokhor Zykov come along and have a smoke in the house, thinking: "When Grisha comes back from service, the place will smell as it should when a Cossack lives in it!" (4, 436).

She mentions Grigory at every possible opportunity. She gets out his old coat and peaked cap and hangs them on a nail in the kitchen. "You see them as you come in from the yard and it makes things seem more homelike — as though he was back again," she tells Dunya, with a guilty, rather pitiful smile (4, 437).

These touching attentions dictated by deep maternal love are infinitely moving. Ilyinichna is overjoyed by a brief letter from Grigory in which he promises to try and get home on leave in the autumn. A new light shines in her old eyes. The artless old woman tells Dunya with unconcealed pride: "...My younger son has remembered his mother! The way he writes! He calls me by my full name too! I bow low to you, dear Mother, he writes, and also to the dear children.... (4, 455). She would drop into Aksinya's of an evening and ask her to read the letter over again, for Ilyinichna had made peace with her neighbour: their love for Grigory had united them. Aksinya would sit in the dark and recite all the contents of the letter, which she knew by heart.

...In a farm-house, in a war-ravaged village in the depths of the Don country, two women sit in the dark. One of them is an old woman, sitting with her toil-worn hands folded in her lap, listening to the words uttered by the other, the mournful but still beautiful Aksinya. Their thoughts, their heartache and love, are turned far, far away, to where Grigory is fighting the White Poles in the Crimean steppe, and the question uppermost in their minds is, when will he return, if he returns at all?

Sholokhov narrates Ilyinichna's drama with wise simplicity. There is a moving grandeur about the whole section of the book that deals with her tragic last days. Her strength fails her and she falls ill, and still Grigory has not returned. Gathering what remains of her strength, she rises one evening and crosses the yard to the threshing-floor.

"Ilyinichna was supporting herself with both hands on the fencing, gazing out into the steppe to where a camp-fire lit by the mowers was glimmering like a distant, inaccessible little star. Aksinya clearly saw the old woman's swollen face lit up by the bluish light of the moon, and the grey strand of hair breaking from under her black shawl.

"Ilyinichna stood long gazing into the darkling steppe, then called quietly, as though he were standing quite close to her: 'Grisha dear! My darling boy!'

"She was silent for a moment, then in a different, low and husky voice, she said: 'Blood of my blood!'" (4, 460-461).

But Sholokhov does not concentrate on Ilyinichna's yearning for Grigory to the exclusion of all else: he reveals her feelings in the most varied circumstances.

On the very next day after his return to the village Mikhail Koshevoi calls on the Melekhovs to see Dunya. Ilyinichna greets him coldly. She has not forgotten that it was he who killed her Pyotr and Natalya's grandfather. She considers him a murderer and tells him so. She forbids Dunya to see him, but the girl loves him and refuses to comply with her mother's wishes, and Mikhail becomes a frequent visitor. He tries to be useful and does various men's jobs in the yard, and also makes a toy for Mishatka. He goes down with malaria, and when Ilyinichna sees the fever shaking him, the tough old woman is finally moved to pity. She tells little Mishatka to carry a blanket to him but then sees that Dunya is already looking after him. That evening she invites him to the supper table and, watching him furtively, realises how terribly thin he has become as a result of his illness. "The more Ilyinichna observed the 'murderer's' bowed figure and waxen face, the more she felt an inward discomfort, as though she were being torn apart. Suddenly an uninvited pity for this man whom she hated so much—that gripping motherly pity which subdues even strong women—awoke in Ilyinichna's heart. Unable to master this new feeling, she pushed a plateful of milk across to Mikhail and said:

"'Eat up, for God's sake! You're so thin it makes me sick to look at you.... A fine bridegroom you'd make!'" (4, 448-449).

Only a mother could feel such a burst of heartfelt pity for a man who had caused her so much grief. But though she might pity him she could not forgive him. He remained an outsider to her. She opposed his marriage with Dunya for a long time, and when she finally gave her daughter her blessing, added in a quivering voice: "Oh, your father ought to see you now.... Do you remember what he said about your groom? God knows how hard it is for me...." (4, 450).

Ilyinichna was making a weak, desperate bid to defend the crumbling edifice of the patriarchal family when she reproached Dunya for disregarding her dead father's wishes. But she had not the strength to prevent her daughter from going her own way.

Ilyinichna spends her last days alone and forsaken. Dunya and Mikhail, embarking on their new life together, are far too concerned with one another and the farm to pay her much attention. Sholokhov surpasses himself in his penetrating analysis of the thoughts and feelings of the old woman whose end is approaching, in the terse, powerful narrative with its bright lyric strain.

Ilyinichna lay alone for hours and all her life passed before her. "It was amazing how short and poor that life had turned out to be, and how much of it was oppressive and bitter, how much she had no wish to recall. For some reason, her memories and thoughts turned most of all to Grigory" (4, 458).

As soon as she thought of Grigory, Ilyinichna would be seized by a choking sensation which only served to hasten her death, yet she could not help yearning for her "young one".

Life was going on as usual outside and echoed in the old woman's heart, evoking all kinds of feelings and distant memories. Sholokhov introduces a wealth of subtle psychological motifs into Ilyinichna's last memories.

The sun was shining brightly outside and the grasshoppers were droning monotonously. As Ilyinichna listened to their incessant chirruping, she caught the scent of the sun-warmed grass and "for a moment she had a vision of the sun-scorched August steppe...". She saw herself young, well-grown and beautiful. It was harvest-time and she was hurrying from the field to feed her Grisha. She reached the encampment and took up the tiny, swarthy child who was crying with hunger. "'My darling, my little son! My beautiful one!... Your mother's famished you with hunger....' Still sobbing offendedly, the little Grisha sucked and bit painfully at the teat with his tiny gums. And beside her stood his young, black-moustached father, whetting a scythe. From under her dropping lashes she saw his smile and the bluish whites of his twinkling eyes. The heat made it difficult for her to breathe, the sweat streamed from her brow and tickled her cheeks, and the light faded, faded before her eyes...." (4, 459-460).

The excitement these recollections caused her was too much for her sick, old heart and she lay still, occasionally sinking into a coma, which was a blissful release from the attacks of choking that she was tormented by. Ilyinichna had recalled the happiest hours of her hard life that had been so poor in joys.

Ilyinichna passed away simply and solemnly as old people who have spent a long life of toil generally die. Death did not disfigure her stern and beautiful face.

3

Sholokhov's account of the Melekhov family drama throws light on all sorts of aspects of the life of the people. In the story of the Melekhovs we can see all that is good in man, which is rooted in a life of toil, and all that is ugly, engendered by private-property instincts.

Summing up the childhood and youth of Alexei Peshkov in *My Universities*, Gorky makes the following terse and wise remark: "...A man is made by the resistance he presents to his surroundings." This aesthetic criterion of Gorky's is a humanistic approval of the strong, active individual, who cannot reconcile himself to evil and sordidness, and wages a constant struggle for a better life.

Gorky's aesthetic discoveries, which reflected the laws of development of life itself, have become a permanent feature of Soviet literature, and with his *understanding of the value and significance of man*, Sholokhov is fundamentally a writer *in the Gorky tradition*.

The courageous fighters for the Revolution, for the transformation of the world, characters like the Communists Mikhail Koshevoi, Kotlyarov, Likhachov, and Podtyolkov, embody the best characteristics of the people. Grigory Melekhov, Aksinya, and Dunya have many fine and healthy qualities. They refuse to submit to force, and proudly and fearlessly uphold their human dignity, their right to give free rein to their feelings. The morality of the old world, with all its customs and unwritten laws, is too narrow for them.

Grigory Melekhov did not go as far as Mikhail Koshevoi in breaking with the patriarchal Cossack way of life. The Communist Koshevoi takes up arms to overthrow the hatefully smug and soulless old world, and consciously rejects class society as a whole. With Dunya Melekhova he fearlessly marches forward into the new world. Grigory Melekhov, on the other hand, broke with the past without accepting the future. He did not go as far as to completely renounce his class views and habits, and this was his tragedy, that which led him to suffer such trials and hardships in the Civil War, where he was to lose so many of his finer qualities, and was to cause the death of Aksinya who lived for this "unfortunate man".

Other characters, like Pyotr and Darya Melekhov, were able to adapt themselves to the existing order and gain advantage for themselves from it. Sholokhov shows how such acquiescence inevitably led to the loss of many wholesome qualities, that the triumph of the principle of private property was detrimental to the human personality. Pyotr has no scruples about pillaging during the war. With his dream of living in style, he reaches the rank of officer by fawning and flattery, wins medals without risking his life, and generally curries favour with his superiors. His wife Darya shared the common lot of women at the time, which was little better than that of a household slave, and she learned the art of clever, cynical deception to get what she wanted.

In Darya Sholokhov has created a vivid picture of a woman formed under the stifling influence of patriarchal life. The attractive, clothes-loving Darya passes before us on many occasions, with her "easy, swinging walk". She mocks both her dull husband and her short-tempered father-in-law. Darya is never at a loss for an excuse to avoid hard work, and Pantelei Prokofyevich is constantly warning Ilyinichna to see to it that she is not allowed to shirk. "Whip up that Darya. She's a lazy woman, and bad. She paints her face and blackens her brows...." (1, 172).

But it was not so easy to keep Darya in order. However vigilant her in-laws were, she always managed to give them the slip. The gay dissolute woman took pleasure and amusement in continual chance amorous adventures.

Darya's loss of decency leads to moral bankruptcy, cynicism and indifference. Her cynicism is sometimes directly described by the author, although more often than not it is implicit in her behaviour.

Sholokhov makes Darya's cynicism a characteristic feature of her moral nature by frequently referring to it: "she was thinking with her native cynicism" (4, 164), "with her customary cynical facetiousness she added...." (4, 181).

Darya was indifferent even towards her near ones. She recovered very quickly from the loss of Pyotr. "Pyotr's death had had the effect of spurring her on and, as soon as she had recovered from the blow, she had grown still more greedy of life, still more attentive to her appearance" (4, 91).

Through her usual thoughtlessness Darya did a great wrong to Natalya, who was always most amicable towards her. Aksinya asked Darya to tell Grigory to come to her, slipping her a ring for the service. "'Is it gold?' Darya inquired in a *practical* tone" (3, 426; author's italics), betraying her avidity for possessions. After examining the ring by the window, she said: "All right, I'll tell him. You can have him for all I care" (3, 426). The deep cynicism in Darya's words reveals her total indifference to what might happen in Grigory's family, and to Natalya in particular. For a ring she was prepared to deal a mortal blow to Natalya who had shared the same roof with her and eaten at the same table for so many years. When some time later she confesses everything to Natalya, she does so in order to gloat over the sufferings of this pure, loving wife.

Although Darya is strikingly handsome, her ugly nature is not infrequently reflected in her expressions, disfiguring her fine features. "Her pale cheeks, untouched by sunburn, reflected the hot glitter of her questing eyes, and in the wilful curl of her painted eyebrows and in the fold of her smiling lips lurked something challenging and impure" (4, 163). And again: "a firm row of small close-set teeth showed under the fine rim of her shrewish lips."

Sholokhov reveals the ugly side of Darya's nature with great subtlety. It is always lurking there behind her fine appearance, her careless gaiety and sharp tongue, and every now and then it comes to the surface either in her expressions or in her behaviour towards other people. Ilyinichna has no love for her, and Pantelei Prokofyevich is always cursing her. The strict, pure Natalya "always had a feeling of pity and distaste about Darya and her unclean amorous adventures" (4, 155). Aksinya says to Natalya: "Though you called me a strumpet, I'm not your Darya. In all my life I have never played about where such things are concerned" (4, 212).

Darya's boundless cynicism is particularly in evidence in the scene with the Communist prisoners. In order to "avenge" the death of her husband, to whom she had been unfaithful during his lifetime, let alone since, she calmly shoots down the defenceless Ivan Alexeyevich Kotlyarov, who was already terribly beaten up.

Grigory hears about it from Dunya, who with indignant tears in her voice tells him what "the wicked crow" has done. He strode across the yard and threw open the granary door. Darya was lying there, having drunk herself unconscious. "Never before had Grigory felt such a savage desire to use his sabre. For several seconds he stood over Darya, groaning and swaying, grinding his teeth, staring with invincible loathing and contempt at the body lying at his feet. Then he took a step forward and setting the iron-shod heel of his boot on her face, on her dark arching brows, he muttered hoarsely:

"'You poisonous snake!'

"Darya groaned drunkenly and muttered something. Grigory clutched his head in his hands and ran out into the yard" (4, 466).

One has only to remember Grigory's usual gentlemanly behaviour towards women to feel the full force of his contempt, anger and disgust at that moment. At the root of this outburst is the same healthy feeling that had made Dunya cry with indignation and Ilyinichna go to the neighbours so as not to have to sleep under the same roof as a murderess.

Darya finally had to pay for her dissipated life. She picked up a "filthy disease" as the result of one of her amorous adventures.

Under the weight of her sudden misfortune Darya reveals quite a new, unexpected side to her nature. She shows great strength and firmness of purpose in her decision to take her own life. She cannot bear the thought of going on disfigured by her disease, unable to live a normal life. "Who will want me in the state I am now? My beauty will fade, I shall go all withered, I shall rot alive.... And I don't want that!" (4, 179). Of course Darya is only thinking of herself as usual. She is afraid that when her beauty fades there will be no more pleasure for her. Yet there is a certain human pride one cannot help admiring in her refusal to resign herself to her fate.

Sholokhov's characters are always complex human beings with a rich and varied nature. They are neither wholly good nor wholly bad. Darya is no exception, although admittedly in her case her moving, human appeal only shows just before her death.

Sholokhov conveys Darya's pusillanimity through her attitude to nature. As if blinded by her own self, by her own attractiveness, she is generally incapable of perceiving the beauty of the surrounding world. Never once throughout the novel do we see her in contact with the world of nature, not once is she moved by a feeling of understanding or being a part of that beautiful kingdom, as Grigory, Aksinya and Natalya so often are—not once, that is, until shortly before her death.... "'Look at the life I've lived. I've been sort of blind; but as I was coming back from Veshenskaya along by the Don, and as I thought that soon I would have to leave all this, it was as though my eyes had been opened. I looked at the Don, and it was all rippling, and in the sunlight it was pure silver, and dancing so that it made my eyes smart to look at it. I turned all round and looked.... Lord, how beautiful it was! And yet I'd never noticed it before....' Darya smiled shamefacedly and was silent" (4, 180-181).

There is something sweet and childish in this shamefaced smile, and we have a glimpse of Darya as a girl running down to the river with her playmates, swimming out far ahead of the others, fighting with the boys.... Yet here she is telling Natalya of her bitter trouble, a broken woman who is "fed up with it all", and for whom "everybody's turned horrible".

Darya's heart aches as she looks back over her past. The gay, easy-going Darya, who had so often poured scorn on Natalya for her purity, for being faithful to her husband, now speaks with unconcealed envy of Natalya's love for "her man", and cannot repress a sigh when talking of herself: "But I've never happened to love anyone very much. I've loved as a dog loves, here, there and everywhere. I wish I could have my life over again, Imight live it different" (4, 187).

Darya parted with this life like a barren flower, leaving nothing behind her, not even a good memory. This was the sentence Sholokhov passed not only on her, but on the whole way of life that so corrupted human feelings.

4

The tragic story of Grigory and Aksinya's love, and Natalya's hopeless love for Grigory, runs its dramatic course through the whole of the novel. It is woven into the very fabric of the epic canvas of historical events and scenes from everyday life and nature, and is an integral part of the Melekhov family drama.

Already a married woman, Aksinya fell head over heels in love with her young neighbour, Grigory Melekhov. But neither of them were free to follow their hearts. "I'd like to marry you," Grigory says, but knows full well it is impossible. Everything is against the lovers: "the law", and the strict moral code of the patriarchal way of life. Aksinya can only suffer in silence as she sees her one and only love leaving her, maybe for ever, to be married to Natalya Korshunova. But in the privacy of her home, she breaks down, and her piercing anguish bursts out in a flood of choking tears.

Natalya trustingly gave Grigory all her pure, youthful love, but met with no response from him. Before long she discovered to her horror that she was unloved, that her "lawful wedded husband" was pining for another.... Then she would run to the shed and weep convulsively for "her desecrated happiness".

Most of the female characters in *And Quiet Flows the Don* are revealed first and foremost in love. In presenting a woman in love Sholokhov discloses her whole personality and rich inner world, the simplicity and charm of the Cossack peasant woman.

Natalya's drama is presented with remarkable psychological penetration. Her image is sombre and pure, her thoughts and emotions are revealed with a subtlety that

171

gives us an insight into the pain of love, and her passionate soul.

Natalya fell in love with Grigory at first sight. Her father was against the proposed marriage: he did not consider the Melekhovs' boy a good enough match for the daughter of the richest family in the village. Mitka did all he could to blacken his former schoolfellow in his sister's eyes. But Natalya made up her mind immediately. "I like Grigory. I'll never wed another," she declared to her mother, and stood firmly by her decision in spite of all the attempts to persuade her otherwise (1, 113).

But life was to play a cruel game with Natalya's feelings. Soon after their marriage she realised that Grigory loved another. He himself made no bones about telling her how he felt: "I don't love you, Natalya; you mustn't be angry...." (1, 190). Life had brought her first sorrows, but she bravely kept her sufferings to herself. In the end, she attempted to fight back and defend her right to happiness, threatening to go home to her parents. But this move backfired. Instead of bringing Grigory back to her it drove him further away and into the arms of Natalya's rival. He left home and went off to live with Aksinya.

Natalya is a particularly touching figure because of the way she combines moral strength with a certain helplessness and defencelessness.

She is not a fighter by nature, and her attempts to take up arms to defend her love always backfire and end in failure. She is quite incapable of dealing with life's hardships, and retreats before her rival, punishing only herself. On receiving Grigory's curt answer to her pleading letter she tries to commit suicide, but only succeeds in disfiguring herself for life.

When she recovers, she makes another bid to win back her husband, who is by now away at the front, this time by going to Aksinya. She turns up at Yagodnoye, covered in dust like a tramp, her neck twisted from the wound she had inflicted on herself, and humbly asks Aksinya to give Grigory back to her. But she only gets further humiliation. Aksinya jeers at her cruelly. When Natalya looks into the cradle, the baby stares back at her with Grigory's eyes.

Several years later, now the mother of Grigory's growing children, Natalya again comes to Aksinya, to learn that she has taken him from her once more. "I've got two children, and I shall know how to stand up for them and for myself, too!" she tells Aksinya with unusual firmness. But this show of firmness was short-lived.

Sholokhov has a way of seizing on those particular traits in characters which are unmistakably theirs and theirs alone. With Natalya they are chasteness, modesty and reserve, and they make her a singularly attractive character.

Blushing in her confusion, Natalya made Grigory a present of a tobacco pouch during their engagement. When Grigory tried to pull her towards him to kiss her, she modestly held him off and said: "I'm ashamed to!" and even when they were married, she remained as bashful and reserved.

When she feels she is about to give birth, she quickly slips out of the house, makes her way into a thicket of wild thorn, and lies down there. She returns home at dusk, carrying twins in her apron. "I was ashamed, so I went out," she explains to the amazed Ilyinichna, turning pale. "I didn't like to ... in front of Father.... I'm clean, Mother, and I've washed them. Take them...." (2, 74).

Natalya never gives free rein to her feelings. Her love for her husband and children can be caught only in her shy, tender glances, and touchingly modest gestures, as in the following scene, where Grigory has returned home on leave. "She blushed, but overcoming her embarrassment, went across to him and sat down at his side. Her boundlessly happy eyes drank him in, and her hot rough hand stroked his arm...." (2, 348).

Natalya's delightful nature cannot fail to charm. One comes to know persons not only by what they do and think, but by the way other people respond to them. Pantelei Prokofyevich, that hot-tempered, difficult old man, doted on his daughter-in-law, and never once raised his voice to her. The stern Ilyinichna loved and cherished her as her own daughter. Dunya shared all her innocent secrets with Natalya. Even Darya turned to her in a moment of difficulty. Natalya won the hearts of everybody around her with her moral strength and purity, her rare kindness and consideration for others, and her remarkable industry.

Natalya's characteristic industry is stressed time and again. Our attention is drawn to her "big, toil-roughened hands", and to her broad "peasant" back. We see her mostly at work in the kitchen garden or on the land, carrying sheaves of hay, ploughing with Grigory, and bustling about the stove at home. While Darya is all the time trying to shirk the hard work and follow her own gay and idle pursuits, with Natalya it is quite a job to keep her from overstraining herself. By comparing these two women, who are so different both in character and behaviour, Sholokhov brings out Natalya's hard-working nature to be the source of her moral strength and purity.

Natalya's character is revealed bit by bit in the most varied situations and relationships: in the Melekhov family's approach to her, in her dramatic clashes with Aksinya, but most of all in her love for Grigory.

When Grigory throws her over she returns to her father. "Father, my life is ruined.... Take me back," she sobs. "Grigory's gone away with that woman. He's left me. Father, I've been crushed into the dust!" (1, 239).

But Natalya's love for Grigory was not killed by this first bitter blow, nor indeed by any of her numerous subsequent trials. She had given her faithful heart to him once and for all time.

All the power of her timid, selfless love for Grigory was expressed in the letter she sent him at Yagodnoye. Her life was indeed "quite lost" without him, and she feels "crushed into the dust". Yet she forgave him and was waiting for him.

After her unsuccessful attempt to commit suicide, Natalya went back to live with the Melekhovs. There she yearned with pain and desire to receive the letters that came from the indifferent Grigory at the front. "A smile trembled like sunlight on her lips. She still hoped for a message from Grigory or the slightest reference to her in his letters, in reward for her dog-like devotion and fidelity" (1, 466).

Grigory's return home transformed Natalya. She was now the happy loving wife and mother. She had "blossomed and improved astonishingly" (2, 345).

In Sholokhov's works, *motherhood* always figures as a feature of all that is *finest and best* in human nature, ennobling a woman and making her more beautiful.

Ilyinichna's love for her sons reveals all that is finest in her. The unknown old woman who saves the life of the captured Red Army man long remains in our memories as a paragon of kindness and nobility. "I'm not the only one, we're all good mothers.... We're sorry for you poor devils, mortally sorry!" (4, 43). In these characters' maternal love were expressed all the best and healthiest feelings that sprang from the life of the toiling masses. In this respect Sholokhov is continuing and developing the best traditions of Russian and Soviet literature, reflecting the moral development of the people.

Motherhood brings Natalya even greater spiritual beauty. Unloved and rejected by Grigory at first, as the mother of his children she gradually wins his love. Sholokhov transmits this new image of Natalya most powerfully through an inner monologue. Grigory's short visit is almost over and he is sitting with Natalya. "She, his wife and the mother of Mishatka and Polyushka, was at his side. For him she had decked herself out and had washed her face. In the kerchief she had hurriedly donned so that he should not see how unsightly she had become since her illness, sitting there with her head bent slightly to one side, she looked so pitiful, so uncomely, and yet so beautiful, radiant with some pure, intrinsic beauty. She always wore high collars, to hide from him the scar which disfigured her neck. It was all done for his sake.... A tremendous flood of tenderness swept over Grigory's heart. He wanted to say something warm and kindly to her, but he could not find the words and, silently drawing her to himself, he kissed her white, lofty brow and mournful eyes" (4, 98).

Sholokhov purposely mentions those marks of Natalya's illness and her wound which mar her appearance in order to stress the inner beauty that radiates from the loving wife and mother. Aksinya, who had always stood between Grigory and his wife, momentarily fades into the background now that Natalya is a mother. The image we have of Natalya through Grigory's eyes is all the stronger in that he has come home straight from several days with Aksinya in Veshenskaya. He was overwhelmed with tenderness at the sight of Natalya radiant with maternal joy.

Yet somehow Natalya falls short of harmonious moral perfection. Her main weakness is the reserved, rather selfish nature of her feelings. She is after all mainly preoccupied with herself, with her own sufferings. She is incapable of coming anywhere near to understanding Grigory's tragedy, and, not feeling his agonising dilemma, she is unable to offer him that feminine pity which would have at least brought him the soothing balm of consolation.

When Grigory tries to make a frank confession to her she replies with unusual roughness: "You've done me wrong, and you've admitted it. And now you're trying to put everything on to the war. You're all of you the same. Haven't I had enough sorrow through you, you devil? It's a pity I didn't finish myself off that time...." (3, 393). She makes no attempt to understand the drama that is racking the soul of the man she loves, but merely heaps reproaches on him for the actions that result from it. Deeply wounded, Grigory bitterly concludes: "We've got nothing to talk about." There is every reason to suppose that it was Natalya's cold lack of understanding that drove Grigory back to Aksinya, sealing her fate.

Natalya's love for Grigory is an all-consuming, quite uncompromising emotion. She cannot forgive the man to whom she gave everything either his love for Aksinya or his casual affairs with other women. She felt his infidelities to be insults to her, the mother of his children, and her whole being revolted against them.

Grigory's new affair with Aksinya was too much for Natalya. It was not only a question of the wronged wife whose pride was wounded by her husband's infidelity: Natalya suffered all the more deeply because she considered Aksinya a dissolute woman, unworthy of Grigory's love. She told her so to her face too, in words full of bitterness and condemnation. "You don't love him, you only hanker after him out of habit. Did you ever love him like I do? It doesn't look like it. You played about with Listnitsky, and who haven't you played about with, you strumpet? When a woman loves a man she doesn't do that" (4, 211-212).

Natalya compared Aksinya's feelings for Grigory to her own true love for her "one and only" Grisha, seeing the former as unreal, merely a "hankering out of habit". Yet Grigory obviously saw things differently. Father of Natalya's children whom he loved and cherished with all his heart, he nonetheless carried on with Aksinya, "the strumpet", which, as Natalya saw it, was soiling true love.

Natalya felt not so much the wronged wife as the insulted mother of Grigory's children.

In the struggle for herself and her children she lacked that inner strength which tempered Ilyinichna's character in moments of trial, and which enabled the tough old woman not only to put up with so many hardships, but to keep the family together and bring up the children.

For several days after her talk with Darya, from which she learned that Grigory was seeing Aksinya again, "Natalya suffered as one does in sleep, when oppressed by a bad dream and unable to awake" (4, 207). Natalya was one of those proud, independent individuals who suffer in solitude, keeping their grief to themselves. But there usually comes a moment when they can no longer suffer in silence and then all their pain bursts forth in a cri-du-cœur.

Natalya's grief is expressed with great tragic intensity against the background of an approaching storm in the steppe. We have already referred to the way Sholokhov frequently heightens the intensity of his characters' feelings in the novel by contrasting them with nature in a totally different mood. But along with the principle of tragic contrast so frequently employed, we find many examples in the novel of tragic parallels, where Sholokhov achieves the highest pitch of emotional intensity by making the movements of a character's soul coincide with the rhythm of nature. Sholokhov uses this method in the scene where Natalya breaks down and curses Grigory.

At first there was nothing to suggest an approaching storm. The sun beat down on Ilyinichna and Natalya who had gone out into the steppe to weed the melons. Natalya had spent a sleepless night and was trying to forget her worries in work. When they sat down for lunch at noon Ilyinichna, who had been watching Natalya for a long time, started up a conversation about Grigory. All the suffering that Natalya has kept to herself for so long suddenly bursts forth, and in a near-frenzy of hysteria she screams out a terrible curse on Grigory.

"Unexpectedly she jumped up, pushed Ilyinichna aside, and, turning her face eastward, putting her tear-stained palms together in prayer, hurriedly, sobbingly screamed:

"'Lord! He's tortured my soul to death! I haven't the strength to go on living like this. Lord, punish him, curse him! Strike him dead! May he live no longer, torture me no longer!'

"A black, rolling cloud crawled onward from the east. Thunder rumbled hollowly. Piercing the precipitous cloudy masses, a burning white flash of lightning writhed and slipped over the sky. The wind bent the murmuring grass westward, sent a pungent dust flying up from the track, bowed the sunflower caps with their burden of seeds almost to the ground. It tore at Natalya's dishevelled hair, dried her wet face, and wound the edge of her grey workaday skirt around her legs.

"Ilyinichna stood for several seconds staring at her daughter-in-law in superstitious horror. Against the background of the black thundercloud which had climbed to the zenith Natalya seemed a strange and terrible creature" (4, 216-217).

The storm in Natalya's heart merges with the approaching storm to form a single tempestuous outburst of quite overwhelming power. "'Lord, punish him! Punish him, Lord!' Natalya screamed, fixing her frenzied eyes on the majestically and wildly gathering clouds, piled into masses by the wind, lit up by blinding flashes of lightning.

"The thunder broke with a dry crash over the steppe...." (4, 217).

The violent storm bursts so unexpectedly as if Natalya's grief was so great as to provoke a response in nature. Although nothing had heralded this storm we have been prepared by Natalya's outburst to accept it as a perfectly natural phenomenon.

At the same time the storm adds to the intensity of Natalya's feelings. This simple woman seems to grow in stature before our very eyes, assuming true greatness as she stands beneath the rumbling thunder, giving vent to her passionate feelings, invoking a terrible curse on the head of the man she loves.

In this mighty burst of feelings, sounds and colours, Sholokhov gives a picture of remarkable tragic intensity and majesty. And what a burst it is! Ilyinichna's superstitious horror as she hears the terrible curse laid on her son, the boundless despair of Natalya for whom life has no meaning without Grigory's love and fidelity, the blinding flashes of lightning, the crashes of thunder in the dark, empty steppe....

Sholokhov has a way of presenting life's most violent transitions. From the happiness of love and the joy of motherhood, Natalya sinks into the most hopeless despair. Natalya had kept her suffering at Grigory's unfaithfulness locked up in the depths of her soul until it finally broke her. Premonition of the approaching catastrophe mounts in sadness and bitterness in the scenes with Natalya. Left alone with Ilyinichna and the children, she worries about Grigory who is away fighting across the Don.

Natalya decides to go and visit her old home. Mikhail Koshevoi had set fire to the Korshunov house and farmstead, and Grandad Grishaka's grave mound lay under the old apple-tree. "Overwhelmed by a rush of memories, Natalya silently dropped to her knees and fell face downward to the ungracious earth, with its everlasting smell of death and decay...." (4, 47).

These poetic forebodings of the impending catastrophe are woven into all sorts of various situations.

Home on leave, in a transport of tenderness, Grigory kissed Natalya's "white, lofty brow and mournful eyes" and thought: "Why had she got such mournful eyes? And something secretive, elusive, kept appearing and disappearing in them. Even in her joy she was sorrowful and somehow beyond his understanding...." (4, 99).

Natalya puts "Ilyinichna's black three-cornered kerchief on her head" when she goes to the gate to see Grigory off. He rides off, "burdened with vague presentiments, which weighed him down with anxiety and foreboding". At the fork, he turned back. "Only Natalya was standing at the gate, and the fresh, early morning breeze was tearing her *black, mourning kerchief* from her hands" (4, 104; author's italics). In Natalya's hands, the traditional black kerchief that was so often worn by old women, and which she had snatched up as she hurried out, becomes a "mourning" kerchief.

This is a masterly detail, powerfully conveying Natalya's imminent death. It was as if life was slowly slipping away, her only link with it her suffering.

Before the storm in the steppe Natalya "fell face downward on the dry, ungracious earth" just as she had when visiting Grandad Grishaka's grave. This repetition of "ungracious" applied to the earth we walk on and on whose bounty we live, stresses Natalya's alienation from the world around her.

All these poetic details, which the author builds up with such emotional lyricism, culminate in the climax of the storm scene when in a frenzy of grief and suffering Natalya cries: "I haven't the strength to go on living like this." When they get back home, she says to Ilyinichna: "I don't want him to die. I said that in my temper.... I can't turn him out of my heart, but all the same, life is hard enough" (4, 220).

The intense family drama ends in a terrible tragedy. Not wishing to bear her unfaithful husband's child, the proud, injured Natalya dies as the result of an abortion primitively performed by an old village quack. But even when she is on the point of death, Natalya does not cease to love Grigory; she thinks of him and forgives him for everything. Well aware that her end is nigh, she tells Ilyinichna her last wish: "Mother, dress me in my green skirt, the one with the embroidery round the edges. Grisha liked me in that one...." (4, 229). Calling Polyushka to her bedside, she says with a feeble smile: "She's the very image of her father; only her heart's not like his, hers is softer..." (4, 234). She is terribly sorry that she will not see Grigory before she dies. "Natalya closed her eyes and said, as though delirious: 'So I shan't see him after all....'" (4, 234). So great is her love for Grigory that she takes it with her to the grave.

Natalya had always longed for the pure joy of a love that was shared, unsullied by struggle and rivalry. Nothing mattered for her apart from her all-absorbing love for Grigory. When the family happiness she had achieved through so much hardship was destroyed, she no longer had anything to live for.

5

Sholokhov's aesthetic judgments became noticeably more profound during his many years' work on *And Quiet Flows the Don.*

In book four of the novel he brilliantly disclosed the splendid image of Ilyinichna as the fine, noble character she was, he brought out Natalya's inner beauty more evocatively and filled in Aksinya's psychological characteristics, giving her a harmonious completeness and perfection.

The reader's attitude to a particular character is based on a direct emotional experience, mind and feelings being inseparably involved. If we are enchanted by a character, it is important to understand what the writer is poeticising and how he evokes this feeling in us.

Gorky said that as he got to know more about life he developed a definite moral code. "'Kick a man when he's down'" is one of the basic dogmas of 'the moral code of the masters', which was as hostile to me as 'the moral code of the slaves', and I developed a third moral principle, 'Support a man when he's rising'."* Bourgeois decadent literature tries to belittle man, to undermine his faith in his own powers. It calumniates man in order to render him inactive, and to put a spanner in the works of the struggle against social evil. Decadent bourgeois art is the true servant of the moral code of the masters. Gorky, the great founder of socialist realism, began his literary career by glorifying man, his powers and potentialities.

Through his romantic figures such as Danko, the Falcon, the Stormy Petrel and Man, and his stern, courageous characters such as Pavel Vlasov, Nil, Sintsov and the Mother, Gorky affirmed life as activity, as the heroic task of serving the people. He supported those who rose up against an unjust social order, and showed how the best side of man's nature revealed itself in his implacable struggle against social evils, with all the results of the property-owner's morality. *"Struggling man is fine"* can be said to be *one of Gorky's basic aesthetic precepts*, a precept that has been followed and developed in Soviet literature.

In his portrayal of the camp of the revolutionary people and in presenting such characters as Grigory and Aksinya, Sholokhov is following the *Gorky tradition* of supporting and extolling the fighter.

* Maxim Gorky, *Collected Works*, Vol. 25, pp. 320-21.

The reader feels great sympathy for Aksinya in her brave revolt against the slavish position of woman in the society she lives in. Her struggle for Grigory, for happiness with him, was a struggle to assert her human dignity and rights. While Darya submitted to the existing order and adjusted herself to it, Aksinya proudly came out in open revolt against the generally accepted patriarchal morality and, breaking with the village in the name of a higher truth, asserted her right to follow her heart, as a true human being.

Long-suffering Aksinya is undoubtedly one of the finest characters in the history of Russian and world classical literature. Sholokhov often refers to her as the *proud* Aksinya. She has a "proud" face; defying the village gossip, she "held her happy, shameful head proud and high" (1, 68). After her quarrel with the Melekhovs, she cuts them dead in the street: she "walked past with satanic pride, dilating her nostrils" (4, 295). Aksinya's pride is not of a superficial nature coming from an awareness of her striking beauty, but is one of the essential traits of her character. It is revealed in her readiness to uphold her human dignity, and is an expression of courage, fortitude and nobility of soul. Sholokhov applied the epithet "proud" to only two women in the novel, Ilyinichna and Aksinya, and indeed they are both models of strength, pride, nobility of soul.

It is Aksinya's proud awareness of her human dignity that determines her sincerity and integrity. "What if I love Grisha?" she cries challengingly to Pantelei Prokofyevich. "Beat me, will you? Write to my husband? Write to the ataman if you like, but Grisha belongs to me! He's mine! Mine!" (1, 71). When her husband returns from the summer training camp, she fights down her fear and goes forward to meet him. "I shan't hide. I have sinned," she admits frankly and simply to his face. "Beat me, Stepan!" (1, 88).

Aksinya is incapable of lying, treachery and deceit. She loathes hypocrisy. When Natalya, having heard it rumoured that Grigory is meeting Aksinya again, goes to ask her rival if it is true, Aksinya at first tries to avoid giving a direct answer. But Natalya had only to suggest that Aksinya is afraid to tell the truth and the latter proudly and bluntly comes out with it.

Aksinya is honest and straightforward by nature. Even in the most dramatic situations, which could have had very serious consequences, she found it impossible to lie. To do so would have meant losing her self-respect. During the Upper Don uprising Grigory and Stepan come face to face in the house of Aksinya's aunt. Aksinya has gone to fetch some vodka and the two implacable enemies, her one and only love and her husband with whom she is now living after a long separation, are seated at the same table, awaiting her return. The poignant psychological drama is brought to the highest pitch of intensity. It is a tense moment and anything might happen. The reader holds his breath in suspense, remembering former meetings between the two men, how at the front Stepan had shot at Grigory, and how the time Grigory saved him from death he had said that he still could never forgive him. When Aksinya returned and saw them together, "terror spurted in her black, dilated eyes". But the shock she experienced on entering the room was nothing to tests she then had to withstand. Stepan, knowing full well why Grigory had come, suggests that they drink to a long parting. Aksinya refuses:

"'But you know—'

"'I know everything now.... Well then, not to any parting. Here's to the health of our dear guest Grigory Panteleyevich.'

"'Yes, I'll drink his health!' Aksinya said in a ringing voice, and tossed off her glass at one gulp" (4, 81).

It was typical of the proud Aksinya that she should fearlessly give free rein to her feelings even in this explosive situation. Once again she reveals her rare courage and disarming spontaneity. For one second Grigory "had felt sure Stepan would strike Aksinya when she drank his, Grigory's, health. But he was wrong. Stepan raised his horny palm, wiped his sunburnt forehead, and after a brief silence glanced in admiration at Aksinya and said: 'You're a great lass, wife! I like you for your daring'" (4, 85).

Pride and daring are the two qualities that make for Aksinya's *nobility of soul*. Mutinous recalcitrance was inherent in her strong, passionate nature. Unlike Natalya who was bowed by the blows of fortune, and giving way, punished herself since she was unable to change the course of events, Aksinya faced danger with her head held high and fought all the way for her right to happiness.

Aksinya was undismayed by the severest trials, such as Grigory's refusal to leave the village with her, the brutal beatings she received at the hands of her husband, the scandal and the shame of her position. She bore it all unflinchingly and at night as she lay awake, she firmly resolved that she would not give Grigory up without a fight, that she would "take Grigory from the happy Natalya, who had known neither the bitterness nor the joy of love" (1, 128). Aksinya was convinced that her resolve was perfectly just and moral. Later, when Natalya came to her at Yagodnoye, she said with stormy hatred: "You took Grisha away from me first! You knew he was living with me. Why did you marry him?" (1, 484). Alone and unaided Aksinya stood up against the whole village, against the prejudices and hypocrisy.

Aksinya's love for Grigory is a single ray of light shining in the darkness of her tragic life. Even in moments of trial, in all the bitter humiliations that fell to her lot, in her conjugal life, in her affair with Listnitsky, her absent beloved was always in her thoughts. Indeed it is in her all-consuming love for Grigory that Aksinya acquires her nobility and that the author reveals his sympathy for her. Aksinya's love for Grigory and her struggle for him was at the same time a revolt against the subservient, slavish position of women in the old society, and thus serves to ennoble her. Her relations with her husband and with Listnitsky, often forced on her by circumstance, were like a dead weight pulling her back towards submission to that unjust order that caused her so much suffering.

Aksinya's whole being revolted against the humiliating position she found herself in as "the young master's mistress". How ashamed she was of her affair with Listnitsky we see from her meeting with Stepan at Yagodnoye.

"'I've heard some story about you and the master's son here.... Is it true?'

"Aksinya's cheeks burned, and tears of shame started from under her lowered lashes.

"'It's true enough. I'm living with him'" (3, 94).

Aksinya gives Stepan a straight answer to his question, but she cannot conceal all the bitterness that has built up inside her during those months at Yagodnoye. Life with her "lawful wedded husband" disgusts her no less and she "frowns with loathing" at the memory of their recent intimacy. In spite of all her sufferings and humiliations, the horror and shame of being raped in her youth. Aksinya is nonetheless remarkably uncompromising all her life. The awakening of Aksinya's love for Grigory is described with great psychological penetration and insight. Already another man's wife, she was frightened by her feeling for Grigory and for a long time tried to fight it. But then, no longer able to repress the feeling which filled her, she defied the whole village by openly having an affair with him. "I'll have my love, I'll make up for all the wrongs I've suffered! And then kill me if you like!" she cries to Pantelei Prokofyevich when he threatens her (1, 71).

Aksinya's love for Grigory is like an all-consuming fire. Grigory recalls "Aksinya's passionate fervour". Her passionate nature, the strength of her feelings, are often compared to a *fire*. We find this in descriptions of Aksinya's love throughout the book. During the mowing, when their affair begins, Grigory "pressed her compliant, burning body to his own" (1, 68). "After the mowing Aksinya was a changed woman: as though someone had set a mark on her face, branded her" (1, 68). Nothing, neither the village gossip, nor her husband's beatings, could put out this fire. "Aksinya went about on tiptoe and spoke in whispers, but in her eyes, sprinkled with the ash of fear, lurked a small spark, left from the flame Grigory had kindled" (1, 99).

Whenever Aksinya saw Grigory, or even thought of him, she burned. She happened to meet him down by the Don once, and "the hot blood beat at her temples" (1, 100). She stops Grigory when he is on his way through the woods with Christonya and Pyotr and "shame and joy flamed in her cheeks and dried her lips" (1, 208). When she answers Grigory's call and throwing up everything, as she has so many times before, goes to Veshenskaya and finally meets him, her "eyes burned with such frantic passion in her white face that Grigory's heart quivered" (3, 523).

While the strength of Aksinya's love for Grigory is expressed in the "fire" of her passion, the depth of her feeling is best seen in her actions, in her boundless self-lessness and readiness to follow him through thick and thin. Grigory was everything for her. "Once more the whole world died when Grigory was absent and was reborn when he was near her" (3, 523). Sholokhov concisely sums up the strength and depth of Aksinya's feelings for Grigory, at the same time conveying her very essence.

Aksinya once referred to herself as Grigory's wife, thereby expressing her awareness that she is bound to him for ever. After Yagodnoye, she returned to Stepan, hoping "to gather up again the fragments of the happiness which had not been hers...." (3, 96). But when she met Grigory again, she realised that neither time nor separation could do anything to destroy her love for him.

Wherever she goes, whatever she does, Aksinya's love for Grigory bursts forth in her heart, often quite unexpectedly, as in the following scene, to which Sholokhov as usual imparts a remarkable dramatic intensity and sharp psychological penetration. In answer to Stepan's insistent plea Aksinya has come to visit him in the trenches across the Don. As she washes her husband's clothes in a nearby pond, she is all the time thinking of Grigory. "As with the utmost clarity she recalled every one of those infinitely precious features, she began to breathe heavily, her face broke into a smile, she straightened up, and throwing her husband's half-washed shirt underfoot and feeling a burning lump in her throat as the sweet tears suddenly started, she whispered: 'Curse you, you've got into me for ever!'" (4, 12-13).

Everything connected with her husband is base, worthless and unnecessary and pales in the light of her feelings for Grigory. It was the same with her affair with Listnitsky. There had been times in the course of her hard life when circumstances had forced her to act against the dictates of her heart. When Natalya, in a fit of jealousy, calls her a loose woman, she turns pale and in a quivering voice says: "'You've got children, but to me he's.... He's all I care for in the whole world. He's my first and my last!'" (4, 212).

Aksinya's pride and courage in her struggle for happiness makes her such a noble figure that even Natalya pales beside her. It is not surprising that Grigory should have turned to her again in his most difficult moments for she was able to understand, console and forgive.

Sholokhov often reveals Aksinya's rich nature and nobility of soul through comparisons with nature. Indeed this applies not only to Aksinya: in expressing a character's nobility he frequently takes into account the environment and by his clever choice of comparisons, reveals his own sensitivity to beauty in man.

In the scene where Grigory and Aksinya meet after he has left home Grigory observes the smell of Aksinya's lips both when they meet and when they part. "She had evidently been running: she was out of breath, and the faint scent of the winter wind, or perhaps of fresh steppe hay, came from her fresh cold mouth" (1, 225). "The agitating scent of her lips remained on Grigory's lips; the scent of the winter wind, or perhaps that faint, faraway scent that comes from the hay after a spring shower in the steppe" (1, 227).

The smell of the winter wind and the smell of fresh steppe hay are far removed from one another in time as natural phenomena. But Sholokhov grasps their subtle relationship. Both transmit an impression of freshness, purity and health. While the first comparison stresses the fact that the scene is taking place in winter, the second is obviously more important, and when he repeats the image at the end of their meeting, it is this that he develops. The smell of "fresh steppe hay" becomes "that faint, faraway scent that comes from the hay after a spring shower in the steppe". Sholokhov widens the image to include the beautiful month of May and the spring rain, thereby enhancing Aksinya's freshness, health and beauty to correspond to the reader's increased sympathy for her after her conversation with Grigory.

A writer's aesthetic values are determined by his perception of life. The images Sholokhov uses to reveal Aksinya's nature invariably coincide with perception of beauty as understood by the people.

Sholokhov uses such images not only to bring out a character's nobility of soul, but also to show changes that have taken place. His imagery is closely linked with the flow of life itself. He compares the young Aksinya leaving to live with Grigory at Yagodnoye to such natural phenomena as symbolise the flowering of life. The scent of hay after a spring shower in the steppe is suggestive of youthful strength and vigour. Many years later, when time and suffering have left their mark on Aksinya, she is compared to a lily of the valley, touched by mortal decay but still beautiful.

Sitting down to rest under a hawthorn bush in the forest, Aksinya "suddenly caught the languorous perfume of lilies of the valley. Groping with her hands, she found the plant. It was growing right beside her, under an impenetrably shady bush. The broad, once green leaves were still jealously protecting from the sun the bent, low-growing stalk, crowned with the drooping snow-white chalices of the flowers. But the leaves, covered with dew and yellow rust, were dying, and the flower itself was already touched by mortal decay: the two lower cups were wrinkled and blackened, and only the upper one, all dressed in the sparkling tears of dew, suddenly flashed in the sunlight with a dazzling, captivating whiteness.

"For some reason, in that brief moment while through her tears Aksinya was looking at the flower and breathing in its mournful scent, she recalled her youth and all her long life so meagre in happiness. She must be growing old.... When a woman is young does she pause to weep because her heart is caught by a chance memory?

"And so in her tears she fell asleep, hiding her tear-stained face in her hands, pressing her wet and swollen cheek against her crumpled kerchief" (4, 17-18).

Let us examine this passage and see just why it is so moving. The first thing that strikes one is the comparison between the aging Aksinya who has suffered so much over the years and now has wrinkles round her eyes, and the lily of the valley, with its drooping cups, already touched by mortal decay. It is hard to imagine a more apt comparison.

Sholokhov's rare sense of beauty is no less apparent in the actual description, where he displays that measure and poetic rhythm that is the hall-mark of the truly great writer. First he describes the flower, and although we remember that Aksinya is looking at it, she is excluded from our field of vision as it were. The signs of decay are chosen with great subtlety; the drooping chalices, the wrinkled and blackened lower cups. Sholokhov is not only describing the flower. Aksinya is watching it fascinatedly, and it is as if a living being is dying, touched by mortal decay. We are witnessing the death of beauty. "The upper one, all dressed in the sparkling tears of dew, suddenly flashed in the sunlight with a dazzling, captivating whiteness." Our feeling of wonder at the beauty of the flower drowns out all other feelings, and we automatically transfer this wonder to Aksinya, who suddenly comes back into our field of vision, so suddenly indeed that it is as if the same description is being continued. For a moment Aksinya and the flower become one. The sparkling tears of dew on the fading flower announce Aksinya's hot tears. Yet at the same time an unfeeling flower and a suffering woman can clearly only be likened just so far.

Sholokhov avoids a lengthy description of Aksinya's thoughts and feelings here by conveying them in her perception of the lily of the valley. Before she saw the flower, she had caught its languorous perfume, and as she regards it now, thinking of herself, of her life, its scent seems mournful to her. By this single, subtle detail, Sholokhov conveys Aksinya's change of mood, the nature of her emotions. The words "she must be growing old" follow straight after the description of her tears and of the flower's mournful smell. They express the intensity of her inner drama. As she looked mournfully and sympathetically at the flower, she was thinking of herself, of her life "so meagre in happiness", of decay. It is as if one hears her speaking. This burst of feeling is moving because it has been prepared for by the detailed description of the dying flower. Sholokhov then adds to the strength of Aksinya's feelings and generalises them, striking a lyrical note with: "When a woman is young does she pause to weep because her heart is caught by a chance memory?"

The description of the dying lily of the valley does not merely serve to give us a deep psychological insight into the aging but still beautiful Aksinya who has suffered so much in her life: it is at the same time a vague hint at what the future holds in store for her. Only a true artist could pack so much into a single image.

The characters in *And Quiet Flows the Don* are shown in a constant process of development and change. Time and events leave an indelible mark on them. Grigory Melekhov advances along a tortuous path towards moral bankruptcy and physical destruction. Pantelei Prokofyevich changes under the impact of his sufferings and losses during the Civil War. Aksinya, too, changes greatly both inwardly and outwardly during the novel.

The Aksinya we see at the beginning of the novel is a beautiful woman in the flower of youth, strong and healthy, happy and confident. Time passes, and she meets Grigory down by the Don after five years of separation from him. Sholokhov gives us a detailed description of Aksinya at this important point in her life. When she got back home, she went straight to the mirror "and stood staring anxiously at her aging but still beautiful face. It still retained its wanton and seductive charm, but the autumn of life was beginning to cast fugitive hues over her cheeks, her eyelids were yellowing, rare strands of grey were entwined in her hair, her eyes were dimmed with mournful weariness" (3, 423-424).

Life had been hard to her. The apparently attainable happiness of living with the man she loved had slipped through her fingers; like the legendary firebird it had shown itself only to move away out of reach when she stretched out her hands to take it. She had to fight for the man she loved, to wrest him from the clutches of ill fortune, she had to reject her husband and struggle alone and unfriended against the Melekhovs and Natalya. All she had had to suffer was reflected in the expression of her eyes, which were "dimmed with mournful weariness". This mournful weariness in her gaze is to feature more and more in the descriptions of Aksinya, it is in her eyes that we can read of the tremendous burden of suffering she has borne. Reunited with Grigory at Veshenskaya, she looked into his eyes "with her own humble eyes. Something in her gaze was so wistfully wretched, yet so harshly desperate, like the eyes of a hunted animal, that it was painful and embarrassing for Grigory to look at her" (3, 524).

In painting his characters, Sholokhov centres his attention on their eyes, more often than not. Aksinya's eyes are the mirror of her inner world. When she returns home from a short meeting with Grigory after he has been demobbed from the Red Army, we once again have a chance to see her state of mind as expressed in her eyes. "Worn out with the agitation she had felt all the evening, she sat with her cheek pressed to the cold, hoar-frosted window-pane, fixing her calm and rather sorrowful gaze on the darkness, which was lightened only very little by the snow" (4, 511-512). Aksinya's gaze now expresses the wisdom that comes with experience, which has led her to doubt the possibility of ever attaining happiness. As she looks out into the darkness, only slightly lightened by the snow, with "a calm and rather sorrowful gaze", it is as though she is looking into her future. And this gaze seems to say that things can hardly get worse than they have been.

The changes that have taken place in Aksinya's character are all linked with the story of her love for Grigory. As her love for him grows so she gradually acquires that nobility of soul which so enchants us. In his subtle depiction of this process Sholokhov reveals himself a past master of the secrets of the human heart. Aksinya loved Grigory so passionately from the start that it seemed impossible to imagine her loving him any more, and yet Sholokhov manages to show how her feelings developed and altered over the years, becoming more profound all the time. To her woman's passion is added maternal tenderness, as we see from a short, but important episode where Aksinya is thinking of Grigory as the young lad he had been in the early days of their love. "And because of all this, Aksinya felt even greater love and an almost motherly tenderness towards him" (4, 12).

This maternal tenderness that so ennobles Aksinya is especially evident in her attitude to Grigory's children. She transfers her feelings for Grigory to his children and after Natalya's death gradually takes their mother's place. When Grigory runs away from Fomin's band and asks her to go to the Kuban with him, she refers to the children as if they were her own. "I'm only sorry for the children," she says, "but I wouldn't say one 'Oh' over myself." The children reciprocated her feelings, and called her "Mummy", and this beautiful word, coming from the lips of the children does much to ennoble Aksinya still further.

In book four we no longer find references to Aksinya's "wanton, seductive charm", her "shamelessly avid lips" or her eyes flashing "with a desperate glint of content-ment". Sober realist that he is, Sholokhov shows Aksinya as a particular type of woman in particular historical conditions. There was indeed something sordid in Aksinya's affair with Listnitsky and in her living with Grigory and her husband at the same time, but one can no longer speak of this after she has shown continuous fidelity to Grigory, and has acted as a mother to his children. It had been consumed in the fire of passion and mistakes. Aksinya emanates a new elevated beauty and has acquired the harmony and perfection of nobility.

Korolenko once said: "Man is made for happiness, just as a bird is made for flight." These poetic words fit very well Aksinya's longing for happiness in her love for Grigory. Aksinya saw her struggle for Grigory in the hard conditions of patriarchal life as a struggle to attain pure, human happiness. But this narrow understanding of the purpose and meaning of life made her terribly vulnerable.

"Whatever she thought of, whatever she was doing, her thoughts were always turning to Grigory. So does the *blind horse* plot the everlasting circle of the water-wheel...." (3, 424; author's italics).

Indeed, throughout the years Aksinya had seen nothing in the world but Grigory, for whom she had suffered so much, whom she had wrested again and again from the clutches of adverse fortune, only to lose once more. She was only affected by the Revolution and the Civil War in so far as they affected her Grigory; her one concern being "was Grigory safe?" Blinded by her love for him, she was not concerned with the issues at stake, with what he was fighting for. And this, indeed, was to prove the undoing of this strong and noble woman.

Aksinya found the life unbearable and tried to break out of it. But in her ignorance she believed that she had only to leave the village with Grigory and go far, far away, over hills and dales, and she would find true happiness. With great wistfulness Sholokhov shows how this was but a dream that could never come true. All their attempts to put it into practice ended in disaster.

When Grigory breaks with his family and asks Aksinya to go away with him, she says: "They can put me in the shafts as long as I'm with you, Grisha. Anything to be with you." On her lips "trembled a joyous smile of happiness fulfilled" (1, 226). Yet she did not find happiness at Yagodnoye. She became the mistress of the master's son, and lost Grigory.

Many years later Grigory returned to Aksinya, who was living in the village again. After Natalya's death it seemed nothing could separate them. When the Red Army defeated Denikin's forces and marched into the Don Province and Grigory decided to retreat, she eagerly set off with him. She looked with eager curiosity at the steppe in its pall of drifted snow, taking delight in everything. Even Prokhor Zykov's gloom and sharp criticism could not influence her high spirits. "She smiled at the thought that the dream which had so long held her captive had so strangely and unexpectedly come true. Now she and Grigory were driving somewhere far away from Tatarsky, far from her native and hated district, where she had suffered so much, where she had spent half her life in torments with an unloved husband, where everything aroused oppressive memories. She smiled as with all her body she felt Grigory's presence beside her, and she did not think either of the price at which she had gained this happiness or of the future, which was enveloped in as dark a haze as these steppe horizons that beckoned her into the distance" (4, 351-352).

Aksinya fell ill with typhus and Grigory had to abandon her amid unfriendly people in strange parts. When she recovered she returned to her neglected house. Her illness had aged her; she took up life again, all alone and without news of Grigory.

Yet Aksinya was to leave home again, this time never to return. Having run away from Fomin's band, Grigory crawls through her window like a burglar one night, and asks her to run away with him to the Kuban to begin a new life with him. She agrees with the following passionate words: "I'll go, Grisha, my darling. I'll go on foot, I'll crawl after you, but I won't stay here alone any longer. I can't live without you.... Kill me, but don't leave me again" (4, 671). "I'll follow you everywhere, even to death," she says with a youthful joy as they set off together. Grigory reminds her of how they had set off to Yagodnoye many years before. "But all the time I'm afraid I shall find I've been dreaming," she says, laughing quietly, and Grigory sees her eyes "shining with happiness" (4, 674). "...The world seemed exultant and bright, as though after a plentiful summer downpour. "'We too will find our place in life,' she thought" (4, 678). And it was in this last attempt to find her "place in life" that she found her death. Far out in the steppe, in a nameless ravine, the grief-stricken Grigory buried his beloved Aksinya. Far from "her native and hated district" this passionate, rebellious woman, so great in love, yet so tragically helpless, was to find her last resting place.

Aksinya's environment was such that she could not imagine a different world where a joint struggle is fought for the happiness of all. All her strength of character was channelled into her all-absorbing love for Grigory. Nothing else mattered to her. This, in the long run, was the cause of her downfall in the harsh conditions of the Civil War.

Sholokhov presents the events of the Revolution as a mighty upheaval that affected every aspect of human life, and put the integrity of every individual to the test. He shows us the drama of the great struggle between the old order that was condemned to perish and the new life that was being born.

Sholokhov touches on practically every aspect of life during this period. An example of this is the amazing variety of Cossack women types he portrays: Ilyinichna, Aksinya, Natalya, Darya, Dunya.... Each one of these highly distinctive characters reveals some new elements in women's psychology, and moreover allows us to see the Cossack world from a new angle, enabling us to better understand the significance of the profound changes brought about by the Revolution. The epoch is perceived through a variety of types and emphatically individualised characters.

6

A truly great writer not only shows us what a man was like, but also enables us to feel his potential mobility. Each character is related to an ideal that lies behind all that the writer creates.

"Remember that all the writers we call universal or simply good and which intoxicate us have one outstanding point in common: they are moving towards some destination and beckon us to follow them, and we feel not merely in our minds but with our whole being that they have some purpose, like the ghost of Hamlet's father, who had a good reason for coming to stir up his son's imagination.... The best of them are realists and portray life as it is, but since every line is imbued with awareness of a purpose, like with sap, we feel not only life as it is, but life as it should be, and this is what captivates us."*

These lines from one of Chekhov's letters express remarkably well both the role of the ideal in literature and its meaning for the writer. The ideal includes not only awareness of the purpose of what is being created but the ability to see real life in its constant development and change, the ability to foresee, or rather apprehend the future.

The progressive ideal in art confirms the close link between art and reality, its dependence on reality. Art is not only a means of self-cognition: it has aims—social, moral and ethical—which are embodied aesthetically, in concrete sensorial form, in the ideal. By giving concrete expression to its ideal, mankind strives to bring the future nearer, that is, to show that it is realisable by realising it in art. The progressive ideal in art is fundamentally revolutionary.

The writer's aesthetic ideal contains an extremely important element of the personal. A distinction must be drawn between the aesthetic ideal of society as a whole and the aesthetic ideal of a particular writer. Even a cursory glance at the works of such writers as Gorky, Sholokhov, Fadeyev, Fedin, Alexei Tolstoi and Paustovsky is sufficient to convince one that while their concept of nobility of soul sometimes coincides, it is more often than not quite different. The more varied these individual aesthetic concepts, the richer the aesthetic ideal of society as a whole.

Art is not only an expression of the aesthetic concepts of a society, it enriches people and helps to mould their

* A. P. Chekhov, *Collected Works*, Russ. ed., Vol. 15, Moscow, 1949, p. 446.

characters. Art leads the way, it is a beacon which embodies mankind's dream of beauty, harmony and perfection, and lights the way to the future. Art ennobles and purifies man, preparing him for ever new struggles for social justice, helping him to master the secrets of his environment.

The artist's aesthetic ideal is apparent in his choice of subject-matter and the way he treats it, in his appraisal of people and their actions.

Socialist realism, following in the best traditions of the classics, portrays the life of the working people. The workers and peasants, the true makers of history, came to occupy the centre of the stage. It is in their life and struggle that the socialist realist writer finds his ideal of what is noble and beautiful. Socialist realism represents a completely new set of ethical and aesthetic principles. Not only do we have a new viewpoint, a new approach to reality, but new principles of portraying it too.

One of the most important of these new principles concerns the relationship between the life of the individual and the fortunes of the people as a whole. The hero's life is not only seen in the light of his inner world but in relation to the life and struggle, the ideals and aspirations of the people. In epic genres this approach to the individual is an important compositional feature.

The hero of 19th-century realist literature was usually a young idealist breaking into "polite society" from the outside, having been brought up somewhere in the back of beyond, far from the contradictions of life. His moral qualities were mainly compared to the morality of the society he now entered, that is, the society of the parasitic ruling classes and, to begin with at least, the comparison was as a rule in his favour. Frankness and sincerity were set off against hypocrisy and deceit, kindness and unselfishness against the general avidity for wealth and success. Beneath the respectable façade of high society the power of money went unchallenged, crippling even the most noble feelings like friendship and love. Everything could be bought and sold in this world which the naïve, ambitious young man was ingenuously striving to enter. For such people as Rastignac, Lucien de Rubempré and

Aduyev junior,* not to mention a host of others, experience meant the loss of all that was noble and fine in their nature. Their naïve dreams gave way to cold cynicism, soulless egoism, and calculating careerism.

Others, like Lermontov's Pechorin, escaped this cruel world, only to find that even in apparently more "natural" conditions, there was no outlet for their high aspirations, no possibility of putting their remarkable talent to any positive use.

Socialist realism began with Gorky's search for the positive hero, the hero who would lighten "the darkness of life".

The portrayal of the positive hero, his life and the purpose of his struggle, was the great innovatory feature of the new literature. The writer's aim was to show man "moulding" the historical process, directing the course of events. The hero was no longer alone, for he had the masses behind him. His character, ideals and endeavours were revealed in the context of the struggle of the whole people. This greatly widened the epic foundation of literature and gave rise to new ethical concepts and aesthetic principles of portrayal.

Naturally the portrayal of the positive hero is not the sole purpose of socialist realist art. Had this been so, it would have inevitably led to its impoverishment. Socialist realism sets out to reveal life in its entirety, to present the lives of people of different social standing and natures.

The writer is obviously not indifferent to the life he is portraying and his attitude is often revealed in his very choice of heroes. By focussing his attention on certain human types, he leads the reader into the turbulent river of history, so full of contradictory currents.

Still, the main task facing the socialist realist writer is to accurately define his hero's place in the historical process. The hero's true relation to his age can only be revealed in the context of the ideals and aims of the life of the people. The writer can only create an authentic character, authentic as regards his social outlook and his individual traits, if he really understands the ideals and aspirations of the popular masses.

* The principal character in *A Common Tale* by Ivan Goncharov.

Of the unquestionably positive heroes in *And Quiet Flows the Don*, none are anywhere near as powerfully drawn, or endowed with such nobility as Grigory Melekhov. Mikhail Koshevoi, who is deliberately set off against him, does not win the reader's sympathy. On the contrary, in his last conversation with Grigory he rather antagonises us with his callous singleness of purpose and his inability and unwillingness to understand Grigory's inner conflict.

According to the line pursued by some Soviet critics it follows that Sholokhov has made a grave aesthetic and compositional miscalculation in letting a character condemned by history—and indeed by himself—occupy the centre of the stage and reveal more depth and nobility of soul than the positive hero, the Communist Koshevoi. In fact, in the arguments which raged round the eighth and last part of the novel, on its publication in 1940, many critics were to take this line. Obviously there was no character in the novel who could be said to embody an ideal, the "highest human perfection".

At the same time, the unprejudiced reader, excitedly following the fortunes of Grigory Melekhov and deeply sympathising with him, would find himself longing for the blundering errant hero to go over to the revolutionary camp, and join the struggle on the side of Koshevoi, Kotlyarov and the others.

The older generation of readers remember how delighted and relieved they were to find in the excerpts from book four published in the press that Grigory had become a squadron commander in Budyonny's army. It seemed that at last he had found his proper place: he had been temporarily misguided, but now everything was as it should be.

Indeed the tragic finale merely confirms this instinctive conviction. It is this that sets the whole tone of the novel and shows where the writer sought and found the truly noble and beautiful in life.

Sholokhov saw the grandeur, heroism and nobility of the people's revolutionary struggle, and his attitude to their unparalleled exploit is the main aesthetic criterion in the book, the yardstick against which humaneness and nobility are measured.

The writer's ideal of the perfect human personality is

in evidence in all the imagery, in the whole narrative structure of the novel.

The positive hero, a living individual, naturally does not correspond entirely to the writer's ideal of perfection. A writer's ideal is usually higher and richer than what we can find in any particular living individual.

A typical feature of Sholokhov's works is his constant loving interest in the life of toiling masses. He gives a picture, tremendous in range and penetration, of the spiritual strength and wealth of simple Russian folk. That Sholokhov's art grows out of the life of the working people is apparent in his very choice of characters.

Beauty and nobility are inseparable from the life and struggle of the people in Sholokhov's works. In his vast, impressive canvases of the life of the people we feel Sholokhov's passionate involvement, his real concern for the victory of the Communist ideal as being truly noble and lofty.

The nobility of soul of Davidov, Razmyotnov, Kondratko and Naidyonov, those fine courageous characters of *Virgin Soil Upturned*, is revealed above all in their active struggle for the collectivisation of agriculture. It was their selfless struggle for the people's happiness that produced and fostered their finest human qualities.

Sholokhov was completing *And Quiet Flows the Don* at a time when the rich spiritual make-up of the Soviet man was coming to the fore in life and literature. The past is thus viewed in the novel from the standpoint of the people successfully building socialism.

The people figure in *And Quiet Flows the Don* as the bearers of nobility and heroism. Heroism and beauty have long been related in the general outlook of the people. The hero of folk songs and tales was always an ideal personality. The popular fancy endowed such heroes with nobility of soul and exceptional strength, the ability to perform amazing feats. He was always close to the people, ready to protect them from their enemies and from the high and mighty, to wage an unremitting struggle against what he considered evil in life. In short, he was the people's wise and strong protector. This is how the artist Vasnetsov depicted the Russian epic hero in his famous painting: constantly vigilant, and ready to defend Russia and the people.

This popular concept of the heroic was later carried over into Russian literature. We find it in Pushkin, especially in his epic poem *Poltava*. Gogol's immortal hero Taras Bulba is in the same tradition. The proud, stern Cossack leader gave himself heart and soul to the people's cause, their struggle against foreign oppression. This great figure rose in the stifling world of Russia under Nicholas I, a reminder of another, free life, of those formidable forces concealed in the people.

In *War and Peace* it is the rank-and-file soldiers or those officers whose thoughts and feelings are most akin to those of the people, such as Tushin and Bolkonsky, who perform acts of heroism. With great perspicacity Tolstoi presented the patriotism of the ordinary people as being the fount of heroism. He was one of the first Russian writers to show how heroism is often concealed under the most ordinary, unassuming façade. The ordinary Russian in a soldier's greatcoat, drew himself up to his full heroic height on the bastions and redoubts of Borodino. In the special conditions of a truly national, patriotic war simple, inconspicuous people like Captain Tushin, the defenders of Rayevsky's redoubt, and the soldiers of Bolkonsky's regiment displayed the heroic side of their nature.

Gorky, with his lauding of the strong and heroic, his passionate appeal for bold, heroic action in order to change the sordid reality of his day, was the stormy petrel of Revolution. In his works such heroic deeds figured as an inseparable part of the ideal. He introduced into literature a new type of hero, the socialist waging an untiring struggle for the realisation of his ideal. In his novel *Mother* and his play *The Enemies*, for example, Gorky showed the heroism the Russian revolutionary displayed in the most prosaic situations of his everyday work.

This theme of heroism is present in all Sholokhov's writings. Essentially a realist writer, he sees the ideal and the heroic in the most mundane situations.

Sholokhov's concept of a true man is of an active, indomitable personality, inspired in his constant struggle by high ideals of goodness, truth and beauty. His heroes either are seeking or have found these socially important ideals.

Several of his very earliest short stories, like *The Bastard*, *Mortal Enemy* and *The Herdsman*, already struck this heroic note. They affirmed the nobility of man acting in the name of social justice, for the victory of the revolution.

Small as he is, Mishatka (the hero of *The Bastard*) performs a deed worthy of the memory of his father, a Communist in the Red Navy. The ex-Red Army man Yefim cannot accept evil and mendacity. His whole being revolts against it and by his death he keeps the flame of humanism and truth burning.

In *Virgin Soil Upturned* Sholokhov often puts Semyon Davidov in situations which reveal the heroic side of his nature: the village meeting, the women's riot, the flashbacks to the Civil War and so on.

The same heroic note rings out loud and clear in such scenes of *They Fought for Their Fatherland* as the battle for the height, the death of Kochetigov, and Lopakhin in the battle against enemy tanks.

The very essence of the character of Andrei Sokolov, the hero of *The Fate of a Man*, lies in the complex struggle between tragic hopelessness and heroic optimism that goes on in this Russian soldier who has lost so much in the war. Sholokhov shows human life, even in the most prosaic situations, to be a heroic struggle in which the real Man reveals his latent powers and abilities.

As a rule Sholokhov avoids elevated romantic pathos, seeing hidden courage, instinctive heroism, as true humanity and nobility.

In *And Quiet Flows the Don* an ordinary worker, a Communist soldier from the ranks, performs a heroic action, blowing up a bridge in the enemy rear. Podtyolkov dies a heroic death, addressing the Cossacks from beneath the gallows and calling on them to come to their senses and realise how they have been deluded by the White officers, firm in his belief that the day will come when Soviet power will be established throughout Russia. The Communist Likhachov also dies a hero's death.

In *And Quiet Flows the Don* Sholokhov draws a clear distinction between heroism and courage. Grigory Melekhov is courageous, but reading about him one never for a moment feels lofty heroism. All the descriptions of battles in which Grigory displays courage and skill contain such details as arouse excitement but not admiration. In these harsh, gloomy scenes he reveals himself a master of the art of war, but his actions are not inspired by a high and noble feeling and thus lack the essential feature which makes all the difference between courage and heroism.

Sholokhov does not consider courage to be a good thing in itself. Everything depends on the end it serves. The noble aim of the revolutionary reconstruction of society and happiness for the people, for which Communists like Likhachov and Podtyolkov were fighting and for which Red Army men and sailors marched into the attack with red banners and singing the *Internationale*, gave the quality of heroism to their courage.

Sholokhov's verdict on deeds and events is manifest not only in what his characters do, but in their very essence, in every aspect of their nature.

By revealing the ugliness in the natures of such characters as Listnitsky, Kaledin, the Korshunovs, Mokhov, Ostrovnov, Polovtsev, Latyevsky and others, Sholokhov was pronouncing his verdict on those social conditions which so debased people. By showing the doomed world of oppression and violence to be devoid of beauty and nobility, he was at the same time affirming the inevitable triumph of the principles of the Revolution.

Art that has its roots in the people invades life itself, revealing the ugly nature of social evil and striking many a crushing blow at it. Socialist realism shows true beauty and nobility to be inseparable from the struggle to establish the new, socially progressive principles: by its very nature it is "of the people".

Mikhail Prishvin made the following profound remark about the link between the ethical and the aesthetic in art: "Goodness does not automatically attract our attention and is convincing only if illumined by beauty. Thus the artist's job is to avoid the temptation of beautiful evil and create beauty with the sun of goodness."*

Sholokhov is one of those great writers of this century whose works most clearly reveal fruitful links with the romantic history of the people reflected in songs, fairy-

* *Nash Sovremennik*, 1956, Book 1, p. 126.

tales, and legends, with the imagery in modern everyday speech, metaphor and so on.

Indeed, one of Sholokhov's basic aesthetic criteria is that art should express the people's aspirations—something only art that is deeply rooted in the life of the people can do.

Thus, in examining the folk-poetical elements in Sholokhov's works, we are considering above all the character of his poetics, and how they link up with folk images and the ethical and aesthetic concepts of the people.

Sholokhov did more than draw on folklore: what the latter contained in embryo was developed in his poetics in the wider framework of the traditions of world literature and thus assumed an inimitable form of its own. His deep penetration into human nature and remarkable talent for moulding characters developed on the basis of 19th- and 20th-century Russian and world literature.

Many of Sholokhov's achievements, such as the principle of epic parallelism, went much further than merely enriching folk poetics; they opened up new paths in literature. His art is truly contemporary, disclosing as it does great achievements of the human genius and a poetic perception of laws as yet undiscovered.

Sholokhov's ideal, his concept of goodness and beauty, took shape under the influence of the ideals of the people, their yearning for good and justice. The recent changes in the social life of the people, however, were the decisive influence.

Good and evil are not abstract concepts, and Sholokhov's attitudes to them bear the stamp of socialist humanism. Scrupulously honest, describing people as they were in concrete socio-historic conditions, he judges them from the high, comprehensive viewpoint of the Communist ideal, which he calls on the reader to follow.

In all Sholokhov's works labour, the will to work, and the life of the toiling masses are poeticised and figure under the aesthetic category of the beautiful. The grim battle scenes, the descriptions of work in the fields, the poetic recollections of the Cossacks torn away from work by the war, and indeed the characters themselves, all reveal the ennobling influence of work. The Red Army men, sailors, commanders and revolutionary Cossacks are all depicted as toilers, whom the Communists had rallied to the united camp of the revolutionary people.

The ennobling influence of labour is evident in the fine qualities it brings out in such characters as Ilyinichna, Aksinya, Grigory, Dunya and Pantelei Prokofyevich.

Work often figures as a yardstick by which Sholokhov measures his characters' worth: "Stepan worked half-heartedly, and went off to smoke, to play cards, to learn the latest news, and Aksinya had to do everything" (1, 55). The joy work gives people is an important theme in *And Quiet Flows the Don*. It crops up especially often in Grigory's recollections of home, but runs throughout the novel, often appearing in small, incidental episodes like the following:

"On the threshing-floor men were threshing by lantern light, taking advantage of the fine weather, and the machinery pulsated with life. A man tirelessly feeding the threshing machine was crying hoarsely and *happily*: 'More, more!'" (3, 75; author's italics).

Sholokhov contrasts the fine qualities and poetic perception of the working people with the emotional bankruptcy of "the educated". Listnitsky, son of a land-owner and a dashing Guards officer, is a poor specimen in comparison with the simple working folk. Ruled by his baser instincts and incapable of real, sincere feelings, he deceives Grigory and takes advantage of Aksinya's grief.

Private property instincts were causing this amorality to penetrate the working classes. Darya's attempts to shirk work and her continual love affairs are shown as being two sides of the same coin. As Pantelei Prokofyevich says contemptuously: "She keeps away from work like a dog from flies, but she's always trying to get the best piece for herself and to have a good time" (4, 172).

Industriousness has always been an ideal characteristic in the outlook of the people, and Sholokhov, by using it to bring out his heroes' finest qualities, is sharing this view. He draws a sharp distinction, however, between the industriousness of the Melekhovs and the zealous husbandry of the Korshunovs. Grigory feels a basic need to work, and is miserable when he is unable to do so for long periods, while for Korshunov his own labour and that of his hired hands is merely a means of accumulating wealth. It was not the work itself, but the fruits of his labours that he delighted in. He was no longer a toiler but a property owner.

Sholokhov shows the ugly nature of this avidity in the merchant Mokhov and the kulak Korshunov, and we see it carried to its inevitable conclusion in Korshunov's son and heir Mitka. Devoid of the most elementary moral principles, Mitka Korshunov seduces Yelizaveta Mokhova, steals from his comrades at the front and plunders the local inhabitants without a twinge of conscience. It is in the description of his army record that he is first likened to a wolf, a comparison that is employed frequently later on. "Smilingly Mitka trod the earth with light, wolfish feet: there was a good deal of the wolf breed in him, in his gait, in the lowering glance of his prominent greenish eyes, even in the way he turned his head. Mitka never twisted his neck, which had been injured by a shell blast; if he had to look round he turned his whole body" (2, 89).

This "wolfishness" in his external appearance later develops as a basic psychological element in the descriptions of his sadism in the Civil War. His fierce hatred of Soviet power drives him to perpetrate unspeakable crimes as member of a whiteguard punitive detachment. His inhuman cynicism and bestial behaviour cause not only the Melekhovs but even his own sister Natalya to turn away from him in disgust.

Sholokhov portrays the life of the Cossack toilers as a struggle between good and evil forces. The noble struggle of Communists such as Mikhail Koshevoi, Kotlyarov, Podtyolkov, Lagutin, Nagulnov and Razmyotnov, men who embody the best features of the people, was a revolt against the egoistic morality of the ruling classes, in the name of the fine principles of revolutionary humanism. Aksinya and Grigory, and Dunya too, are also noble in their refusal to meekly submit to the restrictive pressures of the old society.

Grigory Melekhov's painful search for the right path in the great social upheavals taking place; his hatred for the tsar and the landowners, the generals and officers, for all the parasitic classes; his scrupulous honesty with others and with himself; his ability to face danger without flinching; the strength of his feelings and his devotion to his children: all these are shown as most valuable qualities.

Depth of character and strength of feeling are manifestations of the beautiful for Sholokhov—hence his unreserved sympathy for Aksinya, Grigory, Natalya, Ilyinichna, Pantelei Prokofyevich, Semyon Davidov, Makar Nagulnov and Andrei Razmyotnov.

But the reader is impressed not only by the depth and strength of these characters' feelings, and by their authenticity: Sholokhov so presents people and events that we emerge from this seething stream of life clearly aware of what is good and what is bad in it, admiring some and despising others.

We are moved to sympathy and admiration by the Civil War battle scenes and such episodes as the deaths of Podtyolkov and Likhachov and the behaviour of the prisoner musicians—wherever we are led into the noble world of the defenders of the Revolution.

Beauty and nobility foster the finest feelings in the reader; they are truly educative. Thus, in the episode of the storm in the steppe, Natalya's grief, which is deep and moving in itself, is heightened by the peals of thunder and blinding flashes of lightning. Yet the description of the approaching storm merely serves to give greater expression to Natalya's feeling of outrage. The actual beauty is in Natalya herself, in her inconsolable grief, in her revolt against betrayal, leading her to rise up in the defence of virtue, to keep purity untainted.

In his foreword to the works of Maupassant, Lev Tolstoi insisted that one of the essentials of true literature was that the writer should have a moral approach to the subject he is portraying. Speaking of the heavy responsibility borne by the writer engaged on a vast epic work, he wrote: "The novel has the purpose, even the express purpose, of describing the whole life of one or many persons, so that in writing a novel one must have a clear, firm idea of what is good in life and what is bad."* He goes on to say that the author must know whom to love and whom to despise. "Without knowing this, the reader does not believe the events described and is not interested in them."**

* Lev Tolstoi, *Collected Works*, Russ. ed., Vol. 30, Moscow, 1951, p. 18.
** Ibid., p. 19.

Tolstoi is here making the profound observation that a firm moral standpoint on the part of the writer is a basic condition for truth in art. Only truth can convince the reader and evoke fine feelings, and all the most clever attempts to produce a colourful imitation are doomed to failure, just as imitation flowers are no substitute for the real thing. Naturalistic wallowing in the seamy side of life merely inspires disgust.

The greatness of true literature lies in its ideals and the high demands it makes on man. Socialist humanism, with its respect and love for the working people, enables the writer to produce works of universal import.

Sholokhov poeticises those universal and morally healthy qualities which Soviet society has inherited: the class consciousness and integrity of the Communists, active protest against oppression and coercion, love of freedom, the will to work, maternal devotion, and love.

For Sholokhov people are not only beautiful for having a rich spiritual life and a poetic perception of the world but outwardly too. He is not attracted by cold perfection but rather by warm, mobile faces, just as we usually are in life.

Sholokhov's concept of physical beauty largely corresponds to that of folk traditions. He frequently hits out at the oleographically smooth concept of beauty of "the educated", often with great irony, as in the scene where the new recruits are undergoing their medical examination. The tall, well-built Grigory seemed to be an obvious choice for the Ataman's Lifeguards. The other men of his age did not doubt it for a moment. "The Lifeguards, eh?" they asked, crowding round him when he came out. But the officers had applied their own aesthetic criteria:

"'How about the Lifeguards for him?' the district military commissary asked, bending a black sleek head towards his neighbour at the table.

"'He has the face of a brigand.... Very savage-looking....'

"...As he went towards the door he heard a shocked whispering:

"'It's impossible. Just imagine it, if the emperor saw a face like that? His eyes alone....'

"'He's a cross-breed. From the East, no doubt'" (1, 302-303).

And this of Grigory, who combined strength and courage with a fine, passionate nature. For Aksinya and Natalya he was very handsome; for the officers he had "the face of a brigand".

Sholokhov's heroes are beautiful because their fine character is reflected in their outward appearance. Grigory Melekhov, with his hawk nose, his swarthy complexion and his grim, rather savage look strikes the reader as being handsome. Aksinya's plumpness is frequently stressed, there is a touch of shamelessness in the avid curve of her lips, and there is something irresistible about her proud face, and her dark, shining eyes. Natalya, Dunya and Mikhail Koshevoi are also outwardly attractive because they have attractive natures.

Sometimes Sholokhov uses a sharp contrast between a character's nature and appearance in order to impress the former more strongly on the reader's mind. Thus, Darya's handsomeness is in striking contrast to her empty, cynical nature. Chumakov, one of the members of Fomin's band, who has just killed a man, says: "That's my job these days, to kill people," and this makes Grigory look at him more closely. "Chumakov's clean, ruddy face was tranquil and even cheerful. His glossy blond whiskers showed up strongly against his sunburned face, setting off the darker hue of his eyebrows and well combed hair. He was genuinely handsome and of modest appearance, was this honoured executioner of Fomin's band...." (4, 634-635).

The dissonance between "handsome and of modest appearance" and "honoured executioner" serves to drive home the man's ugly nature with particular force.

Sholokhov does not pull his punches in striking out at the ugly features of class society. Contempt for the people and boundless egoism had penetrated so deeply as to become part of the very nature of such enemies of the Revolution as Listnitsky and Mitka Korshunov. Gross sensuality determined their relations with women, and they would not stop at using force or deception in order to satisfy their brutish desires. Their struggle against the people in the defence of their "sacred" property rights led them to cynicism and moral bankruptcy. One of these degenerates, Ostrovnov in *Virgin Soil Upturned*, is responsible for the most terrible crime a man can commit: he causes his own mother's death.

But property interests had also left their scathing mark on the working masses. They were responsible for the Cossack clannishness, for the contempt in which they held the "muzhiks" and workers. Sholokhov severely condemns these Cossack prejudices in such episodes as the brawl at the mill and by showing the inglorious role a large part of the Cossacks played in the Civil War, fighting against the people.

Pantelei Prokofyevich, that indefatigable worker and loving family man, did not think twice about ruthlessly plundering the families of Cossacks away fighting in the Red Army. Typically, Sholokhov condemns the old man's behaviour through the words of Grigory. "'You're a lot of swine!... No more of that, or I'll pack you off quick! I've given Cossacks a good hiding for that, and here is my father come to plunder the people!' Grigory quivered and panted" (3, 117, 118).

By showing many of Pantelei Prokofyevich's uglier features in a tragi-comic light, Sholokhov seems to be suggesting that many of the prejudices that class society has instilled in the toiler could be eradicated with time.

The negative influence of property interests on the working people is also evident in Darya's attempts to shirk work, her predisposition for easy pleasures, her cynicism and corruptness.

The patriarchal structure of Cossack life and the perpetuation of the Cossacks as a special military caste, produced Uryupin's anti-humanitarian "philosophy", with its cynical denial of the value of human life and the soulless professional maxim, "you're a Cossack, and it's your business to cut down".

Kharlampy Yermakov has similar views. When the White armies are utterly defeated and put to flight, he tries to justify his decision to go over to the Reds with the following extraordinary arguments: "If the Reds allow us to live we'll go and serve them. We're Don Cossacks! Cossacks of the purest blood, without any mixture! Fighting's our job! Do you know how I wield my sabre?... We don't care who we sabre, so long as we can sabre someone" (4, 404).

This is not a soldier talking but a cold-blooded murderer, an empty shell without heart or conscience. And Grigory's refusal to listen is understandable.

The class and property prejudices which Grigory was unable to shake off were to prove the downfall of this gifted man of the people. Sholokhov is full of sympathy for his tragically deluded hero, yet this does not prevent him from condemning Grigory, not only at the end but at many stages of his ill-starred life.

The whole structure of the imagery Sholokhov employs in his narration of the life of Grigory Melekhov gradually develops and changes. The young Grigory, "with his youthfully thin, round neck and the unconcerned fold of his continually smiling lips", is portrayed in totally different colours from Melekhov the insurgent leader. The imagery confirms to the nature of Grigory's emotional experiences, its very quality and the attitude it fosters changing accordingly.

After a talk about the Bolsheviks with Izvarin, a Cossack autonomist officer, at the beginning of the Civil War, Grigory says: "It's hard for me to make head or tail of it. I'm as lost as if I were in a snowstorm in the steppe." This comparison merely expressed what Grigory felt; the author has not as yet let his own attitude intrude.

When Grigory, now commanding a Red Guard division, is returning home on leave after being wounded, he is tormented by doubts as to whether the path he has chosen is the right one. "...The ground quaked under his feet as in a bog, the path branched in many directions and he felt no confidence that he had chosen the right one...." While the imagery here conveys far greater doubts than in the above case, the author is once more neutral.

But in the description of Grigory's state of mind on the eve of the Veshenskaya uprising, we have the following comparison: "Why had his spirit tossed like a hunted wolf in search of a way of escape, of solving contradictions?"

This is more than a cri-du-cœur of the hero; we feel a note of condemnation intruding. Grigory's feelings, now that he is fighting against the Soviet government, are likened to those of a wolf.

Without in any way detracting from the authenticity of his hero or the situations he is describing, Sholokhov chooses images that convey his own attitude and measure Grigory against the yardstick of true humanity, beauty and nobility. He mercilessly points out the changes in Grigory's outward appearance now that he has taken up arms against his fellow toilers. The way Grigory gallops off "flaming with blind hatred" is enough to convey his tragic loss of humanity, for the image of the former Grigory is still fresh in our memories; the Grigory who had stared with such compassion at the inert little ball of down in his hand, when he had accidentally cut a tiny bird in two with his scythe, the Grigory who had been so long tormented by a "dreary inward pain" after killing his first Austrian in the First World War, and who fired a shot at Uryupin when the latter cut down a Hungarian prisoner in cold blood.

There was indeed something terrible about the transformed Grigory who led the Cossack insurgents, and this does not pass unnoticed by Ilyinichna, who studying hard her youngest son, sadly remarks on a "wolfish" quality in his heart. This marks the beginning of the wolf motif, which becomes more insistent as Grigory gradually gets more and more involved in the struggle against the Soviet government. The motif entirely corresponds to the movements of Grigory's heart. Thus, it appears on several occasions during his participation in the uprising, and is dropped when Grigory leaves the insurgents, to reappear in a major key in the descriptions of his activities as a member of Fomin's band.

The remnants of Fomin's band that had escaped the rout by a Red Army squadron, set up their quarters on a tree-covered island in the Don where "only the wolves' litters find a safe shelter in the thickets year after year, spending their days lying in the snow-laden scrub" (4, 616).

The reader cannot help but feel that this is not merely a reference to the band as a whole, but applies to Grigory himself too, and this is confirmed a little later when Grigory compares his position on the island to that of "a wolf cut off by a flood". Sholokhov could not have hit on a better way of conveying the ugly features that had crept into Grigory's nature as a result of his service to an ignoble cause than through this motif—a motif, by the way, which has its origin in the folk tradition, where the wolf is an incarnation of all that is evil and most inhuman. Sholokhov's condemnation of Grigory is all the more forceful for being expressed in "popular" terms.

Naturally, this does not mean that Grigory is now painted entirely black. He still loves Aksinya just as passionately as before, and his tender devotion to his children is undiminished.

Towards the end of the book Grigory loses all his characteristic features. The impoverishment of the image expresses his spiritual depletion and the utter bankruptcy of his life.

The tragic end Grigory's errors brought him to is convincing proof of the destructive influence which working people who belonged to the petty-bourgeoisie suffered from their private-ownership beliefs and habits.

Even the few examples presented above should suffice to refute the naïve opinion that Sholokhov is objective to the point of showing life as it is, without allowing his own attitude to intrude. On the contrary, Sholokhov is perhaps one of the most partisan of writers. The point is, he does not present his views in an obvious didactic manner, but takes his readers into the depths of the struggle, dramas, and tragic contradictions. *Passionate humanism, high moral criteria and tendentiousness are manifest in a truly objective approach to reality and are due to poetic apprehension of what is historically inevitable and desirabl: for the people.*

And Quiet Flows the Don is a broad panorama of the death of the old world and the painful birth of the new. This panorama of great battles, human joys and sorrows, birth and death, in which the tragic life of Grigory Melekhov unfolds, ends in a vision of "the spacious world that lay glittering under the chilly sun". The world seems to have paused after the great upheavals to regain its strength before embarking once more on the turbulent river of progress. This last scene is warmed by the presence of Mishatka — Grigory's little son, a citizen of the new world.

The connection between life and the ideal is dialectical. The ideal contains man's longing for absolute knowledge, perfection and harmony that is infinite, for as he approaches the ideal he replaces it with an even higher one. This is why the aesthetic ideal of the writer who is aware of what is going on around him is constantly developing: it advances hand in hand with life itself. Indeed, this ideal is essentially a keen reaction to social development.

Even the most cursory examination of Sholokhov's works is enough to reveal how the most important, fundamental events in the life of the people were reflected in the writer's aesthetic awareness. While his artistic perception remained unchanged in its essentials, it was nonetheless advancing all the time.

Lopakhin's feeling of personal responsibility for the fate of the country characteristic of all the heroes of *They Fought for Their Fatherland*, from the insignificant old woman in a remote Cossack village to the divisional commander, was seen by Sholokhov as a feature of the new, socialist way of life.

Lopakhin, Zvyagintsev and Streltsov are "blood brothers" not only in that they are prepared to risk their lives in order to come to one another's aid but in that they share the same outlook as regards the point of the war, and indeed on life in general.

In *The Fate of a Man* Sholokhov is poeticising not only the courage and fortitude of Andrei Sokolov, and the life force sending out a strong green shoot even in the ashes of his burnt-out soul—his devotion to his newly adopted son Vanya. When Sholokhov poses the question: "What did the future hold for them?" he has the answer ready. The passage that follows is an affirmation of that strength which could overcome any obstacle "if his country called upon him to do so".

These are new motifs in Sholokhov's concept of man and in his aesthetic ideal, motifs which could not possibly have been present in *And Quiet Flows the Don*.

Book Two of *Virgin Soil Upturned* was to be a hymn of triumph about people striving for socialism, about the victory of the fine and noble in man.

First impressions are almost invariably the strongest, and in the case of true art, unforgettable.

I was lucky enough to hear the last chapters of Book Two of *Virgin Soil Upturned* read by the author himself before an audience of students and teachers at Moscow University on New Year's eve 1959. The weather was warm for the time of year and there were festive crowds in the streets. The seasonal aroma of pine-needles was everywhere. The decorations on the large New Year tree in the University club were sparkling brightly. Silence reigned, there was not a soul about: the New Year festivities had been postponed until later in the evening, and everyone had crowded into the hall, which was full to overflowing.

Sholokhov was greeted by a long ovation. Everybody who had a seat rose to their feet. We looked at his somewhat embarrassed person with close, loving attention.

He climbed onto the stage and in a hesitant, rather hoarse voice that betrayed how moved he was, began:

"Good evening, dear friends!

"As you see, I'm a little nervous. If I haven't come to visit you earlier, there were several reasons. The author of unfinished novels.... You see, I didn't want to come empty-handed.

"Thank you for your warm welcome. I have finished Book Two of *Virgin Soil Upturned* and, well, knowing that you're busy people, I won't take up too much of your time...." (Sholokhov raised one hand to silence the wave of protest).

"Allow me to read you the two concluding chapters of the book, taking it in turns to read with my editor and old friend, Yuri Lukin. We've been friends for thirty years now. He edited *And Quiet Flows the Don* too.

"With your permission...."

A writer of world renown had come to this modest university auditorium not to meet his readers, but, as he himself put it at the end of the evening, "to report to them" on work completed.

Sholokhov left the hall surrounded by a large crowd pressing him for autographs. Flash-lamps blinded one from all sides.

Long after he had left, the staircase, the cloak-room and the courtyard outside were milling with groups of young people eagerly discussing and "digesting" the last chapters of *Virgin Soil Upturned*.

III

Virgin Soil Upturned

Chapter One
THE HISTORY OF THE NOVEL.
THE PLOT COMPOSITION

1

Virgin Soil Upturned has a rather unusual history. Book One was published in *Novy Mir* in 1932. The same year, in his unpublished "Autobiography", Sholokhov announced that he was working on Book Two.

However, work on *And Quiet Flows the Don* was taking up a great deal of Sholokhov's time and energy, and he could not get round to finishing *Virgin Soil Upturned*. Then during the war all the writer's papers were lost, including this unfinished manuscript. As Sholokhov recounted it to K. Priyma:

"All my papers, including the manuscript of *Virgin Soil Upturned*, were completely destroyed in the war years. I had given over the manuscripts of *Tales from the Don, And Quiet Flows the Don, Virgin Soil Upturned*, my correspondence with Stalin and Gorky, and other valuable material to the local archives—as I thought, for safe-keeping. As it turned out, it was as good as throwing them away. I just don't understand how they lost them.... The manuscript of Book Two of *Virgin Soil Upturned* was lost with the rest. I'm now writing Book Two afresh and differently, since I didn't like what I'd written before the war."*

It must have required tremendous courage and will-power to start the book again from scratch after the war.

Chapters of Book Two began to appear in newspapers and magazines from 1954 onwards and, as we have seen, the novel was completed by the end of 1959.

Both in the writer's biography and in the history of Soviet literature the two parts of *Virgin Soil Upturned* exist as one single whole and also as two separate books. While marvelling at the way Sholokhov achieved such

---

* *Sovetsky Kazakhstan* No. 5, 1955.

unity in the narrative despite the long interval in his work on the novel, one can hardly fail to notice how the time each of the books was written has left an indelible impression on their form and content.

This automatically leads us to such important questions as the influence of the time of writing on the content of a novel, the nature of the author's link with reality, and the temporary and eternal in art.

At the time they were published (Book One in eight numbers of *Novy Mir* in 1932 and Book Two in *Pravda*, beginning in 1954) both books of *Virgin Soil Upturned* were *contemporary* in the fullest meaning of the word.

The theme would appear to be the same in both: life in a Cossack village in 1930, collectivisation, the period of sharp and decisive change in social relationships. Yet even the most superficial comparison of the two books reveals, in addition to the unity of the narrative, Sholokhov's new attitude to his characters and events which had evolved under the influence of developments during the intervening years. The Sholokhov who had completed *And Quiet Flows the Don* (in 1940), who had gone through the Second World War and the difficult post-war period, who had seen the tremendous changes taking place in our lives after the Twentieth Party Congress, could not help but have a different outlook to the Sholokhov of the thirties, and this new outlook naturally left its mark on Book Two of *Virgin Soil Upturned*.

At present it is not possible to determine the exact moment when Sholokhov began writing Book One of *Virgin Soil Upturned*, or when he first began to plan it, for it lies in the shadow of *And Quiet Flows the Don* which was taking up most of his energy and attention in 1930.

It is certain, however, that Sholokhov's friends working in local Party bodies repeatedly begged him to write a book about collectivisation—the all-important event in their lives at that time.

P. Lugovoi, then secretary of the Veshensky District Party Committee, confirms this: "I suggested that Sholokhov should interrupt his work on the third volume of *And Quiet Flows the Don* and write a novel about collectivisation, about the great changes in our life that were stirring the whole country and indeed the world at large.... I was apparently not the only one to suggest this to him."

Any writer who comes into contact with people a lot is familiar with such pressure being brought to bear on him, dictated by faith in his talent, and the desire to see contemporary reality portrayed in literature, on the stage, and indeed in all the arts.

This pressure of public opinion is particularly strong at important turning-points in history. The arts cannot fail to reflect the impact of historic moments.

Clearly Sholokhov himself felt the urge to respond to the impact of collectivisation and reflect it in his writing. He was after all personally affected by the changes taking place in the Cossack villages.

Lugovoi tells how some time later Sholokhov appeared at the District Party Committee office and announced that he had put aside *And Quiet Flows the Don* and begun work on a book about the collective farms.

Sholokhov apparently got down to actually writing the book at the end of 1930, and wrote the bulk of it in 1931-1932. This was a period of intense work for Sholokhov, for it must be remembered that he was completing the third volume of *And Quiet Flows the Don* in 1931.

"He began to work even harder, as I noticed by his lamp," Lugovoi goes on. "The point is, the electric light went off between 11 p.m. and midnight in those days, and the whole of Veshenskaya was plunged in darkness. Sholokhov would light a kerosene lamp and burn the midnight oil sitting over his manuscripts. When I came to see him in the morning, I noticed the lamp had run out of kerosene and the glass chimney was black with soot."

"I was writing *Virgin Soil Upturned* in 1930 soon after the events which had taken place in the village and radically changed village life: the liquidation of the kulaks as a class, collectivisation everywhere, and the mass movement among the peasants to join the collective farms," * Sholokhov wrote in 1934.

Sholokhov had just finished book three of *And Quiet Flows the Don* which tells of the most difficult days in the history of the Don Cossacks and in the lives of his beloved heroes—the Upper Don uprising of 1919. He already envisaged the tragic finale, the ruined life of Grigory Melekhov....

* *Pravda*, October 16, 1934.

The events of the Revolution and the Civil War described in *And Quiet Flows the Don* were still fresh in the memory of many of the heroes of the new novel, for only ten years had passed.

Here now was another revolution in the life of the people. The age-old foundations were uprooted in a terrible, fierce struggle. "Life in Gremyachy Log was up on its hind legs, like a restive horse at a tough hurdle" (1, 102).*

How would the Cossacks behave—and indeed not only the Cossacks, for the events described in *Virgin Soil Upturned* were more or less typical of the country as a whole? And what was the peasantry like, now that the Civil War was over and Soviet power had been established?

Sholokhov was not an objective chronicler of events. That was not in his line. The people involved were those among whom he had been born and bred, and still lived. He wrote *Virgin Soil Upturned* (which was originally entitled *With Blood and Sweat*) not simply because he was struck by the drama and the historical importance of the events he was witnessing, but because of a profoundly human inner need to help others find the right path, and thus set up the new world.

2

Virgin Soil Upturned is not just a book about the period of collectivisation. Sholokhov saw much that was universal in the concrete historical conditions of that time.

L. Pasynkov recalls how in a conversation he and Gorky had in the spring of 1932 on "the truth of Soviet books", the latter made the following remark about Sholokhov's books:

"Not everyone in this country yet appreciates how attentively and seriously the more far-sighted people in the West regard the themes of our best books....

"The more intelligent readers there realise that the development of the subject in Sholokhov's two books,

* All quotations are given according to: Mikhail Sholokhov, *Virgin Soil Upturned*, Book 1, Moscow, 1964, Book 2, Moscow 1961.

for example, is not a matter of the author's whim but is a serious reflection of real life, which cannot be ignored in Paris or in Rome. That's why people in Europe regard Sholokhov's books as reality itself."*

Gorky's words "the development of the subject in Sholokhov's two books ... is a serious reflection of real life" underline a very important feature of *And Quiet Flows the Don* and *Virgin Soil Upturned*. Their plot is determined by important historical facts. Sholokhov is at once poet and sociologist: the two are fused inseparably.

The heyday of the novel, the time of its greatest popularity, was the 19th century, the age of realism in the arts. Great works of literature were then full of tortured thoughts on the relationship between man and society, on the purpose of life and on ways of attaining justice and happiness.

The novel is a particularly broad genre which can combine tense, dramatic dialogue with lyrical interludes and the personal thoughts of the author. It can thus produce a real world, with strikingly natural situations and an exceptional degree of authenticity. With the emergence of the novel, literature began to recreate the flux of life, as it were, in all its variety and complexity, before our very eyes.

The 19th-century novel was above all social. The novelist set out to give an overall picture of life, make generalisations, analyse human feelings and show man the world he lived in. The Russian novel, for example, aroused the awareness of the masses, and was an important stimulus to the development of social and political thought.

The socialist realist novel inherited these democratic and realistic traditions.

The alienation of the novel from social reality, which occurred in the 20th century, has led to the form itself losing its characteristic unity, harmony and completeness. Modernisation and new forms merely served to cover up the fact that the novel was gradually losing its original synthetic nature, was ceasing to be an artistic apprehension of the laws and patterns of history, social relations, etc.

* *Znamya* No. 5, 1954.

In the twenties and thirties we were constantly hearing of the decline of the novel. Today the end of the novel is once more the subject of lively discussion in many countries. There are those who are ready to bury it, declaring it to have outlived its time, others who merely shake their heads sadly and limit themselves to talking of a crisis, and yet others who insist that the genre is still in its prime and holds untapped resources.

From 1956 onwards such polemics have been going on in France, Italy, England and many other countries, with leading writers and literary critics taking part.

A discussion about the novel was held in the Soviet Union in 1960 on the pages of *Literaturnaya Gazeta* and *Novy Mir*. Argument about the contemporary novel and its future development broke out again during the broad discussion on humanism organised by the Gorky Institute of World Literature in 1962.

Finally, in August 1963, the question was brought up at the forum of the European Community of Writers.

The reasons for these arguments and disagreements, as I see it, are not the same for the literatures of the socialist world and the literatures of the capitalist countries.

In reply to questions put to him by the magazine *Nuovi Argomenti* (No. 38-39, 1959), Alberto Moravia declared that it was not so much a question of the crisis of a genre as of a crisis in the relationship between contemporary art and reality. Moreover, Moravia considered that socialist realist art was also undergoing this crisis.

Let us investigate how far this is true.

There is certainly no doubt about there being a crisis of the bourgeois novel. It can be seen quite clearly in the loss of the popular epic foundation. Man as a social being, man uniting the individual and the social disappears, and the novel disintegrates. If novelists renounce synthesis and an epic portrayal of reality for the sphere of the subconscious and the pathologically unstable and so on, the novel becomes no more than a code for the initiated, remaining completely unintelligible for the vast majority of readers.

The novel of the absurd, for example, and the heterogeneous new school of the novel in France which would appear to be opposed to it (Alain Robbe-Grillet, Nathalie Sarraute, Michel Butor), are essentially based on subjectivist concepts. They accept *a priori* the theory that man is an unknowable quantity, and deny the novel the epic quality which is its essential feature.

In 1962 *Literaturnaya Gazeta* published an article by André Maurois, a member of the Académie Française, in which he had the following to say about contemporary French writers: "Many of them are extremely talented and very ingenious in their search for new subjects and forms. But they make no effort to be understood by the wide reading public. On the contrary, they are shy of such popularity and try to discourage the reader with disordered thoughts, an absence of connected narrative, and fanciful style. They also discourage him with the sinister picture they draw of life. Their world is the world of the absurd. Man is unable to understand why he has been thrown into this world. He suffers and his sufferings are futile."*

Obviously a crisis of subject-matter lies at the root of the crisis of the contemporary bourgeois novel. I mean the bourgeois novel that is breaking with realism, for wherever the novel is developing according to democratic traditions it is still thriving.

The future development of the novel will depend on the answer to such questions as: can we know man and his inner world, what is the relationship between man and his time, between man and the life of his country, man and his era. Disconnected narrative, the loss of inner artistic logic and the decline of form occur where an integral world outlook is lacking, where human life itself appears to be a disastrously chance and inexplicable thing, and realistic study of life is replaced by mere subjective caprice and horrific nightmares.

Arguments about the contemporary novel here in the Soviet Union and in socialist countries have arisen for quite other reasons.

But first a word or two about the nature of these arguments.

They largely began with some pretty sharp criticism of monumentality and the epic element. Thus, M. Kuznetsov's article "The Ways the Contemporary Novel Is Developing Along" which opened the discussion in

* *Literaturnaya Gazeta*, March 29, 1962.

Novy Mir (No. 2, 1960) quite clearly counterposed lyrical prose to the monumental novel with its sweeping depiction of historical events. Yuri Bondarev, famous for his fine war stories, declared in the magazine *Voprosy Literatury* that the short-story was taking over as the leading genre.

The way the short-story and the novel were contrasted, and the assertion that the former was the leading genre had its origin in the conditions of the concrete situation obtaining which were of a temporary nature. The personality cult had given rise to a tendency towards pompousness and false monumentality in art. One of the changes that came about in the life of society after the Twentieth Party Congress was the reappearance of direct personal experience and individuality in art. "I think so and so", "I saw..." and so on, were back in. The result was a flourishing of lyrical prose, a growth of the lyrical element in literature, the insistence on the short-story as the leading genre, and so on.

It would be wrong to insist too much on the aesthetic value of these new trends. Subjectivity in narrative form inevitably imposes limits on the writer's field of vision and in the long run limits his expression of his social outlook.

Is it indeed true at all that the novel has given way to the short-story and the novelette? Surely it would be more accurate to speak of a certain deceleration, a seeming halt in development, due in my opinion to the important historical changes taking place in Soviet life since the Twentieth Party Congress, changes in the very character of Soviet man, the new relationship between man and society, the moral problems now facing every individual.

The novel is particularly sensitive to changes in social life, psychology and relationships. But the truth is, it has a delayed reaction. A time lag is necessary for really worthwhile novels to appear. Yet once it has collected the facts, so to speak, and had time to digest them, it takes such a step forward in comprehension and aesthetic assimilation of the age as can rarely be equalled by any other genre. A good novel is always a revelation. It leads us along the highways of history, enabling us to interpret the essence of the conflicts determining the development of human society. The novel shows us human life in all its complexity, so that in it we can comprehend man and the age he lives in.

Sholokhov in his novels shows a remarkable ability to create a picture of life, full of powerful action and new characters, a picture that captivates the reader with its variety and wealth of original details and observations, carefully avoiding the casual, temporary or secondary, which is so often mistakenly accepted as important.

One of the most admirable traits of Sholokhov's talent is his ability to portray real life, capturing those features characteristic of the age in bold relief, with classical clarity.

Many novels and stories were written about collectivisation. It was the subject of such works as *Bruski* (1928-1937), a novel in several volumes by Fyodor Panferov; *Hatred* (1931), a short-story by I. Shukhov which Gorky thought very highly of; Y. Permitin's novels (*Claws*—1928, *The Trap*—1930, and *The Enemy*—1933); V. Stavsky's short-story *Running Start* (1930), and *Stanitsa*, a book of sketches written in 1929.

But only Sholokhov's *Virgin Soil Upturned* not merely captured life in all its power and infinite colour and variety but caught the very spirit and meaning of those years.

It was as if Sholokhov was looking back on his time from the vantage point of the future, singling out with remarkable sureness the most important features that were to be essential in life and in the development of his heroes' characters for years to come.

Sholokhov's art is constantly concerned with the relationship between *man and property*, which was already an important theme in Russian realist literature of the 19th century.

In the epic canvases in *Virgin Soil Upturned* Sholokhov showed man gradually revealing his creative potential as he freed himself from the power of the property instincts of the past.

In *Tales from the Don* (1923-1926) Sholokhov could still make "who will win" a vital issue. In *Virgin Soil Upturned* there is no longer any doubt that socialism will triumph, for it is assured by the whole previous development of Soviet society.

The literature of socialist realism sets out to depict reality in all the complexity of the struggle between new and old. In *Virgin Soil Upturned* the battle is fought along the whole wide front of life. There is the struggle between the poor and middle peasants on the one hand and the kulaks and whiteguards on the other, and between two types of leadership represented by Davidov and Nagulnov. Then there are the more personal conflicts, as between Lushka and Nagulnov, and Marina and Razmyotnov, and the gradually developing socialist awareness of the working masses, as in the way Kondrat Maidannikov overcomes his "sneaking regret" for his own property.

The collective-farm plough turned up the virgin soil of property instincts, all the deeply rooted prejudices, views and relationships that had grown up over the centuries. The psychological effects of this revolutionary change were no less important than the socio-historic effects.

The tragic figure of Grigory Melekhov, casting this way and that in his search for the right path, was now fading into the past.

Kondrat Maidannikov's "cursed hankering" for his property and his inner drama were but a weak echo of those spiritual torments which Grigory Melekhov went through in the years of the Revolution and Civil War.

It is no longer the Melekhovs, but people like Maidannikov, Lyubishkin, Ushakov, and Shaly who are now representative of the Cossack village.

The social instability and dual social and psychological nature of the peasant who was half-labourer, half-property owner were slowly becoming a thing of the past as history took its course. Such was the great humanistic essence of the revolutionary changes Sholokhov describes in *Virgin Soil Upturned*.

The whole novel is imbued with Sholokhov's deep understanding of the historical process. While giving a picture of that particular period through its unforgettable concrete events, Sholokhov at the same time shows it as a link in the chain of historical development. The Civil War years are still fresh in people's hearts and memories. Davidov, Nagulnov, Razmyotnov and Kondratko look back upon them with the pride of the victors; Polovtsev and Ostrovnov with the bitterness that comes with defeat, an angry longing to launch a new armed struggle to settle old scores.

Sholokhov shows the present as the outcome of the past (the Revolution and the Civil War), and the seeds of the future germinating in the present. The description of the first spring after the organisation of the collective farm, and the competition in Lyubishkin's brigade at sowing time acquire a special significance as a glimpse of the future of the collective farm, and of the way the characters will develop. The future belongs to such people as Davidov, Razmyotnov, Maidannikov and Lyubishkin.

Sholokhov's faithful application of the historical method in *Virgin Soil Upturned* determined many of the compositional features and elements of the plot.

3

The precipitous development of events in *Virgin Soil Upturned* is especially evident when compared with the epic sweep and leisurely pace of *And Quiet Flows the Don*. The former has almost nothing of the latter's excursions into family history (the Melekhovs, the Mokhovs, the Listnitskys, and the Korshunovs), changes in scene of action (from the Don to the front, to Petrograd, the Kuban and so on) or long digressions by the author which are so much a feature of *And Quiet Flows the Don*.

"The composition of *Virgin Soil Upturned* is better than that of *And Quiet Flows the Don*. There are less characters, and I didn't have to rush from the Don to the Kuban, all the time changing the scene of action,"* wrote Sholokhov.

While we hardly think that words like "better" or "worse" are applicable at all, we do appreciate that compositionally *Virgin Soil Upturned* must have been easier for the author, as there are fewer heroes, a fixed scene of action, and a comparatively limited time-span.

The action of Book One of *Virgin Soil Upturned* takes place in the first five months of 1930. The setting up of the collective farm at Gremyachy Log is described stage by stage, almost entirely in chronological order. March is particularly packed with dramatic events, the happenings

---

* *Bolshevistskaya Smena*, May 24, 1940.

are described day by day, nothing is left out, even such a small matter as Marina Poyarkova, Andrei Razmyotnov's sweetheart, handing in her resignation from the collective farm on the 26th.

Let us take a look at the hidden mainsprings of the action, which produce the upheavals and determine the outcome of the conflicts.

Whereas the 19th-century novel was mainly concerned with the individual, or the relationship between the individual and society, the whole plot of *Virgin Soil Upturned* hinges on an event of great historical importance in the life of the people. The revolution in the life of the peasants which ended in the victory of the collective-farm system, and the implacable struggle of the forces of socialism with the remnants of the world of private-property relationships are what determine the "connections, contradictions, sympathies, antipathies and indeed all human relationships" in *Virgin Soil Upturned*.

The novel contains a most remarkable wealth of characters and human types. There are those like the worker Semyon Davidov, Makar Nagulnov, Razmyotnov, and Kondratko, who dedicate all their thoughts and wishes, indeed their whole lives, to the high and noble aim of building socialism. There are the poor villagers like Lyubishkin, Ushakov, and Shaly, for whom the collective farm means the beginning of a new life in which they gain basic human dignity for the first time; Grandad Shchukar, the notorious story-teller; Khoprov, member of a punitive detachment during the Civil War and now finding the courage to openly oppose Ostrovnov and Lapshinov; Borshchov, who had been bought off by the kulaks. Then there are the kulaks—former Red partisan Tit Borodin, Lapshinov, a fence who also sold candles in church, Frol the Torn and Ostrovnov, and the whiteguards Polovtsev and Latyevsky. In the course of the action all these characters fall into one of two perfectly distinct groups, two irreconcilable class camps. Thus the leit-motiv of *Virgin Soil Upturned* is the socio-historical conflict.

The events described in Book One which serve to reveal a great deal of the characters' natures were largely based on actual events. With a few local variations these developments were typical of collectivisation throughout the country and not only on the Don. Basically, the pattern of events was as follows: a meeting of the poor peasants and Party activists, the beginning of the expropriation of the kulaks, general meetings, the pooling of implements and draught animals, the battle with mass slaughtering of cattle provoked by enemies, the laying in of seed stocks and so on....

In recreating the conditions in which the characters of his novel move and have their being, Sholokhov aimed at maximum authenticity and historical accuracy. He drew on concrete reality even to the point of frequently dating events exactly: "...On February 4th a general meeting of the collective farmers passed a resolution exiling the kulak families from the territory of the North Caucasus..."; "He returned from his journey on March 4th..."; "At evening on the tenth of March a mist descended on Gremyachy Log"; "By the fifteenth of March the seed-grain fund had been gathered in completely"; "On the morning of March 20th the postman arrived in Gremyachy Log with the newspapers that had been delayed by the floods and that contained Stalin's article *Dizzy with Success*"; "On the twenty-seventh Davidov decided to drive out to the first team's field..."; "By May 15th most of the district's grain crops had been sown".

Here we see one of Sholokhov's chief aesthetic principles at work. "When the writer violates the truth even in the slightest detail," he said, "he makes the reader suspicious and think 'perhaps the important details are untrue too'."

Absolute historical authenticity helped Sholokhov to show the great significance of the events described, and also to stress their uniqueness.

Of course, the plot of a work of literature is more than a sequence of events in their correct chronological order. The character grouping, the time the different characters are brought into the action are also important aspects of plot composition, expressing as they do the author's attitude to the events described, his ideological and aesthetic standpoint.

In a radio broadcast on April 5, 1952, Sholokhov had the following to say about the difficulties facing the novelist:

"One can compare work on a novel to a construction job, with the difference that while on a real building site every worker's tasks and duties are strictly assigned and limited, the writer has to be a jack-of-all-trades— the man who prepares all the various materials to be used, architect, mason, and construction engineer rolled into one.... Unfortunately, it frequently happens that due to a change in some important aspect of the writer-architect's plan while work is in progress, what the writer-mason has already done is razed to the ground."

This interesting comparison gives us a clear idea of the nature of the novelist's work and the difficulties involved. What is more, the possible drama in the relationship between architect-planner and mason-builder that Sholokhov states so clearly, helps us find the right approach to studying the plot composition.

But then the way events are strung together in a novel is very different from the strong framework of a building, which has nothing of the flexibility, give and freedom, which is such an essential feature of the continuous flux of life.

In *Virgin Soil Upturned* it is not only the socially significant events of collectivisation which make up the subject. Through their particular relationships with one another, the characters exert a considerable influence on both the course of events and their nature.

Chronological order is not observed at the beginning of the novel. Davidov has in fact arrived in Gremyachy Log before Polovtsev. We hear of his arrival from Ostrovnov: "They say some worker or other came here this evening from the district to drive us all into the collective farm" (1, 26).

If one tries to put the events described in chapters one and two into chronological order one finds that the plot loses considerably. It is more than a question of interest and arousing the reader's curiosity: the dramatic mainspring of the action is wound down and the socio-historic conflict which lies at the root of the novel reveals its true content and meaning far less strikingly.

The talented writer organises his plot by concentrating events, shuffling them and rearranging them in what appears to be the only possible order which reveals so well the characters, "connections, contradictions, sympathies, antipathies and indeed all human relationships".

The first three chapters of *Virgin Soil Upturned* are a good illustration of the masterly way in which Sholokhov creates the inner links between events and reveals the social and psychological factors that condition his heroes.

First the secrecy that surrounds Polovtsev's arrival, and the aura of mystery around Ostrovnov. In chapter one we have learned that Polovtsev is a former Cossack captain and that he has come to Gremyachy Log from a long way away. But we are kept guessing as to why he has come and who Ostrovnov is.

Here the natural sequence of events is interrupted. Our attention is switched to other people: the Secretary of the District Party Committee, the Leningrad worker Davidov, local Communists Nagulnov and Razmyotnov, and the group of Cossacks outside the building of the village Soviet, including Grandad Shchukar.

In that very first conversation with Davidov about the Association for Joint Working of the Land, Razmyotnov mentions Ostrovnov: "The chairman they need is Yakov Lukich Ostrovnov. There's a man with a head on his shoulders!... He grunts a bit when we come down on him for his taxes, but he's a good farmer, he has a certificate." Nagulnov shakes his head doubtfully (1, 23).

Ostrovnov appears in his true colours in chapter three, when the purpose of Polovtsev's visit is revealed—to rouse the peasants to revolt against Soviet power.

Davidov's arrival was the impulse giving rise to those important events which revolutionised life in Gremyachy Log and, indeed, throughout the country.

The fact that Polovtsev's arrival coincides with that of Davidov is obviously a device of the author. The two figures, who never actually meet face to face, are opposite, both as representatives of different social forces and as personalities.

Being the products of the forces of history, they are largely responsible for the turn of events and for the destinies of other characters in the novel. Each of them has the strength and firm conviction to make them a centre of attraction, and they polarise the contending forces in Gremyachy Log.

However, freedom of action and freedom of historical choice are different for Davidov and Polovtsev. The former's actions are determined by clear awareness of the laws and regularities of historical development, and the humanistic ideal of the general weal. Polovtsev tries not only to hold up the inevitable course of events but even to turn back the tide and restore those conditions that existed in Russia before the Revolution.

Crippling defeat in the Civil War did not reconcile him to reality, but embittered him and made him thirst for revenge.

Polovtsev rides into the village under cover of darkness. Sitting in the kitchen of Ostrovnov's house, "from under his prominent wolfish brow he cast a swift glance round the room" (1, 10). There we already have clearly, if indirectly, expressed the author's attitude to one of the two forces that are about to come to grips.

Thus, in the very first chapters of the novel the forces and even individual characters that are going to enter into violent conflict in Gremyachy Log have already been indicated. The position they take is dependent on their attitude to the incipient collectivisation.

The present is linked up with the past it grew out of— the Civil War. Polovtsev persuades Ostrovnov that collectivisation spells ruin for the Cossacks. "Do you remember, in Yekaterinodar I think it was, during the retreat, I had a talk with my Cossacks about Soviet rule? Even then I warned them, remember?... 'The Communists will get you under, they'll twist you like a ram's horn....' Wasn't I right?" (1, 27).

The truly epic nature of the plot comes out in chapter four, at the meeting of the poor peasants, where the popular masses come forward to take an important part in events. The collective portrait, the polyphonous dialogue, and the characters on whom the spotlight falls (the former partisan Lyubishkin, Arkashka the Bargainer, the sharp-tongued Dyomka Ushakov and Borshchov, that gloomy, cowardly defender of the kulaks) give a striking picture of the real hopes and fears of the Gremyachy Log peasants.

The dynamics of "through action" develops rapidly (we learned that the meeting was to take place in the very first chapter from the words of Ostrovnov; the meeting also marks the beginning of Davidov's work in Gremyachy Log).

The scene is an epic fusion of the general and the personal. The action was set off by an impulse from above and meets with strong response and support from below.

"'Don't give us your propaganda! We'll come into the collective farm body and soul!...'

"'We agree with the collective farm!'

"'If we're together we can do anything.'

"'But it's got to be run proper'" (1, 35).

The crowd scenes in *Virgin Soil Upturned* show the "revolution in the minds of men" which took place during collectivisation, and how slowly but surely, and not without occasional reverses and retreats, the new collectivist outlook gradually replaced property feelings and prejudices.

The crowd in the novel is never a faceless, impersonal mass, it always has distinct social and psychological features, whether it be the crowd of activists and poor peasants of Gremyachy Log receiving the news of collectivisation as the answer to their most vital needs (chapter four), or the wider circle, as regards social composition, present at the general village meeting, where the middle farmers' voices were also heard—the voices of people like Maidannikov who are all for the collective farm, of the waverers, who would rather sit on the fence and "see what happens", and of those who are openly opposed, either sucking up to the kulaks or themselves outright enemies of the people (chapter nine). Or again, there are those Cossacks who recoiled from Polovtsev for their own personal reasons yet spoke as one man when it came to condemning his activities as anti-popular and unpatriotic (chapter twenty-seven); or that jubilant, excited crowd greeting the blacksmith Ippolit Shaly with jokes and words of encouragement when he was rewarded publicly for fulfilling his repair-work plan in record time (chapter twenty-six).

What we are shown is the triumph of the new not only in the hearts of certain individuals, like Kondrat Maidannikov or Ippolit Shaly, but in whole social groups of the working Cossacks. The individual characters and their actions are filled out and gain body through the description we have of the way socialist ideals penetrated the masses, including the most backward section. Sholokhov gives a remarkably complete picture of the people's advance towards socialism. There is surely not a single social group in Gremyachy Log whose position during the period of collectivisation was not truthfully, comprehensively shown from many angles. While during the Civil War the majority of the Don Cossacks followed the kulaks and whiteguards, they had now largely come down on the side of the Soviet government. The middle farmer Kondrat Maidannikov ends his application to join the collective farm with the words: "I ask to be allowed into the new life, as I am in full agreement with it" (1, 92).

Nevertheless, getting the collective farm started was no easy matter. There was even active resistance: the villagers slaughtered their cattle and carted away the seed grain, and the women almost beat Davidov to death. Yet even in their open resistance the Cossacks tried to keep within the bounds of Soviet law—as they understood it, of course. Rather than force the locks on the barns, they try to get the keys from Davidov, the collective-farm chairman, and make Razmyotnov, as chairman of the local Soviet, to open a meeting.... However much they might hesitate and waver, the villagers of Gremyachy Log in 1930 are Soviet people, and no enemies can get them to rise against Soviet power. The most they can do is provoke their discontent and temporarily pull the wool over their eyes, by capitalising on the difficulties encountered in organising the collective farm and their deep-rooted habits and property prejudices.

The whiteguard camp can find no firm support even among the Cossacks who are most hostile to the collective-farm system. When Polovtsev shouts at an old Cossack who is a member of the counter-revolutionary organisation he has formed, for referring to Stalin's article *Dizzy with Success*, a "stocky Cossack of about forty ... stepped out from the men crowded against the wall and spoke challengingly, fiercely: 'Don't start yelling at our old men, comrade ex-officer, you did enough yelling at them in the old days. We've had enough of your high and mighty ways, now you've got to talk to us polite. Under the Soviets we've got out of the habit of such treatment, understand?'" (1, 257).

These were the words of one of the Cossacks Polovtsev had carefully chosen as the core of future insurgent detachments, of a man who considered himself "wronged" by Soviet power. It is not difficult to see why Polovtsev failed to incite the Cossacks to revolt.

These Cossacks, on whose support to judge by all appearances Polovtsev could reasonably have been expected to count, came out with a whole system of arguments evidencing their unwillingness to take action against Soviet power. Their words express awareness of the invincible strength of Soviet power and a deeply patriotic attitude towards the "allies", whose support would lead to the enslavement of Russia, and a memory of their personal hungry existence in exile. There is a feeling of injured dignity in the words of the Cossack: "Under the Soviets we've got out of the habit of such treatment...."

In shifting our attention from one social group to another, Sholokhov shows us how the process of revolutionary reconstruction gradually moulded that unity which brought the Soviet people victory in the war against nazi Germany. "...It seems this here newspaper will be parting us from you," an aged Cossack tells Polovtsev on behalf of the others, after they have read Stalin's article in *Pravda* and *Molot*. "We're not against Soviet power," says another, "we're against the disorders in our own village, but you wanted to turn us against the whole Soviet power. Nay, that won't suit us!" (1, 258).

When, during their first conversation at the beginning of the book, Ostrovnov asks doubtfully: "How will people look at it? Will they support us?" Polovtsev answers confidently with the following cynical remark: "The people are a flock of sheep. They've got to be led" (1, 30-31).

The decisive defeat of Polovtsev and his like exploded once and for all the counter-revolutionary upper-class myth of the historical inertia of the masses.

The real historical awareness and activity of the masses is strikingly revealed in the crowd scenes of *Virgin Soil Upturned*.

In *And Quiet Flows the Don* the people in the crowd scenes were often nameless Cossacks, soldiers, Red Army men and sailors who stood out sharply in the composition of the epic. The revolutionary masses were mainly presented in the crowd scenes, and through minor or incidental characters.

In *Virgin Soil Upturned* on the other hand, the Cossack masses and the major heroes are almost always directly related in the crowd scenes. This is the case with Davidov and the Gremyachy Log activists (chapter four); Davidov and Maidannikov at the general meeting for the establishment of the collective farm (chapter nine); Razmyotnov at the meeting which took a resolution to evict the kulak families, and chose a name for the farm (chapter thirteen); Davidov, Ostrovnov and Grandad Shchukar at the enlarged production meeting of February 12, where the coming spring sowing was discussed (chapter twenty-one); Polovtsev and Ostrovnov with the Cossacks recruited to the Union for the Emancipation of the Don (chapter twenty-seven); and Davidov, Razmyotnov, Nagulnov, Ostrovnov and Shchukar during the women's riot and the village assembly—all scenes which illustrate the true nature of the ties between the Party and the people, and reveal the actual relationship between the Cossacks and Polovtsev and his supporters.

The relationships between the main characters (Davidov—Nagulnov, Davidov—Ostrovnov, Razmyotnov—Nagulnov, Polovtsev—Ostrovnov, and so on) develop as an integral part of the intricate pattern of events, and are to a great extent determined by the movement of the popular masses towards collectivism and their gradual shedding of property instincts.

In Book One *the crowd scenes serve as nodal points in the plot.* Each hinges onto what goes before and at the same time marks the beginning of a new chain of events. The hidden undercurrents burst to the surface in the crowd scenes, and the laws of historical action, human relations, and the characters' natures are laid bare.

Thus, when the meeting of village activists passes a resolution to evict the kulak families, all the events recounted in the fifth to ninth chapters are in some way connected with this decision, however indirectly.

The basic idea behind *Virgin Soil Upturned* is expressed with naïve directness and uncompromising power of feeling in Nagulnov's account of his childhood and how he came to leave his father's prosperous farm: "I can breathe easier, dear comrade worker, now I've heard that we're going to take all farming property into the collective farm. I have had a hatred of property since I was a lad. It is the root of all evil; our learned comrades, Marx and Engels, were right" (1, 44).

Tit Borodin, the kulak, wounds Davidov, who is carrying out the decision to evict him. Collectivisation has turned Nagulnov and Borodin, the former friends and comrades-in-arms, into implacable enemies.

"'Makar! Remember!' Titok shouted like a drunkard, shaking his bound hands. 'Remember! Our paths will cross! You've trampled on me, but next time I'll do the same to you. I'll kill you whatever happens. Our friendship is buried!'

"'Get going, you counter-revolutionary!' Nagulnov dismissed him with a wave of the hand" (1, 76).

This episode illustrating the tragedy of a property-corrupted man has not lost its significance as a clear warning even today. It also serves to shed light on the character of Makar Nagulnov: "The pain of it curdles your blood," he says, referring to Tit Borodin. Yet although devoted and loyal in personal relationships, he is able to resolutely sever all bonds that tied him to property.

As a rule the past of the heroes in Book One of *Virgin Soil Upturned* is presented to us without obvious digressions or suspensions in the action, in the course of the development of the basic events. The conversation between Polovtsev and Ostrovnov in chapters one and three serves to link events connected with the underground activities of the counter-revolutionaries, and also sheds light on the past of two of the leading characters. The accounts we hear from Davidov and Nagulnov of their childhood, and from Razmyotnov and Davidov about the Civil War years are also woven into the action.

In chapter five there is an apparent "suspension", when we are given a detailed account of Razmyotnov's past in the form of a flash-back. But here too, his past is connected with the present through the conversation with Marina Poyarkova about the collective farm. This flash-back also has an inner link with the subsequent development of the action. The dramatic moment in chapter nine when Razmyotnov says he's not working any more ("I'm not working any more.... I'm not going to dispossess anyone any more") can only be properly understood in the light of the man's tragic past, his short-lived happiness as a husband and father. When Nagulnov's cold response to his empassioned outburst is "have a cry", he exclaims: "I will cry! Perhaps my little boy...", and breaks off (1, 78).

The cruel drama of the time pours salt on Andrei Razmyotnov's festering wound from the loss of his son, bringing his humanity to the surface.

Andrei's outburst leads Davidov to reveal his innermost feelings in turn. "You pity them. You're sorry for them. Did they pity us? Did our enemies cry over our children's tears?" he burst out, and there follows his impassioned account of his bitter childhood years. Then Nagulnov is able to contain himself no longer and "explodes". "'Swine!' he spat out in a vibrating whisper, clenching his fists. 'Is this how you serve the Revolution? Sorry for them?'" (1, 78, 79). He then begins to writhe in one of the fits he is prone to as an after-effect of wounds received at the front.

What an outburst of passion and suffering at this meeting between three friends and associates after a hard day's work at the village Soviet!

The dramatic situations in the plot of *Virgin Soil Upturned* give an authentic picture of a great turning-point in the life of the people.

The drama gradually builds up. The general meeting in chapter nine is more than the natural, inevitable outcome of the events that precede it. A middle peasant decides to join the collective farm, a decisive condition for its success. The story of Kondrat Maidannikov's past is woven into the continuously quickening pace of events of the collectivisation: the socialisation of cattle and the eviction of the kulaks (chapter ten). The murder of the poor peasant Khoprov, who had once been with the counter-revolutionary punitive forces and who now found the courage to break with Ostrovnov and Lapshinov (chapter twelve) is connected with the historical changes taking place in the Cossack village while at the same time serving to spark off subsequent events—the decision to evict the kulak families from the region (chapter thirteen).

This decision dealt a crippling blow to the whiteguard-kulak camp. Polovtsev was thrown into a violent state of agitation: "They're driving us into a corner, cutting away our last support! We must kill, kill, kill without mercy!" (1, 201).

4

The dynamics of the plot where the sequence of events is based on real life, is calculated to probe and reveal those concrete historical conditions in which the people's progressive cause triumphs.

The most dramatic events during collectivisation in many villages occurred in connection with the collection of the seed funds and the beginning of the spring sowing. A decisive trial of strength took place: if the spring sowing campaign was jeopardised, the country would be left without grain the next year.

Polovtsev sends Ostrovnov and Latyevsky a letter containing the slanderous claim that "this grain will be exported abroad and the farmers, including the collective farmers, will be condemned to cruel starvation", and the order that it was "absolutely essential to prevent the collection of grain" (1, 216).

A propaganda team arrives in Gremyachy Log. Such teams, usually consisting of industrial workers or employees from regional offices, were sent to the villages for short periods during collectivisation to help the local Party and Soviet organisations carry out their political and economic campaigns. As always in Sholokhov's novels, this authentic historical fact is presented in an artistic form and is motivated by the imaginal structure of the work.

A singularly important element in the construction of a plot is what we may term setting off characters by means of foils.

The characters are a mobile element. When they are brought together, they set one another off by force of contrast or similarity. The appearance of new characters on the scene or the retirement from the action of "old" heroes is often dictated not only by the development of the action, but also by character-drawing considerations.

The commander of the propaganda team Kondratko and the Komsomol member Ivan Naidyonov live their own, individual lives and also a "general" life, in complex aesthetic relationship with the other heroes, especially with Davidov and Nagulnov.

Both Kondratko and Naidyonov, who are essentially incidental characters, have that sharp individuality about them which is typical of all Sholokhov's personages and which enables them here to fulfil the function of foils for the major characters of the novel.

Kondratko is older and more experienced than Davidov. A Lugansk worker, in the Civil War he had marched "through the Cossack villages, aflame with whiteguard insurrection, to Tsaritsyn". Now, ten years later, older-looking and having put on a lot round the girth, Kondratko was helping to set up the collective farms in those same villages.

With a few deft strokes Sholokhov creates a remarkably vivid picture of the old Bolshevik and Red Army veteran from recollections of the Civil War years, "whose undying echo still lives in the hearts and memories of its fighters", a passing reference to the valour of Kondratko, the calm, quiet dignity and strength of purpose he reveals in talking with Davidov and the village Communists.

Placed alongside Davidov, Kondratko serves to set him off, showing more clearly the features that constitute the essence of a certain *type* common in that epoch.

Though men of different generations and character, Kondratko and Davidov share a common aim. Basically they both represent the same type of worker-revolutionary. What we have here is rather like a relay, with Ivan Naidyonov, the Komsomol member employed at an oil mill, taking the baton at yet another change-over.

Typically, Sholokhov is seeing to it that before the decisive battles begin the reader is clearly aware of the forces that stand "for Davidov".

At the same time "Old Square Sides" as Kondratko's comrades jokingly call him, enables us to see in Davidov something that so far existed merely as a vague hint, a disturbing possibility, a danger of which he himself was as yet not fully aware....

Davidov had refused to give any of "his" collective farm oats to feed other people's horses, the other people being the men of a propaganda team. He "suddenly felt cold with embarrassment and disgust at himself....

'That's the small property-owner's mentality! And it's beginning to get hold of me too', Davidov thought. 'I never felt anything of the kind before, that's a fact! What a blighter I am!...'" (1, 198).

Kondratko replies with the wise, sly humour of a man who was not born yesterday: "You'd make a right good farmer, you would ... mebbe even a kulak" (1, 198). This good-natured reproach is enough to make Davidov feel ashamed and put him on his guard against himself.

It is paradoxical and unexpected to say the least, that a Communist organiser should revert to the property-owner mentality. Yet in Book Two we see how the chairman of Tubensky collective farm moves into a kulak house and catches the "kulak spirit", permitting hay to be lifted from another collective farm....

Ivan Naidyonov appears in the novel at a very crucial point. The argument between Davidov and Nagulnov about what line to adopt with the Cossack masses was coming to a head.

The peasants are not bringing in the grain for the seed fund. Nagulnov beats up Bannik for sneering at Soviet power and has several Cossacks arrested. Davidov is livid, and Razmyotnov disapproves, although "the thought stirred in his mind too: 'Maybe Makar is right after all? If we pushed them a bit harder, we'd have the whole lot in in one day!'"

At a Party meeting Nagulnov is given a severe reprimand. As Davidov says: "You're using the old partisan methods, but the times have changed.... Look at the new generation: our Komsomol lad from the propaganda team, Vanyusha Naidyonov, the wonderful things he's doing!... And the ones he talks to bring in their seed without any beating up or 'solitary', that's a fact" (1, 231-232). Nagulnov swallows his pride and goes around with Naidyonov the next day to see how the "young one" sets about it.

In the scene at Akim Beskhlebnov's house Nagulnov is merely a spectator who sits there morosely, with his guarded mistrust of the "property-owner".

The Beskhlebnov "case" seems an impossibly difficult one for him. As he says on the way there: "You won't move those two Akims in a hurry, they're the tightest pair in Gremyachy. And scaring them won't work either. Akim the younger served in the Red Army and, taking things all round, he's a good Cossack and one of us. But he won't bring in his grain because of his meanness and love of property" (1, 235).

It is typical of Nagulnov that he thinks of "scaring" and "moving" the Beskhlebnovs. This was the line he would adopt in cases of difficulty. Yet to his surprise Naidyonov is behaving quite differently, showing respect for the household and being frank, forthright and straightforward.

Naidyonov's approach is to arouse good, human feelings in the peasants, appealing to their working Cossack instincts.

While Nagulnov always puts himself above the masses, Naidyonov puts himself on an equal footing with them. He does not even ask himself whether the Beskhlebnovs will hand over the grain or not. He doesn't doubt it for a moment. All he has to do is to convince them that it is necessary for the great cause of the Revolution. He tries to rouse a feeling of class solidarity, appealing to the sympathetic, open heart of the toiler.

In this psychological duel, Naidyonov gains a decisive moral victory over Nagulnov. Yet this difficult man, severe to the point of cruelty on occasion, is pleased to recognise his defeat, and his joy shows the fine, human qualities he possesses.

Thus Naidyonov stresses Davidov's essential nature and at the same time rejects the repressive methods and threats against the peasants that Nagulnov uses, affirming that humanism is essential to the behaviour of the Communist manager. Naidyonov "sets off" both Davidov and Nagulnov, the former in point of likeness, the latter in point of contrast.

5

The climax of Book One of *Virgin Soil Upturned* is the women's riot (chapters thirty-three to thirty-five).

Here again the factual basis of the plot shows through, for these riots were a typical event during collectivisation. A. Plotkin describes in his memoirs such a riot in Veshensky District. However, I feel it is unlikely that Sholokhov was basing his account purely on local material. The artistic fabric of *Virgin Soil Upturned* is woven out of the material of numerous observations.

In the novel these events are packed with great significance and emotional power. The conflict between old and new with all its undercurrents and everything that had slowly been building up under the surface, suddenly bursts forth into the open in a decisive battle. The chairman of the Soviet Andrei Razmyotnov is arrested, Davidov is manhandled, and the seed grain is plundered.

But even the greatest triumph of the forces of the past—open action by some of the Gremyachy Log peasants against the collective farm—ended in their total defeat. Moreover, they were defeated without any outside help whatsoever.

These unfortunate outbursts of violence reveal just how tight the links between the Party and the masses are, and the greatness and moral strength of Davidov, Razmyotnov and Nagulnov, ordinary people aware of the historical importance of collectivisation. The people follow them. They at last seem to accept Davidov, who has so far been an outsider, a stranger in their midst, as "one of them". "Let's make it up, Davidov, let bygones be bygones, eh?" a voice pipes up in a deeply moved tone at the village assembly that follows. Those that had gone astray ask to be taken back into the fold, and the spring sowing gets underway.

Parallel with, or rather woven into the pattern of these historic events, we have the personal drama of Makar Nagulnov—the meeting of the District Committee bureau, his expulsion from the Party, and his despair and contemplation of suicide.

Sholokhov's plots throw the characters right out into the turbulent mainstream of history. The great flood of life seethes through his novels, carrying all before it, tearing away everything from the past that stands in its path. The life of individuals and that of the whole people at turning-points in history are merged and developed in the plot as a single current.

The personal relationships are "hooked" to the crowd scenes, which are the turning-points in the plot. The individual and the social are interwoven and the hidden dramas of everyday family life are worked out in direct bearing to the events of collectivisation.

These events are the cause of the break-up between Andrei Razmyotnov and Marina Poyarkova. The first hint of profound disagreement comes during the conversation they have immediately after the meeting of the poor peasants.

"'I won't join. No matter what you say!...'

"'Well, look out then, it'll be good-bye'" (1, 57).

Andrei's threat worked. Marina joined the collective farm. But Andrei and Marina's feelings for one another were not of the lasting sort. Later she shows her true colours, when at the time the farmers began to desert the collective farm *en masse* she declared that to be in the collective farm was "to go against God". Andrei's efforts to make her change her mind were in vain. Marina was adamant: "...I don't want to be in the collective farm! I won't have anything to do with your sinning!" (1, 284).

Casual, unstable ties break up. In calmer days Nagulnov and his wife might have dragged on their marriage indefinitely without things coming to a head.

When her lover Timofei the Torn had left the village with the other kulaks and their families "she had shrieked hysterically and thrown herself down in the snow".

That had been the last straw for Makar and he had told her to prepare to leave. "I've known a lot of shame loving you, but you've reached the end of my patience! You got tangled up with that son of a kulak—I didn't say anything. But when it comes to wailing out loud before all the class-conscious collective-farm people—my patience won't stand any more! With a woman like you around I'll never live to see the World Revolution, and I may go off the rails altogether. You're just a burden to me in life. Well, I'm chucking that burden off. Understand?" (1, 143).

Contemporary reality can only be properly understood in the light of its significance in the history of human society and its influence on the intrinsic essence of human nature and individual destinies.

It is just this awareness of the laws of history that accounts for the social optimism of Sholokhov's novels, which are a powerful poetic affirmation of the ceaseless advance of history. This is why we must reckon with Sholokhov's novels "as reality itself".

An important feature of Book One of *Virgin Soil Upturned* as regards composition and style is the continual contrasting of day and night, and the parallel drawn between the approach of spring and the movement of the Gremyachy Log peasants to join the collective farm.

Virgin Soil Upturned tells of people who have freed themselves once and for all from the crippling, stifling influence of private-property instincts. It tells not of the individual, but of the peasant masses in their millions who have forever renounced their fettering private-property mentality.

Our awareness of the importance of the changes taking place, our impatience for the complete triumph of the new order that will free man for creative labour, is strengthened by the ardent anticipation of spring and hot, fruitful summer that is present throughout. This theme runs through the book like a captivating and subtle musical melody. We have a few bars in the description of the countryside in the very first chapter and then it is lost in the turbulent torrent of events to come up here and there until it once again bursts forth loud and clear in the descriptions of spring, the exciting scenes of the socialist competition in Lyubishkin's team at the ploughing and sowing, the blessed rain after which everything was green and burgeoned in the collective-farm fields.

The countryside plays an important aesthetic and compositional role in *Virgin Soil Upturned*. Like the first stream to cut its path through the melting snow, the descriptions of the countryside carry the reader headlong towards spring, constantly turning his thoughts to it. It is not calm and silence that emanates from these descriptions but irrepressible élan.

Compare these two passages. "The cherry orchards smell good after the first thaw at the end of January. In sheltered parts at noon (if there is any warmth in the sun) the faint melancholy smell of cherry bark mingles with the vapid dampness of melted snow, with the powerful and ancient odour of the earth just beginning to appear from under the snow and the dead leaves of the previous autumn" (1, 7).

"February.

"The earth is crushed and wrenched by the cold. The sun rises in a white glare of frost. Where the winds have licked away the snow, the earth cracks loudly at night. The mounds in the steppe are furrowed like overripe water-melons with snake-like rifts. Outside the village, on the autumn-ploughed land the snow-drifts shine dazzlingly, unbearably bright. The poplars along the stream are engraved in silver. Orange columns of smoke rise straight as building timber from the village chimneys of a morning. And on the threshing floors the wheat straw smells even stronger of golden August, of hot dry winds, of the summer sky" (1, 127-128).

While in January the only hints of distant spring are the faint fragrance of the cherry bark and the damp smell of the earth beginning to appear from under the melted snow, in February the strong smell of wheat straw carries us across the months, making "golden August" and "hot dry winds" an almost tangible presence. Despite the cold which makes the earth cringe summer seems just around the corner. Sholokhov purposely mentions August, the fruitful month when the harvest is gathered in and the results of man's labour are everywhere visible.

In *Virgin Soil Upturned* the descriptions of nature figure neither as a background, nor as pantheistic studies, complete in themselves, but are an inseparable part of the events described, giving the reader a feeling of suspense and anticipation of great and wonderful things to come and helping him sense the grandeur of what is taking place.

One of the most important places in the novel for the wealth of meaning and emotion it carries is the description of the night (chapter twelve) following the account of the distribution of confiscated kulak clothing. The poorest of the village poor, "their dark faces brightening with trembling hesitant smiles, hurriedly crumpled up their old patched and repatched garments and donned new outfits through which their flesh no longer showed" (1, 161).

It is more than a question of people, many of whom had never worn decent clothing in their lives, receiving the good-quality kulak articles. Poverty was being banished for ever from the Cossack village to become but a bitter memory of the past, and as Kondrat Maidannikov tosses and turns, unable to sleep, he has a vision of Moscow at night.

"Separated from Gremyachy Log by a thousand miles, great Moscow, city of our fathers, lives even at night. Engine whistles call out loud and long, motor horns sound like the chords of a huge accordion, tramcars clang. And behind the tomb of Lenin, behind the Kremlin wall, borne up on a cold blustering wind, a red flag flutters in the glowing sky. Lighted from below by the white glare of electric light, it blazes and streams like flowing scarlet blood. Its heavy folds droop for a minute and then the strong wind lifts it and whirls it about, and again it flutters and flaps, pointing now west, now east, blazing with the purple flame of rebellion, and summoning to the struggle...." (1, 166-167).

This epic vision of Moscow and the red flag "blazing with the purple flame of rebellion, and summoning to the struggle", throws into relief the great importance of the events taking place in a far-off Don village, by drawing them into the broad mainstream of historical development.

The epoch as a whole and events in Gremyachy Log are qualitatively related. This is a fine example of the epic sweep of the novel. Sholokhov has managed to give poetic expression to the relationship between what took place at Gremyachy Log and the world at large.

The description of the still winter night at Gremyachy Log which follows is in sharp contrast to the morning stir, when "the Moscow wind" blows on the village from the north, the wind of ceaseless movement forward, and of restless endeavour for improvement and the happiness of mankind.

At the first formal meeting ever held in the village, Ippolit Shaly the blacksmith is rewarded "for his really excellent work, which every member of the farm should try to equal". The scene of the presentation ceremony follows hard on a description of the coming of spring to Gremyachy Log; rapidly melting snow, upland waters pouring down to the lowlands in countless stream, which overflowed their banks, flooding orchards, "and the luring call of a wedge-shaped flight of cranes breasting the intense blue of cloudless skies". As usual, Sholokhov gives a very concrete picture of nature's re-awakening.

"A heat haze flows and trembles over the mounds; a blade of grass forces its sharp green sting through the dead stubble of the previous year and reaches up to the sun. The wind-dried winter rye seems to be standing on tiptoe to offer its leaves to the light-bearing rays" (1, 243).

The whole scene of nature bathed in light with all living things stretching up with longing towards the sun is a poetic prelude to the description of people finding happiness in working for the good of the community, and beginning to learn the value and significance of that work.

Ippolit Shaly, "who had never been spoiled with overmuch attention, and had never in his life made a lengthy speech, and whose only reward for his work had been a glass of vodka now and again from one of the villagers, was quite knocked out of his usual balanced state of mind by the management's gift and the impressive circumstances attending its presentation" (1, 245). He was at a loss for words. A clamour of voices arose. The collective farmers, who had so recently been individual peasants, shouted words of encouragement and friendly jokes. They were proud of him, and happy for him. In this short, humourous scene Sholokhov captures admirably the feelings of the man who for the first time in his life transfers his attention from his own little acre to the world at large and for the first time in his wretched life feels respect for his neighbour not because of his business acumen and wealth, but for his conscientiousness and work.

Andrei Razmyotnov, who was the master-of-ceremonies, had quite a job bringing the meeting to order: "Cool down a bit there! What are you yelling about again? Feeling the spring?" (1, 245).

Razmyotnov has accidentally hit the nail on the head. The villagers are really feeling the spring, which has caught them up in its flood-waters and is carrying them towards a life quite different from the miserable existence they have hitherto known.

Ippolit Shaly finally plucks up the courage to speak. He ends his stumbling, faltering speech: "Thank you, Comrade Davidov and the collective farm ... thank you very much!" (1, 246). These simple words straight from the heart express better than any others just what he felt—and with him the majority of farmers present at the meeting.

The end of Book One contains the seeds of new conflicts and betokens new class battles. Timofei the Torn, son of an exiled kulak, returns to his native parts; and Polovtsev and Latyevsky turn up again at Ostrovnov's house as foreign agents.

7

Until such time as the draft versions of Book Two become available it will be impossible to form a complete picture of the book in the process of writing, as one of the main points requiring our attention is the actual subject-matter of the novel.

The rough notes for Book Two were apparently made in 1932 right after work on Book One. Sholokhov expected to finish *Virgin Soil Upturned* at the same time as book four of *And Quiet Flows the Don*, if not before. However, he was forced to put aside his writing for some time, due to the difficult situation that arose on the Don in 1932-1933.

In a conversation with a reporter from *Literaturnaya Gazeta* in 1934, Sholokhov made a clear statement to the effect that work on *And Quiet Flows the Don* kept him from completing *Virgin Soil Upturned*. His exact words were: "Work on the last book of *And Quiet Flows the Don* has prevented me from finishing Book Two of *Virgin Soil Upturned*.... As soon as I finish *And Quiet Flows the Don* I shall get back to *Virgin Soil Upturned*."

In the same interview Sholokhov speaks of the time of the action of Book Two and the heroes.

"I have now overcome the main difficulty which slowed down work on part one—the abundance of material and my efforts to choose what was most essential. Book Two, like Book One, will show the establishment of the collective-farm system in the countryside. It covers roughly the same period (1930-1931), but a later stage. All the main characters in Book One are carried over into Book Two, but in addition to them the reader will also meet new heroes. These are mainly Party workers from the district."

He then went on to say how he intended taking certain criticisms into account in Book Two. "I accept the criticism that in the first book of *Virgin Soil* the role of the

Komsomol in the collectivisation of the countryside is poorly reflected and that women activists are not shown at all. This shortcoming must be corrected in the work plan for Book Two. As to how, I don't know yet."*

In a conversation with an *Izvestia* correspondent a year later, Sholokhov again confirmed the period of time the action of Book Two would probably cover: "Book Two will also be the last. It covers 1931, the period during which the collective farms were well and truly established."

The arrangement of the key figures was to be the same as in Book One.

"The figure of the middle peasant joining the collective farm will be the central theme as before, despite the fact that this imposes certain limitations on the development of events.... The trio with Davidov at the head remains, Grandad Shchukar will not, I hope, lose all his joviality, and the people from the district offices will become more intelligent and cultured. Polovtsev and Timofei will join a small renegade band.... I want Book Two, like Book One, to be a novel of everyday life. There's a peculiar vigour and fascination in collective-farm life.... Everyday life needs describing and it's an honour to do it!"**

Judging from the final version, Sholokhov's plans underwent some quite considerable changes. Kondrat Maidannikov, "a middle farmer joining the collective farm", has definitely passed into the background and becomes no more than an incidental figure. Nor was this, obviously, dictated by fears of "certain limitations on the development of events". The truth is that the social and psychological content of Kondrat Maidannikov was practically exhausted in Book One (his break with the past, overcoming of his hankering after what was "his own" and so on). All the events in Book One lead up to the moment when he joins the Party, which marks his civic coming of age.

It was thus quite natural that he should fade into the background in Book Two. Other characters—like Ippolit Shaly, Ustin Rikalin and Ivan Arzhanov—are brought into the foreground. Each of them has his past filled

* *Literaturnaya Gazeta*, February 6, 1934.
** *Izvestia*, March 10, 1935.

in with a fair degree of detail, thus historical perspective is created, and one is given a strong feeling of the passage from the old days to the new life. The laws of history are more consistently manifest here than in Book One.

Sholokhov completely changed the fate of Polovtsev and Timofei the Torn, finding a much more dynamic solution. The scene where Nagulnov kills Timofei is one of the most powerful in the whole novel. Here is such a wealth of tragic motives as one could hardly have expected to find if Sholokhov had followed his original intention of having Timofei meet Polovtsev, describing how the band was formed, and so on. Timofei's feelings come to the fore and determine the outcome of events: he feels he must see Lushka, and tries to meet her. He fires at Nagulnov, and all his class hatred, memories of former injuries, and bitter jealousy mixed up together go into that shot....

It is interesting to note what became of Sholokhov's plan to show the people from the district offices much more clearly in Book Two. During the thirties Sholokhov was bound by close ties of friendship with many of the Party and Soviet workers in Veshensky District, and he took everything that happened in the district very much to heart. He took part in all the sowing and harvesting campaigns and so on. Sholokhov's creative work was closely linked to work for the Party and the Government.

Men like P. Lugovoi, P. Krasyukov and T. Logachev did not only meet Sholokhov on "business". There were the hunting and fishing outings, gatherings at Sholokhov's house, such as the gay New Year celebrations, when the children would have to solve verse riddles composed by the writer himself and the grown-ups would sing folk songs, and laugh and joke together.

An *Izvestia* correspondent wrote in 1935: "Sholokhov is obviously very much wrapped up in this type at present, he feels he has a debt to pay the district men. He is continually comparing them with the average intellectual in the West, and marvelling at the integrity, thirst for knowledge, and clarity of purpose and outlook of the people who are leading the districts forward.

"'Writers, myself included,' he says frankly, 'have a debt of gratitude too great to be repaid to these remarkable people who are so quickly acquiring knowledge and culture in the widest sense of the word.'"*

Sholokhov "paid off the debt" with Nesterenko, the Secretary of the District Party Committee, in Book Two of *Virgin Soil Upturned*.

One cannot help wondering whether Sholokhov had intended writing of the gross distortions in the policy of collectivisation which had such tragic consequences in 1932 and 1933. That is a question that cannot be answered without the help of the author.

Almost every mention Sholokhov made of his plans which we know of, shows that he had no avowed intention of continuing the action beyond 1931. In the final published manuscript, indeed, the events do not take us beyond 1930.

As the tight mainspring of the action unwinds, it becomes clear that the author's main attention is focussed on the events and historical significance of the *beginnings* of collectivisation.

Be that as it may, however, like any true work of art, Sholokhov's book transcends the bounds of the time in which it is set and is a valid comment on many questions of our whole age.

Book Two of *Virgin Soil Upturned* is by no means an impassive chronicle of events that are over and done with. Although it deals with events far removed in time, it is permeated with the spirit of today. Indeed, Sholokhov was able to see much of what he described all the more clearly for viewing it from the vantage point of a later day.

Since the development of the action is determined by the active influence the Communists exert on the social processes it is only natural that Davidov, Razmyotnov and Nagulnov should occupy the centre of the stage.

Rather than ignore the humdrum and everyday aspects of reality Sholokhov draws strength from them. His artistic vision has an immeasurable range. He sees how some men are ennobled by their awareness of the historical aims of society and by working for their attainment, while others are the slaves of the small property-owner mentality and this leads them to moral degradation.

* *Izvestia*, March 10, 1935.

He sees how the shoots of the new struggle up in every sphere of human feelings, even the most eternal and intimate.

If in Book One the poetry of social transformation rings out loud and clear in a jubilant key, Book Two strikes a more lyrical note with the *moral education* of the man for whom the future was opening up.

The social theme often appears in Book Two as an intrinsic part of the moral element.

Hence such features of the plot as deceleration of the action, numerous "confessions" full of hidden meaning (Ivan Arzhanov's confession and advice to Davidov to think about the "kinks" in human nature), lengthy conversations (Ippolit Shaly and Davidov, Nesterenko and Davidov and so on), increased interest in relationships which reveal the more intimate side of human nature (Davidov—Lushka—Varya Kharlamova; and Nagulnov—Lushka).

The author's "tone" has changed considerably. Whereas in Book One he only addressed the reader directly once, in Book Two his own attitude makes itself felt on numerous occasions and he openly projects himself into the world of his heroes as a sympathetic friend. The lyricism of the language gives a very special note of sincerity and intimacy to the narrative.

The author's feeling suddenly bursts into the hitherto objective account of Varya and Davidov's ill-starred love: "What are you crying for, dear?" (2, 93); "Poor little ox-driver, only seventeen years old!" (2, 98).

This tender note of sympathy on the author's part is often present in accounts of Davidov and Razmyotnov, and builds up to the moving requiem for Nagulnov and Davidov at the end of the book.

"...And so the nightingales of the Don have sung farewell to my dearly cherished Davidov and Nagulnov, the ripening wheat has whispered it, the pebbles of the nameless stream that flows from somewhere at the top of the Gremyachy ravine have murmured it. And now it is all over" (2, 456).

This requiem born of the writer's love and sympathy for his heroes arouses a strong note of response in the reader, making him feel the loss as a personal one.

The strong lyric element already observable in the later parts of *And Quiet Flows the Don* is typical of almost all Sholokhov's post-war works. In fact, the prominence of the subjective element in epic narrative is a typical feature of modern prose. It takes the form of lyricism, and is also manifest in the changed character of the period, the bold combinations of various kinds of speech (narration by the author, the heroes, represented direct and so on), and in the wide use made of represented direct speech, which permits the author to subtly introduce his own standpoint into even the most intimate thoughts and experiences of his heroes.

Throughout Book Two Sholokhov debates such subjects as true humanity, humanism and historical necessity.

The actions of Semyon Davidov, Makar Nagulnov and Andrei Razmyotnov are determined by their aspirations for their cherished ideal of socialism, which for them was a dream of new social relations coming true. These men were free from slavish attachment to "cursed property", their land and their chattels.

The humanistic ardour in *Virgin Soil Upturned* indeed arises from this rejection of that world of unbridled property instincts where class egoism withered the human spirit.

The struggle for socialism brings out the best qualities in any Sholokhov hero—that is, his personal concern for the common weal and his social consciousness.

Virgin Soil Upturned is not only orientated towards the present day. The high ideals it is imbued with make it a bridge to *the future.*

Chapter Two
SEMYON DAVIDOV

1

In May 1960 the workers of the Kirov (the former Puti-lov) Works in Leningrad congratulated Sholokhov on his Lenin Prise award for *Virgin Soil Upturned* and invited him to pay them a visit.

"I'll be with you at the first possible opportunity," Sholokhov cabled back.

In March 1961 a large "Sholokhov delegation" including the writer and his family and people from Veshensky District—collective farmers and Party workers—arrived in Leningrad.

A meeting was held in the Works Party Committee room. Sholokhov introduced the delegation with the following words: "Your Davidovs are old-age pensioners now and these are young representatives of Gremyachy Log, representatives of the collective farms, people who have distinguished themselves by outstanding achievements in farm production, who are carrying on the good work of the pioneers of the collective-farm movement."*

Sholokhov told the Kirov workers how he created Semyon Davidov: "I'm often asked why Semyon Davidov is a Baltic sailor and not a Kharkov or Mariupol man. I'll tell you quite frankly: when I wrote *Virgin Soil Upturned* I was paying a tribute of admiration to the Petrograd working class to which the Putilov workers belong. Why a sailor? I was paying a tribute of admiration for a second time—to the sailors of the Baltic Fleet.

"That's how I created a character that was one of your lads. I am proud of the fact that he is your son.... And how grand it is to see the new generation that owes its experience and schooling to Semyon Davidov and his

* *Literatura i Zhizn,* March 3, 1961.

255

contemporaries and has also inherited their best traditions."*

The question of "prototypes" for Sholokhov's novels is a purely derivative one. The factual basis of his novels cannot be reduced to any concrete people or events. His characters were the product of countless impressions and observations in the school of life.

An essential feature of Sholokhov's novels is that throughout we feel the presence of a mind striving to assess the fundamental problems of human life. In creating his characters or recounting events he tries to show them in their historical perspective and reveal all the complex links between a man and his time.

As a philosopher, thinker and "lyric", Sholokhov does not limit himself to showing what people were like in 1930, but tries to comprehend man historically, in the perspective of the country's rapid development. Sholokhov examines the qualities which, born of reality itself, transform the human personality and make the most ordinary people of Gremyachy village approach the ideal harmony and perfection of the truly beautiful, noble individual.

This alluring light of the ideal creates a special, intellectual and moral atmosphere in Sholokhov's novel.

2

Sholokhov has a remarkable way of disclosing the warming glow of the noble and beautiful in the most humdrum everyday circumstances, and singling out in intense emotional struggles those fine features which ennoble his favourite heroes and give the reader an idea of what a real man should be.

In Book One Davidov's essential nature is revealed mainly in how he behaves in the events of great social importance.

Davidov rallies all the best, most progressive forces in Gremyachy Log around him. Kondrat Maidannikov, with his pure heart, reflective mind and painful doubts is drawn to Davidov and expects advice and support from

* *Leningradskaya Pravda*, March 3, 1961.

him. Davidov helps and advises the village Communists Nagulnov and Razmyotnov, poor peasant activists like Lyubishkin and Ushakov, and has quite an influence on them.

In the modest appearance of this mechanic from the Putilov Works with his cap, an overcoat with a worn sheepskin collar, and an old pair of shoes, there's nothing to suggest the truly heroic qualities that will come out in crucial moments.

From our very first meeting with Davidov, during his argument with the Secretary of the District Party Committee who is a "careful" man, and "a bit shaky on the right leg" when it comes to dealing with the kulaks, we feel ourselves in the presence of a man of great integrity. He may not always find the right words during a heated argument, but he thinks carefully before making a decision and once he has made it sticks to it.

His integrity and firmness immediately arouse trust and sympathy. On returning home after his first meeting with Davidov, Andrei Razmyotnov "remembered Davidov's stocky, solidly built figure, his determined, tightly bunched face with its firm folds at the sides of the mouth, and the humourously wise expression of his eyes.... And as Andrei remembered this, he decided joyfully, 'No, that one won't let us down'" (1, 58).

Davidov's great inner strength and sense of purpose come from his awareness of the vital importance for the nation of the mission the Party has sent him on and his feeling of oneness with the masses.

At the very first meeting of the Gremyachy Log poor peasants Davidov managed to explain the collective farm in such a simple straightforward manner that the assembled peasants immediately declared their support: "'But we're heart and soul for the collective farm!'

"'We'll start tonight, if you like!'

"'Take our names down now!'

"'Lead us to smash the kulaks'" (1, 39).

Davidov's strength and directness is reflected in his speech. He tries to choose words that cannot possibly be twisted or misconstrued, so that there is no room for ambiguity. He speaks clearly, concisely and to the point. His words, fired by strong conviction and iron logic, always find their mark. "The Party is planning complete collectivisation so that it can hitch you up to a tractor and haul you out of your poverty. What did Comrade Lenin say before he died? The only salvation from poverty for the toiling peasant is in the collective farm. Otherwise he's done for. The vampire kulak will suck him dry. And you must take the path that has been pointed out to you, absolutely firmly" (1, 33-34).

True, his speech at times seems rather blunt and journalese, but behind it one feels the passionate enthusiasm of the Bolshevik capable of great self-sacrifice. When the kulaks were being dispossessed Tit Borodin struck him with an iron bar. That very evening Davidov, with his head bandaged, presides at a meeting. He answers all the questions put to him carefully and intelligently, and convincingly tells the peasants of the advantages of the collective farm. There is an uproar in the overcrowded school-house. Some support the collective farm, others are hesitant and yet others are openly hostile to it. It almost comes to an open brawl. When the shouts die down, a belated voice full of malice is heard: "'You can't herd us together like sheep! Titok blooded you once, and it can be done again.'

"Something seemed to strike Davidov like a whip. For a minute he stood pale-faced, his gap teeth parted, in the tense silence, then he shouted hoarsely:

"'You there! Voice of the enemy! So you haven't had enough of my blood! I'll live to see the day when we'll bury your kind, everyone of you. But if it's necessary, for the Party, for my Party, for the cause of the workers, I'll give every drop of my blood! Do you hear, you kulak swine? All, to the very last drop!'" (1, 88).

There in the crowded school-house, in the tense silence that follows the enemy's threat, Davidov's words sound like a vow taken before the battle.

Less than a month later Davidov finds himself alone facing a furious crowd aroused by kulak propaganda. The kulaks have spread the rumour that the seed grain is to be exported abroad, and a large number of the Cossacks dash to the public barns and demand that Davidov give them the keys so that they can share out the grain.

Davidov tries to calm the crowd by addressing them in a cool, self-assured, authoritative manner. "...But the women hemmed him in, shouting deafeningly with the silent approval of their menfolk at the back." He tries to gain time for help to arrive and says that the keys are at his lodgings, then that they are at Nagulnov's. On the way the women start to beat him. "His ear was bleeding, his lips and nose were cut, but he still smiled with his puffy lips, showing his missing front tooth, and with mild unhurried movements warded off the women who attacked him with particular fury." Yet Davidov does not lose control of himself. In the end he has been knocked about so badly that he can hardly stand and sits down in the road. "'But it's for you, curse you...' Davidov said suddenly in an unusually resonant voice and looked round with a strange new light in his eyes, 'it's for you we're doing all this. And you're killing me. Blast you! I won't give you the keys, understand? Fact I won't! Well?'" (1, 343-344). There is readiness to meet death steadfastly, without faltering, and deep pity for the deluded people in his words.

"...But that's not the stuff we, Bolsheviks, are made of, citizens, and nobody's going to squeeze us into the shape they want! I was beaten up by the cadets in the Civil War and even they couldn't knock the stuffing out of me! The Bolsheviks have never gone on their knees to anyone, and they never will, fact!" Davidov says at a meeting where he addresses the villagers, including those who have beaten him and are now shamefacedly keep quiet (1, 361).

From scattered biographical facts and from the way Davidov behaves at dramatic and often unexpected turns in the bitter struggle for collectivisation, there gradually emerges a picture of a Bolshevik, a man of unbending will and courage. Davidov is so attractive because this is not a declarative image but a character revealed in concrete actions and situations. What we are told of him and what he tells us of himself is in full accordance with his actions.

Davidov says that he is prepared to shed his blood "to the very last drop" for the Party, and we are able to note that this is so, for we see him go alone and unarmed against an angry mob, we admire the dignity with which he bears himself when he is almost beaten to death, we see him rise to his feet and, wiping away the blood, stagger weakly to the barns to prevent them being plundered. The cadets who had beaten him got nothing for their pains and we know that this is no empty boast. This detail sheds a little more light on his character, showing us how he was tempered in the crucible of the Civil War. Thus, in the figure of Davidov, Sholokhov has created a remarkably *authentic and convincing* character.

As soon as he hears that there is trouble in Lyubishkin's team during the spring ploughing, Davidov leaves the managing to his assistant and is off to the fields. Not to give them a rating, but to "teach them to work", for as he himself says: "That's what leadership is!" When Razmyotnov protests, he replies: "Do you think I haven't seen any good commanders in my time? The good ones lead by example when they're in a tight spot. And that's what I've got to do" (1, 370-371).

Leading means teaching people how to work, and there is no better way of teaching than by example. Such are the rules of Bolshevik leadership that Davidov applies in his practical work.

The episode where Davidov goes ploughing for the first time in his life, and sparks off socialist emulation in Lyubishkin's team is certainly one of the most exciting and poetic in Book One.

In striving to emulate Davidov and one another, the men in the team learn the joy of labour for the common weal. The spirit of the new life has got into them, dictating their actions without their even noticing it.

"Our breed are not bad workers," shouted Antip the Rook, one of a group Davidov had dubbed the "low-power crew" and which suddenly shot to a top place. He was probably not aware of the fact that with that old worn expression he was expressing something quite new, that he was no longer working just for himself, but for the collective farm and hence for the whole country.

Davidov takes a kind, considerate interest in other people. He notices Lyubishkin and upbraids the village Communists for having neglected the former partisan and failed to educate him. As a result of Davidov's attention Lyubishkin is made a team leader and once the spring sowing is over is accepted into the ranks of the Party. Davidov also rewards Shaly the blacksmith for his good work and praises Kondrat Maidannikov for being "a real shock-worker". He is able to arouse the best feelings in a man, and in all he does we feel the strength of the Party which is capable of waking the creative energy of the masses and directing it toward building a new life.

Davidov goes about with great awareness that he is a master of the new life, its builder and creator.

"The way he walks, the son-of-a-bitch! As if he was lord of creation! As if he was walking about his own house!" Yakov Lukich Ostrovnov thinks with anger and fear, sure that Davidov has come to arrest him for the murder of the poor peasant Khoprov. Davidov does not understand what Yakov Lukich is so frightened about. He liked the man's good, sensible speech at the meeting and has come to him for advice and to get some agricultural magazines to read.

In the scene in Ostrovnov's house Sholokhov has created a tense, highly dramatic situation, bringing Davidov into contact with his enemies, whose existence so close at hand he did not suspect for a moment. In this first engagement Davidov wins a clear moral victory. Yakov Lukich cringes and fawns before Davidov when he learns what he has come to see him for, while Davidov listens attentively to his advice about farming, questioning him carefully, little guessing that his clever host is his enemy. Polovtsev stands in the cold best room listening "with intense hatred" to the hoarse young voice of his enemy, separated only by a door. "'Shouted himself hoarse at his meetings, the dog! I'd take you and.... If only I could do it now!' Polovtsev pressed his blood-swollen fists to his chest and dug his nails into his palms" (1, 134).

Sholokhov contrasts the destructive hatred of the vulture Polovtsev awaiting chance prey and the base sabotage of the white-livered Ostrovnov with Davidov's constructive life, courage and humanism.

While Polovtsev and Ostrovnov fight for their former or possible future privileges in the name of "sacred private property" Davidov is giving all his strength—and is prepared to give even his life—for the well-being of all the working people. In this lay his strength and his superiority over those pitiful isolated enemies with their feeble attempts to put a spoke in the wheel of progress.

Davidov's rich nature is reflected in his speech, in which we hear now a passionate note ("I am for the Party"), now a harmless joke, now the iron logic that goes with conviction, now tremendous energy, or firmness.

There is nothing sentimental about Davidov, however. On occasion he can even be intentionally sharp and blunt, as when he upbraids Nagulnov for putting up with the conduct of his "loose" wife who has got "tangled up" with the son of a kulak. We sometimes feel he is too strict with himself and ought to relax a little and that he does not have enough experience to be able to understand another's heart. When Nagulnov explains what kind of a man Tit Borodin, now a kulak, was in the glorious days of the Civil War, fighting as a Red partisan, Davidov twice interrupts him impatiently and urges him to "make it shorter". "You can't make a thing like this shorter," Nagulnov retorts. "The pain of it curdles your blood." To Davidov, impatient for the meeting to pass a resolution evicting the kulaks and their families, Nagulnov seems to be merely "telling tear-jerking tales".

Davidov is often unnecessarily serious, "gloomy" even. Whereas Andrei Razmyotnov is often quite carried away by a joke or a funny story, Davidov never loses sight of the "business in hand". But certainly there's no denying he has his share of worries. "Collectivisation is so young and terribly vital. Everyone must go along with us," he says. He has given himself heart and soul to the task of organising "young collectivisation" and it never ceases to worry him, giving him no time at all to think of himself.

Lushka realises this and cunningly worms her way into his heart by getting him to talk about collective-farm affairs.

Whenever the farm suffers some set-back or other Davidov feels it as a personal tragedy. By the time Razmyotnov has finished telling him of the wholesale slaughter of cattle in the village "splintery wrinkles had gathered round his eyes, and his face seems to have grown older"; when he learns that Ostrovnov had maliciously let the farm oxen get frostbite, "his eyes fill with tears of anger".

However, Sholokhov does not only test his hero in the events directly linked with collectivisation, the most important matter in hand, but in all life's circumstances, in family, everyday, and personal relationships.

The story of Davidov's relationship with Lushka occupies an important place in Book Two. Though it may not appear so at first sight, it is in fact closely connected with the main theme of collectivisation.

The hero seems to "fall" before our very eyes. The village youngsters would run along the street teasing the pair of them as Davidov walked arm in arm with Lushka in defiance of Cossack custom. Andrei Razmyotnov smiles knowingly, and Makar Nagulnov is genuinely distressed.... "Why, he used to live in my house, he saw what sort of a menace she was, he saw me battling with that domestic counter-revolutionary all the time, and now he's in a mess! And what a mess! When I looked at him just now, believe me, my heart bled for him. Thin as a rake, that guilty look all over him, his eyes darting this way and that..." (2, 60).

There is also a stern note of condemnation in the author's account of how Davidov had changed. "Somehow, without noticing it himself, Davidov had grown a bit slack. An unaccustomed irritability appeared in his character...." He had changed in outward appearance too: "His shoulder-blades jutted out from under the jacket that was draped over them, his hair had not been cut for a long time and thick black curls dangled from under the cap on the back of his head, reaching down his broad brown neck to the greasy collar of his jacket. There was something unpleasant and wretched in his whole appearance."

Ippolit Shaly's words contain even severer condemnation. "...You're chairman only at meetings; for everyday work it's Ostrovnov. That's where all the trouble arises.... You're not chairman of the collective farm, but a kind of hanger-on, as they say." He goes on to enumerate to Davidov his failings, his loss of vigilance, his political irresponsibility, his failure to see his enemies' plots: "...you, lad, don't see these dangers at all. All your young goings-on have darkened your mind...." (2, 159 and 161).

Is the hero being debunked? If so, how is it that the reader is still so well-disposed towards Davidov?

Sholokhov shows us his hero from all sides, both his strength and his weaknesses, testing his whole character in the actual circumstances of "bitter-sweet" life. At the same time, he presents people and events in such a way that the reader is always aware of a character's essential nature, be it Davidov, Nagulnov or Razmyotnov, and also of the kindness and excellence which determine their real and undeniable worth. There is no doubt about it, Davidov's weakness is condemned, yet this does not tarnish his human beauty and rather serves to enhance it by casting a new light on it. The hero has grown a bit slack, but he will find the strength to pull himself together and correct his mistakes. In this lies the true strength and beauty of Davidov, whose number one concern is the well-being of the village peasants.

Sholokhov's tremendous triumph is the skill with which he manages to arouse ardent faith in man, in the inner strength, the great humanity, and the honest and noble intentions of the Communist leader.

From any number of situations where Davidov meets other people, and from the ensuing conversations and thoughts, we can observe with what consummate skill and tact Sholokhov preserves the reader's faith in his hero.

Upset by his shameful relationship with Lushka, Davidov drives out to Agafon Dubtsov's ploughing team. "Davidov felt a pleasant thrill when he saw how everyone rose together from the table.... As he strode forward, hands stretched out to greet him and smiles gleamed on the dark sunburnt faces of the men and the lightly tanned faces of the girls and women.... Davidov smiled as he glanced at the familiar faces. These people had got to know him well; they were genuinely glad to see him and welcomed him as one of their own...."

One has only to compare a few episodes from Book One and Book Two that show the Cossacks' attitude to Davidov to appreciate the tremendous change that took place in the Cossacks' whole outlook, and to gain a clear picture of the political and moral authority Davidov won among the villagers of Gremyachy in a comparatively short time.

At first the villagers had given Davidov the cold shoulder, adopting a cautious "wait-and-see" attitude. A few months later, at the meeting held after the "women's riot", "a warm and cheerful bass said in a deeply moved tone: 'Davidov, the chicken's liver for you! Good old

Davidov! For not bearing a grudge in your heart ... for not remembering old wrongs. The folk here are all worked up ... we don't know which way to look we feel so ashamed. And the women are all a-flutter. But we've got to live together...."

"We've got to live together"—these words were recognition of the fact that Davidov's work in Gremyachy was necessary. The Cossacks came to trust him, for they saw that even in the most difficult circumstances, Davidov did not let himself be guided by motives of personal injury and desire for revenge, but by the high moral principles of revolutionary humanitarianism. Stirred up by his enemies, the women had almost beaten him to death, and yet the very next evening, still rather the worse for the rough treatment he had received at the hands of the women, Davidov told a silent gathering of villagers in the school: "The Bolsheviks do not take revenge, they punish mercilessly only enemies.... You are wavering middle peasants that have temporarily gone astray, and we shall not take administrative measures against you, but we shall open your eyes to the facts." These words serve to melt the last ice of estrangement, fear and doubt.

This faith in the ordinary labourer who may waver and go astray, but in the long run will understand where his place is, this faith in the ultimate triumph of the collective-farm system as "terribly necessary" for all, this readiness to give himself heart and soul for the well-being of the working folk was bound to find a response in the Gremyachy Cossacks.

A little later Dubtsov's team welcome Davidov "as one of their own" and are "genuinely glad to see him". The feeling of closeness that has arisen between the Petrograd worker and the Gremyachy peasants in the struggle for the collective farm is growing and developing.

A major criterion by which man is judged in Soviet literature is his relationship to the people and their just struggle. The subjective intentions of a character are put to the decisive test in the concrete circumstances of the life of the people, and in the last analysis it is this that determines a writer's aesthetic standpoint.

Davidov "stands trial" before *the supreme court, the people*, in Book Two of *Virgin Soil Upturned*. He has got tangled up with Lushka, and has committed a number of serious mistakes in his work. Yet we see that he has achieved the most important thing through his work and human qualities—he has earned the trust and love of the people. It is this love, indeed, demanding and critical as it is, that helps Davidov overcome his weaknesses and errors, and find his way again.

In this respect the conversation between Davidov and Ippolit Shaly, the village blacksmith, is extremely important. Shaly's words express both the uncompromising, high demands the people make on their leader and their faith in him. This frank conversation was triggered off by the careful blacksmith's fear that the kulak's son Timofei the Torn who had escaped from exile might make an attempt on Davidov's life. "That's why I asked you over, to warn you". This stern, direct expression of genuine anxiety for Davidov's safety was an involuntary recognition of what he meant to the villagers.

Davidov's deep humanity, his understanding, sympathetic nature, are apparent in the way he reacted to Ivan Arzhanov's dreadful confession about how, when still a lad in tsarist times, he had killed his father's murderers. Indeed, the very fact that a man who "had crawled into his shell in childhood" locked himself up and wouldn't let anybody into his soul, confided so freely in Davidov is a sign of tremendous faith in his human qualities.

Here is the same Davidov we knew in Book One, and yet not quite the same, for while having lost none of his former inner strength and integrity he is the richer for many essential, new qualities.

Davidov changes noticeably as a result of the class struggle in the village, his serious mistakes, and his catastrophic love affair.

In Book One Davidov is occasionally criticised even by Razmyotnov and Nagulnov, his closest comrades, for adopting too rigid an attitude and lacking the necessary tact and sympathy in cases involving complex moral conflicts (Razmyotnov during the expropriation of the kulaks, and Nagulnov when talking about Borodin's past, about Lushka and so on).

Anticipating an unpleasant conversation about Lushka, Nagulnov makes a rather sly dig at Davidov: "How am I to talk to you?... If I go a bit wide of the mark, you're down on me with 'Anarchist! Deviationist!'" A little while later he exclaims: "You're like a rod of iron" (1, 144).

The Davidov we meet in Book Two has "softened" somewhat. This appears first and foremost in his relationships with other people, about which we have already spoken, but also in what would seem to be insignificant minor details.

Davidov arrived on his visit to Dubtsov's ploughing team at lunch time. He sat down to table without any ado and when he had finished "boyishly licking his wooden spoon, he looked up".

This boyish movement shows us the chairman of the collective farm in a new light. Davidov has already been described eating in Book One: "He immediately bit off a huge lump of bread, and as he chewed, the muscles rippled in his flushed cheeks.... Soon Davidov was eating in gulps" (1, 139).

In Book One we have a harassed man who is tired and hungry, upset by a piece of unpleasant news. The Davidov who sits down to lunch with Dubtsov's team in Book Two is quite different. What is it about Davidov licking his spoon boyishly that is so important as to merit our attention? Surely, if the writer wanted to mention a habit left over from Davidov's hungry childhood, he had opportunity enough to do so earlier.

The fact is that for Sholokhov "childishness" is a manifestation of untouched purity, goodness, naïve faith in others, and a certain charming defencelessness in the face of the dramas and tragedies of the big world. This "childish" quality was just not present in the "gloomy looking" Davidov of Book One. It only makes its appearance after Davidov has known the torments of passion for Lushka, the exhausting struggle between duty and desire which was really below his dignity both as a man and a leader.

But Davidov does not go down, and after this he listens with undivided attention and great sympathy to Arzhanov's confession, and behaves terribly carefully and considerately towards Varya Kharlamova when she falls in love with him.

The "childishness" Sholokhov draws our attention to in Davidov has the force of a sudden illumination. As is the case with all truly great art, the external detail of appearance leads us straight to the very roots of the character.

The colourful, "metaphoric world" in which the hero's relationship with his environment is revealed is tremendously important in a work of art.

The milieu in which a character lived and was brought up, his biography in the widest sense of the word, his temperament and so on, are reflected not merely in the actual words he utters in direct speech, but also in the images and constructions the author uses in narrating.

In this respect Sholokhov undoubtedly encountered the greatest difficulty in creating Semyon Davidov. A Petrograd worker and sailor of the Baltic Fleet is transferred into a totally different social milieu, where everything, from the way of life to social outlook and even language, was unfamiliar and strange to him.

Right from the first the Cossacks were quick to note Davidov's hard Russian "g", and realise that he was not "one of their own" from the Don, but an "outsider"....

The link that grew up between Davidov and the villagers was based on the realisation that they had common historical interests, on the humanitarian aims of the revolutionary transformation of the countryside.

As it happens, what we learn of Davidov's character does not alienate him from the villagers, since Sholokhov avoids stressing local characteristics that would make the "townee" and "worker" stand out too much from the "peasant" and "Cossack".

Sholokhov did not fall for the easy bait of describing superficial traits "typical" of this or that milieu. He was too aware of what they had in common. But neither does he overlook features that could only belong to a man representing a particular social layer.

Thus the passage in chapter thirteen where Davidov is thinking over his first week in Gremyachy is full of associations and comparisons with his life at the factory in Petrograd.

"To him the village was like a complex new machine and he tried intently to understand it, to study and get the feel of every part, to hear every irregular note in the incessant daily throbbing of this queer machine" (1, 122).

Even the sudden change in his train of thought, when he passes from his recollections of the factory to his work in Gremyachy is expressed by an image connected with factory work:

"Then his mind would suddenly return to Gremyachy, as if someone had firmly *put over a switch* and sent *the current of his thoughts* down a new channel" (1, 121-22).

This restricted choice of terms is perfectly justified psychologically. Davidov still feels a part of the factory and has not yet fully adapted himself to the transfer from his old job at the factory to his new life in the village.

However, for this Davidov the first simile in the passage seems very unexpected: "Like a trapped wolf, he would try to break out of the circle of thoughts connected with the collective farm; he would recall his shop at the factory, his friends, his work" (1, 121). This image is hardly one that would occur to a town worker, it belongs to the life that is still strange to Davidov. In leaps to the eye all the more in view of the "factory" terms that follow: "tractor engine", "lather", "the current of his thoughts" and so on.

It is interesting to compare this image with one in book three of *And Quiet Flows the Don*, bearing in mind that it was finished just before Book One of *Virgin Soil Upturned* was written. "Why had his spirit tossed like a hunted wolf in search of a way of escape, of solving contradictions?" One feels that an image which was extremely effective when applied to Grigory Melekhov and his tormenting doubts has lost all its power when "misapplied" to Davidov. But was it in fact a question of misuse? Is it really an example of mental inertia on the part of the writer?

Imagery is never neutral. Any comparison contains a tremendous charge of emotional judgment, which is transmitted to the reader.

The writer does not force the reader to accept his view: he seems to be merely expressing things as they really are without comment. But as a rule the poetic expression of the connections observed by the writer hides a certain tendentiousness and partiality.

The comparison with a trapped wolf was intended to express the great strain Davidov was living under during his first few days in Gremyachy and his painful search for the right solutions.

However, this comparison has certain overtones. Strictly speaking, only a man with some form of moral guilt can be compared to a wolf, someone whose behaviour does not conform to the popular concepts of good or is decidedly antisocial. Grigory Melekhov could rightly be compared to a wolf since he was at the time actively engaged in the struggle against Soviet power, as he galloped across the empty steppe to take part in the Upper Don uprising. Not so Davidov, whose nature and future activity would seem to exclude such comparisons.

But so far we have said nothing of the content of the imagery that characterises Davidov. As a rule, both in the author's narrative and the direct speech this imagery is constructed on a broad lexico-semantic basis common to the masses.

The everyday speech of the Cossacks was full of images that originated in folklore. Davidov also uses the odd folklore image, and when he does so it is always to the point.

"A horse has four legs but it can still stumble, so they say," Davidov says to Nesterenko (2, 110). The "so they say" is sufficient indication to show that he is not seeking to justify himself with a proverb, but is merely recognising a sad fact.

Davidov has no great difficulty in entering the peasant's world of imagery. His hard-working past is a help to him here. Even the fact—at first sight insignificant perhaps—that in the Civil War he had manned a machine gun mounted on a horse-driven cart helps him find a common language with the villagers relatively easily.

At the assembly of the village poor, where he first meets the people of Gremyachy Log, he effectively squashes Lyubishkin with his well-aimed remark: "First you've got to create a collective farm, then worry about the machines. But you want to buy a collar first, then fit the horse into it" (1, 38).

The general mirth and shouts of approval that this is greeted with ("Ho-ho!".... "But we're heart and soul for the collective farm!".... "He got it right there, about the collar....") were the natural response to an apt remark which illustrated an important historical principle through a simple everyday image.

When Ivan Arzhanov is driving slowly on the way to Dubtsov's ploughing team, Davidov asks grimly: "Do you think you're carrying pots to a fair, Uncle Ivan? Afraid of breaking them?" (2, 63).

Such a comparison is quite natural for Davidov after six months in the village, for he is quick to catch and imitate the way of thinking of the environment in which he lives and works. It testifies to the way he has come to understand the villagers and really become "one of them".

Once, waxing lyrical, Davidov says to Lushka: "Lushka, darling, you're like a flower! Even your freckles have a scent, and that's a fact! Do you know what they smell of?... A sort of freshness, like the dew or something.... You know what—like snowdrops. You can hardly smell it, but it's good" (2, 39).

There is something terribly natural and convincing about the way Davidov's private world comes to light and we hear that lyrical note which could not have sounded in the difficult first months of the struggle to set up the farm. But with the spring floods over, and the passage of the flocks of birds towards the north, when everything is in flower and the nightingales sing their song, the "ex-sailor" appears to us in quite a different light.

He does not rest content with comparing Lushka to a flower, but instinctively seeks just the right comparison to express most exactly what he feels. His feelings and imagination work like those of a poet. "All lovers are poets," and Davidov is not satisfied until he has found the best possible image. "Like snowdrops. You can hardly smell it, but it's good."

This alone testifies to subtle powers of perception and susceptibility to beauty. We have been shown yet another aspect of Davidov's nature. Poetic imagery in the hero's speech is one of the most adaptable of instruments enabling the writer to reveal his character's inner world.

This poetic side of Davidov's nature is also reflected in the author's descriptions, such as the following passage where Davidov's mind suddenly goes back to the past....

"Breathing deep of the heady scents of the grass and the moist black earth, Davidov gazed at the long line of ancient burial mounds in the distance. Those distant blue barrows reminded him in some way of the storm-roused waves of the Baltic and, unable to fight a sudden rush of melancholy, he sighed heavily and quickly averted his misty eyes..." (2, 62).

The connection Davidov saw between the Don steppe and the sea, speaks of his poetic imaginativeness. He had to feel an attachment to the steppe, in order to visualise sea waves in those rows of burial mounds. The heady scents of the grass and the black earth had become as dear to him as the waves and the tang of the sea.

This is just another reason why the peasants in Dubtsov's team should welcome Davidov as "one of their own".

The author extends the comparisons between Davidov's former life in the Navy and his present, bringing out more and more subtle emotional links.

"Steppe, the boundless, rolling steppe. Ancient barrows in a light-blue mist. A black eagle in the sky. The soft rustle of wind-blown grass.... Davidov felt very small and lost in this huge expanse, as he gazed wistfully over the tormentingly endless plain. His love for Lushka, the grief of parting, the unrealised desire to see her, now seemed trivial and unimportant. He was oppressed by a feeling of loneliness, of isolation from the whole living world. Something like this he had experienced long ago, when he had stood watch at night in the bows of his ship. What a long time ago that had been! It seemed like an old, half-forgotten dream."

The associations and connections seem to arise automatically here. The steppe is as boundless as the sea, and both inspire feelings of awe at the grandeur of nature which makes the temporal seem "trivial and unimportant". The feeling of loneliness and isolation from the living world that the boundless steppe evokes is naturally reminiscent of what it was like to be on watch at night in the open sea.

In a true work of art characters are not given a cut-and-dried portrayal, and only a person who is insensitive to art seeks ready-made patterns.

The author's tenderness, anger or indignation can be revealed gradually and imperceptibly, evoking a response from the reader's heart with the inspired imagery, and the subtle power of beauty.

3

Sholokhov's love for his fellow men is especially in evidence in Book Two of *Virgin Soil Upturned*, where it can all the time be felt in the increasingly poetic narrative and the lyrical digressions.

The time is still 1930, the early period of collectivisation with its bitter class conflicts and clashes.

The clashes between Davidov, Razmyotnov, Kondratko, and Naidyonov on the one hand, and Nagulnov on the other did not only involve moral principles: more often than not they turned into political arguments about methods of leadership.

In a number of episodes in Book Two Sholokhov shows the method of persuasion, based on the democratic traditions of the Party and the very essence of the Soviet regime, as against the method of coercion, which Nagulnov considered the most effective means of overcoming the private-property prejudices of the Cossack masses.

Much in Book Two is relevant to vital present-day issues. One of the most interesting of these passages is the one where Davidov clashes with Ustin Rykalin. As usual with Sholokhov it is not abstract ideas and views that clash but living people whose characters are expertly portrayed.

Davidov is furious because the Cossacks have left off work at the busiest time of the season and are sitting round playing cards. He comes galloping up and starts shouting and threatening, quite beside himself. Ustin Rykalin decides to take Davidov down a peg or two, and his replies, questions and drawn-out views are exaggeratedly calm and ironic.

What cuts Davidov to the quick is not so much the provoking questions about days-off, as Ustin Rykalin casting doubt on the sincerity of his motives.

"You only want to fulfil the plan, that's why you're making all this fuss about the hay.... You're trying to show the district authorities what you can do, the district's trying to show the region, and we have to suffer for the jolly lot of you. Do you think the people don't see anything? Do you think they're blind? They see everything, but how can they keep away from climbers like you? We can't push you, or your like, out of your jobs, can we? Oh, no! And so you just do what you think you will. And Moscow's far away, Moscow don't know what tricks you get up to, here" (2, 198, 199).

Davidov a "climber"! Surely nothing could be more insulting than that. Even though it came from Ustin, a White, and a counter-revolutionary.

This dramatic scene is handled with remarkable skill. The "external action" and the inner workings of Davidov's turbulent thoughts and feelings are inextricably interwoven.

On the surface of it a duel is going on between Davidov and Ustin, and Davidov has to defeat the arguments of his sharp-tongued, sharp-witted opponent and show up what is noxious and unsound in them.

At the same time he is boiling inside. Davidov's blind fury and resentment are ready to erupt at any moment in a savage act of violence. But they are checked by his sense of duty, his awareness of his responsibilities as a leader who must defeat Ustin not through the power his position gives him, by resorting to threats, but through ideological superiority, strength of conviction, unquestionable truth, and last but not least, his moral superiority.

Davidov does not merely "knock Ustin flat" but he also overcomes the Nagulnov in himself.

The "fearless" Ustin's words are a remarkable mixture of foolish kulak talk and desperate defence of his human dignity, his right to think and speak as he thinks fit.

"But how do you set about it?" he asked Davidov. "Almost before you've got here you're shouting at the top of your voice: 'Why aren't you working?!' Who talks to the people like that nowadays? Soviet power has come, and the people, you know, they've dug their pride up out of their big chests, and they don't fancy being shouted at.... And you and Nagulnov ought to realise by now that times have changed, and you'd better give up the old habits...."

Nesterenko, the Secretary of the District Party Committee, had said as if in passing but obviously intentionally: "Some very incompetent ways of doing things have taken root in our Party life and we've got fitting expressions for them. We talk about 'taking shavings' off a man, 'sandpapering' him, and 'scouring' him, as if we were talking about a chunk of rusty iron instead of a human being. Is that right, I ask you? And the people who use these expressions most, mind you, are people who've never taken a shaving off metal or wood in their lives, and probably never had an emery wheel in their hands either. People are very sensitive, and you've got to be terribly careful how you treat them!"

Davidov can hardly have remembered these words during his clash with Ustin. But as a Communist, he was perfectly aware of the fact that "you've got to be terribly careful how you treat people". This, indeed, is the source of that "inner self-criticism" which is an essential factor determining his behaviour, and makes him such a noble character.

Davidov is a merciless judge of his own behaviour. He has a strong Party conscience, he always knows for whom and for what he is living, and this prevents him from making serious mistakes.

Bitterly dissatisfied and angry with his own behaviour, Davidov had frankly to admit to himself, "that he had unconsciously begun to adopt the rough, Nagulnov way of treating people; he had 'slipped the collar', as Andrei Razmyotnov would say". Moreover, he found the courage to declare for all to hear: "As a matter of fact, I needn't have bawled at you like that, you're right there, Ustin."

Although Davidov has not yet cooled down after the encounter and is still convinced that Ustin is "an open enemy of collectivisation", he is nevertheless prepared to listen to old Osetrov's account of Ustin's hard life.

His heart, ever responsive to human misfortune, is moved by what he hears, and he immediately begins thinking about how to help clothe and feed Ustin's numerous children and see that they're sent to school.

Sholokhov does not have a narrow understanding of the purpose of art and does not limit himself to posing or answering "questions" of social importance. A "problem" interests him in so far as it enables him to understand people, to understand the motives for their actions.

Thus, the argument about methods of leadership has the wider implications of a serious reflection on the essence of humanism, on the new kind of social relationships, on honour, and all that which is finest in man.

Sholokhov is a "thoroughly earthly" writer for whom the very concepts of beauty are intrinsically bound up with concrete reality.

Davidov's fine qualities are evident not only in his thoughts and convictions but also in practice, in his everyday behaviour and relations with other people.

Davidov's inner beauty, as we have already noted, is revealed not only in events of great moment and socio-historical importance. No less important for understanding his character is Varya Kharlamova's pure, innocent love for him, which is contrasted with Lushka's cynical, calculating feelings. Whereas his relationship with Lushka lowered Davidov, "smeared him with tar" as Shaly put it, Varya's love ennobles him.

Grigory and Aksinya's love in *And Quiet Flows the Don* which, especially at first, swept them up in a mighty storm of passion and desire, is told dramatically. The story of Varya and Davidov is narrated with remarkable tenderness, and has all the bitter-sweet pain, innocence and artlessness of first love.

Varya, with her swiftly changing moods, her joy and pain, tears of disillusionment and the gay laughter, is indeed "as pure as the sunrise on a fine morning".

This love, which Sholokhov describes with his usual deep understanding of the human heart, helps us understand a great deal about Davidov. He is tormented by his strong carnal lust for Lushka, and his going out to the distant fields where Dubtsov's ploughing team was working was like "the shameful flight of a man who desired yet feared the final untying of a love-knot".

At first he is indifferent to Varya's love, but his attitude to her feelings is so clean, it reveals such kindly understanding and sensitivity as speak of a really fine nature.

The reader may find it difficult to reconcile his picture of Davidov with the passage where he trudges wearily behind the plough in his sweat-stained, tattered shirt, desperately trying to hide from Varya's innocent eyes the obscenity that has been tattooed on his stomach in his foolish sailor days.

Sholokhov seems to be telling us that if we look closely at this "thoroughly earthly man" who is far from perfect, and has many mistakes and failures behind him, we shall see those fine qualities which the struggle for the Revolution and Soviet power had instilled in him, and also great spiritual beauty.

This is perhaps the main message of Sholokhov's novel for contemporary literature—that there is no need for "romanticising", no need for the "exceptional", for in our present life the future is being born, and the *fine*, *noble man* of the future is already emerging.

"Where did you spring from and what do I need of you, you sweet kid? Davidov thought absently, regarding the girl's violently blushing face. And what do you need of me? You've got so many young fellows running after you, and you look at me, you blind little thing! Why, I'm twice your age; all scarred and ugly, and half my front teeth are missing; but you can't see it.... No, I don't want you, poor little Varya. Grow up without me, my dear."

That was when he first realised that Varya was in love with him. Later, when he knew her a little from having worked together in the fields with her, he began to sadly reflect that with a girl like Varya it was all or nothing, and he had best leave her alone. The fact that his thoughts are so down to earth only serves to stress the purity and sincerity of his motives.

"No, that kid can only be loved seriously, my conscience wouldn't let me just fool around with her. Why, she's as pure as the sunrise on a fine morning, and her eyes are so clear when she looks at me.... So if I haven't learned to love properly, if I don't understand that side of things yet, then there's no point in worrying the girl's head for nothing. Now it's a case of cut your moorings, seaman Davidov, and be quick about it! And I think I'd better keep away from her in future. Yes, I'll just tell her gently, so she'll understand, then keep away, Davidov decided with an involuntary sigh."

Without knowing it Davidov learns what true love is, and still distrusting himself he goes out to meet this love, the one and only he is to cherish all his life. His passion for Lushka disperses like mist in the warm rays of Varya's love.

At first, thinking about Varya Davidov wished that Lushka would gaze at him "with such selfless devotion and love".

Later that day, out in the field Varya bent down to give him his jacket, and their heads almost touched. "His nostrils twitched as he caught the fragrance of her hair. Her whole body smelled of the midday sun, the sultry grasses, and that singularly fresh and bewitching scent of youth that no one has ever yet been able to describe in words. "What a sweet kid! he thought, and sighed."

That evening, back at camp, Davidov was falling asleep when he heard Varya laughing, and her laughter reminded him of the "cooing of a turtle dove". "What a sweet kid, he thought as he dropped off to sleep. She's grown up though, fit to be a bride, but she has the mind of a child. Good luck to you, Varya dear."

Words of endearment like "sweet" and "dear" acquire especially moving overtones coming from the rather gruff, reserved Davidov.

Yet there is really nothing so surprising in the fact that tender poetic epithets and comparisons should well up unawares in the heart of a man with such strong feelings as Davidov.

It was certainly no accident that Davidov first thought of marriage when he came across an abandoned nest in a salt-marsh. The sudden thought seemed "absurd and foolish". Apparently he did not suspect for a moment that it was Varya who had aroused in him the eternal human longing for a family.

Such was the consummate artistry with which Sholokhov "set the scene for" the decisive conversation between Varya and Davidov.

As is almost invariably the case with Sholokhov, an external event suddenly brings to a head with amazing dramatic force something seemingly unimportant that has been building up for some time. This dynamic leap gives a new turn to the mood, emotions and feelings of the characters.

Varya tells Davidov that her mother is trying to marry her off to Vanka Obnizov. Davidov is plunged into "utter confusion" by the news.

"Dismayed, numb with surprise, his heart pricking painfully, he gripped Varya'a hands and, taking a step back, looked into her tearful downcast face, not knowing what to say. And only now did it dawn on him that for a long time perhaps, without acknowledging it even to himself, he had loved this girl with a love that for a man like him with all his experience of life was strangely fresh and pure, and that now he stood almost face to face with the two sad friends and companions of nearly all true love—parting and loss."

A sad premonition has crept into this terse description of Davidov's feelings. Davidov and Varya could hardly have imagined on that night which seemed to unite them, that they were soon to be parted for ever. The lines pack tremendous heart-breaking sorrow, pain and tenderness.

Davidov's love is no blind, egoistic passion. His main concern is for Varya and her future. It took real self-sacrifice on his part to ask Varya to be his "lawful wedded wife" and then send her straight off to town to study at an agricultural college. By so doing he is helping her make sure she's not making a mistake.

There was another important consideration behind this decision. Davidov evidently wanted Varya to break out of that narrow world she lived in and plunge with all the ardour of youth into intelligent life, so that she could become his true partner in their common struggle.

Sholokhov is too laconic to explain all this in detail, and thus merely mentions Davidov's decision, leaving the reader to draw his own conclusions as to the motives.

Another motive behind Davidov's decision to marry Varya deserves our attention as throwing further light on his character. It is difficult to say what was uppermost in his mind that sleepless night when he decided to "take the plunge": awareness of his love for Varya or compassion for the large and needy Kharlamov family that had long been without a proper breadwinner.

Davidov always tried terribly hard to hide his sympathetic heart behind a wall of sternness and almost roughness. He was always ready to come to the aid of those in need, to lighten other people's burdens and help wherever possible.

The appearance of the fine features of the new, Communist morality in Davidov, a man who seemed so ordinary and unassuming on the surface, is presented most convincingly. It is as if we can see the light of the future shining forth in a still far from perfect reality, the age-long artistic ideal of the strong, good and noble man being made flesh.

Chapter Three
MAKAR NAGULNOV

1

Makar Nagulnov, Secretary of the Gremyachy Party group, is a sharply-drawn character from early on in Book One. Since childhood he has had a fierce loathing for property, for the way it divides people and turns them into wild beasts. "I can breathe easier, dear comrade worker, now I've heard that we're going to take all farming property into the collective farm. I have had a hatred of property since I was a lad. It is the root of all evil; our learned comrades, Marx and Engels, were right," he tells Davidov (1, 44). Nagulnov rose in arms against property when he was a lad and, leaving his father who was a well-to-do Cossack, hired out as a labourer. In the Civil War he commanded a cavalry squadron and got shell-shocked at Kastornaya after which he suffered from periodic fits. Later he was awarded the Order of the Red Banner, which still "warms his heart" (1, 45).

But Makar Nagulnov's passionate hatred for the old world of property relations is purely instinctive and takes the form of blind revolt. He quotes Marx and Engels frequently enough, but does not understand the actual way the class forces are drawn up at all, and in the complex class struggle during collectivisation is often unable to distinguish between middle peasants who have gone astray and real class enemies.

Nagulnov's selfless devotion to the revolutionary cause, to "his" Party which had been mother and father to him, his romantic preoccupation with the future and the way he feels the sufferings of all oppressed mankind as if they are his own go side by side with the naïve conviction that "our middle peasants have got to be taught a threatened lesson". "No, it's no good talking to them, you've got to clout them over the head and tell them, 'Don't listen to the kulak, you dirty swine! Don't learn a love for property from him!'" (1, 148).

There is a note of warning in the very first description we have of Makar: "He would have been handsome in a restrained masculine way but for the *savagely arched* nostrils of his smallish hawk-like nose and the dull film over his eyes" (1, 20, author's italics). In many descriptions later on we find him likened to a bird of prey, as in the following: "Nagulnov had dug his nails into the table like a kite clawing its prey" (1, 78).

These can hardly be chance details. References to his appearance and behaviour, to the lightening speed of his reactions and so on, are insights into his essential nature with his readiness to be cruel if he thinks the situation demands it.

When, instigated by the kulaks the villagers begin to slaughter their cattle Makar is for having the more malicious of the cattle-slaughterers shot. His fanatical obsession makes him ready to go to the extremes of brutality. When Andrei Razmyotnov voices pity for the children of the kulaks he has been sent to dispossess Nagulnov cries fiercely, almost hysterically: "Is this how you serve the Revolution? Sorry for them? Why, I'd ... give me thousands of old men, children, women.... And tell me they've got be done away with.... For the sake of the Revolution.... I'd do it with a machine-gun ... every one of 'em!" (1, 79). One of his fits comes on, and he thrashes and writhes in agonising convulsions.

He lacked those qualities which Davidov possessed in such abundance—consideration for others, the will and the desire to understand the needs of every single individual and help him wherever necessary.

"You're living in a dream, Makar!" Davidov says reprovingly.

Nagulnov indeed lives as in a febrile dream, thronged with world catastrophes and upheavals, and he still seems to see the revolutionary fires, lighted in different parts of the world, during the Civil War. The villagers of Gremyachy Log interest him only in so far as they can delay or speed up the "world revolution" for which he is impatient.

Nagulnov is least of all concerned with their present-day interests. If there is the slightest hitch in the vitally important revolutionary task of collectivisation, he is ready to "get things moving" again by any form of coercion: threats, and if that doesn't work then at gunpoint.

It was as if he imagined himself to be some stern, incorruptible executor of historical necessity, which he anyway misunderstood.

That is why there was often such a tragic rift between his aspirations and his actual deeds, between his lofty humanist aims and the means of achieving them.

But Nagulnov sincerely believed that this was what was best for the common cause, and indeed for these people, if not today, then in the future. In this he differed radically from Davidov, a true Leninist Bolshevik, who considered it right that people should receive material benefits in the present too.

Collectivisation was carried out in order that the villagers of Gremyachy Log should have an easier, better life. As Davidov put it: "Collectivisation is so young and terribly vital. Everyone must go along with us."

This was the root of the clashes that occurred between Davidov and Nagulnov and which were essentially a reflection of the struggle between two styles of leadership: one the true Leninist approach, which sought to patiently explain and convince, and the other an anti-Party approach, which sought to overcome difficulties by frontal attack using threats and coercion.

Brought to task by his comrades, and time and again unable to defend his attitude in an argument, Nagulnov says challengingly to Davidov: "You've got into the habit of sucking up to those property-owners of yesterday, but I treat them as my partisan conscience dictates" (2, 191).

Sholokhov has avoided making Nagulnov a tailor's dummy on which to hang mistaken methods and erroneous policies. There are indeed unpleasant aspects to his nature, and far be it from Sholokhov to hide them. Indeed, true humanist writer that he is, he is quite merciless in exposing them. Yet there is even more about Makar that is admirable.

Nagulnov is first and foremost a fighter prepared to sacrifice himself without hesitation for the cause should the need arise. Life has no sense for him without this "service" to the Party and the people. "I can't live without the Party!" he exclaims at a meeting of the District Committee bureau which has decided to expel him for distorting the Party line during collectivisation. "Makar ... spoke slowly, as if thinking to himself:

"'Where can I go without the Party? And what for? No, I won't give up my Party card! I've put my whole life into ... my whole life...' and suddenly he began to grope about the table in pitiful confusion, like an old man, muttering indistinctly. 'Then you'd better take me and ... tell the lads to ... I'd better be done away with. There's nothing else.... I don't need life now, expel me from that too.'"

Out in the empty steppe, by an ancient burial mound, Makar broods on suicide.

The decision to expel him from the Party wounded him deeply but it cannot kill him. The thought of his enemies rejoicing in his suicide is enough to decide him against it.

As Nagulnov hastens back towards the village he has no idea of the violence that has broken out in his absence. Davidov is being beaten up by the infuriated women for refusing to hand over the keys to the barn, Razmyotnov has been arrested and locked up, and the Cossacks are intent on prizing open the barn doors to share out the seed grain.

"With aching regret" Makar surveys the "black untended ploughland in its terrible nakedness". And this love for the good earth which is in the blood of peasants is linked in Makar's heart with hatred and fury against those who are hindering the building of the new life. "They won't come out to sow because the idea of property is stamping and rearing up inside them. The bastards! I'll go back and drive the whole lot of them out into the fields! Every man jack of them!"

Once again we see the former Makar, lively, abrupt and ever ready to struggle against the idea of property and its power over men's hearts.

"He may be a bungler, but he's one of us and no mistake," Davidov thinks.

When the collective-farm book-keeper, an elderly Cossack who had once been a regimental clerk, speaks scornfully of Nagulnov's "lack of education", Razmyotnov silences him with a very apt answer: "It's the uneducated chaps that have to face the music these days....

You're mighty educated, you are, you make a fine row with those abacus beads and put all those squiggles on your handwriting, but it wasn't you they fired at, it was Nagulnov."

Sholokhov gives Nagulnov many tragi-comic traits. This mixture of tragic and comic elements enables the writer by using the peerless method of contrast to bring out all that is truly great in Nagulnov, to lay bare his turbulent hidden passions, and ridicule the "unearthly rubbish" he often spouted, his taste for asceticism and self-sacrifice, and so on. Thus laughter becomes one of the means of criticising his character.

In Book Two Sholokhov boldly brings together two characters that are poles apart and would seem to be totally incompatible: the gloomy and reserved Nagulnov and merry old Grandad Shchukar, the biggest fibber and boaster in the village.

Nagulnov makes no secret of his contempt for Grandad Shchukar, calling him "a blatherer" and "an upstart", and frequently cutting the old man short. For his part Grandad Shchukar jibes at the way Nagulnov rants on at meetings. "Last May Day, Makar, old chap, you talked about the World Revolution from midday till sunset. Boring it was, I must say—same old thing, all the time. Why, I curled up on the bench and had a nap in the middle of it...."

Yet, in Book Two we find them sitting up nights together getting on with their "various advanced studies". However it is their common admiration for the harmonious crowing of cocks that really brings them together.

"Near midnight, in the unbroken stillness that reigned over the village, he and Grandad Shchukar listened solemnly to the first cocks and each in his own way rejoiced at their harmonious crowing.

"'Like an archbishop's choir!' Shchukar whispered reverently, lisping with emotion.

"'Like a cavalry regiment!' Makar said, gazing dreamily at the soot-caked lamp chimney" (2, 59).

Nagulnov's unsuccessful attempts to learn English, Grandad Shchukar's "reading" the thick Russian dictionary and picking up a staggering number of unfamiliar words there, and the delight both take in cock crowing are all "kinks". The things that draw them together are worthless and ridiculous.

Nagulnov's absurd friendliness for Shchukar reveals humorously his point of greatest vulnerability—his naïve, head-in-the-clouds enthusiasm.

Shchukar acts as a foil to Nagulnov, bringing out in sharper relief those traits of the latter's character which would otherwise not be so clear and distinct.

Yet besides humour there is also something rather sad and touching in this budding friendship between two basically very lonely men. The talkative old man with always a ready joke brightens up the cheerless life of Makar, still suffering and lonely after his wife has left him yet too proud and reserved to open his aching heart to anyone. At the same time Nagulnov, like Davidov, arouses kindly, paternal feelings in the childless old man.

Nagulnov is a tragic figure above all in his relationship to the popular masses, in the contradiction between his bursts of high idealist enthusiasm and his actions, which are often cruel and rough. At the same time his personal life is full of violent, tragic clashes—his ascetic rejection of family life, his continual sarcastic allusions to his "former wife", the gay, "loose" Lushka who was supposedly merely a burden to him, a revolutionary, and his secret, hopeless love for her.

Nagulnov has no illusions about Lushka, as is clear from what he says to Davidov when he "sums her up". "She didn't give a rap for the collective farms, or the state farms, or Soviet power either! All she wanted was to fool around with the men and do as little work as possible, that was the whole extent of her non-Party programme.... Now, how could you or I keep a four-footed flirt like that? Were we to chuck up the revolution and all our everyday Soviet work just for her sake? And club up to buy an accordion? We'd be done for! Done for and degenerate as any bourgeois! No, let her go hang herself on the first branch she comes to, it's not for me or you, Semyon, to betray our Party spirit for the sake of a worthless slut like her!" (2, 193-194).

When it came to reasoning, Nagulnov was perfectly aware that Lushka was a slut, and the power of her grip on his heart was all the more frightening. He could not master his love, it was there to stay.

For Sholokhov violent passions are one of the measures

of a man's greatness. Nagulnov's secret unrequited love gives us a totally new angle on his character.

Dynamism and laconicism—two of the outstanding features of modern prose—are eminently present in *Virgin Soil Upturned*, bearing an inimitable Sholokhov quality.

While Sholokhov does sometime describe a character's inner world directly, he shows a marked preference for a more subtle approach. Thus, in Book Two of *Virgin Soil Upturned* artistic methods which we might well sum up for the sake of convenience as "theatre" figure extensively: *dialogue* and *action* play an increasing role and *gestures pack a far greater psychological significance*, and there is a greater tendency to hint at characters' feelings by *overtones*.

A good example is the night Nagulnov and Razmyotnov come to arrest Lushka. The situation is a tense one. Nagulnov suspects Timofei the Torn, who has returned clandestinely from exile, of taking a pot at him, and has a feeling that Lushka has not forgotten her old "boy friend". He knows that jealousy or hunger will drive Timofei to Lushka's house if she does not turn up at the agreed rendezvous.

We know nothing so far of Nagulnov's true feelings for Lushka but the very atmosphere of the scene and the dramatic tension it packs prepare us for anything.

The scene that follows is a psychological duel between the provocative Lushka, who is perfectly self-possessed, and Nagulnov, who behaves not at all as one would expect a man who feels nothing but contemptuous indifference for his ex-wife.

"Lushka appeared barefoot, with a shawl over her naked shoulders. Her smooth brown calves showed up the pure white of her lace-trimmed underskirt.

"'Get dressed,' Razmyotnov ordered. And shook his head reproachfully: 'You might have put on a skirt.... Lor', you're a shameless hussy!'

"Lushka surveyed the visitors with an intent and inquiring glance, then gave them a dazzling smile:

"'But we're all kith and kin here, why should I be shy?'" (2, 180).

Lushka has wasted no time in starting her cruel game. "We're all kith and kin here" is pretty sure bait. But

Nagulnov does not rise to it. He keeps quiet, as if leaving it to Razmyotnov to do everything that has to be done.

Nagulnov's outward calm is underlined: "Makar regarded her with heavy calm, and with the same heavy calm in his voice, replied"; "Makar said still as calmly, without losing his control"; "his cool restraint was such a surprise to Lushka that she lost her temper".

For the reader, who knows Nagulnov's usual rashness and hot temper, this "cool restraint" comes somewhat as a surprise. There is something alarmingly tense about it, and one cannot help wondering what might be the reason for it, and what secret pain and suffering it might be a cover for. Nagulnov even tries not to look at Lushka, as if afraid of some tumult in his heart that might suddenly burst its floodgates.

While Razmyotnov admired the half-naked Lushka, "Makar stared at the old mistress of the house (Lushka's aunt—*author*), with a heavy unblinking gaze".

Even when they remained alone, and Lushka was getting dressed, Makar avoided looking at her. "She threw off her night-dress and underskirt. Naked and radiant in her compact, youthful beauty, she walked unembarrassedly to the chest and opened it. Makar did not look at her, his indifferent gaze was fixed on the window" (2, 182).

Lushka, who apparently guessed by some demonic intuition what Nagulnov really felt, hit out where it hurt most, with calculating spite shamelessly reminding him of her affair with Davidov. Thus, although perfectly aware what they had come for, she feigned innocence.

"'What can I do for you, my dear guests?' Lushka asked, hitching up the shawl that kept slipping down with a movement of the shoulders. 'You aren't looking for Davidov by any chance, are you?'" (2, 180).

Again, a little later, she asks: "Why did you follow me? What did you want? I'm free as a bird, I can go where I like. And if my boy friend Davidov had been with me, he wouldn't have thanked you for dogging our footsteps!" (2, 181).

This is almost too much for Makar, who for a moment is practically thrown off balance and almost lets his pain and jealousy get the upper hand. "The muscles under Makar's pale cheeks bunched sharply, but with a tremendous effort of will he controlled himself and said nothing.

His knuckles cracked audibly as he clenched his fists."

Here again Nagulnov's feelings are not explicitly described, but their exact nature is becoming clear to the reader. Only at the end of the episode when he is returning from the village Soviet where Lushka and her aunt have been locked up, are we given a direct insight into his great suffering.

"But it was not the former gallant and upright Makar Nagulnov who walked back through the deserted streets of Gremyachy Log in the blue darkness of early dawn. His shoulders drooped and he walked slowly, with hanging head, from time to time pressing his big broad hand to the left side of his chest" (2, 184).

Not once throughout the whole scene is direct mention made of the sufferings tormenting Nagulnov's soul. The real cause is subtly hinted at in such outward features as gestures, glances, tone of voice, the way he moves.

Sholokhov never resorts to half-tones and lyrical understatements, and hidden passions always end up by bursting into the open, into actions. The most ordinary working people that figure as heroes always have strong feelings, which helps reveal their true greatness of character.

One of the most important features of Sholokhov's art is the way he reveals strong human characters to the full in all the powerful intensity of their passions. This forms a link between him and the great tragedians of the past.

The proud, reserved and hot-tempered Nagulnov could only show his real greatness and superiority by containing himself, and not giving vent to his feelings.

Nagulnov's apparent numb calm and outer indifference in the scene with Lushka hide violent undercurrents of passion that are to burst forth in violent drama in the murder of Timofei the Torn and the final parting with Lushka.

Both these scenes have the two essential features only truly great art combines: apparent inevitability and staggering unexpectedness.

When Ippolit Shaly saw Lushka with Timofei the Torn one night outside the village, his first thought was for Davidov's safety. It was only natural that Davidov should be the main target of the son of a kulak who had been exiled to Siberia, for he was after all the heart and soul of the collective farm, and it was with his arrival that the expropriation and eviction of the kulaks had begun.

However, Timofei fired his first bullet at Nagulnov. The two men had old scores to settle. Nagulnov accepted the challenge.

At daybreak, near Lushka's yard a shot rang out. "Dropping his rifle and crumpling at the knees, Timofei slowly, or so it seemed to Makar, fell backwards.... Even in death he was handsome, this women's darling. A dark lock of hair had fallen on the clear white forehead that the sun had never touched, the full face had not yet lost its faint rosiness, the curling upper lip with its soft black moustache was raised a little, exposing moist teeth, and a faint shadow of a surprised smile lingered in the blooming lips that only a few days ago had kissed Lushka so avidly. Seem to have been eating well, lad! Makar thought.

"As he calmly surveyed the body of the dead man, Makar felt neither his recent anger, nor satisfaction, only a crushing weariness. Everything that had moved him through long weeks and years, everything that had once sent the warm blood rushing to his heart and made it contract with bitterness, jealousy and pain—all that had passed away with Timofei's death, never to return..." (2, 185-186).

"Before he turned away, Makar glanced at the dead man for the last time, and only then did he notice that the embroidered shirt he wore had been freshly washed, and the khaki breeches darned neatly at the knees, evidently by a woman's hand. So she did you proud, Makar thought bitterly, lifting his leg heavily, very heavily, over the stile" (2, 187).

It was not merely jealousy that possessed Nagulnov as he pressed down on the trigger of his revolver. After all, it had never occurred to him to hold anything against Davidov; he rather pitied him for having been a victim of Lushka's charms.

Timofei the Torn was for him a kulak escaped from exile, a bandit who had taken up arms against Soviet power. Nagulnov fired his shot first and foremost at a class enemy, and only secondarily at a man who had ruined his life. Timofei, the best accordionist in the village and a "women's darling", was a man who enjoyed a soft life. Lushka with her pleasure-seeking, parasitic outlook had found a "kindred spirit". They had no scruples about quite thoughtlessly trampling another man's life in the mud.

These lovers of an easy life laughed at him, making this ascetic, selfless man seethe with silent fury.

Nagulnov fired his shot at the wolf-like features of the property-owning kind, with their calculating egoism and callousness. He saw Lushka's liaison with a bandit and son of a kulak as a direct challenge to himself as secretary of the local Party group and to his "Party spirit" that caused him to place the common good above everything.

There is a note of melancholy throughout this scene, sadness at a wrecked human life and the imperfection of human relations.

We have only to compare the harmonious beauty, the wondrous light that radiated from Varya and Davidov's budding love and friendship, that pure, "ideal" quality it contained, with the gloomy, tragic discord between Lushka and Nagulnov to feel the true depth of Sholokhov's insight into the human heart and mind, the high moral demands he made on man.

There is a sharp dissonance between Lushka's physical beauty and ugly nature. And here is a man with many fine and noble qualities hopelessly loving such a woman.

Sholokhov finds one last, "final" detail which reveals the smouldering strength of Nagulnov's love. After killing Timofei he frees Lushka, thus saving her from certain conviction. He says good-bye to her, knowing they will never meet again. "Makar fumbled awkwardly in his pockets. Then he held out a crumpled lace handkerchief that was now grey with dirt.

"'It's yours. You left it behind when you went away.... Take it, I don't need it now'" (2, 188).

In the Cossack villages a gift of a handkerchief or a tobacco pouch from a girl is traditionally the first token of love.

To have kept the lace handkerchief left behind by Lushka testified to the youthful strength and purity of his love. Had he kept it nursing the faint hope that she would one day return?

Surely it would be impossible to describe faithful, unrequited true love in a simpler, more down to earth manner, yet with such lyrical evocativeness.

Makar was not humiliating himself at this last moment of parting. "They parted in silence, never to see
one another again. As he walked down the steps of the
porch, Makar nodded a careless farewell. Lushka
watched him go, then bowed her proud head. Perhaps at
this last meeting she saw someone different in that stern
and rather lonely man. Who knows?"

The author's question is at the same time a criticism
of Lushka's blindness and narrow-mindedness and a
statement of the beauty and nobility of Nagulnov's
restless soul.

Chapter Four
ANDREI RAZMYOTNOV

When Ivan Arzhanov is discussing what different people will be doing if "a fire" breaks out in the village, he puts Andrei Razmyotnov "in charge of the job". "It'll be us, the collective farmers, who'll do the putting out. Some with a bucket, some with a hook, and some with an axe.... And the man in charge will be Razmyotnov, there's no one else fit for the job" (2, 65).

During "the fire" everyone gets his job according to the way he lives, according to his character, and Arzhanov's appraisals are very shrewd.

Andrei Razmyotnov is fond of a joke and a bit of light bantering. He is one of Grandad Shchukar's most grateful listeners. He is also fond of "occasions". When Ippolit Shaly is presented with a gift at a big general meeting as a reward for good work Andrei says in his artless way: "Take a deep breath now and speak up. Please, Sidorovich, make us a good speech, with plenty of learning in it. You're the hero of the occasion, you know, you've got to make a proper speech, a real lengthy one" (1, 245).

But we would indeed have a very poor understanding of Andrei Razmyotnov's real, essential nature if our knowledge of him were confined to these rather sweet human weaknesses.

Right from the outset Sholokhov stresses Andrei's essential humanity. Absolute implicit faith in others comes as natural to him as breathing. When the poor peasant Borshchov refuses to vote for dispossessing Frol Damaskov, a grasping kulak, Razmyotnov asks: "'Did he ask you to stand up for him? Did he bribe you with money or grain? You can admit it, don't be afraid!... Tell us what he promised you.' And *ashamed of the man* and of his own blunt questions, he smiled awkwardly" (1, 40, author's italics).

After a conversation with members of the regional GPU administration, who told him of their suspicion that Polovtsev, the ex-whiteguard officer they were looking for, was hiding up in Gremyachy, Andrei sat deep in thought for a long time.

"Who of the villagers could be mixed up with that damned Polovtsev? He went over all the men of Gremyachy Log in his mind and could attach no real suspicion to any of them" (2, 318-319).

He was unable to believe that a Soviet man could possibly be mixed up with the enemy. He was trusting to the point of credulity. Yet he was not as naïve as might at first appear. It was he who refused to believe that the purveyance officials' documents were real, and from certain things he saw that they were frauds.

We feel we know a lot about Andrei, and then well on in Book Two comes the description of how a pair of wild rock-pigeons settled in his yard.

In folk poetics pigeons embody pure joy, peace and the imperishable beauty of true love.

At first sight such poetic symbolism appears totally absent from Sholokhov's account. His description of the arrival of the two pigeons and the early stages of their mating game is told in a matter-of-fact manner, very circumstantially and without any elements of romanticism and poetisation: "The hen was mincing hurriedly on dainty legs round the edge of a puddle of thaw water, pecking at something as she went. The cock would take a short run after her, then stop for a little while, go round in a circle bowing and almost touching the ground with his beak and crop, coo energetically, and once again set off in pursuit, fanning out his tail and pressing his body to the damp and still wintry earth."

The eternal song of triumphant love rings out as simply as if played on a shepherd's reed pipe....

The two pigeons reminded Andrei of his youth and marriage. During the Civil War he was at the fighting fronts. When he finally returned home, it was to learn of his wife's death by her own hand. She had been raped by a whiteguard Cossack, and could not bear to live with the shame of it. His small son had died a few weeks later.

The pigeons billing and cooing made Andrei's heart sore....

"Smiling wistfully with misty eyes he watched the beautiful young hen-pigeon greedily pecking at the wheat while her sturdy mate kept running round in circles in front of her, displaying tireless energy without pecking a single grain himself.

"Twenty years ago he, Andrei, as young and sturdy as this cock-pigeon, had preened himself before his sweetheart. Then had come marriage, service in the army, the war.... With what terrible and disappointing haste had life swept by! Thinking of his wife and son, Razmyotnov murmured sadly: 'I didn't see much of you when you were alive, my dear ones, and I don't visit you often now.'

"The cock-pigeon had no time for food that brilliant April day. And neither had Andrei Razmyotnov. His eyes were no longer misty but blinded with tears as he stared out of the window and saw not the pigeons, not the tender blue undertones of spring beyond the window-frame but the sad image of the one woman whom he had really loved, more than life itself, it seemed, without ever knowing the fulness of that love, and from whom black death had parted him twelve years ago on just such a sparkling April day as this" (2, 321).

We often engage in senseless violent arguments over which is more important in art: the personal or the general, and what the connection between the two should be.

This is surely a case where there can be no question of argument, when we're dealing with truly great art, that is. Man can be cognised perfectly well through small details. It obviously all boils down to the writer's ability to feel and think.

Sorrow can make an empty shell of a man, or break him like a straw. One might have expected Andrei's heart to contain nothing but the hot embers of hatred for the people who had taken away his family and his happiness.

Andrei Razmyotnov always reminds me of Andrei Sokolov in *The Fate of a Man*. The one drank the cup of sorrow to the full in the Civil War, the other in the war against the nazi invaders.

Our gratitude is due to the writer who revealed so well the modest greatness of the Russian man who came through incredible suffering and deprivation spiritually unscathed, without losing his kindness, responsiveness, and compassion.

Andrei preserved his love for his wife and his memory of his son throughout his life. It was as if these two casual victims of the harsh class struggle had bequeathed him love and concern for all the people in the world.

Andrei's spiritual richness, fused with sorrow, is especially in evidence in the graveyard scene. He had come to his dear ones in answer to the voiceless call of love.

The desolate glumness of the graveyard makes a striking contrast with the pigeon's billing and cooing.

"In those difficult years the dead were not in favour with the living. The old blackened crosses were crooked or fallen, some lay face downwards, others face upwards. Not a single grave was tended and the east wind sadly stirred dead weeds on the clayey mounds and ran caressing fingers through the strands of wilted colourless wormwood. A mingled scent of decay, rotting grasses, and thawed black earth hung persistently over the graves....

"Why had Andrei come here on this spring day of brilliant sunshine, filled to the brim with awakening life? To stand clenching his short strong fingers and gritting his teeth and to stare with half-closed eyes beyond the misty rim of the horizon, as though striving to discern in that hazy distance his unforgotten youth and short-lived happiness? Perhaps so. The dead but beloved past can always be seen well from a graveyard or in the dumb shadows of a sleepless night" (2, 322-323).

Sholokhov uses contrast to the maximum of psychological tension, to the point where feelings burst forth into the open. He makes it a sad generalisation about the power of memory of "the beloved past".

The skill with which the sad melody of feeling and thought and the essential objective narrative elements like pictures of the setting, portraits and so on, are combined in one period of the author's narration is further evidence of the perfect conciseness of Sholokhov's prose.

The introductory question: "Why had Andrei come..." is a way of addressing the reader directly, which is typical of Sholokhov's prose. Very often Sholokhov seems to be reflecting together with his heroes, sharing their hopes and sorrows, everything that happens to them. This lyrical note of concern on the part of the author is an important stylistic element of Book Two.

Sholokhov addresses Andrei as a dear friend. But since this is a question from the author it can be continued without any strain on the reader's imagination and feelings, and can automatically lead straight into a description of the situation in which the hero found himself at that moment: "on this spring day of brilliant sunshine..." and so on.

The suppositions as to the true reasons that had brought Andrei to the graveyard gradually reveal his mood perfectly naturally and unconstrainedly.

"To stand clenching his short strong fingers and gritting his teeth and to stare with half-closed eyes beyond the misty rim of the horizon..." is like a continuation of the author-and-friend's question.

It is only later that the actual nature of Andrei's feeling is disclosed as memory of his unforgotten youth and short-lived family happiness.

Sholokhov seems to be employing a very widespread form of speech, the rhetorical question, a question normally asked purely in order to attract attention. But Sholokhov infuses it with his own sincere feeling of deep concern.

He expresses a whole wealth of feelings in Andrei's sufferings: undying love and yearning for his dead wife and son, woeful regret at his lost youth, and sad anticipation of approaching old age. There is much down-to-earth beauty and fermenting tenderness, faithfulness and inerasable sadness of heart wounded for ever. The triumph of Andrei's undying love for his dead wife and son over death and decay speaks for the whole man. In it we have the very essence of Andrei Razmyotnov.

It renders any description of his activities as chairman of the Soviet quite superfluous. We already know that he is not one to hurt a man unnecessarily, that he will help an old woman who comes to him to complain about some injustice or other, and we are sure that he will be happy to receive a young couple come to register their marriage. In big things and little things he will always be a man, a man working in the interests of the people.

Once again we see the persistence with which Sholokhov returns again and again to speculation on the real meaning of humanity, on true beauty that ennobles man, awakening in the reader's heart a moving sensation of moral perfection.

However, the artistic solutions Sholokhov adopts in Book Two are not always so successful and striking. It is difficult to explain, for example, what follows the passage about Andrei and the pigeons. After this episode, which is perfect for its poetry and emotional intensity and the classical precision of its words and tone, there comes an episode where Andrei's "childish" enthusiasm for the pigeons leads this no longer young and by all appearances self-respecting man to declare war on the village cats. The slanging match between Andrei and old mother Chebakova goes beyond the borderline separating humour from buffoonery. Where is the humour in Andrei's demanding that an old woman hand over her cat for capital punishment as being a threat to his pigeons? The "flicker of youthful Cossack mischief" Andrei still retained, the "miraculously preserved spark of bluff humour" would hardly have found satisfying food in baiting old women over cats. Yet we are told that the chairman of the village Soviet found "great pleasure, even delight" in such verbal battles.

This strange war declared on cats and the altercation with old women is out of tune with Andrei's character and with the mounting tension of the class struggle.

Ivan Arzhanov's confession ends up with an important remark about "kinks".

"'Suppose you've got a cherry-tree with a lot of different branches. I come along and cut one to make a whip-handle—cherry-wood makes a good strong whip-handle. When it was growing, it had all kinds of kinks in it, with its knots and leaves. Beautiful it was in its own way. And now I've whittled it down, here it is....' Arzhanov pulled his whip out from under the seat and showed Davidov the brown gnarled cherry-wood whip-handle. 'Here it is! Nothing to look at! And it's the same with a man. Without a kink, he's bare and wretched like this whip here. Take Nagulnov—he's learning some strange language—that's his kink; old man Kramskov has been collecting all kinds of match-boxes for twenty years—

that's his kink; you've got yourself mixed up with Lushka Nagulnova—that's your kink; a drunk goes down the street, trips up and rubs his back on the fence—that's another kink. Yes, dear chairman, and if you take a man's kink away from him, he'll be as bare and flat as this whip-handle here'" (2, 78).

Arzhanov makes a rather sly dig at Davidov, telling him to think it over and "mebbe you'll see things clearer...".

Obviously this is what the writer is advising us, his faithful companions, to do. He is also addressing men of letters, protesting against the gloomy monotony of paragons of virtue in art and suggesting that we examine man more carefully and seek the causes for his oddities, not neglecting even seemingly insignificant details in trying to understand man.

While we can accept Sholokhov's advice, we feel bound to recall that there are kinks and kinks. Nagulnov's interest in learning a "strange language" disclosed something extremely important in his character, his longing for the world revolution, which, naïve and even amusing though it was, was nonetheless an organic part of his personality and experience. This "kink" deepens our understanding of Nagulnov. The fascination with cocks crowing which brought Makar and Grandad Shchukar together helped disclose the comic in his character, for there was a humorous dissonance between the "high" idealistic impulse which drove Makar to strive with such enthusiasm and obvious futility to master a "strange language" and his frank "base" passion for harmonious cock crowing.

Davidov's love for Lushka was likewise a "kink" which enables us to see into the man's moral principles.

Andrei Razmyotnov's fierce war against the village cats was a fortuitous, unnecessary kink, which adds nothing and is merely out of place. It merely casts a shadow on the true humanity of a character Sholokhov has moulded with such power.

Chapter Five
KONDRAT MAIDANNIKOV.
THE MASSES

1

Virgin Soil Upturned is remarkable for its perfect composition, and the natural manner in which the dunamic plot is constructed. The characters are masterfully arrayed from the very start with the classical clarity of a chess composition, and one is immediately struck by the depth of the author's penetration into the philosophy of the age, and by the socio-historical and psychological authenticity. There is perfect cohesion and dynamic interaction, nothing is superfluous. In the foreground the group of Communists with Davidov at their head stands out sharp and clear; Polovtsev and Ostrovnov lurk in the shadows; Kondrat Maidannikov looms large in the turbulent village crowd....

The hero of *And Quiet Flows the Don* was Grigory Melekhov, whose life embodied the doubts and vacillation of millions of "the semi-petty bourgeois and petty bourgeois masses". In its extreme form this wavering was their downfall.

In *Virgin Soil Upturned* the spotlight is on the Communists affirming the new life and people like the middle peasant Kondrat Maidannikov whose whole life had prepared him for accepting collectivisation as a vital necessity.

During the Civil War Kondrat had fought with the Red Army. His old worn cavalry cap which he hasn't the heart to part with tells us more of his past than any words.

Kondrat Maidannikov's doubts and wavering are not expressed in his actions (he is among the first to join the collective farm), but in his inner struggle to overcome that "sneaking regret" for his own property.

Naturally Sholokhov saw, knew and understood that the majority of those who doubted and hesitated during collectivisation were middle peasants. The dramatic "flux and reflux" was connected with this section of the peasantry. But as a writer and thinker Sholokhov went further and deeper in appreciating the nature of the historical conflict.

Sholokhov's attention was drawn to the fundamental aspect of the period, which was "how the property-owner voluntarily gave up his scrap of land".

The conflict became an inner, spiritual one. The struggle between reason and prejudice in Kondrat's heart revealed the mighty historic significance of what was happening throughout the countryside. Sholokhov showed how joining the collective farm was but the first stage in the painful birth of the new.

This indeed was one of the central ideas of the novel, an idea which is developed with deep psychological penetration—the drama of parting with property, cardinal changes in life, and decisive turning points.

Kondrat Maidannikov is a generalised figure. The ordinary, inconspicuous Cossack from Gremyachy Log who was sharp and aware enough to recognise in himself the "cursed hankering" after property and struggled against it with all his might, was thereby performing a historic feat and raising himself to the level of those heroes of literature who can serve as an example and a model....

The individual struggled with himself in order to better and ennoble himself, to bring his own life into line with the historical aims of society—such is the wider significance of Kondrat Maidannikov, testifying to Sholokhov's profound understanding of the essential nature of the social conflicts of the time.

Kondrat has no doubts about the collective farm being the only way to bring about a better life. His doubts come later, and not from the fear that he and his family will be worse off in the collective farm. He is worried about something quite different as he lies in bed at night unable to sleep: "What would it be like in the collective farm? Would everyone feel and understand, as he understood, that this was the only way, that there was no going back?... And what if everybody gives it up after a week because they're afraid of the snags? Then I'll say good-bye to Gremyachy for good, and go off to the mines. We'll have nothing left to live on here" (1, 91).

If collectivisation failed it would be a personal disaster for Kondrat, dashing so many hopes.

This understanding of the historic importance of collectivisation is one of the essential features of Kondrat Maidannikov's nature. This is indeed what sets him apart somewhat from the average middle peasant he is supposed to typify. It was only after much doubt and hesitation that the middle peasants came to identify the general historical interest with their own.

Nikita Morgunok from Tvardovsky's poem *The Land of Muravia* typifies the attitude of this section of the peasantry. He dreams of the peasant land of Muravia, where:

"The land from end to end, it all
Belongs to you...."

It is only much later, after having gone through all sorts of trials and seen his former dreams and ideals shattered that Nikita Morgunok finally decides to join the kolkhoz.

Kondrat Maidannikov is a different, new type of peasant. Educated by years of revolutionary struggle, he has come to understand the indestructible connection between his own destiny and that of the whole country that was building socialism, feeling the general interest to be his own. He is set apart by the way he thinks on a nation-wide scale, something which was later developed by Sholokhov with a great wealth of motifs in the characters of his novel *They Fought for Their Fatherland*.

Kondrat thinks and worries a lot about the initial difficulties in getting the collective farm going and comes to the conclusion that the biggest danger to the new life is "a sneaking regret" for one's own property. He himself is unable to suppress it entirely. He is oppressed by it in the silence of the night and it will not let him rest; it creeps up on him when he is on duty in the collective-farm stables, and he gives "his own" horse the best hay; when "his" horse's neck is rubbed by the yoke, he "can't eat the whole day afterwards".

Sholokhov shows that the thing is not only a property "instinct" that has built up over the generations. The psychological explanation will be found in the actual circumstances of Kondrat's life. Kondrat collected his modest property at the cost of tremendous toil, and self-denial for himself and his family. He himself guesses the reason for his "cursed hankering": "It's all because it was so hard to get what we had. I reckon people that were up to their eyes in wealth wouldn't feel it so bad" (1, 171).

One of the secrets of great art is the authenticity that comes from direct, personal knowledge. You, the reader, "alone" are privileged to be offered an insight into the secrets of another person's life. This is very true of Sholokhov's art.

Sholokhov gives us a very full picture of Kondrat Maidannikov's life, his everyday interests, his dreams and hopes. We feel the author's sympathy and concern as well as his deep understanding of the inner world of the peasant toiler.

We are told how difficult Kondrat's life had been. Kondrat with his one poor nag really knew what poverty was. He could not wait for his cow to calve. "How many times of a cold night had Kondrat woken up as if someone had shaken him, and, pushing his feet into his boots, run out to the stable in only his underpants to see if the cow was calving. The frosts were bitter and the calf might get frozen as soon as its mother had licked it clean..." (1, 90). The bull grew up and worked for Kondrat "in summer and winter cold". When the time came to drive the bull to the collective farm his heart bled, and he wept, finding relief in tears.

With one short remark the author seems to sum up all Kondrat has suffered and experienced: "Collective farming did not come easy to Kondrat. With tears and blood he tore apart the belly-cord that bound him to his property, his bull, his scrap of land" (1, 92).

Yet however much Kondrat's heart might ache for his own property, however difficult he might find it to get rid of his "cursed hankering" after his horse or his bull, he gradually becomes more and more concerned for the collective-farm property.

"But none of the horses belong to other people now, they're all ours," he says, thereby expressing his new concern for common property as for his own.

Kondrat transfers all his zeal to the collective-farm work, making everything his business and never missing the slightest lapse. He not only notices that the litter for the horses is used wastefully—there's enough to feed the sheep and the goats—but gets Davidov to cancel Ostrovnov's sabotaging instructions. He notes that Kuzhenkov leaves the watering of the horses to young boys who drive them back before they have drunk their fill. He is quite prepared to fight Atamanchuk for not ploughing deep enough and, moreover, going out in the rain, when it can do the oxen irreparable harm. "I won't let you harm the collective farm!" Kondrat shouts. This same personal concern for the collective farm determines all Kondrat's actions.

Kondrat's concern for the welfare of the collective farm does not boil down to refusal to put up with slackness from others. He is equally demanding on himself and works so well that Davidov praises him before the whole team. The poetry of the new life bursts forth in the novel in a jubilant key. Kondrat drives his oxen into camp after dark, having worked solidly since noon, without even breaking off for a smoke. He has ploughed more that day than any of the others and his eyes are shining with the triumphant light of a man who has experienced the joy of labour for the common good. The new principles of collective labour are becoming a part of him.

After supper Davidov thanks the farmers for their work on behalf of the management, and says that special thanks are due to Maidannikov, for "he's been a real shock-worker". Kondrat's wife isn't quite sure if that is a compliment: "It sounded like praise ... but what is it—a shock-worker?" Although he has heard the term before, Kondrat doesn't know exactly what it means. Nevertheless he makes a brave attempt to explain. "A shock-worker? Ah, you foolish woman! A shock-worker? Hm. Well, it's a.... How shall I put it so you'll understand? In a rifle, for example, there's a pin that strikes the cap of the cartridge, and the shock makes the rifle fire. That pin's a shock-worker, you can't fire without it. And it's the same in a collective farm, the shock-worker is the main person in it, see? Now get to sleep and don't come worrying me!"

In the person of Kondrat Maidannikov Sholokhov shows us the complex and contradictory process of the new socialist man being born out of the property man, of the victory of the new in the mind of the peasant toiler.

If Kondrat is such a sharp, clear-cut character, it is in no small measure due to the way Sholokhov lets his own attitude filter through his words, thoughts and feelings.

In Sholokhov's action-packed, dramatic novels, the way a character speaks and expresses his thoughts is of primary importance as a revelation of his inner world.

Kondrat Maidannikov's thoughts about the collective farm and his family pass naturally and simply to thoughts about the whole country and the whole world. His thoughts are at first of narrow, personal, everyday matters and worries—"people don't want to look after the horses, no one wants anything to do with them", "mustn't forget to tell Davidov tomorrow how Kuzhenkov watered the horses...", "Khristina's running about barefoot. Say what you like, but she ought to have some slippers!" He goes on to thinking about "the need the country is suffering while it carries out the five-year plan", and addresses a wrathful speech to the workers in the West "who do not support the Communists".

His thoughts are not a soliloquy, they are really a dialogue. His sharp reproach is at the same time a warm appeal straight from the heart: "You'll feel ashamed, brothers...." Kondrat believes that the workers in the West that he is addressing will ally themselves with the Communists and become faithful friends of the land of the Soviets, and this is why he addresses them so. He is an inspired propagandist of the new life.

2

In Book Two there are considerable changes both in the nature of the subject-matter and the principles on which the Cossack masses are portrayed.

Sholokhov no longer shows the Cossacks in a crowd, or only very rarely. Unfortunately, even one of the important scenes, the open Party meeting where Kondrat Maidannikov, Agafon Dubtsov and Ippolit Shaly were admitted to membership,—a scene which might well have been one of the "pivotal" episodes in the novel—did not have the impact it should have for this reason.

Sholokhov was mainly endeavouring to deepen and give further details of that epic concept of the social processes taking place in the masses that Book One gave, and to reveal more fully the influence of the social on the moral and ethical.

Kondrat Maidannikov is an extremely important character in Book One. It is he who helped us see into the tortured soul of the peasant, who had been attracted to join the collective farm because he was perfectly aware where his own interest lay, yet at the time was tormented by the "cursed hankering" for "his own" property. Now, in Book Two, he fades into the background, having fulfilled his artistic purpose. Book One prepares us psychologically for his admittance to the Party, Book Two merely gives us "the event".

In Book Two Sholokhov singles out several characters who had hitherto been "dissolved" in the masses so to speak, and makes them into clear-cut striking individuals. They include: Ippolit Shaly the blacksmith—whom we already know from Book One but who is essentially revealed anew as it were—Ivan Arzhanov, and Ustin Rykalin.

Ippolit Shaly and Ivan Arzhanov tell their stories themselves, while we learn about Rykalin's past mainly from the words of his old relation Osetrov.

Arzhanov and Shaly's life accounts are like complete short-stories inserted in the narrative, and can easily stand by themselves. Yet in actual fact they are not the arbitrarily inserted stories in their own right that they seem, but are organically linked to the mainstream of the narrative by a thousand inner threads.

Certainly, one cannot help admiring the wealth of imagination involved here. As regards the amount of action and the completeness of the character-drawing there is enough material in the story of Ivan Arzhanov's life alone for a whole novel.

Each of these "autobiographies" is an insight into the moral and ethical experience of the people. It is significant that they are in each case told to Davidov, thus enriching his political and life experience and his knowledge of men.

The past comes into the present to light up the bright goals of the future.

A taut thread of human pride runs through the life-stories of these people from the masses, a feeling of jealously guarded human dignity.

Sholokhov shows how by maintaining at all costs their human dignity, people from the masses, people who lead a "real" life of work, are at the same time defending the dignity of the people as a whole. He detests abject servility.

Sholokhov is making a poetic acclamation of proud defence of one's dignity, active refusal to submit to injustice, and readiness to stand up for the "insulted and the injured" as fine human qualities.

The young Arzhanov watched his father's murderers "like a young wolf watches a bird from the rushes", waiting to have his revenge. But he was not merely blinded by passion, and longing for revenge for the fact that the men had made an orphan of him, doomed a large family to dire poverty, and placed such a tremendous burden of cares and sorrows on his young shoulders.

His father's parting words were: "Now listen to me, son.... You're twelve years old now, and when I'm gone, you'll be master here. Remember this: it was Averyan Arkhipov and his two brothers, Afanasi and cross-eyed Sergei, who beat me up. *If they'd killed me straight out, I wouldn't be holding anything against them.* That's what I asked them to do down there on the river, while I was still conscious. But Averyan said to me: 'You won't have an easy death, you dog! You can live for a bit as a cripple and swallow as much of your own blood as you like, then you'll die!' That's why I've got a grudge against Averyan. Death's at my bedside, but I've still got a grudge against him. You're only small now, but when you grow up, remember my sufferings, and kill Averyan!" (2, 72, author's italics).

Ivan kept his promise. He was not simply avenging them for killing. But for subjecting the man they killed to cruel torments, for making brutal mock of him first. It was his memory of his father's sufferings which drove him to carry out his deed of vengeance.

Obviously Arzhanov's actions can be judged in various ways, but there is no overlooking the human pain in them.

Davidov is the first man Arzhanov has ever told the terrible story that has haunted him all his life. He knows he has found a man who will understand him.

Davidov's moral exigence, his keen sense of the border-line between revenge and crime are clearly expressed in his reaction when Arzhanov tells him how he shot Averyan, and mentions that he took his money.

"'Why did you take the money?' Davidov snapped fiercely.

"'Why not?'

"'Why did you take it, I say?'

"'I needed it,' Arzhanov answered simply. 'In those times poverty was gnawing at us worse than a shirtful of lice'" (2, 76).

The direct cause of the clash between "the village proletariat", Ippolit Shaly, and Selivanov the landowner was the former's highly developed sense of justice which led him to stick up for the "little man" when he was being "insulted and injured".

"I come out, and there, in a light wicker carriage, under an umbrella was Selivanov, the most famous landowner in our district, a terrible proud man, and the worst bastard the world's ever seen.... His coachman was as white as a sheet and his hands were trembling as he unbuckled the trace from the left-side horse. He'd been careless and the horse had lost a shoe on the road. And now this landowner was pitching into him about it: 'You so and so, I'll fire you, I'll put you in prison, you're making me miss my train' and so on and so forth" (2, 163).

The scene where the resourceful blacksmith derides the pompous sire, and completely squashes him making him quite berserk with rage, is full of typical Sholokhov humour.

"You see, lad, he went on calling me a lout and a scoundrel and everything else under the sun, and in the end he nearly choked himself and started stamping on the floor of the carriage. 'You filthy socialist! I'll have you gaoled!' And in those days I didn't know what a socialist was.... Revolution—I knew what that meant, but not 'socialist', and I thought it must be the very worst swearword he could think of.... So I answered him: 'You're a socialist yourself, you son-of-a-bitch,' I says. 'Get out of here before I set about you!'" (2, 166).

Shaly may not have known the meaning of the word socialist and thereby made a boob, but Selivanov grasped perfectly well the link between the man's proud defence of human dignity and the revolutionary spirit of the masses.

Shaly and Arzhanov's tales are more than little windows onto the past; they revive the past as a sort of artistically palpable reality.

There is always a subtle, significant "time link" in Sholokhov's novels. It is worth noting how Shaly's account of the Selivanov incident follows hard on his story of how a "responsible" district manager had come to take up lodgings with Shaly and his wife the year before.

"...He wouldn't speak a word, neither to her nor to me; he thought that was beneath him. He'd sit down at table—not a word. He'd get up from table—still not a word. He'd come back from the village Soviet—not a word; and when he went out again—not a word. Whatever I asked him, whether it was about politics or household matters, he would grunt: 'That's none of your business, old man.' And that's as far as we got. Well, our lodger lived with us very quiet-like for three days, and on the fourth day he opened his mouth.... In the morning he puffs out his chest and says to me: 'Tell your old woman to bring me my potatoes on a plate, not in a frying pan, and tell her to put some kind of napkin on the table, and not a dish towel. I'm a cultured man,' he says, 'and what's more, I'm a responsible worker from district headquarters and I don't like such common ways.'

"That put my back up proper and I says to him: 'You're a stinking nit, not a cultured man! If you were cultured, you'd eat off what people gave you, and wipe your mug with what they gave you. ...Take your brief-case, my dear man,' I says, 'and get out of here, because I've got no use for someone as stuck up as you'" (2, 154-155).

Beneath the surface humour lies serious food for thought. Shaly's tale was a direct hint, a "parable" for Davidov. Look at us a little closer, he seems to be saying. We're not quite as simple as we may seem. We're proud, and if you want to be our friend just you remember that and respect it.

Sholokhov uses his powerful literary gift to convey the beauty of the people's pride and dignity, confirmed and strengthened by the revolution, and to appeal for a considerate regard for man.

His novels are pervaded with the genius of the people, and their demanding conscience.

At the same time these life-stories are a poetic testimony of the historic revolution in the minds of the masses.

Arzhanov and Shaly, who are both secretive men and not without a touch of cunning, open up naturally to Davidov, "the Party man", who had become "one of their own".

This is at the same time testimony of the people's trust in the leader, their faith in the nobility of the Communist's ideas, and a profound expression of the indissoluble link between the Party and the people, which the years of the Revolution and Civil War, with all their battles for socialism have forged.

It was no accident that Shaly started talking to Davidov on the subject of universal responsibility.

Sholokhov is once again returning to one of the major themes of his novel—the Party and the people.

Chapter Six
THE ENEMIES

Sholokhov never takes sides openly by artificially "touching up" characters to serve his purpose. His art does not admit of arbitrary subjectivity.

Sholokhov's own stand is apparent in his deep understanding of the people's interests, his winged dream of human happiness and his knowledge of the paths of historical development.

"The main arteries of historical development" are what determine the structure of his novels. By appreciating the laws and regularities of history, and what is inevitable and desirable for the people, he is able to be perfectly objective in his aesthetic and ethic judgments.

Sholokhov's artistic quest brings him to a comprehensive study of the extent to which a man, his life, his mind, his political views and social sympathies, are influenced by the stand he takes in social upheavals.

In *Virgin Soil Upturned* we are shown those who had made it their aim to "shake Soviet power" at a sharp turning point in history: we are shown them in all sorts of situations.

The motives, aims, and social ambitions of the kulak and whiteguard elements were presented clearly enough in Book One. We saw how egoistic class interests emerged in open conflict with the interests of the Cossack masses. Even those Cossacks who had fought against Soviet power in the past were no longer giving their support to the whiteguard conspirators and their stooges. The fact that the anti-popular cause is doomed to failure from the outset becomes a powerful motif of the novel.

We have already mentioned on several occasions the humanism and the moral and ethical content of Book Two.

Sholokhov raises such questions as the essence of true humanity, the relationship between humanism and historical necessity, and what leads to a man's moral ascent or fall.

In Book Two we once again meet our old acquaintances Polovtsev, Latyevsky and Ostrovnov.

True art does not permit ready-made conclusions to be dealt out wholesale and forced on the reader who must form his own opinions through thinking over what the writer has shown him.

Thus for the superficial reader—some literary critics also fall into this category—Yakov Lukich Ostrovnov could seem a rather enigmatic figure.

Some critics did, in fact, think Ostrovnov a contradictory character. They found it difficult to reconcile his hatred for Soviet power and the farmers with the pleasure he took in the day-to-day business of the farm, and his acts of sabotage with his efficient work and bold plans.

Some asked if Sholokhov was perhaps not getting carried away by the dialectical complexity of this character, while others made no bones about launching open reproaches at him for doing so.

Sholokhov won through thanks to the power and truth of his artistic thought, just as he had in that infinitely more complicated case, his treatment of the history of the Cossacks in the Civil War in *And Quiet Flows the Don*.

Prejudice and preconceived opinions which so often ruin interesting, important observations of young, immature writers are quite foreign to Sholokhov. He teaches us not to overlook in our view of things any social or psychological factors, any factors at all that go to produce a particular character, social phenomenon, etc.

Yakov Lukich is indeed a complex character. But then for real art there is nothing simple in life, and only a swift or superficial glance can give one the impression that there is.

Collectivisation brings out rather important historical contradictions in Ostrovnov. He knew and loved the land. He had the necessary knowledge of agronomy. He was a man of vision with a bold approach to farming which required machines, large areas of land and large manpower. He naturally felt cramped on his own "lawful" portion of land.

So it was that collectivisation seemed to offer him the opportunity for following all his inclinations and desires, and putting all his abilities to good use.

And paradoxical though it may seem, this was another example of the humanistic essence of upheaval begun in the countryside, but it was a historical process which entered into irreconcilable conflict with egoistic property interests and prejudices.

Ostrovnov might give Davidov some sound advice as regards the land, he might be unable to repress if only a temporary feeling of excitement when bold plans were being discussed which the individual farmer of the past could not even have dreamed of. But this excitement went as soon as it conflicted with personal egoistic interests, and then the man with ambitious plans became a malicious wrecker, causing oxen to get frost-bite, a petty trouble-maker, ransacking the farm larder, wickedly using Davidov's name for cover.

All his life Yakov Lukich had dreamed of building up his farm in a big way, of buying a steam-mill, owning a car, and sending his son to military college to become an officer. His one aim in life had been to get rich, his only joy—accumulation at the expense of others.

The Revolution had cut the ground from under Yakov Lukich's feet. Now with collectivisation there was no longer any going back.

Everything in Ostrovnov's nature was subordinate to his class instinct as a property-owner. He hated Soviet power because it blocked his way, prevented him from getting rich, dashed his hopes of owning his private steam-mill with hired labourers, and of seeing his son an officer. Before the Revolution his life had "glistened and crackled like a new bank-note", the new bank-note that had been the ideal for which he had lived. "If it wasn't for this hounding of the rich, I might be the first man in the village by now with my ability," he complains to Polovtsev. He doesn't hesitate for long before throwing in his lot with Polovtsev and is soon his right-hand-man in Gremyachy Log.

Working for Polovtsev, Ostrovnov recruited members for an anti-Soviet underground organisation, and joined the collective farm where he was able to make use of his position to freeze the oxen so that they'd be no good for ploughing. He was the first to begin slaughtering his cattle: "he does not want the meat of his sheep to feed some worker in a factory, or some Red Army man". He stirs up the Cossacks to open revolt against the Soviet government by spreading the most malicious rumours. Davidov apparently did not suspect for a moment that those hostile forces he came up against at every step were led and guided by his thorough and efficient farm manager. The trials of the Revolution and the Civil War had compelled Ostrovnov to learn the art of camouflage. Besides he was only too well aware of the strength of "the other side". Duplicity was henceforth the only line open to him.

Ostrovnov is not merely cunning and resourceful: he is vicious and unscrupulous. When the poor peasant Khoprov who has got entangled in the kulak net declares, "I won't rise agin the government and I don't advise others to either", Ostrovnov, fearing that he will inform on them, takes Timofei the Torn with him and goes straight to Polovtsev. "Why did you bring him here?" Polovtsev asks. Their eyes met and they understood each other without words. That same night Khoprov and his wife were murdered in their home.

True, Yakov Lukich is a bit of a coward. He can't stand the sight of blood, for example. But he masters his weakness and becomes Polovtsev's trusty servant. He is occasionally assailed by doubts and torments. He doubts Polovtsev's strength, and is not very fond of Latyevsky. "How will the people look at it? Will they follow us?" he asks Polovtsev at their very first meeting. He realises perfectly that any revolt that does not have the support of the masses will be doomed to failure. As it happened this support was in fact not forthcoming.

Yakov Lukich begins to look to the West for salvation. "The people were so cussed nowadays" they were loyal to Soviet power and refused to rise in defence of the Latyevsky, Polovtsev and Ostrovnov. "None of your Polovtsevs will stand up to 'em, no matter how much brains they've got. Straw can't stand up to force...." Ostrovnov concludes disconsolately. Yet he does not give up hope that his day will come. "There's no parting with Soviet power yet, but mebbe we'll have better luck next time" (1, 417). So Yakov Lukich sits down to wait patiently for "deliverance", which he is firmly convinced now can only come from abroad. Ostrovnov, Polovtsev and Latyevsky show a sad lack of patriotic feeling and a deep hatred for the people.

In the first chapter of Book Two we see Yakov Lukich alone with his troubled thoughts about the path he has chosen.

"I ought to have waited, old fool that I am, kept in the background for a bit, not sworn myself like this to Alexander Anisimovich Polovtsev. If they'd got the better of the Communists, I could have joined up with them and reaped the benefit, but now I may be finding myself in the cart before I know it. But look at it this way—with me hanging back and others doing the same, what'll happen? Are we to let this cursed Soviet government ride on our backs for the rest of our lives? That won't do either!" (2,15).

Ostrovnov indeed had good reason to worry. He could see that the Cossack masses were not supporting the plotters. He could also see the strength of Soviet power. "The Bolsheviks will smash us, sure as God they will! They're good at it. Then it'll be all up with us who rise against them."

Book Two is the book of reckonings. Sholokhov has wide recourse to *"climax scenes"*, where the *dominant feature of a character's nature is revealed in action, in direct, intense experience.*

We have already had cause to mention some of these scenes, like Davidov's marriage to Varya Kharlamova, Nagulnov's murder of Timofei the Torn and his parting with Lushka, Andrei Razmyotnov and the pigeons....

The logic of the struggle leads Ostrovnov, who "cannot stand the sight of blood", to commit the most heinous crimes. Suffice it that he took part in the murder of the Khoprovs, he starved his own mother to death for having gossipped to some other old women about the presence of the officer conspirators in their house.

Probably nowhere else in all Soviet literature will you find such a damning criticism of the evil property can be, of the abysmal depths to which a man can sink by going against the people and the progressive course of history.

Sholokhov uses sharp changes in emotional tone and unexpected twists in the composition to achieve a high pitch of tragic intensity. The tremendous power of the tragic account of the mother murdered by her own son required a great sense of authentic inner emotional development, balance and rhythm.

Ostrovnov's fear of being discovered takes the form of hatred turned against his mother. "Ruined by my own mother! She's killed me!" Ostrovnov is driven to distraction by the thought. He is terrified of what Polovtsev might do, and goes in to see him "cringing like a dog".

Polovtsev leaves Ostrovnov's house. His parting words are words of advice: "Just think a little about your mother, Lukich, won't you. She might upset all our plans. Think about that...."

Lukich "thought" about it all right; out of pure, blind egoism, his one idea was to save himself, and in the grip of unreasoning fear he came to his terrible decision.

"Ostrovnov returned home and, when he had got into bed, pushing his wife unusually roughly towards the wall, said: 'Listen to me. Don't feed mother any more. And don't give her anything to drink. She'll die soon anyway.'"

The composition and emotional tone of the narrative change suddenly. The dark world of heartless brutality and the cynicism born of fear is suddenly pierced by a ray of light: his mother's tender feelings for him, her trust in her only son, her darling Yakov. She hears his footsteps approaching the door, and unaware of his sinister purpose, she thinks of him with boundless tenderness, remembering his whole life, from his carefree childhood to maturity.

"She has long been accustomed to telling his presence by that sound. And how could she have failed to learn the sound of her son's footsteps, even from afar? Fifty years ago, then a young and handsome Cossack woman, she would pause in her housework or cooking and listen with a smile of pride and delight to the uncertain, faltering patter of bare feet on the floor in the next room, the little feet of her first-born, her one and only darling Yakov, a little toddler who had only just learned to walk. Then she heard the clatter of little Yakov's boots as he skipped up the steps coming home from school. In those days he had been quick and frolicsome as a young goat.

She could not remember him ever walking at that age—
he always ran. And he didn't just run, he skipped along,
yes, just like a young goat. Life rolled on, a life like everyone else's—rich in long sorrows, poor in brief joys—
and soon she was an elderly mother, listening disconten-
tedly at night to the soft, stealthy footsteps of Yakov,
a lithe, sprightly lad of whom in secret she was very
proud. When he returned late from courting, his boots
seemed scarcely to touch the floor-boards, his youthful
tread was so light and swift. Before she noticed it, her
son became a grown-up family man. His tread acquired a
ponderous confidence. For a long time now the house had
echoed with the footsteps of its master, a mature man,
almost an old man, but for her he was still 'little Yakov',
and she often saw him in her dreams, a lively little tow-
headed boy....

"And now, too, on hearing his footsteps, she asked in
her reedy, old woman's voice: 'Is that you, Yakov?'

"Her son made no reply. He stood a moment by the
door, then went out into the yard, for some reason
quickening his pace. I've reared a good Cossack and a
thrifty master, thank God! the old woman thought as she
fell asleep. Everyone's abed, but he be up and about,
looking after the farm. And a proud maternal smile
touched her pale wrinkled lips" (2, 24-25).

The most powerful thing here is the sinister contrast
between childhood innocence, carefree youth, maternal
pride, and the deliberate cruelty of the object of this
great love, who was committing the most atrocious of
crimes, taking the life of his own mother who had given
him life.

The tragic clash of feelings here reaches tremendous
intensity. Ostrovnov is condemned and damned for his
crime by the boundless love of his victim, the woman who
bore him and raised him.

The event Sholokhov describes here would appear to
follow from an extremely unusual set of dramatic circumstances. Yet as is so often the case, Sholokhov makes the
tragic and out of the ordinary serve as a merciless disclo-
sure of the typical. In the chaos of life the triumphant
note of regularity sounds. In recounting how Ostrovnov
killed his mother, Sholokhov laid bare the cruel callousness inherent in property and egoistic class interests,

and placed it before the unforgiving judge that represents authentic kindness, humanity, and virtue.

Sholokhov does not deny the enemy natural human feelings, acts and affections. Even Polovtsev, who is frequently compared to a wild beast, particularly a wolf— (Polovtsev has a "prominent wolfish brow", when he was in a rage over some set-back he would talk in a "low growl", with a "hollow choking in the throat" (1,202); in a moment of danger he jumps up, "and going purple in the face, leans forward alert and tense, like some great beast of prey ready to spring" (1, 112); "there, in the parlour, like a vulture on a grave mound, sat Polovtsev, frowning and terrible in his solitude" (1, 203)—even this man can suddenly reveal human feelings.

"I love cats, Lukich! The horse and the cat, they're the cleanest of all animals. At home I used to have a Siberian cat, great big, fluffy fellow. Always slept in my bed... cats I'm devilishly fond of. And children. Little ones. Terribly fond of them, almost too fond. I can't bear the sound of children crying, it makes me heave..." (1, 253).

But just compare this sentimental avowal with the description of Polovtsev bringing down the axe on Khoprov's wife, and take a look at how after the murder he drank brew at Ostrovnov's house and "fished a stewed pear out of the jar, munched it and walked away, smoking a cigarette and stroking his plump bare chest..." (1, 121) as if nothing had happened. The glaring contrasts here reveal the true nature of this "champion" of the Cossacks' cause.

Sholokhov is struck by the incompatibility of normal human feelings and actual abhorrent behaviour, an egregiously distorted manifestation of naturalness. By using the power of contrast in a masterly fashion, he allows us to see the other, dark side behind the natural, human façade....

The inherent logic of the struggle against the people reveals terrible cynicism, emptiness and moral bankruptcy in these characters.

Ostrovnov was incited to murder his mother by the "dashing cavalier" and "passionate nature" Polovtsev. That, at least, is how Polovtsev saw himself:

"Sinking on both knees, Polovtsev held out the sword on his upturned palms, his head thrown back as if to admire the dull gleam of the silver; then he clasped it to his breast and in a trembling voice said: 'My beloved, my beauty! My true old friend! You shall still render me devoted service!'

"His massive lower jaw quivered slightly and tears of frenzied delight welled up in his eyes, but he managed to control himself and, turning a pale, distorted face towards Ostrovnov, asked loudly: 'Do you recognise it, Lukich?'

"Ostrovnov swallowed convulsively and nodded. He recognised the sword. He had first seen it in 1915, worn by the young and dashing Cornet Polovtsev on the Austrian front" (2, 11).

The theatricality of all this, the way Polovtsev is puffing himself up with all his might, is revealed by his worthy "companion" Latyevsky.

In a work of literature there are no disconnected characters. The connection may not be directly afforded by the plot, but taken together as a "character system", they form a single canvas, expressing the writer's mind.

The characters that are close to one another in the action often serve as "catalysts" to one another. They may have the same social background and way of life like Grigory Melekhov and Prokhor Zykov in *And Quiet Flows the Don*. Here Sholokhov used the very different characters of the two men to make Prokhor Zykov a tragi-comical version of the truly tragic Grigory Melekhov, thereby setting off and drawing attention to what was purely individual and personal in the latter's life. Characters may also have a very different background, as regards externals at least, like the "aristocrat" Latyevsky, scion of one of the most blue-blooded noble families, and the "plebeian" Polovtsev, who are brought together by the changeful circumstances of the uprising being prepared against Soviet power on the Don.

Polovtsev's imperious, stern power is maintained by the carefully nursed conviction that he, a fighting Cossack officer, a man of honour and duty, is fanning the flames of revolt in the interests of the working Cossack masses of the Don, and that he has no motives other than "sworn hatred" for the Bolsheviks and the Soviets.

He tries to "open the Cossacks' eyes" to their historical error of giving up and laying down their arms in the Civil

War, which has brought them the even harsher misfortune of collectivisation. He tries to arouse in his supporters the feeling of dashing Cossack bravado that goes with the idea of an autonomous Don region, which has been exploited by the whiteguards in inciting Cossack uprisings against Soviet power several times during the Civil War.

When the Cossacks refused to follow him any further, after reading Stalin's article *Dizzy with Success*, it was too much even for the hardened officer and he broke down and wept. "'I weep that our cause has not succeeded—this time,' Polovtsev said loudly and, sweeping off his white cap, dried his eyes with it. 'The Don has grown poor in true Cossacks and rich in scum, in traitors and scoundrels...'" (1, 261).

The somewhat theatrical gesture (the way he sweeps off his cap and dries his eyes with it) does not detract from the impression that this is a truly genuine outpouring of feeling.

The cynical Latyevsky, who has been through "fire and water" is a perfect "foil" to Polovtsev. He has long since ceased to believe in any ideals, and is merely a clever, vicious adventurist. Polovtsev's romantic pose as a defender of the Cossacks' interests merely gets on Latyevsky's nerves. He is too intelligent not to see that the Cossacks will not go along with Polovtsev and his kind. He even causes Ostrovnov great embarrassment with his frank cynicism.

"What the hell made you join up with us, you old stick-in-the-mud? What the devil made you do it? Polovtsev and I, of course, we've nowhere to turn, we're facing death. Yes, death! Or else we shall win. But let me tell you, you poor lout, the chances of victory are grievously small. One in a thousand, not more! But that's for us; we have nothing to lose but our chains, as the Communists say. But you? If you ask me, you're just a sacrificial offering. You could have had years to live, you fool. Granted I don't believe that a lot of louts like you could ever build socialism, but all the same ... you might stir up a little of the mud in the world swamp. As it is, there'll be a rising, you'll catch a packet, you grey-haired old devil, or else you'll simply get taken prisoner and be sent off, as one of the ignorant, to Arkhangelsk Province, where you'll be chopping down pines till the second coming of communism. You poor fool!" (1, 213).

For him, Ostrovnov, who is generously placing his house at the disposal of the officer conspirators, is just "a grain-taker and a grain-eater! A dung-beetle!" He even goes as far as to scornfully throw at his host: "Weren't enough of you Cossack sons-of-bitches killed off in the Civil War!" (1, 214).

The Cossack officer Polovtsev with his idea of a popular uprising seems hopelessly out-of-date to Latyevsky, and even rather amusing and awkward in that international game that had developed around collectivisation.

For this Polish nobleman—guards officer turned spy—an uprising is "a game on which everything was staked", which even if it were lost might be some help to the West. Patriotism was entirely foreign to him.

Indeed, perhaps his vicious sarcasm, the caustic, mocking tone he adopted towards Polovtsev was produced by a feeling of inability to influence the course of history, a cold sober realisation that they were outcasts, so much driftwood floating on the surface with absolutely no anchor in the life of the people, and that they were doomed to solitude.

Polovtsev nearly always suffered defeat in his verbal duels with Latyevsky. The stern Cossack officer somehow turns a funny and awkward side to the reader. Latyevsky tears the mask off Polovtsev with his ironic comments on his words and actions. When Polovtsev sinks to his knees and holds out his sword, with tears springing to his eyes, Latyevsky sneers at him.

"'A touching reunion!' he said hoarsely. 'The rebel's romance, I suppose. Ugh, how I hate these sentimental scenes puffed up with false emotion!'"

Polovtsev then advances threateningly on Latyevsky, holding his sword in one hand and with the other clawing at his collar, and is met with open mockery.

"'Pure theatre!' Latyevsky said, smiling contemptuously, his solitary eye fixed on the ceiling. 'I have seen all this before, more than once, on second-rate provincial stages. I'm tired of it!'" (2, 12).

The ridiculing of Polovtsev comes from the clash of characters, without the apparent interference of the author, is yet another triumph of Sholokhov's realism and great artistry.

Of course Polovtsev was not merely putting on an act, but was expressing genuine devotion to his sword, which reminded him so vividly of those bygone "glorious" days. His tears were not only an outpouring of emotion, but were produced by a nagging awareness of the fact that the tarnished St. George sword-knot of which he had once been so proud had been secretly smuggled to him in a cramped little parlour where he was forced to hide up for fear of discovery and arrest. And when Latyevsky continues to make fun of him, referring to his sword as "a policeman's flapper", Polovtsev suddenly resumes his usual powerful commanding tone.

"'Look here, you Polish sw... squireen!' Polovtsev interrupted him rudely, and his voice had suddenly regained its usual firmness and metallic commanding ring. 'You dare to mock the weapon of St. George?! If you say another word, I will cut you down like a dog!'

"Latyevsky sat up on the bed. His lips had lost all trace of their former ironical smile. With affected seriousness he said: 'Now that is something I believe! Your voice betrays the complete sincerity of your intentions. I shall therefore shut up.'" (2, 13).

Sholokhov has an uncanny knack for sensing the possible moral and emotional response of his readers. He possesses that "purity of moral feeling" which Lev Tolstoi described in his foreword to the works of Maupassant as the sine qua non of true artistic genius.

Latyevsky could not possibly remain purely an ironic commentator, a witty, mocking "foil" for Polovtsev. He had to show his true face sooner or later.

This comes much later on when he describes to Polovtsev his preparations for a revolt in the Kuban four years previously and the murder by him of the two GPU men who came to Gremyachy posing as purveyance officials.

Latyevsky tells with absolutely cold-blooded cynicism of the way he once betrayed four Cossack conspirators to his interrogators. "So I thought, let them shoot or exile those four idiots, but I shall get away and my life is far more valuable to the organisation than the lives of these cattle" (2, 427).

Now, in Gremyachy Latyevsky recognised one of the two "purveyors" who forced themselves uninvited into Ostrovnov's yard. The man had interrogated him that time in Krasnodar. Taking one of his fellow conspirators with him, Latyevsky brutally murders the two GPU men out in the steppe. When the two bodies are found, one of them attracts special attention. "The left eye of the herdsman, whom the bandits had turned over on his back in the course of their search, had been crushed out, judging from the marks, by the heel of a boot.

"The chairman of the village Soviet, a hard-boiled Cossack, who had been through two wars, said to the militiaman: 'Look at that, Luka Nazarich, one of the swine took a kick at a dead man'" (2, 430).

The brutality with which this "old score" is settled exposes the true essence of the "gay", "jolly" officer.

One is reminded of how Makar Nagulnov killed the bandit Timofei the Torn. "No, Makar Nagulnov was no kulak swine who would shoot an enemy in the back. Without changing his position he said loudly:

"'Turn round and face death, you snake!'"

He surveys the body of his enemy who had caused him so much suffering feeling neither anger nor hatred but only a crushing weariness.

Latyevsky shot his enemy in the back, and then kicked his dead body ferociously.

Mutual rancour is unavoidable in the class struggle. But Makar Nagulnov managed to remain a human being even when he had to be brutal, whereas Latyevsky sank to savage, furious bestiality.

Chapter Seven
"A SENSE OF HUMOUR IS A SPLENDID HEALTHY QUALITY"

Sholokhov does not simply show the new features that were gradually becoming a part of life and people's very nature, but paints a broad and sweeping picture of the fight between the old and the new in all its social and historical significance. He presents it as a ferocious class struggle between two clearly defined camps—on the one hand, the poor and middle peasants led by the Communists, embodying the creative strength of the people and their passionate dedication to the cause of building a new, better world, and on the other hand, the kulak and white-guard camp, with Polovtsev and Ostrovnov at the head, representing the forces of the past. Now as a furious, ceaseless struggle within the heart of Kondrat Maidannikov, where the past is cut off at the very roots by the collective-farm plough. Or again that past will suddenly rear its head and peep through in the comic figure of Grandad Shchukar, to leave the battlefield shamefully, its head hung low, amid merry peals of laughter.

Sholokhov has a wonderful sense of humour. His ability to see the funny side of life as well as the tragic is one of the most precious qualities of his talent.

Lenin once said to Gorky: "A sense of humour is a splendid healthy quality.... There's probably as much of it in life as sadness, no less...."*

Some critics have suggested that humour plays a purely subordinate role in Sholokhov's works, that aware of the need to entertain his readers in a lighter vein, to let them "unwind" after tense, dramatic scenes, Sholokhov provides humorous relief just in the right places.

* M. Gorky, *V. I. Lenin. A Literary Portrait*, Moscow, 1970, p. 56.

This is not the case however. Humour in fact plays a far more serious role in his works.

In his superb examination of the nature of comedy and tragedy Karl Marx wrote: "History is thorough and goes through many phases when carrying an old form to the grave. The last phase of a world-historical form is its *Comedy*. The gods of Greece, already tragically wounded to death in Aeschylus's *Prometheus Bound*, had to re-die a comic death in Lucian's *Dialogues*. Why this course of history? So that humanity should part with its past *cheerfully*."*

The great importance of comedy and humour in literature lies in the fact that man parts with the past by laughing at it, and laughter clears the way for the present and lays the foundations for the future. Laughter educates man, helping him to free himself from many of the ugly traits of the past.

In his *Poetics* Aristotle defined comedy as a form of art which portrays "the worst sort of people, not in all their imperfection, but in an amusing manner". "Humour is a component of ugliness," he went on. "It is ugly and monstrous, but without pathos." The "worst type of person" is the way he is for the simple reason that the past is more deeply rooted in him than in others. In real life it is already so much over and done with, that it cannot be connected with suffering, it has become ugly and monstrous, and laughable.

Let alone exposing the old world and showing the need and inevitability for its fall, Sholokhov ridicules the past where men were often disfigured and crippled. This laughter is full of respect for the working people, and helps them to cast off the worn, frayed garments of the past, pull themselves up to their full height and get down to actively building the new life.

Of all the comic old men in Sholokhov's gallery Grandad Shchukar is without a doubt his greatest success. Pantelei Prokofyevich, Grandad Sashka and Avdei Brekh in *And Quiet Flows the Don* all pale beside him. Grandad Shchukar was like a walking compendium of all the features of the village boaster and fibber.

* *Karl Marx and Frederick Engels on Art*, Russ. ed., Moscow and Leningrad, 1937, p. 166.

Pantelei Prokofyevich in *And Quiet Flows the Don* changes considerably in the course of the novel, to finally appear as a tragi-comical figure in Book Four. His boisterous, belligerent tone when it's only a matter of talking, and his constant attempts to slip home from the war he is fed up with and doesn't understand; his vain boasting about his son's valour loaded with strong implications that he is a chip off the old block, and his own cowardly desertion; his thrift, which once verged on meanness and miserliness, and his attempt to see things as worthless so as the easier to bear their loss in the vicissitudes of the Civil War—were all humorous touches to the character of Pantelei Prokofyevich. This humour was a façade hiding tragic exhaustion with the war, with the losses and hardships that had befallen the family, painful bewilderment and complete failure to understand what was going on.

Grandad Shchukar on the other hand is a thoroughly comic figure. While the humorous in Pantelei Prokofyevich lay in the contrast between his thoughts and feelings and the reality of the Civil War years, there is not a shadow of suffering in Grandad Shchukar. The features of the past in Grandad Shchukar are not such as to create a dramatic clash between his personality and reality. On the contrary, his sympathies are wholly on the side of the new reality, which brought a wonderful improvement into his existence.

The comic in Grandad Shchukar arises from the disparity between what he is in fact and what he imagines himself to be.

A conflict arises between progressive ideals and those remnants of the past which are deeply rooted in man. Sholokhov presents this conflict in humorous form in the figure of Grandad Shchukar.

Shchukar sees himself as a "martyr for Soviet power", a "hero", a bold, resolute, and on occasion passionate man, ready "when his blood's up" to "slaughter" not only the cur which has ripped his coat to shreds, but Titok and Titok's wife too. His ideal is in the present and he would love to be like Davidov, Nagulnov and Razmyotnov. He would like to copy active and worthy people, but his own life had been lived in other times that were now over and done with. He had become the village fibber, an astronomical boaster, and essentially a rather empty person. What were the conditions that had moulded human nature so unsuccessfully?

"Ever since boyhood, my life's had a twist in it, and it still has," Shchukar begins his life-story to Davidov. "It's like a wind carrying me along, scraping me agin this, bashing me agin that, and some days it just about knocks me out" (1, 299).

Misfortune after misfortune had befallen Grandad Shchukar in his long life. He didn't even get as far as putting an old nag to use on the land. People reacted in different ways to the harsh reality: some became déclassés, others, people like Demid the Silent, retired in gloomy solitude. Grandad Shchukar found refuge in hyperbolic bragging. At least in his boasting the old man found compensation for his joyless existence in real life. When entertaining the Cossacks with his amusing stories at village gatherings, or at the fence of an evening when they gathered for a smoke, the old man, though unaware of it himself, was regaining his self-respect in the attention he received and the grateful laughter of his audience. In his account of Shchukar's life, Sholokhov is showing how and in what concrete historical conditions there arose such an absurd gap between what a man wanted to seem and what he in fact was.

Grandad Shchukar had been a braggart and a fibber long before the Revolution. But he could only become a completely comic character without a trace of suffering in the new conditions of his village. It is no accident that he does not appear as a fully developed character in the novel until the major difficulties are already over, that is, when the collective farm has already been set up and the spring sowing is underway.

Grandad Shchukar's "ideal" altered considerably along with the changes that took place in life. In his tall stories set in pre-revolutionary days, he figured as the "efficient" farmer with his head screwed on the right way, astonishingly successful in all kinds of business deals and undertakings. Once the old order had been swept away Grandad Shchukar felt and understood that the new times gave a poor peasant like him every opportunity for a really full life. He is for Soviet power, and likes to think of himself as an activist. But he has already lived long and got too set in his ways to be able to change his personality.

He even took it into his old head that it wouldn't be a bad idea to join the Party. After all, he wasn't born to spend all his life with stallions, and "all the Party men ... have got positions", and carry brief-cases. "That's what I've come for," he tells Nagulnov. "I want to know what sort of position I'll get, and so on. Just give me an example of what I've got to write and tell me how to write it."

Sholokhov skilfully creates an extremely humorous situation here: on the one hand there is Shchukar, a tongue wagging bumpkin, tangled up in a web of dark prejudices but fully convinced that as an activist, a "hero", "a martyr for Soviet power", he can expect to be taken seriously and to command full and undivided attention; on the other hand, there is the stern, gruff, and short-tempered Nagulnov. If Davidov had been there in the place of Nagulnov the clash would probably never have taken place. Davidov would have laughed and somehow found a way of explaining to Shchukar in terms he could understand why there could be no question of him joining the Party. Not so Makar. His high almost jealous regard for the Party and Communists made the very idea of someone like Grandad Shchukar joining the Party seem preposterous. At first he managed to check himself and changed the subject. "'Did the priest call on you at Easter?' he asks.

"'Course he did.'

"'Did you give him anything?'

"'Well, o' course! Couple of eggs and half a pound of bacon.'

"'So you still believe in God?'

"'Well, not so very strong, as you might say, but if I gets ill, or some sort of upset happens, or there's a big clap of thunder, then o' course I say a prayer, I turn to God'" (1, 399).

The very order in which the questions come show how Makar is gradually getting worked up. Shchukar's long-winded artless explanations make Nagulnov fume, and he finally explodes.

"What the hell does the Party want with such a bumpkin?" he cries. "Are you trying to be funny? Do you think they take any old rubbish for the Party? The only job for you is wagging that tongue of yours, telling a pack of lies. Get along, don't make me upset, I'm a man with a nervous disorder. My health won't allow me to talk calmly with you. Go, I said!"

Grandad Shchukar knew full well that Nagulnov was likely to be as good as his word, and beat a hasty retreat.

The whole passage brings a smile to our lips, but the crowning touch of humour is when Shchukar hurriedly closes the gate behind him, thinking regretfully: "Picked the wrong moment! Ought to have tried after dinner." It isn't so easy to shake Shchukar's high opinion of himself. He wouldn't be Shchukar if it were!

The humour in this episode arises from the clash of two very different characters, both of which have certain comic features. In the case of Nagulnov this time it is his intention to be patient as he had intended and explain to Shchukar calmly and clearly why he cannot be accepted as a candidate for the Party and his outburst of characteristic wrath.

An important element of a comic situation is the margin between a character's words and deeds. Grandad Shchukar often refers to himself as "a terror". "Get out of here, woman! Get out this minute!... Get out, or I may be a-doing a murder next! I'm a terrible man when I'm roused!"; "I'm a terror when I'm roused, you know"; "If it hadn't been for that dog, Titok would never have escaped from me alive! I'm dangerous." Shchukar considered "a terror" and expressions such as "like a hero", and "a martyr for Soviet power" to be the most favourable and at the same time most apt epithets that could possibly be applied to him.

But Shchukar chooses the most inappropriate moments to let slip what a terror he is. Thus he bravely drives the village leech from the room, threatening her with murder, just after being saved from her clutches by Davidov. In one breath he mentions how Titok's cur had almost torn the clothes off him, and how lucky the whole tribe of Titoks were to have escaped with their lives. Knowing that people take what he says with their tongue in their cheek, he piles detail on hilarious detail. He "recalls" how Titok's wife set the dog on him. "'Seize him!' she shouts. 'Seize him, Serko! He's the worst of them all!'"

and makes himself out to be Davidov's saviour: "So I hurled myself to the rescue like a hero and knocked that bar out of his hands. If it hadn't been for me, it would have been all up with Davidov!"

"You may be an old man, but you lie like a trooper!" Nagulnov interrupts him. "Some says as how you were running away from a dog and fell over, and he started twisting your ears like a pig's," put in another of his listeners. "Rubbish!" Grandad Shchukar would exclaim without batting an eyelid and skilfully change the subject.

More often than not, Shchukar's tales are about himself. Sholokhov uses the devise of "self-exposure" and the old man's stories reveal most clearly the rift between what he is and what he would appear. It is sometimes as if he is making fun of himself, and joining in the general hilarity at his own expense.

During the anti-Soviet "riot" by a large body of the Gremyachy peasants, Shchukar had hidden in a hayloft. On emerging he tells Davidov how it had been. While he was lying there he had felt someone creeping across the hay. "Oh, Mother! I thinks. They must be looking for me, they're after my blood.... And then he treads right on my face! I make a grab with my hand—and it's a hoof, and all in fur!... It's the devil! I thinks. It was terrible dark in that hayloft and all evil spirits are fond of darkness. Now he'll get hold of me, I thought, and tickle me to death. I'd rather be put to death by the women. The terrors I went through—there's no counting them! If it'd been anyone else in my place, one of the cowardly kind, I reckon he'd have pegged out right away from failure of the heart and guts. That always happens when a man gets frightened too quickly. But I only went a bit cold and kept lying there."

The comic effect here lies in shameless exaggeration of the real danger, and the combination of the most primitive superstition—so out of tune with the image he has of himself as "an activist"—with abject cowardice. Still weak and trembling at the knees from his recent "shock", the *real* Shchukar stands before us.

We see how he really behaved, and this makes his boasting after the event—his attempt to show that in spite of all the "terrors" he went through he was not "one of the cowardly kind"—even more comical than usual. As for the "terrors" (a goat which he imagined to be the devil), they are so ridiculous and far-fetched that only someone like Shchukar who believed in God and also stood in awe of "the dark powers" could possibly have been assailed by them. Shchukar's adventure is presented with the most improbable details, yet everything is so "in character" that you accept it all and have a good laugh. What is highly improbable at first sight in fact contains a strong germ of truth. Exaggeration and selection of certain specific characteristics in such a way as not to destroy the character's authenticity produces a highly comic effect.

It is typical of Shchukar that he behaves as an onlooker rather than as a participant in events. "I'd better hide or they'll go and kill Davidov and then get after me, and then who will there be to give evidence to the inspector about Comrade Davidov's death?" he says with a grave, self-important air to Davidov, who is just about able to stand after being beaten up by the women. This position of an "observer" that Grandad Shchukar more often than not adopts adds to the comic nature of the hapless would-be "activist".

Shchukar has a very high opinion of himself as a speaker. He is convinced that his words are full of worldly wisdom and are the fruits of experience. "I may not talk much, but when I do it's to the point. You can be sure that my words'll not be in vain!" "Wise words, like mine, are silver..." he remarks during one of his regular "attacks of garrulity" which provokes an unceremonious "When are you going to shut up?" from Nagulnov, and "Finish off, Grandad! Your story's not to the point," from Davidov.

Apart from his amazing capacity for getting into absurd predicaments, Shchukar has a rare ability for noticing the funny side of things, and the comic in life. His faded eyes frequently light up with a sly, merry, knowing twinkle.

When Grandad Shchukar decides to "enlighten" everyone as to how Demid got nicknamed "the Silent", he tells his story like a born artist, using his imagination to embroider on true fact. He skilfully creates a fine life-like episode—the priest's questions at confession and Demid's silence—and provides his own inventive commentary. Describing the priest's amazement at not hearing a single word in reply to his questions, Shchukar gives a masterly finishing touch to his story. The reverend got wild and "What a bang he gave Demid between the eyes with his little candlestick!"

"'That's a lie! He didn't hit me!' came Demid's rumbling bass.

"'Didn't he really, Demid?' Grandad Shchukar said in great surprise. 'Well, it's all the same, he wanted to, I bet.'" This "he wanted to, I bet" better than anything else sums up Grandad Shchukar, that unquestionably talented story-teller and one of the nameless creators of folklore. The priest ought to have given Demid a bash with his candlestick, for otherwise the picture would not have been complete and would hardly have caused the roar of merry laughter that followed it.

In Book Two Grandad Shchukar goes on for a long time by sheer inertia. Sometimes he simply repeats himself as for example in his ironic remarks about Nagulnov's long, high-flown speeches. Sometimes his tomfoolery detracts from his characteristic comic seriousness or is "out of place" in plot development (as in the scene where Maidannikov, Dubtsov and Shaly are being accepted into the Party).

Shchukar's "adventures" which add nothing new and throw no further light on his character occupy an unwarranted amount of space. In this connection, his journey to fetch the land surveyor immediately springs to mind.

Not until the epilogue, when he is overwhelmed with grief at the loss of his dear ones, Davidov and Nagulnov, does Shchukar become his "powerful" self again.

Let it not be thought that we say this in the interests of "critical balance", or in order to show the famous "objectivity". The fact is, we think far too highly of Sholokhov not to mention what seems to have been written on a level well below what with his inexhaustible talent he is capable of.

The novel closes tragically with the death of the main heroes, Davidov and Nagulnov.

The place of the fallen is taken by their friends and associates. Razmyotnov is chosen secretary of the Party group, Kondrat Maidannikov becomes chairman of the collective farm. Varya Kharlamova will continue with her studies in the town, and then return to the village to tend the grave of her beloved Davidov, to live, overcome and build.

The counter-revolutionary plotters are destroyed, and life in the Cossack village continues its advance towards socialism.

And so we reach the last page. One feels one has spent a whole lifetime with Sholokhov's heroes, and yet the action of the novel covers barely a year. A year is not long, but the book is so packed with events and we delve so deeply into human nature that a whole age seems to have passed before us.

For this we have to thank a truly talented writer, who has given us the incomparable joy of true art; the joy of getting to know and understand life, people and their thoughts and feelings—the joy of recognising goodness and beauty.

IV

WAR EPIC

The Science of Hatred

They Fought for Their Fatherland

The Fate of a Man

During the war Sholokhov joined the armed forces like the majority of Soviet writers, working as war correspondent for *Pravda* both during the bitter days of retreat and the bright hours of victory. In 1945 he was awarded the Order of the Patriotic War, First Class, for his literary services to the war effort.

Sholokhov's articles "On the Don", "In the South", "The Cossacks", and so on, were published in the press and in separate book form in the very first months of the war.

His short story *The Science of Hatred* (1942) enjoyed wide popularity during the war years.

All the Soviet literature of the period has as its leitmotif the moral and political superiority of the Soviet people over the fascist invaders.

The author's publicistic fervour is very much in evidence in *The Science of Hatred*, but as usual Sholokhov the publicist clothes his political ideas in the flesh of concrete artistic images.

The story is told in the first person by Gerasimov, a lieutenant. This factory mechanic from the Urals did not quite realise the enormity of the danger that threatened the country or the true nature of the enemy. Gerasimov was fond of reading and was familiar with German classics. In the course of work he had often seen and operated German lathes and machinery and was used to thinking of the German people with respect. Sholokhov's character is an ordinary Soviet worker and Communist with a broad technical and cultural education, taciturn, reserved and kind. Even when he came up against the fascists in the first battles Gerasimov saw them merely as deluded working people.

Sholokhov draws a sharp contrast between the humaneness of the Soviet soldiers and the brutality of the fascist invaders. When Gerasimov is wounded and taken prisoner he has to suffer the most monstrous humiliations, and see his own comrades perish before his very eyes. By a miracle he manages to survive and escape.

Gerasimov is not broken by the terrible trials he underwent while a prisoner. His implacable hatred for the enemy is combined with boundless love for his country and a fine awareness of the high aims of the Soviet people's struggle.

Now and then this love for his country, people, and the Party wells forth in the narration of this reserved, stern man, who has gone grey before his time. It shows through when he speaks of his family, of his parting with his near and dear ones, his last conversation with the secretary of the district Party Committee, and in the moving account of how he managed to keep his Party card safe in prison camp.

Sholokhov's studied symbolism serves to produce the desired effect of making Gerasimov's tale a generalisation representative of the mood and feelings of the whole people. A landscape description precedes and prepares the ground for Gerasimov's account of his trials and sufferings. A mighty oak-tree survives on a battlefield.

"In the early spring a German shell hit the trunk of an old oak-tree growing on the bank of small, nameless stream. Half the tree had been shot clean away leaving an even, yawning hole, but the other half bent towards the water by the explosion miraculously came to life in the springtime and was covered with fresh green leaves. And probably to this very day the lower branches of the mutilated oak-tree bathe in the flowing water, while the higher ones still stretch out their leaves greedily towards the sun."

The author's first words "In wartime trees, like people, each have their own destiny" prepare us for the rather remote parallel between the epic grandeur of the image of the oak-tree scorched by the fire of battle yet still full of life and vigour, and the trials lieutenant Gerasimov suffered. At the end of the story this parallel is re-echoed, this time as a direct comparison: "...This thirty-two-year-old lieutenant, reeling under the terrible hardships he had suffered, but still as tough and strong as an oak-tree...." This comparison both enables us to grasp one of the main features of the hero's character and appreciate the fundamental qualities of the Soviet people at war—their tremendous vital strength and staunchness.

In 1943 and 1944 the first instalments of a new novel by Sholokhov began to appear in *Pravda* and *Krasnaya Zvezda*. It was entitled *They Fought for Their Fatherland*.

In an attempt to capture the essential features of the Great Patriotic War Sholokhov focussed most of his attention on the ordinary Soviet working men defending their socialist country in fierce, bloody battles. By choosing the rank-and-file soldiers of the Soviet Army as the heroes of his novel, Sholokhov was showing the significance of the valorous feats accomplished by the masses in the Great Patriotic War.

Maxim Gorky held that in war the rank-and-file representative of the popular masses should be portrayed in literature as the force deciding the outcome of the conflict. This focus on the ordinary people who are the makers of history is natural to socialist realism.

Sholokhov, who always portrayed the ordinary working people with especial warmth and penetration, now wrote of the rank-and-file soldiers of the Soviet Army as of a "single heroic unit".

Throughout Sholokhov's works we find a constant concern with the complicated, and often dramatic processes that produced the new moral make-up of Soviet man. In Sholokhov's novels the life of an individual—whether it be Grigory Melekhov and Mikhail Koshevoi in *And Quiet Flows the Don* or Semyon Davidov and Kondrat Maidannikov in *Virgin Soil Upturned*—is always related to and conditioned by the historical destiny of the people as a whole. All this is likewise true of the chapters of the novel *They Fought for Their Fatherland* that have so far been published.

It is significant that Sholokhov draws on new material in his works of the war and post-war years. While in *Virgin Soil Upturned* and *And Quiet Flows the Don* he was almost entirely concerned with the Don Cossacks, his new heroes were people like Lieutenant Gerasimov, a factory mechanic from the Urals (*The Science of Hatred*);

Lopakhin, a miner from the Donets Basin, and Zvyagintsev, a harvester operator from the Kuban (*They Fought for Their Fatherland*); Andrei Sokolov, a lorry-driver from Voronezh (*The Fate of a Man*).

Moreover, one of the main heroes of *They Fought for Their Fatherland*—for just about the first time in all Sholokhov's works—is an intellectual, the agronomist Nikolai Streltsov.

All this testifies to a considerable broadening of Sholokhov's observations of life, which was undoubtedly connected with the events of the war.

The action of the published chapters of this book begins in the summer of 1942, when the Soviet Army was retreating to the Don. The battle scenes in the Don steppes are a sort of prelude to the tremendous battle on the Volga.

The battle of Stalingrad was the great turning point of the Second World War. Sholokhov's account of it makes the reader feel like an eye-witness. The very choice of time and place testifies to the epic range of Sholokhov's plot.

The Great Patriotic War fought by the Soviet people was of such enormous significance for the world as a whole, and was so full of heroism and tragedy, that for a long time to come it made one of the most important themes in art and literature.

And literature which wished to be honest, truthful, and genuinely popular in the original sense of the word, had to try and explain that "inner potential" which enabled the Soviet peoples to stand up to the most cruel, crippling blows, and gradually gathering more and more strength, go on to free many of the enslaved countries of Europe on their march to the very heart of the Third Reich.

Soviet writers were concerned above all with exploring the spiritual make-up and moral qualities of the common soldier who bore the main burden of the war.

Sholokhov once said of *They Fought for Their Fatherland*: "I am interested in the lot of the ordinary people in the last war. Our soldiers fought like heroes in the days of the Great Patriotic War. The whole world knows of the Russian soldiers, their valour and their Suvorov qualities. But this war showed them in an entirely new light. That is my aim: to show in a novel the new qualities of the Soviet soldier that so uplifted him in this war...."*

In his unfinished novel *They Fought for Their Fatherland* (the introductory chapter was first published in *Leningradsky Almanakh* in 1954 (No. 8), subsequent chapters appeared in *Pravda* in 1943, 1944 and 1949, and were later collected together in the magazine *Moskva* No. 1, 1959, and in *Roman Gazeta* No. 1, 1959), and also in his short-story *The Fate of a Man* (*Pravda*, December 31, 1956, and January 1, 1957), Sholokhov presented the war not only as a heroic feat of arms performed by the people, but as a tremendous test of all the moral qualities of Soviet man. Here an impressive portrayal of the people's patriotism is combined with a movingly lyrical account of the fate of individuals in the general sea of troubles and trials affecting the whole country.

In his writings about the war Sholokhov remains true to the democratic line of his work. The central figures are simple folk, those who fought the great war in the ranks, working people like Pyotr Lopakhin the miner, Ivan Zvyagintsev the harvester operator, Nikolai Streltsov the agronomist, and Andrei Sokolov the lorry-driver....

The depth and fulness of life is a remarkable quality of Sholokhov's novel, the soldiers speak about the fate of their country, they discuss the aims of the war, recall peacetime, their families, children, and sweethearts.... The tragic intensity of battle may be suddenly followed by comic scenes and episodes.

The words addressed to Lopakhin by a nameless old woman from a Don village: "Everything concerns me, duck" are extremely important as a key to the main message of the novel, the theme of common responsibility, and the connection between the life of the individual and a life of the people as a whole.

What Lopakhin says to his mate Kopitovsky just before they go into battle for the river crossing sounds like a direct challenge. With quite "unusual" seriousness he says: "I've just got to make a stand here, while the others get across. Did you see how much equipment was brought

---

* I. Aralichev, "At Mikhail Sholokhov's", *Vympel* No. 23, 1947, p. 24.

up to the crossing in the night? That's the point. I just can't leave all that good stuff to the Germans, my conscience won't let me."

One has only to compare the heroes of *They Fought for Their Fatherland* with the Cossacks and soldiers in the trenches and dug-outs during the First World War in *And Quiet Flows the Don* and remember their feelings and attitudes to realise the tremendous difference in their moral make-up, and understand the essence of those historical changes which so altered the character of the Russian people.

Consideration of the radical changes that have taken place in the mentality and position of the people in Soviet times is the *determinant factor influencing the structure of Sholokhov's narrative.*

Lopakhin's "conscience" was an overtly publicistic statement of the Soviet people's attitude to their state, of the feeling of a man who realised he was master in his own land.

The novel abounds in monologues and "confessions", meditations, dialogues, now winged and dramatic (Streltsov and Lopakhin, Nekrasov and Lopakhin, etc.), now in a lighter, humorous vein (Lopakhin and Zvyagintsev, Lopakhin and Kopitovsky); and speeches like Sergeant Poprishchenko's address to the soldiers at the grave of Lieutenant Goloshchokov, and Colonel Marchenko's speech to the remains of the battered regiment, drawn up before him with their banner out.

In all of them, in the most various situations we find this "conscience", this patriotism and hatred for the enemy. A personal, frank note is combined with overt publicism.

Sholokhov has a way making his heroes pass very smoothly from personal feelings to general reflections about the enemy and what the war was being fought for.

Zvyagintsev picks an ear of corn which has survived at the edge of a field where the wheat has been burnt down. He is a farmer, a man who knows the value of every ear, every grain of corn. For Zvyagintsev corn is the source of the eternal renewal of life. In the springtime the shoot will push up through the soil, turn green, and stretch towards the sun.... For him an ear of corn is like a living thing.

"Zvyagintsev sniffed the ear of corn, and whispered inaudibly: 'You beauty, you've got proper smoked, you have. You smell about as strong of smoke as a gypsy.... That's what the Jerry's done to you, the soulless bastard.'"

The burnt-out ripened corn across a vast expanse of steppe affects Zvyagintsev as a personal sorrow, arousing a bitter feeling of loss. In his sorrow and regret his thoughts automatically turn to the war, to the enemy who is so pitiless towards "everything living".

"What a load of flaming parasites you Germans are, eh! Got into the habit of trampling other people's land like you own the place, you swine. But what about when we come and bring the war into your country, eh? Then what? You've been lording it around here, lording it good and proper you have, wiping out civvies, women, and kids, and look at all this wheat you've burnt, and you don't think nothing of destroying our villages.... But what about you then, when the war moves to your Jerry land?"

Sergeant Poprishchenko addresses his men straight from the heart: "Comrade soldiers, my lads, men! We are burying our lieutenant, the last officer in our regiment", and goes on to speak of Lieutenant Goloshchokov, about the family he left behind him in the Ukraine, and then, after a short pause, "said in a voice that had become different, wonderfully strong and full of great inner force:

"'Look what a mist there is all around, my lads! See it? Black sorrow just like that mist hangs over the people who have been left behind under the Germans there in the Ukraine and other places. Sorrow that won't let people sleep at night, and sorrow that in the daytime they can't see world around them through.... And we must always remember that: now that we're burying our comrade, and later, when an accordion may be playing nearby us during a halt. And we'll always remember! We went east, but our eyes looked westwards. Let's keep on looking that way until we've struck down the last German on our soil.'"

This type of passage where the hero's personal feelings and "the general" are combined in a manner perfectly justified by the characters and the situation is an important feature of the hitherto published chapters of the novel.

Sholokhov does not always achieve such an impressive unity of what seem to be emotionally heterogeneous elements. Occasionally, especially when Lopakhin is speaking, the publicistic overtone is too strong, and the "general" drowns out the personal so that artistically justified publicism becomes pure rhetoric.

The new in Sholokhov's heroes appears in numerous forms. It is present in Lopakhin's publicistic speech and the deeply hidden thoughts and feelings of Nikolai Streltsov; it also peeps through in Ivan Zvyagintsev's humorous, good-natured tales. The Cossack harvester operator from the Kuban speaks of machines with touching affection. He is as interested in news of the Machine and Tractor Station where he worked before the war as he is to get news of his family. In almost every letter home he asks his wife: "How are things at the MTS? Who of the mates is still there? What's the new manager like?"

The main idea underlying the novel—the invincibility of the new social principles that have penetrated the life of the people to the very roots—is expressed through the attention Sholokhov accords to the new qualities in people of the most varying nature and background. Faith in ultimate victory over the enemy shines through even in the most dramatic passages of the book, where the fiercest battles and most terrible losses are described.

The narrative develops on two planes as it were: the "background" scenes of the soldiers' everyday life, and the epic canvases of heroic battles.

There is a sharp difference in the emotional and stylistic levels of the two planes: the high-flown-heroic and the humorous mundane. The scenes that show the everyday life of the soldiers are more often than not coloured with humour: Zvyagintsev will start to tell of the misfortunes that befell him in his family life, or Lopakhin will chirp in with his usual witty remarks, or the heroes will find themselves in some funny plight. It is these scenes from which we mainly learn about the characters' lives in peacetime, and the ties of friendship that bound them in the war.

The many battle scenes are imbued with frank admiration for the feats of arms of the ordinary Soviet people. Sholokhov tries to show mass courage as typical of the Soviet Army. Though mortally wounded lance corporal

Kochetygov summons up enough strength to throw a bottle of flaming petrol from his destroyed emplacement and burn up a German tank. Lopakhin puts a German aeroplane and several enemy tanks out of action. Zvyagintsev's cool-headedness and tenacity are equally admirable. Captain Sumskov musters his last remaining strength to crawl after his men as they counter-attack, after the red regimental banner flying in the thick of battle. "Now and then the captain would lie on his left shoulder for a moment and then crawl on again. His face was chalky white like death, but he still went forward and raising his head shouted in a breaking voice, high-pitched like a child's: 'Forward, my lads, give it to 'em!'"

This passionate longing for victory that gives strength even to a dying man is a beautiful extraordinarily moving instance of heroism. People like Sumskov, Kochetygov, Lopakhin, Zvyagintsev and Streltsov can be killed but not defeated.

Sholokhov adheres to the essential socialist realist concept of man as a fighter by nature, a victor over the forces of the dying world of imperialist aggression and oppression.

Side by side with the heroic in the battle scenes we find humour too. This bold combination of dramatic and everyday moments, of high-flown passionate lyricism and humour, is very characteristic of Sholokhov's works.

It is not just that Sholokhov tries to give the reader a rest with episodes in a lighter vein after emotional tension and suspense, but this combination of apparently heterogeneous elements enables him to give a fuller picture of his heroes, ordinary people, with their moments of fear and doubt, yet at the same time capable of feats of valour. This ability to render the heroic by way of the ordinary mundane is also a feature of Alexander Tvardovsky's great poem *Vasily Tyorkin*.

Sholokhov's novel deals not only with the soldiers and officers at the front. In a situation that was changing with catastrophic speed, places that until recently had lain in the peaceful rear became the frontline, and so people who had suddenly been plunged into all the horrors and hardships of war kept coming into the author's field of vision—old folk, women.

By alternating civilian life and short lulls in the fighting with sudden fierce battles involving dozens of tanks, aircraft, mortars and heavy guns, Sholokhov gives a complete picture of the *people at war*.

Both *And Quiet Flows the Don* and *Virgin Soil Upturned* depict the collective efforts of the people to transform life. The same is true of *They Fought for Their Fatherland*, where Sholokhov sets out to depict *the heroic endeavour of the people* in the war.

The "peaceful" scenes are imbued with heroism just as the battle scenes are. Thus, the account of the battle for the height, where a handful of soldiers, without liaison, without artillery cover, or tanks, held up the nazis and even threw them back at bayonet point, where we have Captain Sumskov's moving heroism, is preceded by a chapter about a "peaceful" respite....

There is "the small irate-looking old woman in a worn blue skirt and a dirty blouse" whom Lopakhin asks for a bucket and some salt to cook the lobsters he is longing to taste. She starts off by giving him a severe dressing down for retreating, for leaving towns and villages at the mercy of the enemy. Her words are full of restrained grief, and injured pride.

"I've three sons and a son-in-law at the front, and a fourth, my youngest was killed at Sevastopol town, see? You're a stranger, that's why I'm talking to you friendly like, but if my sons were to turn up here right now, why I wouldn't let them into the yard. I'd give 'em a bash on the skull and tell 'em a thing or two as their mother. 'You went off to fight, so fight like men, damn you,' I'd say to 'em, 'and don't drag the enemy after you right through the land, and shame your old mother publicly!'"

This ability to show the beautiful and noble through the everyday is a characteristic feature of Sholokhov's talent and humanism.

The original "visual" impression changes noticeably, and is greatly enriched. "What their mother has to say" represents the hopes and fears, the thoughts and worries of millions of mothers.

The figure of the old woman from the Don village has all the moving significance of a generalisation while losing nothing of its concreteness. She is like an incarnation of the proud and sorrowing Soldier's Mother, of

Motherland speaking the bitter truth to fighting sons.

Sholokhov again returns us to the particular circumstances of the moment, to what is now going on in the mind of the vexed and ashamed Lopakhin—"What the devil possessed me to come here!"—and to how the old woman brings him a bucket and some salt.

But then the concrete, the particular once more slides into the general, universal. "...The little old woman, weary and bent with age and work, went past *with such grave majesty* that to Lopakhin it seemed that *she was twice as tall as him and looked down on him with scorn and pity...*" (author's italics).

The nature of the images Sholokhov employs testifies to the way the apparently romantic "device" can be organically combined with the concrete and realistic in modern prose.

In *They Fought for Their Fatherland* and *The Fate of a Man* Sholokhov's realism is imbued with a publicistic acuteness, symbolic imagery and sudden romantic generalisations without losing any of its tremendous clarity, genre detail or inspired psychological penetration.

The discovery of new means of expression, which with Sholokhov is tied up with a constant attempt to single outstandingly heroic in the ordinary and mundane, and show it to be an essential element in the character of Soviet people widens the possibilities of realism endowing it with new traits as compared to nineteenth-century realism.

The personal, lyrical note sounds much more strongly in Sholokhov's post-war works. In *The Fate of a Man* the author "projects himself" into the narrative. His thoughts and feelings as the narrator strengthen the emotional intensity of the tale and help bring out the fortitude, strength and sheer greatness of the hero, Andrei Sokolov, an ordinary Russian man. This tale of irreparable losses and terrible grief is imbued with faith in life and the human race.

The "cyclic" composition of the story (at the beginning the narrator meets Andrei Sokolov and his adopted son Vanya by the ferry over a river that has burst its banks in the spring flood, and at the end takes his leave of them there) rounds off in a closed circuit so to speak the story of Andrei Sokolov's life.

The writer has set himself a very impressive task—
that of telling the story of a human life in relation to the
events of the Second World War, the tremendous test
the people and the state were put to, and the tragedy
of one of the individuals who went through all the terrible hardships of the war.

Out of the boundless spring steppe a man appears
"tall and rather stooped", leading a little boy of five
or six by the hand.

And off they go again at the end, "Two orphans, two
grains of sand swept into strange parts by the tremendous
hurricane of the war..." (50).*

How could these two lives be told in the genre that
we call a story? The fate of a man is more than a mere
story. Indeed, the title itself, with the philosophical
and aesthetic meaning it embodies, demanded an epic
solution. And Sholokhov found an extraordinarily com-
pressed, striking form, that combined epic with laconicism, remarkable single-mindedness with tremendous
range. *The Fate of a Man* represents the discovery of
a new form, which can conveniently be called *the epic
short story*.

There has been a tendency in literary criticism over
the last few years to exaggerate the significance of so-
called lyrical prose (see, for example, "Current Developments in the Novel" by M. Kuznetsov, *Novy Mir* No.
2, 1960). We often overlook the fact that the epic which
developed in Soviet literature out of the "normal conditions" of the novel has in its turn an important influence
on the present-day novel and on the short story, novelette
and so forth, endowing them with a number of important
new elements both in form and content.

At first it seems as if Sholokhov is returning to the
original short-story form that has been neglected of late,
where the author listened to the account of a narrator
who was a direct participant in or witness of events.
A tale from life told by someone: only then could one
speak of a short story. Hence the traditional beginning:
where and in what circumstances the author heard the
tale.

* All quotations are given according to Mikhail Sholokhov,
The Fate of a Man, Moscow, 1971.

In as far as Sholokhov uses the traditional beginning, he is in a way renovating the old tradition. But here the similarity ends. *The Fate of a Man* is not a "personal story", in the accepted sense of the term. Sholokhov selects from Andrei Sokolov's life only those features which reveal the individual human life in the context of the tragic events of the age and form a sympathetic generalised portrayal of Man at War in broad historical perspective, showing the contrast between the humane hope-inspiring and peace-loving world of socialism and the cruel, barbarous world of fascism that has unleashed the war.

Such is the complex socio-philosophical and concrete historical foundation on which Sholokhov's story is built.

There are two voices then in the story. Andrei Sokolov tells the story of his life, and is thus the main narrator, while the author is in the role of listener, a chance acquaintance who asks the odd question, says something now and again when it is impossible to remain silent before the stranger's grief, or suddenly bursts out, unable to contain his emotion at the moving tale he is hearing....

The author plays an active role as commentator in the story.

"When I glanced at him sideways I felt strangely disturbed. Have you ever seen eyes that look as if they have been sprinkled with ash, eyes filled with such unabating pain and sadness that it is hard to look into them? This chance acquaintance of mine had eyes like that" (9).

The sudden close-up we are given of these eyes penetrates so deeply into the man's hidden suffering that it almost takes your breath away.

They are seen by a man who is extremely sensitive to other people's grief and needs. He sympathises with all his heart and soul and infects us with his noble and purifying compassion.

Andrei Sokolov begins his frank confession. "His emotion communicated itself to me," the author says simply. Full of sympathy for the other man's sufferings, he says quietly, straight from the heart: "Don't let it get you down, friend, don't think of it" (15).

The tale of irreparable losses continues, until, once again, Andrei Sokolov is too overcome to go on and falls silent. "We lighted up...." The two men have been brought very close by the feeling of mutual understanding that has grown up between them.

In that minute of involuntary silence, the author looks around him, and the sunny, early spring day seems somehow to have changed.

"The sun shone as hot as in May," we are told at the beginning of the story. "It was so hot..." the author repeats a few lines later. He felt a tremendous peace and calm descend on him. "It was good to sit there alone, abandoning myself completely to the stillness and solitude" (7).

Now, after being infected by the other man's deep, inconsolable sorrow, everything seems to have become veiled in a grey shroud of gloom.

"The warm breeze still rustled the dry leaves of the alders, the clouds were still floating past in the towering blue, as though under taut white sails, but in those minutes of solemn silence the boundless world preparing for the great fulfilment of spring, for that eternal affirmation of the living in life, seemed quite different to me."

The author's words are not just a sympathetic commentary. They help us to understand a human life and not just see it, to understand it in the context of the time, and grasp its universal content and significance.

The subdued reference to "the eternal affirmation of the living in life" returns us to one of the most vital and personal themes that constantly reoccurs throughout Sholokhov's works. Here it sets the stage for Andrei Sokolov's account of how he buried his "last joy and hope", his son Anatoly, in foreign German soil; how he was left completely alone; how he came to meet Vanya. "At night, I can stroke him while he's sleeping, I can smell his curls. It takes some of the pain out of my heart, makes it a bit softer. It had just about turned to stone, you know" (47).

The reference to "the eternal affirmation of the living in life" is a prelude for the author's reflections on the future of the stranger and his new son, which are the culminating point of the whole story, the philosophical résumé of all that has gone before. The narrative passes from the melancholy key of tragic hopelessness to the jubilant key of heroic faith and optimism.

But the author is a human being, with a human heart, and a very human heart at that. The last chord is a short cry of pain from a heart wounded by another man's grief.

"I felt sad as I watched them go. Perhaps everything would have been all right at our parting but for Vanya. After he had gone a few paces, he twisted round on his stumpy legs and waved to me with his little rosy hand. And suddenly a soft but taloned paw seemed to grip my heart, and I turned hastily away. No, not only in their sleep do they weep, these elderly men whose hair grew grey in the years of war. They weep, too, in their waking hours. The thing is to be able to turn away in time. The important thing is not to wound a child's heart, not to let him see that unwilling tear that burns the cheek of a man" (50).

There was a third voice in Sholokhov's story—the clear, pure voice of a child, apparently not fully aware of all the hardships and misfortunes that fall to a man's lot.

With his eyes as bright and clear as the sky, his pink cold hands and the touching way he presses trustfully against the knees of the author, a complete stranger, Vanya is like a vision of innocent childhood itself. "I'm not an old man, Uncle," he replied to the author's friendly appellation, with a surprised expression and the directness common at his age. "I'm only a boy, and I'm not chilly either. My hands are just cold because I've been making snowballs" (8).

Having appeared at the beginning in such a brightly carefree key, in the final scenes he will be a direct participant in a great human tragedy.

The theme of injured, wretched childhood has long been one of the most tragically intense, social themes in humanistic Russian literature. The very concept of humaneness, whether in connection with individual behaviour or society as a whole, has been vividly expressed in relation to childhood.

The humanistic condemnation of war and fascism in *The Fate of a Man* is equally present in the story of Vanya and that of Andrei Sokolov.

Andrei Sokolov speaks of the child with painfully restrained grief. "'Such a little fellow and he'd already learned to sigh. Was that the thing for him to be doing? 'Where's your father, Vanya?' I asked. 'He was killed at the front,' he whispered. 'And Mummy?' 'Mummy was killed by a bomb when we were in the train.' 'Where were you coming from in the train?' 'I don't know, I don't remember....' 'And haven't you got any family at all?' 'No, nobody.' 'But where do you sleep at night?' 'Anywhere I can find'" (44-45).

This orphan's sigh is a heavy weight on the scales of history, condemning those who began the war.

Andrei Sokolov's decision to adopt the child reveals to us the store of kindness in the man, his ineradicable humaneness. He was returning the joy of childhood to the little boy, he would shield him from pain, suffering and grief. There was a *heroic* quality in this step, for here was a man who had lost all, whom the war had left depleted, yet even in his terrible, soul-destroying loneliness he had managed to remain a Human Being.

It was in Andrei Sokolov's attitude to Vanya that humanism won its greatest victory, triumphing over the inhumanity of fascism, over destruction and death itself.

The life-asserting motif which comes in at the beginning of the story, in the description of "the eternally young, barely perceptible aroma of earth that has not long been liberated from the snow", is taken up again a little later in the reference to "the eternal affirmation of the living in life", and is rounded off in the dramatically heroic intonations of the finale, with its note of passionate humanity, warmed and lit by the child's smile.

As you read Sholokhov's story it is as if before your very eyes there arises above the world a man in army boots, roughly patched khaki trousers, and a quilted jacket scorched in several places—like a living war memorial, an incarnation of sorrow, suffering and loneliness. Behind him is a long chain of bitter experiences—concentration camp, the death of his wife and children, his home in ruins, the loss of his comrades-in-arms....

"Sometimes I can't sleep at night, I just stare into the darkness and I think: 'What did you do it for, life? Why did you maim me like this? Why did you punish me?' And I get no answer, either in darkness, or when the sun's shining bright.... No, I get no answer, and I'll never get one!" (9).

What a passionate condemnation of war we have in this cri du coeur at the beginning of the story.

Nor is this merely a condemnation of what is over and done with. It sounds as a passionate appeal to the present too, to the whole world, to every single man and woman, to stop for a moment and reflect on what war brings, what it could still bring.

Just before the end of the story the author comes in again, this time with a calm reflection, the reflection of a man who has seen a lot in his time: "I wanted to believe that this Russian, this man of unbreakable will, would stick it out, and that the boy would grow at his father's side into a man who could endure anything, overcome any obstacle if his country called up on him to do so" (50).

Here we have an affirmation of the greatness and beauty of true humanity, an apotheosis of courage and firmness, a glorification of the man who had stood up under the blows of war and borne the impossible.

The two themes, the heroic and the tragic, the feat and the suffering, intermingle throughout the story, forming a polyphonic whole.

Nothing is left to chance in the composition of the work. I would call it musical, symphonic even. The main leitmotifs and principal images stand out very clearly. The story falls naturally into very distinct parts, as regards subject-matter and also the emotional overtones. They are the introduction, the three stages of Andrei Sokolov's story, and the final scene. This division is reinforced by the alternation of the voices of the hero—story teller and the author—narrator.

Sholokhov has found just the right "setting" for the story, with his usual, unfailing accuracy—juncture of winter and spring, when it is still cold but already warm, the first triumphant days of spring coming with "rare drive and swiftness". The first spring after the war. The streams are bursting the ice and flooding madly. At the spot where the story of a whole human life, with all its pain, passions, achievements and losses is to be unfolded in a flash (only two hours pass between the departure and return of the ferry), in a great cri du coeur, at the spot where the author met Andrei Sokolov, "there was that kind of stillness that falls on deserted places only late in the autumn or at the very beginning of spring" (6).

One feels that only here, only in this setting, could the story of this Russian soldier and working man be told with that gripping frankness of a confession and the powerful impact of tragedy.

In the very first description right at the beginning of the story we already come across the motif of "a hard road". At first it is the road of the author who had to go on a journey to see to some urgent business or other. "Where the going was particularly heavy for the horses we got out and walked. It was hard to walk through the slushy snow, which squelched under our boots, but the roadside was still coated with a glittering crust of ice, and there it was even harder" (5). Note the insistent reiteration of "hard", "heavy".

The description of the author's road prepares for the appearance of Andrei Sokolov and Vanya. They were going along the same hard road, moreover, they were going along it on foot. The "hard road" acquires added overtones. A note of weariness accompanies the account of the appearance of the travellers: "They tramped *wearily*....", "taking the half-empty rucksack off his back, the father sat down *heavily* beside me..." (author's italics).

Gradually the motif of the "hard road" acquires more and more overtones and shades of meaning as a philosophical generalisation.

Andrei Sokolov's words addressed to the author: "No, it's no job for a man to be travelling with someone like him, not on foot anyway," already have the broader interpretation of *road* and *journey* and *human life*.

The motif develops into a tense, dramatic tale with its staggering wealth of content made of the very stuff of life, a tale of a *hard road of life*, the fate of a man along *the paths of war* where he had a "good bellyful of trouble".

This "musical" development of the theme, the wealth of motifs and the philosophy and shades of meaning they contain, are typical features of Sholokhov's works. What we have is a story that is at the same time a reflection on the fate of people, raised from the particular and the concrete to the universal.